PHOTOGRAPHS OF THE NETHERLANDS EAST INDIES AT THE TROPENMUSEUM

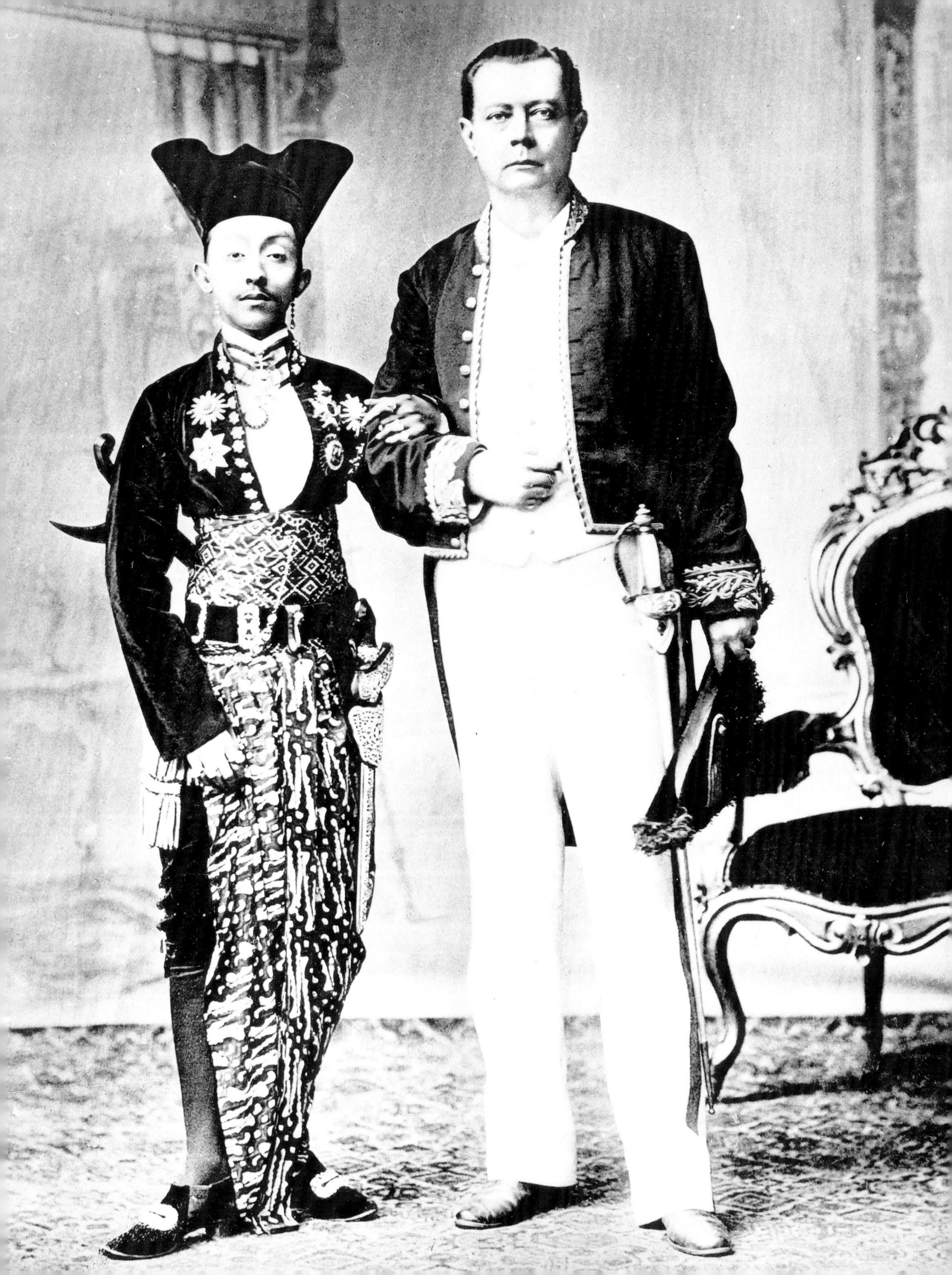

PHOTOGRAPHS OF THE NETHERLANDS EAST INDIES

at the Tropenmuseum

JANNEKE VAN DIJK
ROB JONGMANS
ANOUK MANSFELD
STEVEN VINK
PIM WESTERKAMP

WITH

WIMO AMBALA BAYANG

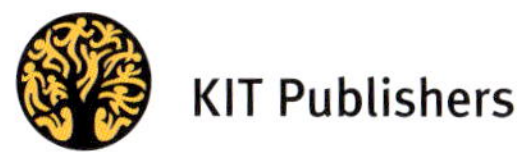

KIT Publishers

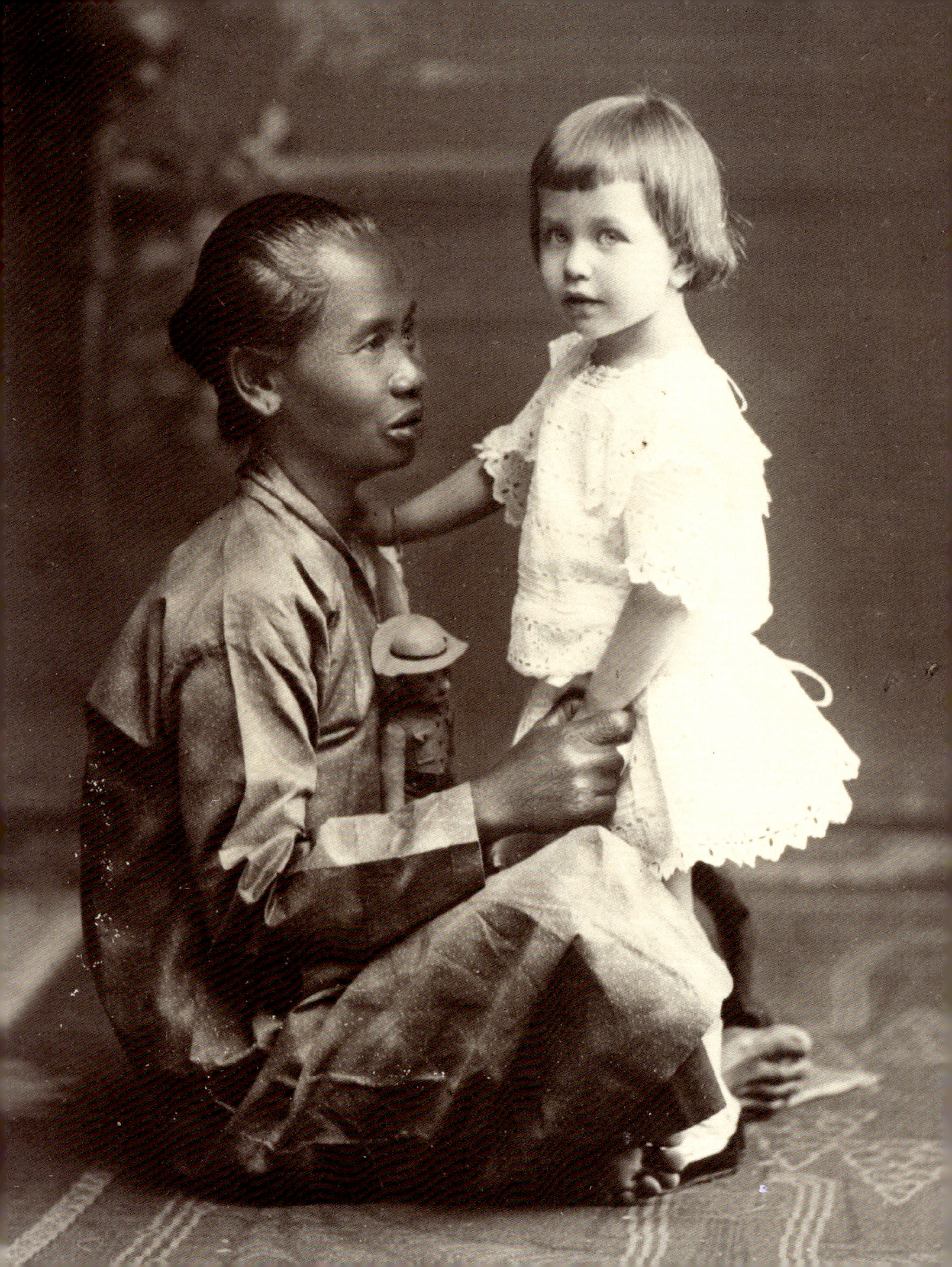

CONTENTS

<< 1
Studio portrait of *Susuhunan* Paku Buwono X of Solo, and Resident Willem de Vogel, Surakarta
Photographer: unknown
gelatin glass negative
1897
9 x 12 cm
60014590. Gift: Royal Dutch Geographical Society (KNAG)

< 2
Studio portrait of Antoinette Westerman and her nanny (*babu*), Java
Photographic Studio: Charls & Co. (Semarang)
gelatin printing-out paper
1915–16
10.1 x 6.6 cm
60027454. Gift: J.H. de Groot-Verschoor van Nisse, 1985. Former collection A.E.M. Westerman

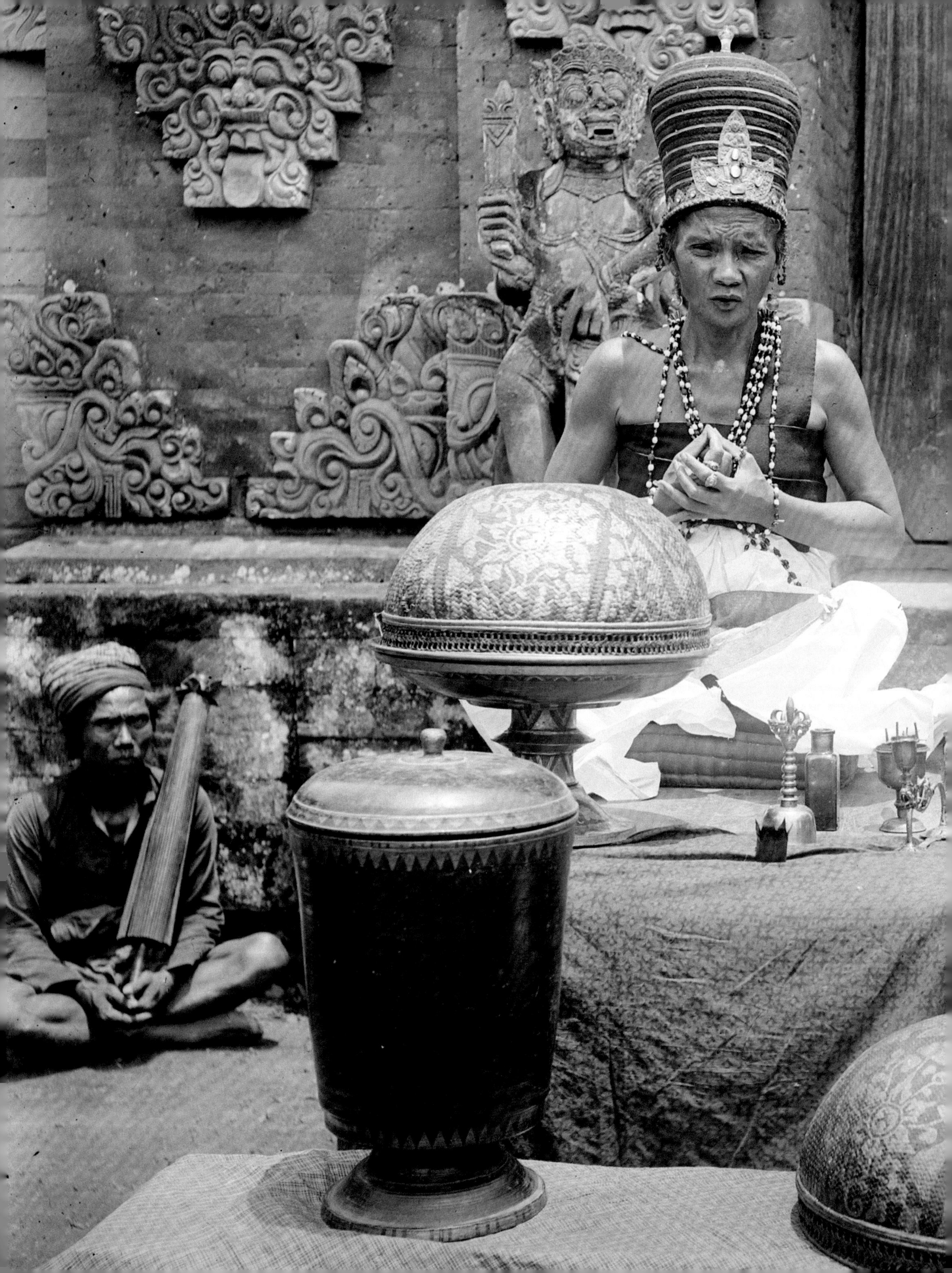

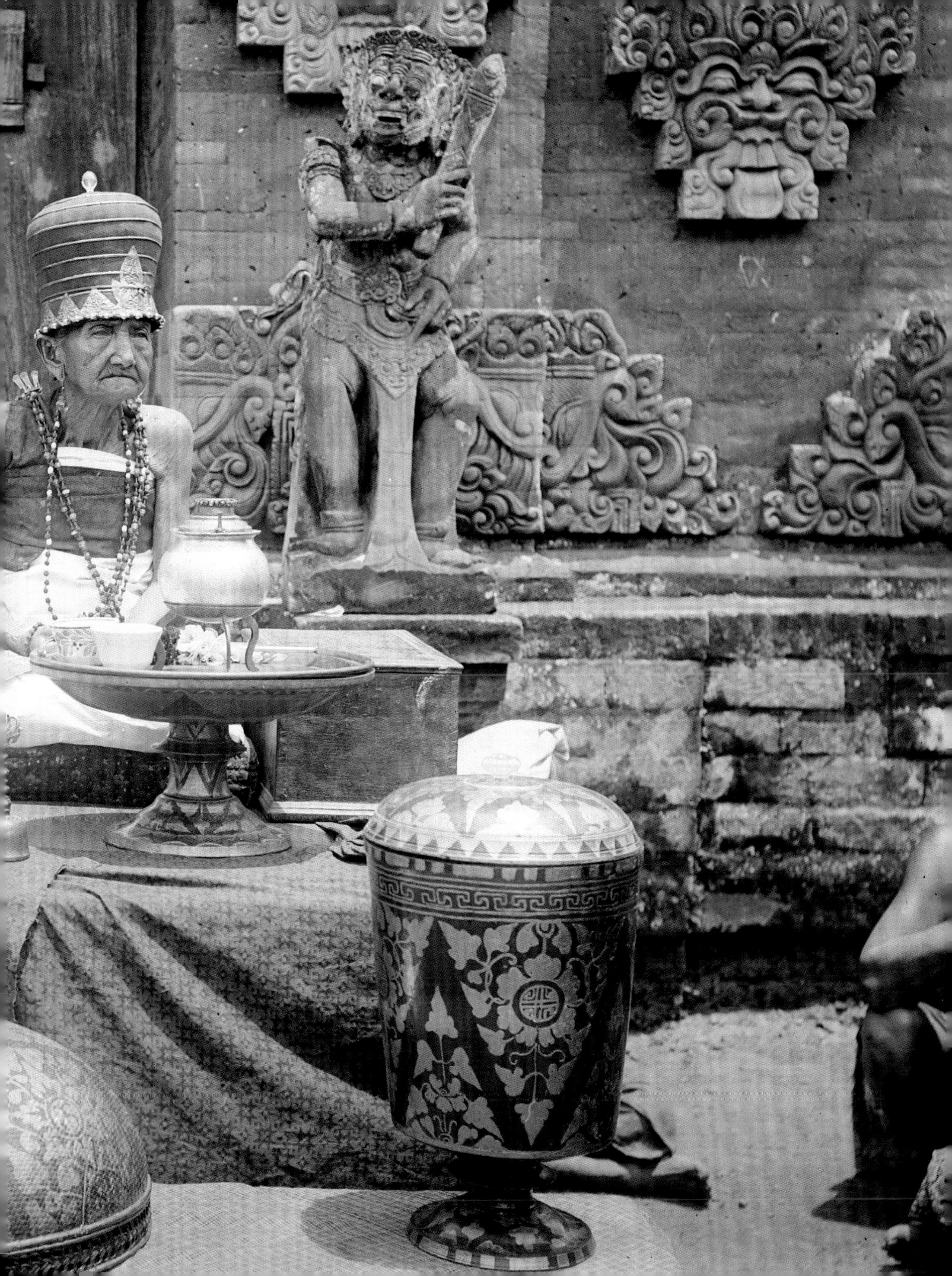

FOREWORD

A museum collection is much more than an assembly of objects. Considerable history is attached to each and every object. Viewed in this light, a museum collection serves as a gateway to an endless number of stories, some of which concern the culture in which these objects originally functioned. They say something about the people who made them, saw them, used them and experienced them. Other stories concern the manner in which the objects passed from their initial owners into the hands of others, including traders, colonial officials and missionaries, collectors, anthropologists and art lovers. And there are also stories about how the objects made their way to their new destinations, where they continually acquire new significance. These stories are about curators and educators, restorers and designers, viewers and readers.

The Tropenmuseum is located in the unique historical building of the Royal Tropical Institute (Koninklijk Instituut voor de Tropen, KIT). The collection is closely linked to Dutch and world history, and documents the numerous types of contacts that occur between different peoples, cultures and nations.

The museum has reinvented itself several times since it was founded. It traces its origin back to a 19th-century colonial collection that was brought together in a museum in Haarlem. In 1910, this collection became a part of the Colonial Institute Association (Vereniging Koloniaal Instituut), newly founded at the time, which had new premises built in Amsterdam. The museum then gained great renown as the Colonial Museum (Koloniaal Museum). After the Second World War, it was renamed the Indies Museum (Indisch Museum), and in 1950 became the Tropenmuseum. As a part of the Royal Tropical Institute, the museum profiled itself as a post-colonial museum with a focus on global economics, trade and culture. In the 1970s, the museum was radically transformed into a presentation centre for development-related issues and was supplemented with a children's museum.

< 3
See Fig. 56

The most recent transformation was completed in 2009: the Tropenmuseum as a dynamic institution focused on world culture, a place where a richly variegated balance is sought between colonial collections, classic ethnography, contemporary art, intangible cultural heritage and popular art. It continually strives to play a significant role in society, and seeks contact with people and communities that recognise themselves in the heritage that the museum manages and in the stories that it tells.

A museum collects, studies and exhibits. Yet a museum also continually reflects on its own mission and provides access to its knowledge. For several years now, this has meant that the collections have been made available online. The museum also felt a strong need to publicise the most important objects in the collection, the related stories and the museum's history as a series of ten volumes. *Photography of the Netherlands East Indies at the Tropenmuseum* is the fourth volume in the series. The other volumes will appear over the next couple of years. The structure of the series is based on the areas of specialisation embedded in the Institute, including cultural regions and several themes.

Of course, the books can only reveal the tip of the iceberg. We are nonetheless convinced that publishing these books in all their glory might well entice the reader to seek out and enjoy all the objects and stories that the museum houses.

Photographs have been collected since the inception of the colonial predecessors of the present museum. Most of the time, however, they have been regarded and treated not as museum objects, but as useful material that is suitable for illustrating the Institute's other activities. It was only in the 1980s, long after the colonial chapter had closed, that new generations developed new perspectives and rediscovered the rich and unique photographic collections. Since then much work has been done to restore, digitise and research the approximately 250,000 images in the museum's holdings. This book presents a small but carefully made selection from this amazing pictorial

archive, and frames it within the complex history of the Tropenmuseum and the Institute of which it forms a part.
I would like to extend a word of thanks to all the authors, editors, researchers, photographers and designers associated with KIT Tropenmuseum and KIT Publishers who have helped to bring this vast project to life. Immense appreciation should be expressed to the Ministry of Foreign Affairs/ Development Cooperation, which has made our museum's work possible for so many years. A word of thanks is also owed to the BankGiro Loterij, which has allowed us to use part of the funds we have received since 2006 to further develop the collection, and specifically to create this historical series of books on the museum's huge collection.
I wish you much reading pleasure and look forward to seeing you at the museum.

Peter Verdaasdonk
Director of the Tropenmuseum

PREFACE

Arguably no other collection in the Tropenmuseum is as closely linked to the history of the Institute as the photograph collection. The collection not only provides richly variegated insights into Dutch colonial history but also informs us about the way in which the Colonial Museum, and later the Tropenmuseum, dealt with this history.
The photographs that are related to the former Netherlands East Indies form the bulk of the Tropenmuseum's photographic collection. Approximately 80 per cent of the material comes from the Netherlands East Indies and Indonesia. The remaining 20 per cent was taken in Suriname and the Dutch Caribbean Antilles (former Netherlands Antilles) North Africa, India, China, Japan and Europe. In its current form the total collection comprises approximately 485,000 objects that can be broadly divided into five categories: c. 2645 historical photograph albums, c. 325,000 photographs, c. 120,000 negatives made with various techniques, c. 26,000 slides, and another c. 10,000 different objects such as transparencies, picture postcards and photomechanical prints. All in all, a sizeable collection that was brought together from around 1870.
Photographs were already being actively collected in the last quarter of the 19th century. The emphasis was on contemporary collecting, so that the images could be used as illustrative documentary or educational material. As the images aged, the photographs were classified as 'rejected', because they no longer fulfilled their documentary purpose from a contemporary point of view. During the colonial period the photographic collection was continuously supplemented with new topical material, brought together in great variety by companies, public, private and scientific institutions and individuals. The rejected images were either consigned to the attic or were disposed of.
After Indonesia declared independence in 1945, little attention was given to the Dutch colonial past and the historical photographs were temporarily placed in a vacuum. Instead, the Institute actively collected new visual material to document changes and developments in various regions around the world. It was only from around 1970 that interest in the historical material was reinvigorated, in response to requests from the large group of Indo-Europeans living in the Netherlands who had a nostalgic desire to revisit an important part of their earlier lives by means of the photographs. For them the images portrayed a lost and increasingly romanticised society in which nature and culture played important roles. This need for nostalgic visual material was gradually supplemented with a more academic interest in documentary photographic material. The photographs were a previously unknown source of information for historical research. The appreciation for the historical photographs as objects has changed since the 1980s and they are being collected again with renewed interest. The aesthetics of the photographs and their place in the history of photography also received attention. The photograph collection also started acquiring museal status after a start was made on professionally cataloguing and opening up the collection. This publication is a long-awaited part of this process. It contains 120 photographs, which are discussed within the context of their creation in Indonesia, the Dutch colonial context, and with reference to the museal history of the Netherlands.
The first chapter is an introduction to the world of photography and to the photographers who were active in the colonial society in the Netherlands East Indies. The second chapter explains how the collection was built up and used, from the first acquisition in 1876 to the most recent types of digital distribution. It is evident that over the years the photographs have been viewed from a range of different viewpoints. The remaining chapters discuss thematic clusters in the collection, from anthropological, historical and art historical perspectives, to broad topics such as society, commerce and personal themes such as family and portraiture.

In an era in which attention for photography as an independent medium became more pronounced, this important photograph collection raises numerous questions, not only about technical and aesthetic developments, but also about (self-) representation, and importantly about the role photographs played in the complex colonial society at the time. Numerous researchers have shown that not only the images themselves, but also the ways they were collected and classified, contributed to a negative representation of colonised peoples. These scholars have proposed a variety of interpretations and frameworks for exploring the complex category we now designate as colonial photography.
This book does not claim to provide detailed answers to all of these questions raised by the collection but offers readers at the very least a thorough introduction and some new insights into one of the world's most important collections of photographs from the Netherlands East Indies, in the hope that this will lead to further research and interpretations.
As readers of this book will be well aware, any choice of language for writing about the colonial period can be a complex issue. In translating words, titles of people, places, concepts and so on, some of the nuances of the original language may be lost. Moreover, translations have political implications. For simplicities sake we have chosen to use words as they were used at the time. We have chosen to use the term 'Netherlands East Indies' as the name for Indonesia before independence in 1945; this is also in line with some of the most recent academic literature on this region. Whenever a place name, for example, appears for the first time in the text, its current spelling or name is placed in brackets (e.g Batavia (Jakarta) and Buitenzorg (Bogor)). This is only done for geographical names that have changed significantly over time. Names of which only the spelling has changed are presented in their current form, for example, Surabaya and not Soerabaja.

The authors

>> 4
Salt production at a company near Kalianget, Madura
Photographer: unknown
gelatin printing-out paper
c. 1914
12.9 x 21.4 cm
60048731. Gift: U. Jansz, 2004

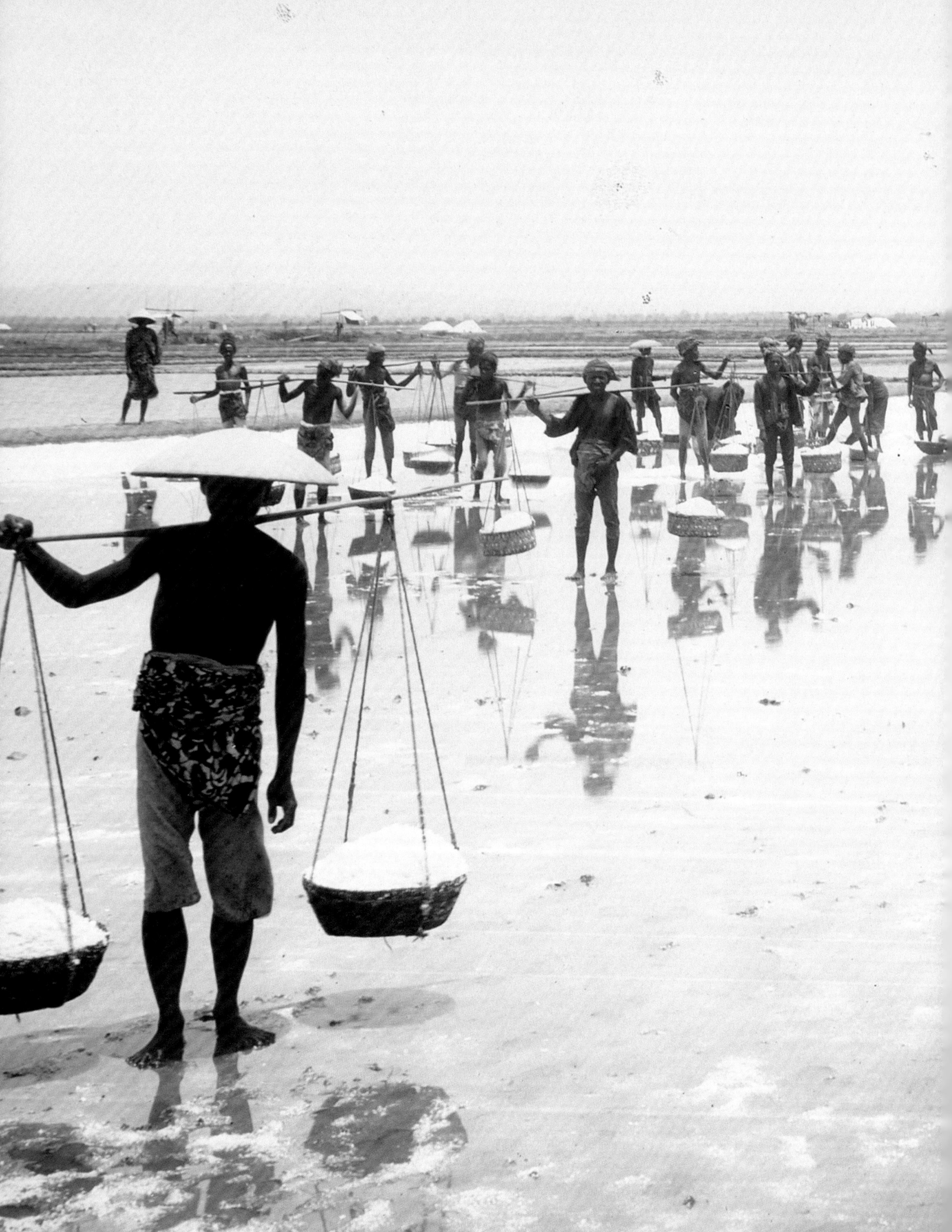

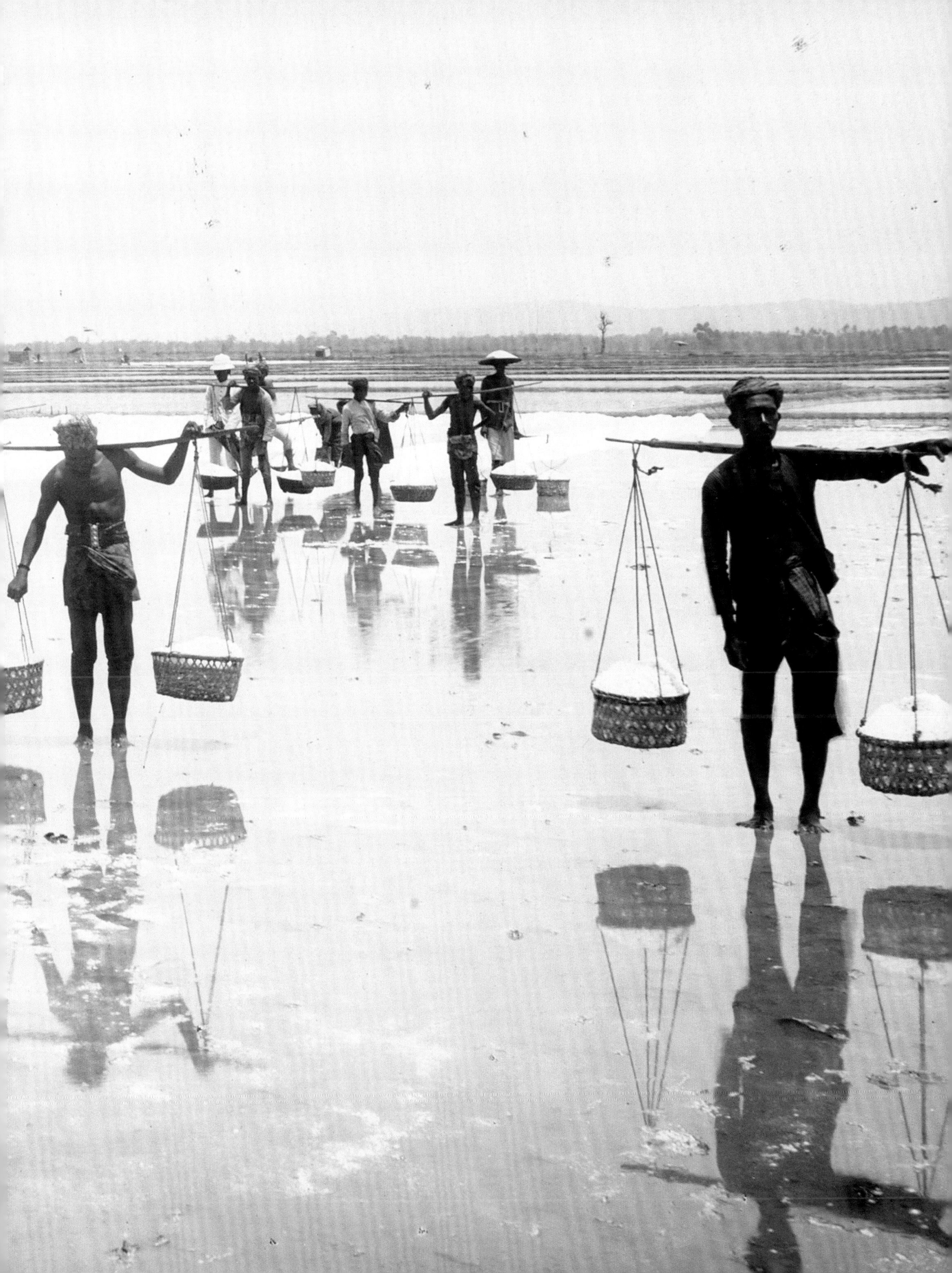

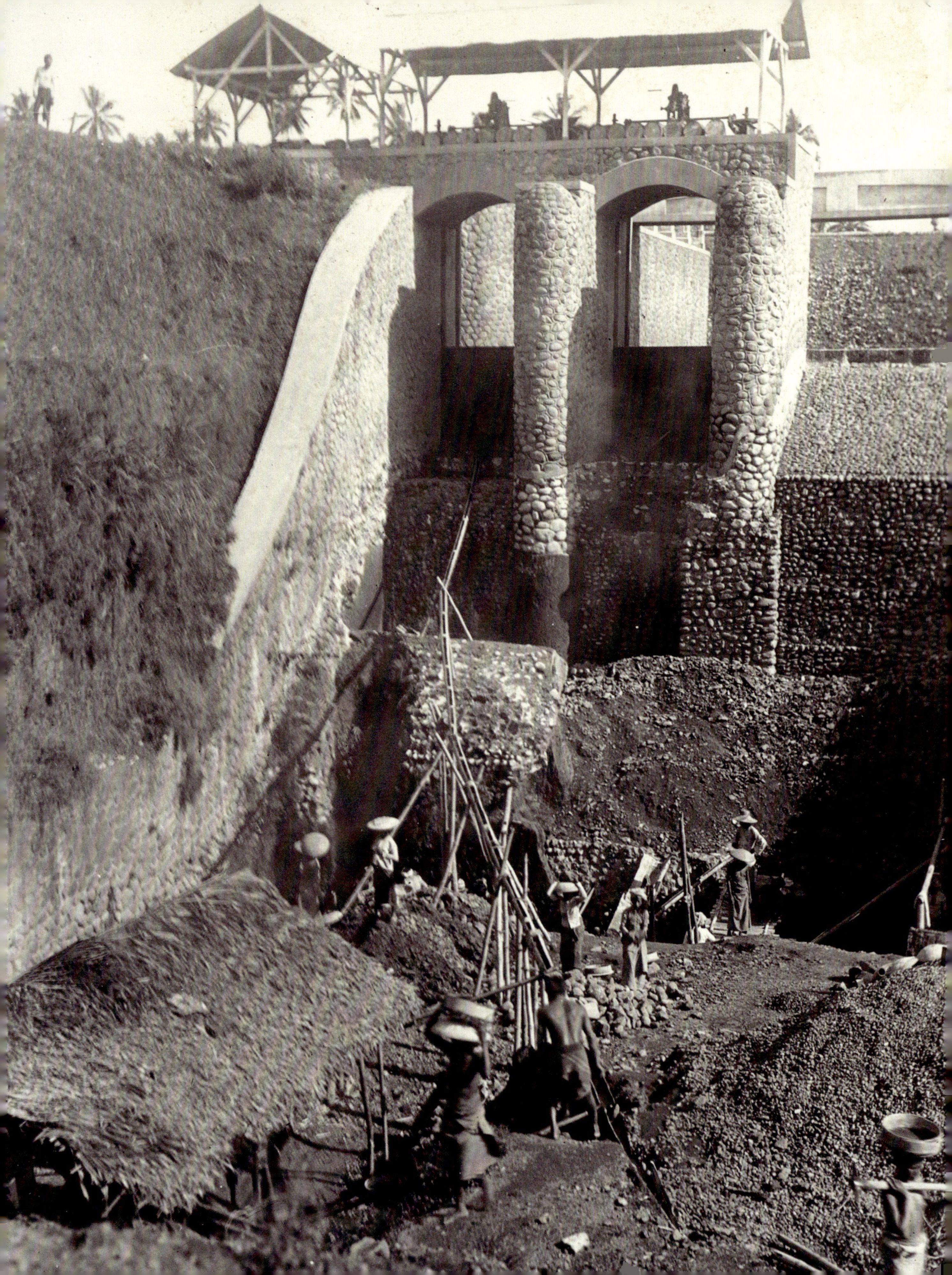

PHOTOGRAPHY FROM THE NETHERLANDS EAST INDIES:

changing perspectives, different views

< 5
Construction of a dam at Denpasar, Bali
Photographer: unknown
gelatin printing-out paper
1910–20
11.3 x 8.2 cm
60026355. Gift: J.B. van Heek, 1984

ROB JONGMANS AND JANNEKE VAN DIJK

In 1877 the Dutch King Willem III (1817–90) was presented with an album of photographs by the Batavia-based photographic studio Woodbury & Page.[1] A large box covered with blue velvet and embossed with silver metal letters, this album contained 50 albumen prints of Aceh (Sumatra) that had been glued onto card stock. A second, this time successful, military expedition had been undertaken in this area from December 1873 to January 1874, but the Dutch king saw no evidence of this; instead the photographs provided him with a different impression of the area: the roadstead at Koetaradja (the capital, Banda Aceh), various military encampments, street views, the European middle class who had settled there, and the sultan's *dalam* (palace). The caption below the photograph of the Willemstoren Lighthouse identifies it as being built during wartime in 1875, and it was dedicated to peace as a lasting monument to the fallen. The Dutch flag flutters proudly on the top of the lighthouse. This album does not contain any images of hostilities or military group portraits.[2] Based on the photographs the Dutch king could do nothing but conclude that the resistance in Aceh was a thing of the past.[3] The battle for Aceh seemed to be won! But this turned out to be an illusion – the Aceh War would only come to a definite end in 1914 after ruthless military force had been used, resulting in much loss of life. This album of photographs reveals a lot about the development and use of photography in the Netherlands East Indies, how it helped to shape perceptions of the colony, the role of photographers and of those who commissioned the photographs, and the way photographs were used in the colonial context.

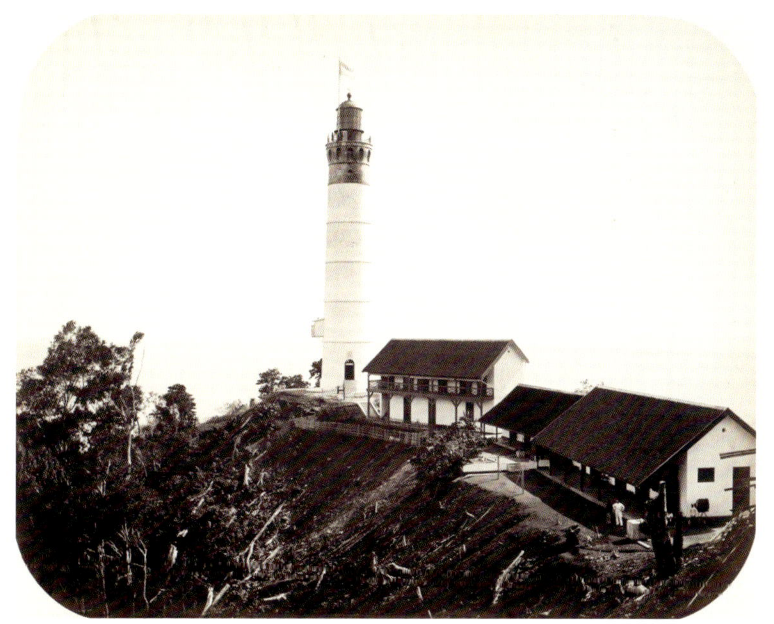

6
The 'Willemstoren' lighthouse, Poeloe Bras (Pulau Breueh, Aceh)
Photographic Studio: Woodbury & Page
albumen print
c. 1877
19.1 x 24.1 cm
60001920. Gift: Royal Archives, 1969

The 19th century: economic and political development

The new medium of photography was introduced to the Netherlands East Indies in the middle of the 19th century. This was at a time when the economy was making a gradual transition to a free economy. The entire archipelago would eventually succumb to Dutch control in the wake of several wars. There were also significant changes in demographics, with increasing numbers of Europeans moving to the Netherlands East Indies, a trend that would continue into the 20th century.

The Cultivation System ('Cultuurstelsel') that was introduced to Java in 1830 and ensured a steady flow of money to the Dutch treasury slowly waned from the 1860s. The obligatory deliveries of coffee, sugar, pepper and indigo – products that were shipped to and traded in Europe, and the requirement that the indigenous Javanese population provide free labour (*corvée*) for constructing and maintaining roads and bridges – were facing severe criticism in the Netherland East Indies and in the Netherlands. Abuse and famine – the latter partly caused by the fact that lucrative commercial crops were replacing the staple crop, rice – did not go unnoticed and was criticised from within (Multatuli's book *Max Havelaar)* as well as in the Dutch parliament. Exploitation of the local population and the one-way traffic of the millions earned in profit were no longer accepted as the natural course of affairs.

The introduction of Agrarian Law ('Agrarische Wet')

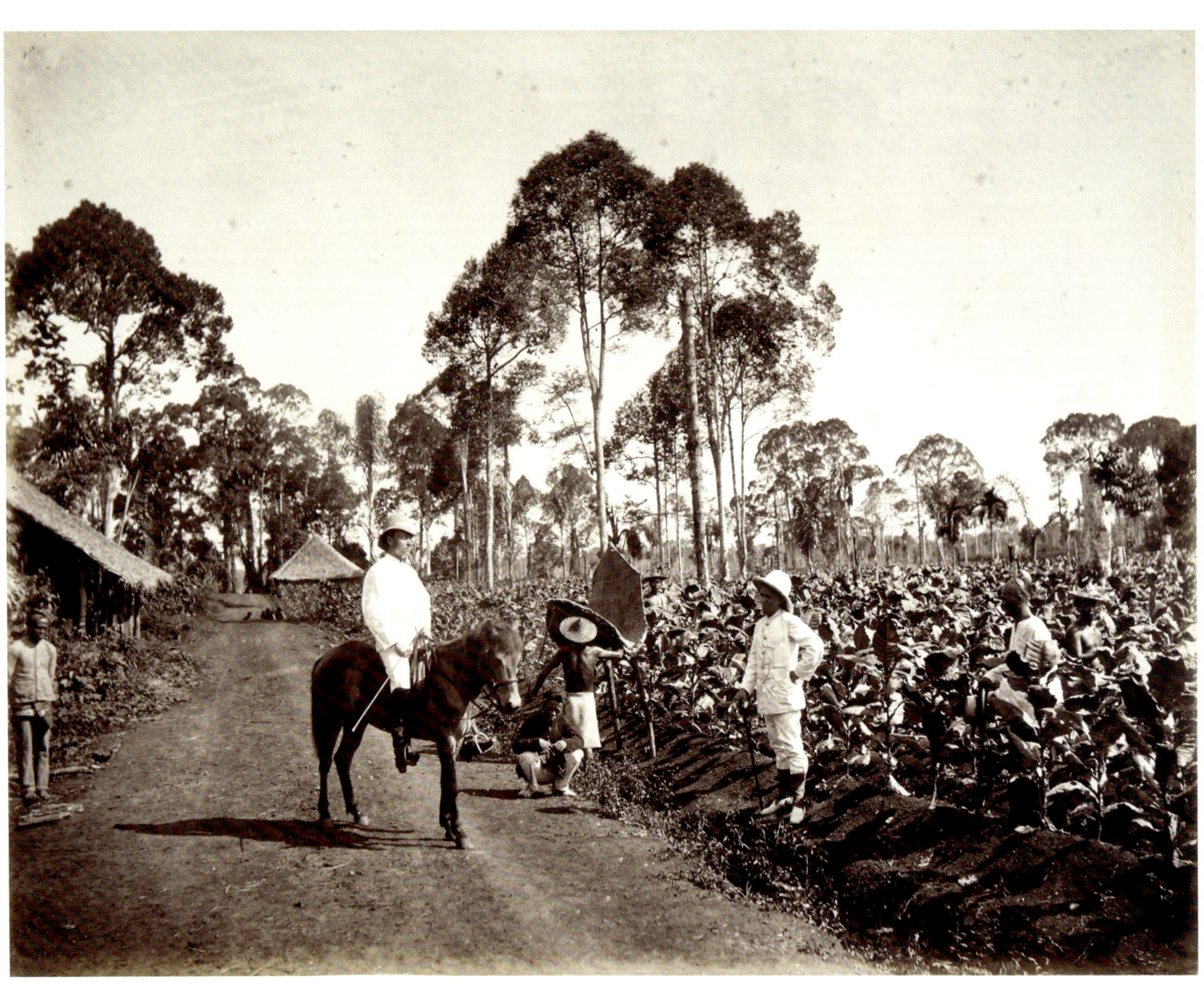

7
Planters in discussion at the Bekioen tobacco plantation, Langkat (Sumatra)
They are supervising the contract labourers in the tobacco fields.
Photographic Studio: G.R. Lambert & Co
albumen print
26.6 x 34.7 cm
1885–91
60001824. Provenance: unknown

in 1870 resulted in the definite end of the Cultivation System. This law made it possible for European entrepreneurs to obtain uncultivated areas on long-term lease. Two years later the trade in colonial products was liberalised. These two measures had the result that from the second half of the 19th century there was a gradual upsurge in the cultivation of commercial crops on West and East Java as well as on Sumatra, where there was much uncultivated land. During the 19th century planters went from being landowners with princely status and lifestyles to being plantation managers. From the 1870s growing numbers of old Indo-European planter families in Central Java, which until this time had lived luxuriously in spacious houses in close proximity to and in plain sight of the local population, started leaving the plantations and relocated to pretty houses in cities like Surakarta (Solo) and Yogyakarta. They also relocated their *pieds-a-terre* to Europe; contact with Europe had become much more frequent and easier because of the opening of the Suez Canal in 1869 and the rise of steamships.[4]
The liberalisation of agriculture attracted many enterprising Europeans, whose numbers doubled in the last 30 years of the 19th century.[5] They also sought economic success in the Outer Regions ('Buitengewesten'[6]), especially on Sumatra's east coast. Wide-scale tobacco cultivation during the second half of the 19th century was wildly successful; rubber plantations followed.
Only a handful of European civil servants governed this vast colony. Around 1860 there were only 175 European civil servants to a population of 13 million on Java.[7] Batavia (Jakarta) was the administrative centre. Peace was upheld by the presence of the Royal Netherlands Indies Army (Koninklijk Nederlands Indisch Leger, KNIL). Contact between the Netherlands and some parts of the Netherlands East Indies had been maintained for centuries, especially Java and Ambon. The administration confined its activities in the Outer Regions to superficial contacts with local rulers. There were areas, still unknown to the Dutch, that were populated by relatively isolated communities, and where no trade or administrative relations were maintained. In other regions, such as Aceh, Lombok (1894) and Bali (1906, 1908), extreme violence was used to coerce the inhabitants into acknowledging the colonial administration.

The 19th century: the arrival of photography

As elsewhere, in the middle of the 19th century 'painting with light' was still in its infancy in the Netherlands East Indies. Much had to be worked out by trial and error. It became evident almost immediately that working in tropical climates was considerably more complicated than in the more temperate West Europe. The few potential clients (government, private individuals, army) doubted if the usefulness and advantages of photography were as good as was being claimed in comparison to traditional drawing and painting. The Ministry of Colonial Affairs awarded the earliest commissions, which involved photographing archaeological monuments on Java. As far as we know, Jurriaan Munnich (1817–65), an officer of health, was the first person to receive a commission, in 1840, to photograph the Borobudur. Unfortunately, the results were disappointing. In 1845, his successor, the German photographer Adolph Schaefer (d. 1873), who lived in The Hague, had more success. In that year he made 58 daguerreotypes of the Borobudur.[8] He opened the first photographic studio in the Netherlands East Indies soon after his arrival in Batavia in 1844, where he made portrait photographs. He later established himself as a portrait photographer in Semarang, Surabaya and Sumenep (Madura).[9]
On 26 August 1851, the Belgian painter, decor painter, lithographer and theatre maker, Isidore van Kinsbergen (1821–1905), arrived in Batavia. As a flamboyant artist and pioneer of photography and the first to arrive from the Low Countries, he became a familiar figure in Batavian art circles. Although van Kinsbergen is in no way a model of the 19th-century photographer, his career does offer some charming insights into the professional practice of a photographer at that time. In 1855, the year Van Kinsbergen began taking photographs, 4145 Europeans lived in Batavia.[10]
In 1863 the Batavian Society of Arts and Sciences (Bataviaasch Genootschap van Kunsten en Wetenschappen) commissioned him to make a comprehensive and expensive photographic documentation of Javanese antiquities, including the Borobudur. How he photographed these various subjects was left to his own expertise. This freedom resulted in a monumental approach, in which

Van Kinsbergen showcased his recently acquired knowledge of photography. He produced a number of catalogues with prints of the photographs that were submitted to a several world exhibitions from 1873 onward.[11] This brought Javanese antiquities to the attention of an international public and simultaneously enabled the Netherlands to profile itself as a colonial power with a scientific approach to archaeology.

Besides photographing the Javanese antiquities Van Kinsbergen also took portraits, landscapes, city views, 'ethnic types', art reproductions, still lifes of fruit, and nudes. This is, however, not what made him unique, as working in different genres was characteristic of the 19th-century photographer's multi-faceted activities, and they frequently wanted and had to exploit all segments of the market to make ends meet. What did distinguish him from his contemporaries was the way he incorporated his skill as a theatre maker to create imaginative, theatrical images. Van Kinsbergen possessed that all-important and defining quality of a photographer: he had an excellent pair of eyes.

His talent as a theatre director is reflected in the portraits he made in the 1860s in his photographic studio in Batavia and at the courts of Yogyakarta, Surakarta, Madura, Buleleng (Bali) and Bandung. It is not merely the symbolic function and status of these high-ranking individuals that is evident in these images; Van Kinsbergen also maintained less distance from his subjects than was usual (see pp. 122-123). This can be clearly seen in his portrait of the three daughters of the Sultan of Yogyakarta.

It is important to note that he utilised his knowledge of Western classics when arranging the girls' poses. The Leiden scholar P.J. Veth (1814–95), has commented extensively and with great enthusiasm about these 'Javanese Graces', named after the three sisters from Classical mythology,[12] but perhaps in making this photograph Van Kinsbergen was also inspired by the reliefs on the Candi Lara Jonggrang, also called the Prambanan temple complex, near Yogyakarta.

There were limits to the number of potential clients in the European colonial administration and the local aristocracy who wanted to have portraits of themselves; the government was somewhat frugal when it came to commissions. Nonetheless, a commercial business dedicated to photography and selling photographic supplies opened premises

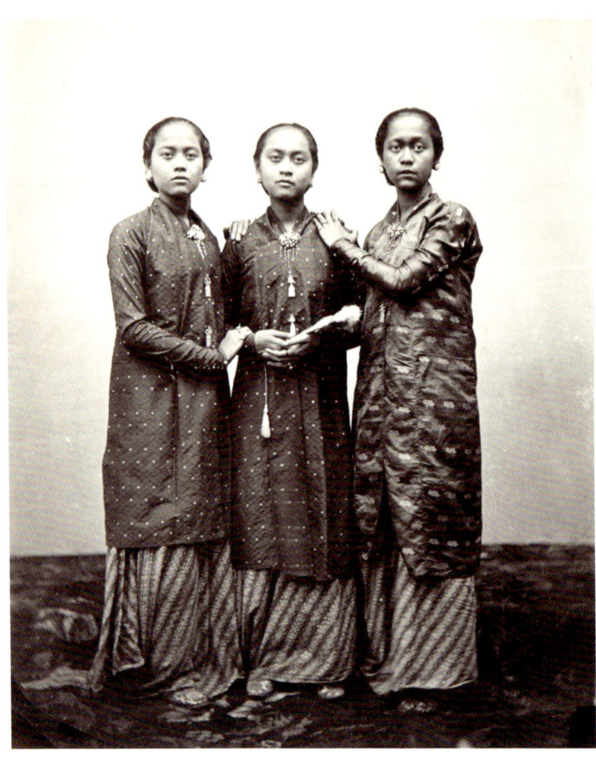

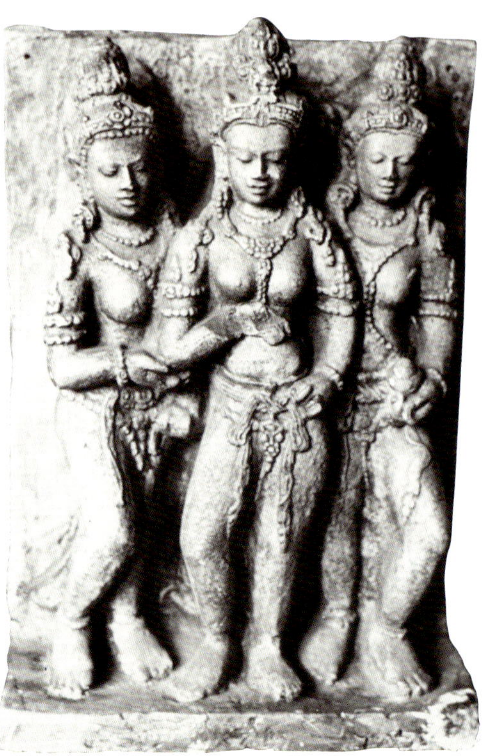

> 8
Studio portrait of three daughters of Hamengku Buwono VI, Sultan of Yogyakarta
Photographer: Isidore van Kinsbergen (1821–1905)
albumen print
18.2 x 15.1 cm
1862–65
60002137. Provenance: unknown

>> 9
Plaster cast of a relief from the temple dedicated to Shiva on the Candi Lara Jonggrang, or Prambanan temple complex, exhibited in Enschede as part of the Colonial Institute's travelling 'Indies Exhibition'
Photographic Studio: Brusse Press Photography Agency
silver gelatin developing-out paper
16.8 x 11.7 cm
1941
60059877. Provenance: unknown

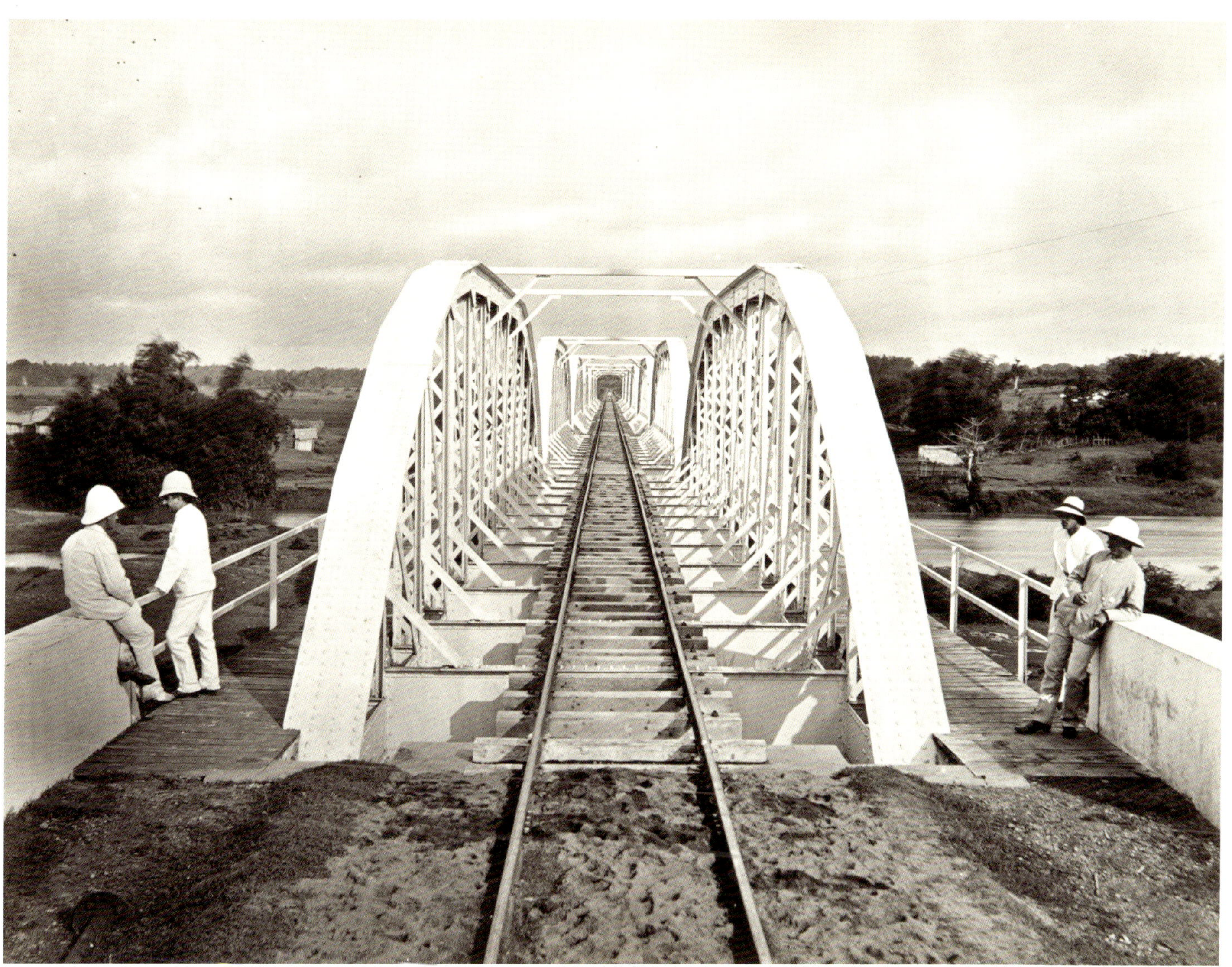

10
Railway bridge in the region of Solo, Java
Photographer: unknown
albumen print
18.2 x 23.5 cm
1870–1900
60005499. Provenance: unknown

in Batavia and other large towns on Java. Six years after Van Kinsbergen's arrival, in 1857, the British photographic studio Woodbury & Page opened a branch in Batavia, where they continued operating until 1908. Extremely ambitious, they frequently took to the road themselves or dispatched other photographers to capture images of the archipelago. Their landscapes, city views and 'ethnic types' were included in many European souvenir albums. As a result, Woodbury & Page clearly made their mark on the way the Netherlands East Indies was represented and perceived in the 19th-century, both figuratively and literally: they pioneered the practise of 'signing' their prints with the stamp of a photographic studio.[13] Working as commercial photographers they also captured the damage caused by natural disasters and offered these for sale.[14] They gave lessons to amateur photographers, and sold cameras and other props. Photography supplies were also sold in bookshops and pharmacies, indicating that there was a guaranteed market for this expensive hobby from the start.[15]

Travelling photographers were a common phenomenon in the Netherlands East Indies in the early days of photography. They would settle somewhere for a couple of months, announce their presence in the local newspaper and hope that as many people as possible would make use of their services. If there were enough clients (private or corporate), they would open a studio; photographers who did this include Hendrik Veen (1823–1905) in Malang (see p. 41), J.A. Meessen (1836–85) in Batavia, and Charls & Van Es & Co. (1880–1915) in Surabaya. Using these locations as a base, they would scour the surroundings for work, or close their studios for a while to work elsewhere in the archipelago. Photographers also worked together and helped each other out – during their travels they used each other's facilities, shared roughly the same photographic styles and exchanged knowhow and techniques. For example, Van Kinsbergen worked for a year from March 1878 with the recently arrived photographer Herman Salzwedel in the Kinsbergen & Salzwedel Photographic Studio in Batavia.[16]

Photographers would take over each other's negative archives if one of them left Indonesia or went bankrupt. The steady stream of European civil servants and entrepreneurs who moved to Indonesia after 1870 was a guaranteed new market for their photographs.

During the 19th century most of the photographers on Java resided in cities where most of their potential clients lived. On Sumatra this was in Medan, where the first travelling photographers from nearby Singapore settled around 1870. After a journey through Deli and across the Karo plateau, the Dane Kristen Feilberg (1839–1919) took the first photographs of Lake Toba, about which little was known at the time and had only been seen by a handful of Europeans. The photographers followed in the wake of the development of these promising Outer Regions. After a trial phase during which Jacob Nienhuys (1836–1927) succeeded in starting a tobacco plantation in 1863 and founded the Deli Company in 1869, Sumatra's east coast was rapidly developed and tobacco was planted on a wide scale. Photographs were taken of all the activities, from the extensive felling of virgin forest to packaging the end product in the tobacco factory. Photograph albums show the planters' successes, while reinforcing ideas of progress and modernisation. The downside, the abuse of contract labourers on the plantations, as described in the broadsheet *De Millioenen uit Deli* (1902) and the *Rhemrev Report* (1904), were not documented.[17]

A branch of the Singaporean photographic studio G.R. Lambert & Co. operated in Medan from the 1880s until the 1890s.[18] It was the commercial drive of this international firm that made it one of the first to open a branch on Sumatra. Around 1900, their clients could select images from a catalogue with no less than 3000 examples. It included 'views and types' and covered a large part of Asia; in fact, it was the largest image archive in South East Asia.[19] Originally, the German photographers Heinrich Ernst and Carl Josef Kleingrothe and the Swede Herman Stafhell worked in the branch in Medan before they opened their own studios. Of these early photographers, Kleingrothe eventually became the most important photographer and distributor of images of Sumatra's east coast. After the turn of the century he published loose-leaf portfolios with heliogravures made after photographs in the archives of Stafhell & Kleingrothe, the photographic studio he continued running under his own name after his business partner left. Elsewhere on Sumatra, in Padang on the west coast, C.B. Nieuwenhuis (1863–1922) opened a photographic studio in 1891. He had photographed landscapes during his travels and also had a keen eye for the local population and their cultural practices.

In 1901 he travelled with a military expedition to Aceh under the command of General Van Heutsz, resulting in the book *De expeditie naar Samalanga. Dagverhaal van een fotograaf te velde*, in which he published the photographs and recorded his own experiences.[20]

Despite the familiarity of some of these names, we do not know who took most of the photographs. What is certain is that until 1900 a large majority of the photographs were taken *by* Westerners *for* Westerners, and it is interesting that more non-Dutch than Dutch photographers tried their luck in the Netherlands East Indies. Additionally, assignments also came from the indigenous aristocracy, who by that time had started commissioning photographs, recognising the importance of photography and the role it could play in asserting status. Local rulers gave away signed portraits as souvenirs, following the practise in Europe. As far as can be ascertained, the

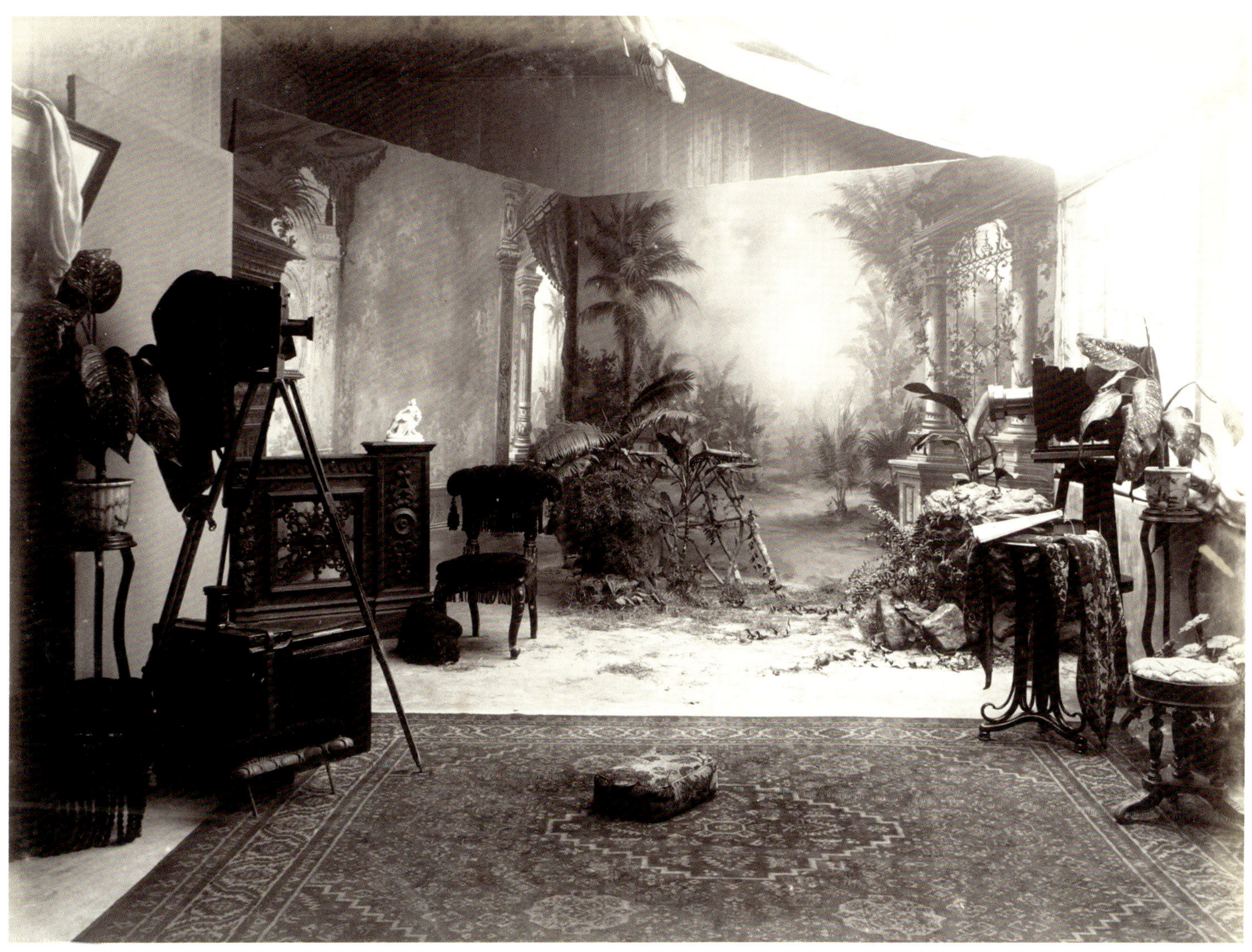

11
The interior of Stafhell & Kleingrothe photographic studio in Medan
albumen print
26.2 x 34.1 cm
c. 1898
60001724. Provenance: unknown

photographers included a few Chinese nationals, such as Tan Tjie Lan in Batavia.

The Javanese Kassian Céphas (1845–1912) is especially noteworthy. This photographer became famous among a wide public, particularly for his series of aesthetic portraits of Javanese women. The Archaeological Society (Archaeologische Vereeniging) commissioned him to make photographs of the Candi Prambanan, Candi Sewu, Candi Mendut and Candi Borobudur temple complexes and sanctuaries around Yogya. It is noteworthy that he appears among the temple ruins in his own photographs, in all likelihood leaving the camera operation to an assistant. Céphas was court photographer to Sultan Hamengku Buwono VII of Yogyakarta (1839–1921). He made a variety of portraits and documented the various cultural practices in the *kraton* (palace).[21] He made the photograph album with portraits of the sultan and his family that was lavishly decorated with velvet and silver mountings, which was presented in 1891 by the sultan to the departing civil servant, Resident J. Mullemeister (1838–1926) (see p. 122-123).

A photograph album seemed to be a fitting gift for such an important occasion. Another striking example of the status that photography had acquired is the presentation by Sultan Hamengku Buwono VIII (1880–1939) of an album of photographs to Queen Wilhelmina (1880–1962) on the occasion of her Royal Silver Jubilee in 1923 (see p. 34).

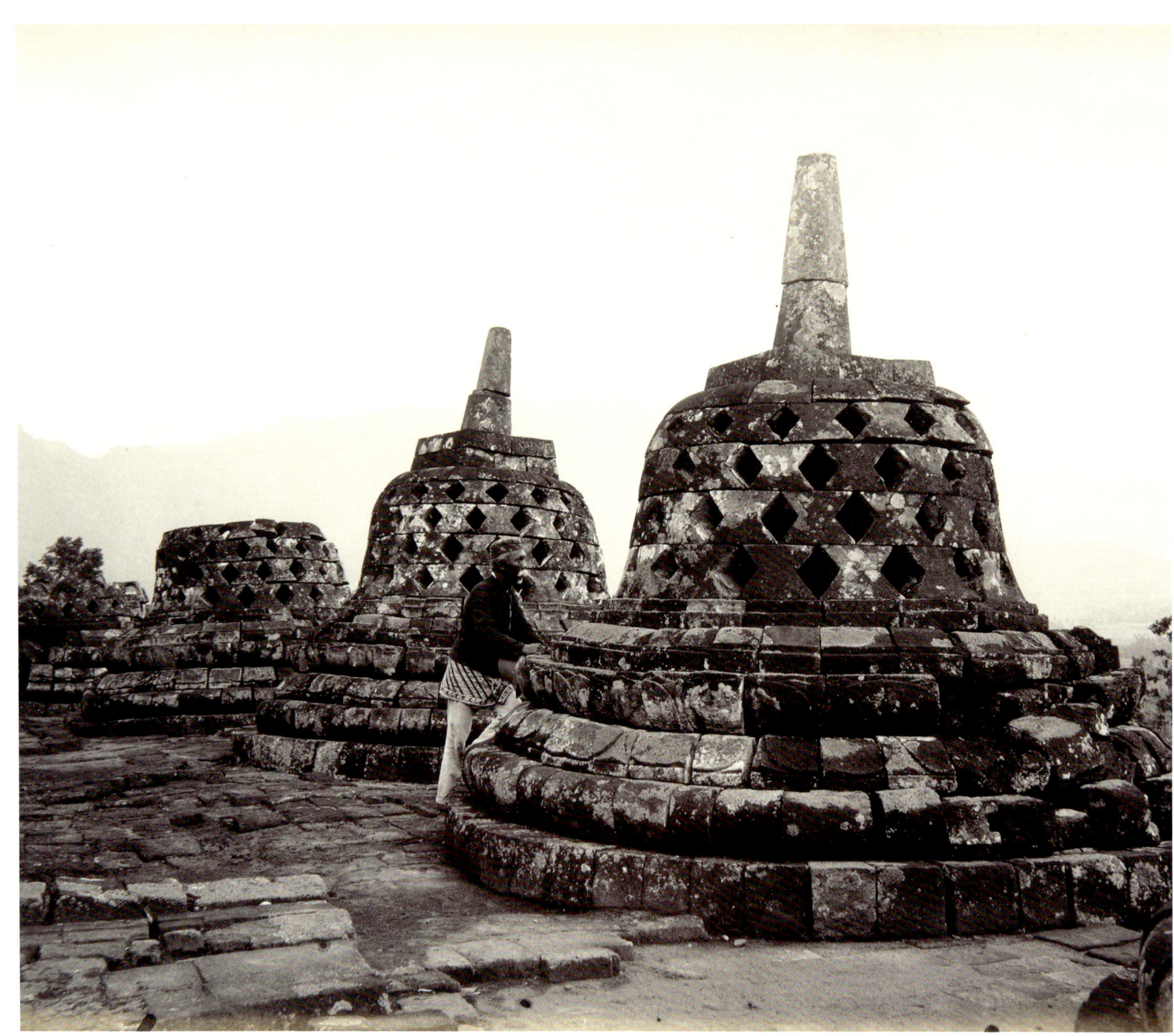

12
Kassian Céphas at the stupas on the Borobudur
Photographer: Kassian Céphas (1845–1912)
albumen print
16.2 x 21.8 cm
c. 1890
60005095. Provenance: Prof Dr J.C. van Eerde, 1930

The 20th century: introduction

Mr and Mrs Boekenoogen travelled to the Netherlands East Indies in 1920 and 1921. The photographs of their voyage and places they thought interesting are contained in five sturdy photograph albums, richly finished with dark red leather and gilt edging as a visual *souvenir de voyage*.[22] These albums present the Netherlands East Indies as a safe place to explore, with many places of interest, and that the nature was overwhelming. Although the Boekenoogen's took a significant number of the photographs themselves, the majority were selected from a local professional photographer's catalogue of stock images. These depicted places they had not visited, or which the professional photographer had captured in more artistic and atmospheric ways. Photographs made by Céphas in 1901 were still available and are included in the albums. Characteristic of 20th-century photograph albums is that personal impressions predominate; they were complemented with existing professionally made images (in time, less of these were used). Socio-economic (tourist infrastructure, good travel facilities), political (peace prevailed), and photographic (no longer a complicated process, everyone could take their own photographs) developments seem to converge in this family's travel albums.

The 20th century: economic and political developments

In her Queen's Speech of 1901, Queen Wilhelmina announced a new direction in colonial politics. After centuries of one-way traffic of wealth from the Netherlands East Indies to the Netherlands, now the welfare of the local population became a focal point. Specific focus points in this Ethical Policy (Ethische Politiek), which was framed as a paternalistic ideal couched in a colonial and modernising language, were the development of local agriculture and the infrastructure (road construction, railways, irrigation), and creating access to and improving health care and education. Executing this policy required much expert manpower. Well-educated Dutch citizens such as engineers, agronomists, doctors and teachers were encouraged to go to the Netherlands East Indies to take the local population, as they imagined it then, by the hand and lead them towards a brighter future. Special institutions were created to disseminate information in the areas of agriculture, health care, or extending credit; research was conducted into how crops and farming methods could be improved. The expansion and improvement of the education system enabled a part of the local population to eventually acquire a position in the colonial system, but only if they were loyal to that system. Opposition was not tolerated. The government actively countered the rising nationalism that denounced the inequality in the colonial relationship. The army, which barely played a military role after the first decades of the 20th century (the entire archipelago was virtually under Dutch control), were assigned ever more police tasks.

The Netherlands East Indies became an even more complex society in the 20th century. The European population increased rapidly, especially on Java.[23] The new arrivals were mostly young, enterprising people who had obtained their initial work experience in the colony. A general rule of thumb

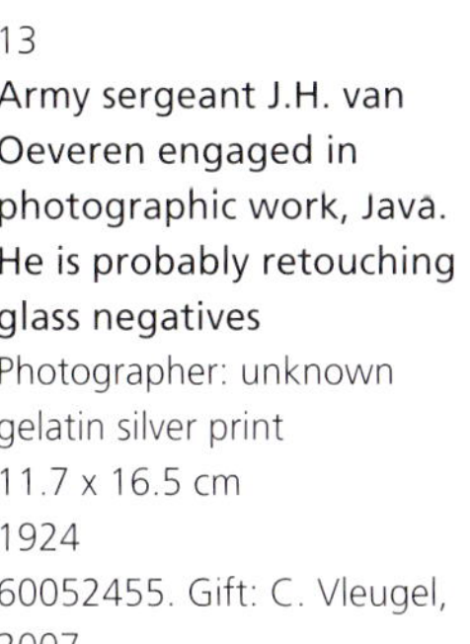

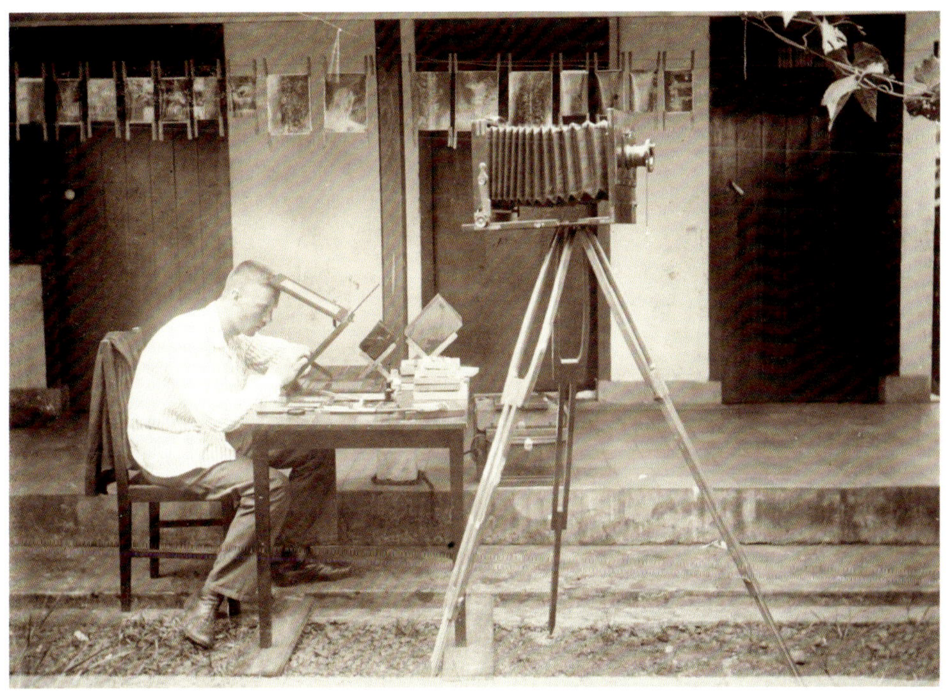

13
Army sergeant J.H. van Oeveren engaged in photographic work, Java. He is probably retouching glass negatives
Photographer: unknown
gelatin silver print
11.7 x 16.5 cm
1924
60052455. Gift: C. Vleugel, 2007

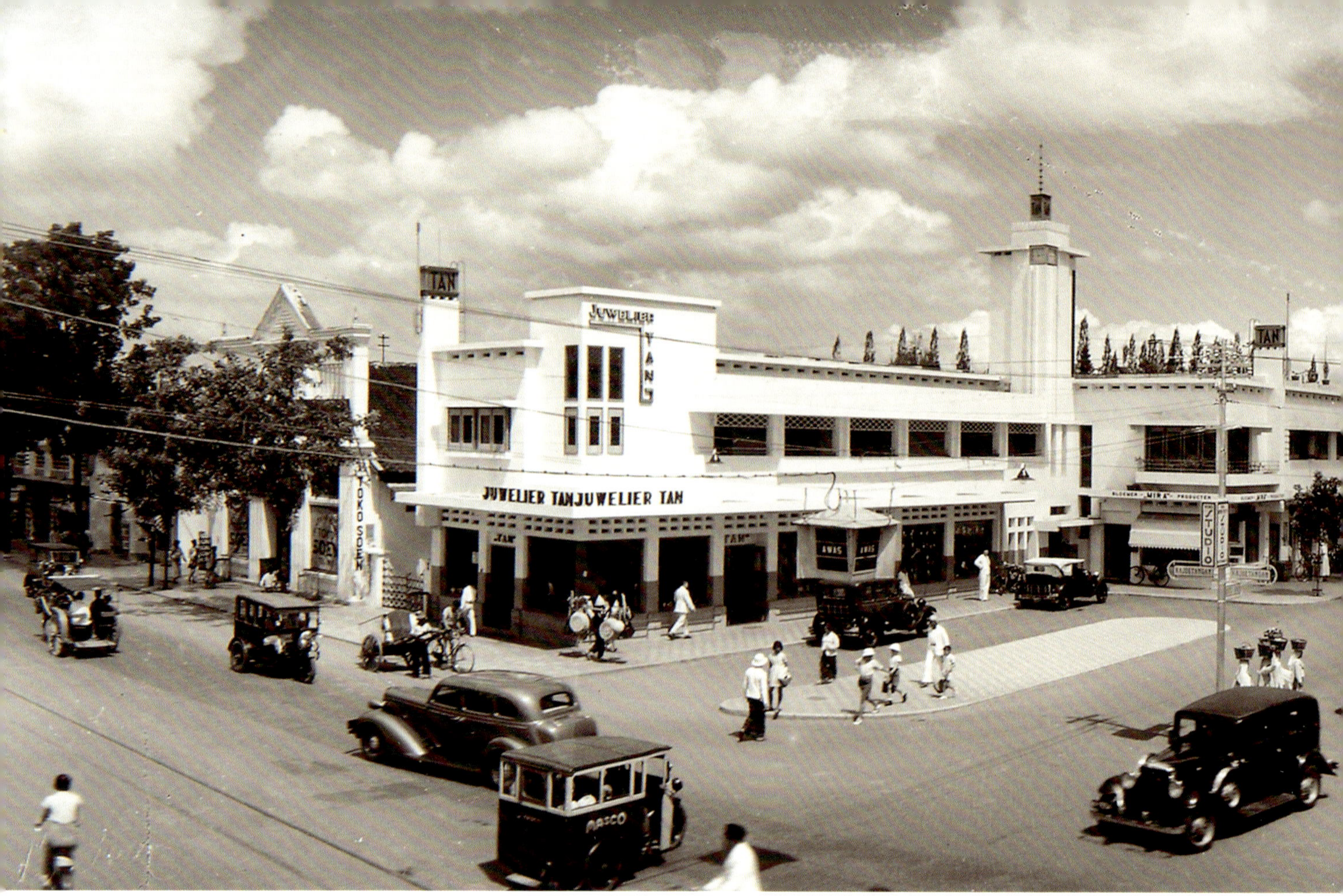

was that a better education secured a better place in society. Some of the Indo-Europeans[24] and the Indonesians made use of this opportunity, but the managerial positions were reserved for the new arrivals. The population was divided by law into Natives ('Inlanders'); Europeans (the Japanese and Armenians shared the same privileges); and 'Foreign Orientals' ('Vreemde Oosterlingen'), comprising Indians from British India, the Chinese and the Arabs. Each group had to abide by rules specific to that group, which also had an impact on education, for example. Another frequently used classification was that of the 'Inheemse' (indigenous), the 'Indische' (Indo-European) and the *totok*.[25] There were differences and discrepancies in welfare, class, social environment and status between these groups, but these also existed within the groups themselves. Unlike the situation in the 19th century, economic developments were not confined to Java and parts of Sumatra. Income was now not only derived from commercial crops. Raw materials such as oil (Borneo/Kalimantan), coal (Sumatra), and gold, silver and tin (Sumatra, Billiton/Belitung) ensured that the Outer Regions became more economically important. Where possible, the work on the plantations was increasingly mechanised.

In the political arena there were slow and cautious steps towards participation, although it was limited to a select group. The creation of the People's Council ('Volksraad') in 1918 was perceived as reflecting this. An elite group, the members of which fulfilled the important requirements relating to income and legal status, chose some of the Council members, while others were appointed directly by the highest authority, the Governor-General.

At the local level, town councils were assigned more and more responsibilities. The 20th-century colonial civilising mission in the Netherlands East Indies was brought to an abrupt end by the Japanese invasion in 1942, taking many by surprise. The consequences were far-reaching for both the local population and the colonial elite.

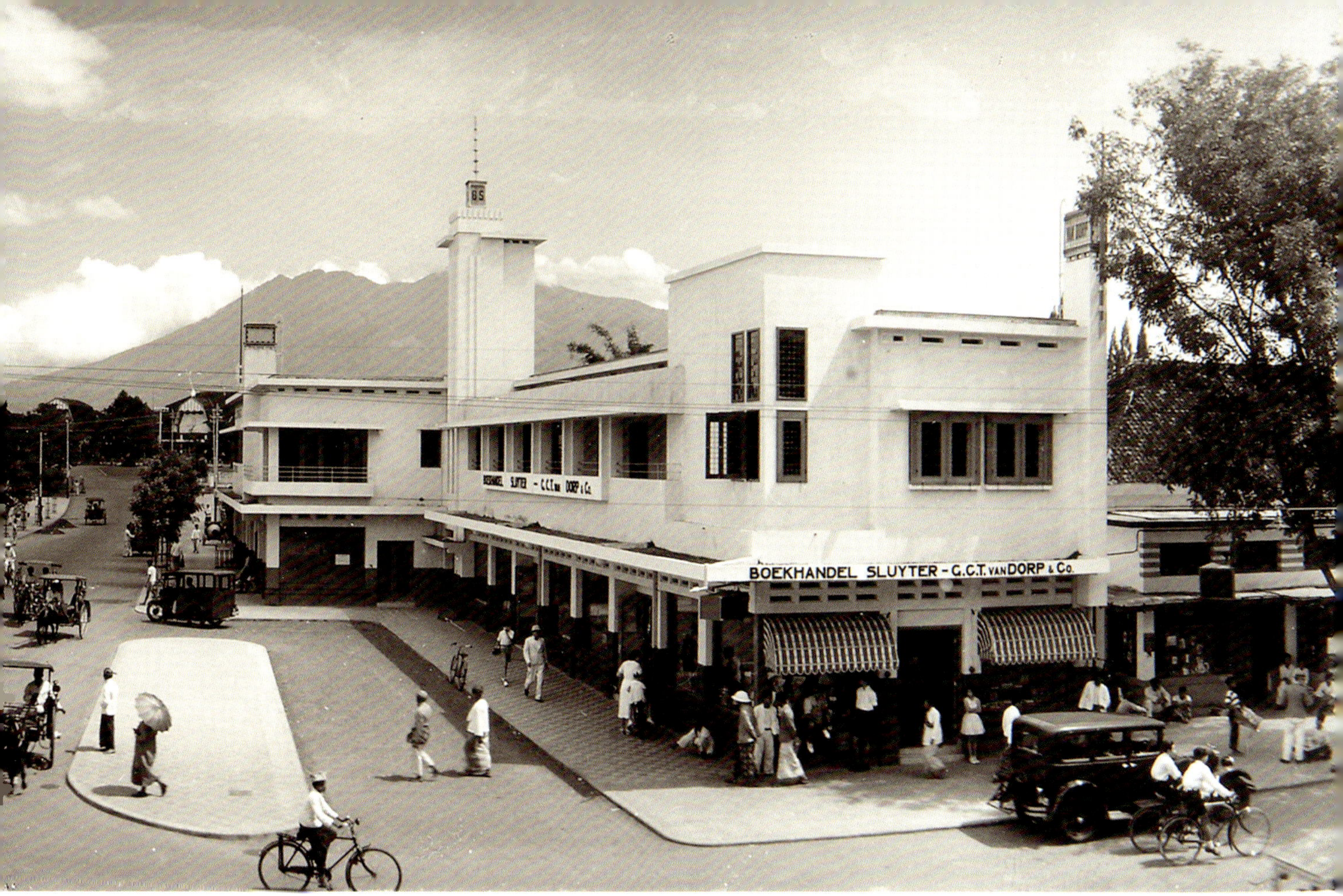

14
View of the junction at the Kajoetangan-, Van Riebeeck- and Smeroe streets and Tjelaket in Malang
Photographer: Tiek Sen
silver gelatin developing-out paper
8.2 x 26.3 cm
c. 1935
60005877. Provenance: unknown

The 20th century: the coming of the age of photography

The previously very complicated procedures involved in photography were as good as resolved during the 20th century. Cameras were easier to use and the growing numbers of photographic shops developed the photographs and sold the necessary equipment and accessories. Anyone who could afford a camera could start taking photographs immediately.
The number of professional photographers and photographic studios increased enormously during the 20th century, as did their area of distribution. At least one photographic studio could be found in almost every large town throughout the archipelago.[26] It is noteworthy that there were comparatively fewer European photographic studios than in the 19th century: now they were primarily run by Chinese and Japanese. Photographic studios seemed to reflect the social hierarchy: European photographers served the colonial upper class, while those who could afford photographs, but found the European photographers too expensive, went to the more affordable Chinese *tukang potret*. These were craftsmen who sometimes made their own, modest wooden cameras that they fitted with German lenses. Chinese photographic studios were family businesses. Cousins or former fellow-villagers travelled directly from China or sometimes from Singapore and worked as apprentices, after which they opened their own studios and in turn taught an apprentice who likewise came from China. This phenomenon gave rise to a steadily growing network of photographers and appears to have been widespread throughout South East Asia.[27]
The Chinese studios also sold photographic equipment and accessories and processed films brought in by clients. In all likelihood the Chinese photographers also worked for their own Chinese community, but this falls beyond the scope of this study. The Tropenmuseum's collections probably include more photographs by Chinese photographers

than we presume, but more research will be required to confirm this. Although the photographer's names are frequently unknown, their approach to photography – especially for an official commission – would have differed very little from that of their European counterparts. Much as now, in the early 20th century the client would also have made his wishes clear, overriding the personal preferences of the photographer.

A great deal of the work done by professional studios and photographers such as Kurkdjian & Co in Surabaya, Lux Studio in Garut (see p. 28), Fotax in Malang and Surabaya, the Van Felde Photographic Studio in Batavia, and Wijnand Kerkhoff (1886–1974) on Java, took the form of commissions. Private agricultural and industrial companies and government bodies such as town councils were important clients that were willing to spend money on glorifying their achievements on film. Studio portraits remained an important genre and source of income. Unlike in the 19th century, photographers rarely travelled through the archipelago; at most they would leave the towns to take photographs of a beautiful landscape or of the local population that they would sell to the growing numbers of tourists. Photographers were still hired for official events, but significant family moments were increasingly captured on film by family members themselves as mementoes or to send to their families in the Netherlands. For families, photography became a binding agent between Indonesia and the Netherlands, and vice versa. Family photographs from the Netherlands were inserted between the colonial photographs in many family albums.

After 1900 the photographs gradually started depicting how Europe was being transplanted to the colony. The European influence became increasingly apparent: comfortable homes, better infrastructure. The archipelago was believed to have become more 'liveable' for European women. Notions of courage and deprivation, used to described earlier European inhabitants in the colony, were soon replaced with feelings of pride and contentment: 'Something monumental is being achieved there' ('Daar werd wat groots verricht').[28]

15

Man, woman and child drying coffee beans, with Batur volcano (Bali) in the background

Despite being rather static due to the careful staging, this image is nonetheless simultaneously alluring and misleading.
Photographic Studio: Kurkdjian (1888–1936)
gelatin printing-out paper
16.8 x 23.1 cm
1890–1920
60027662. Gift: W. van Tets-Ruygrok, 1985

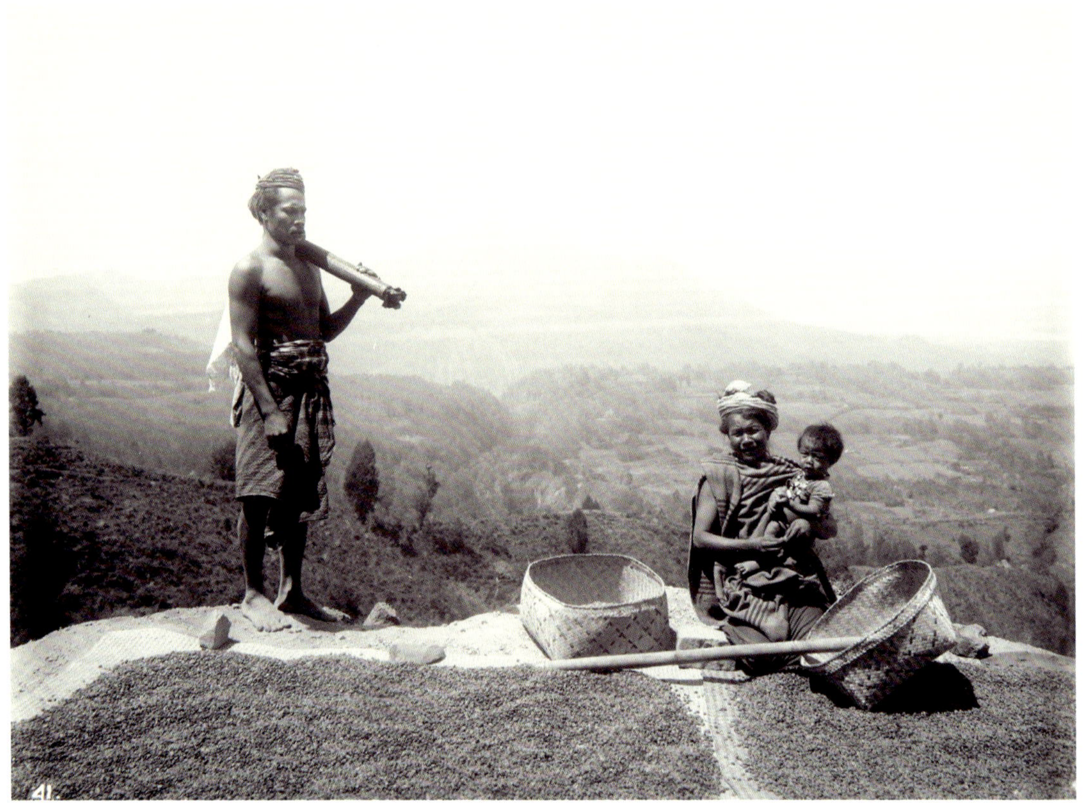

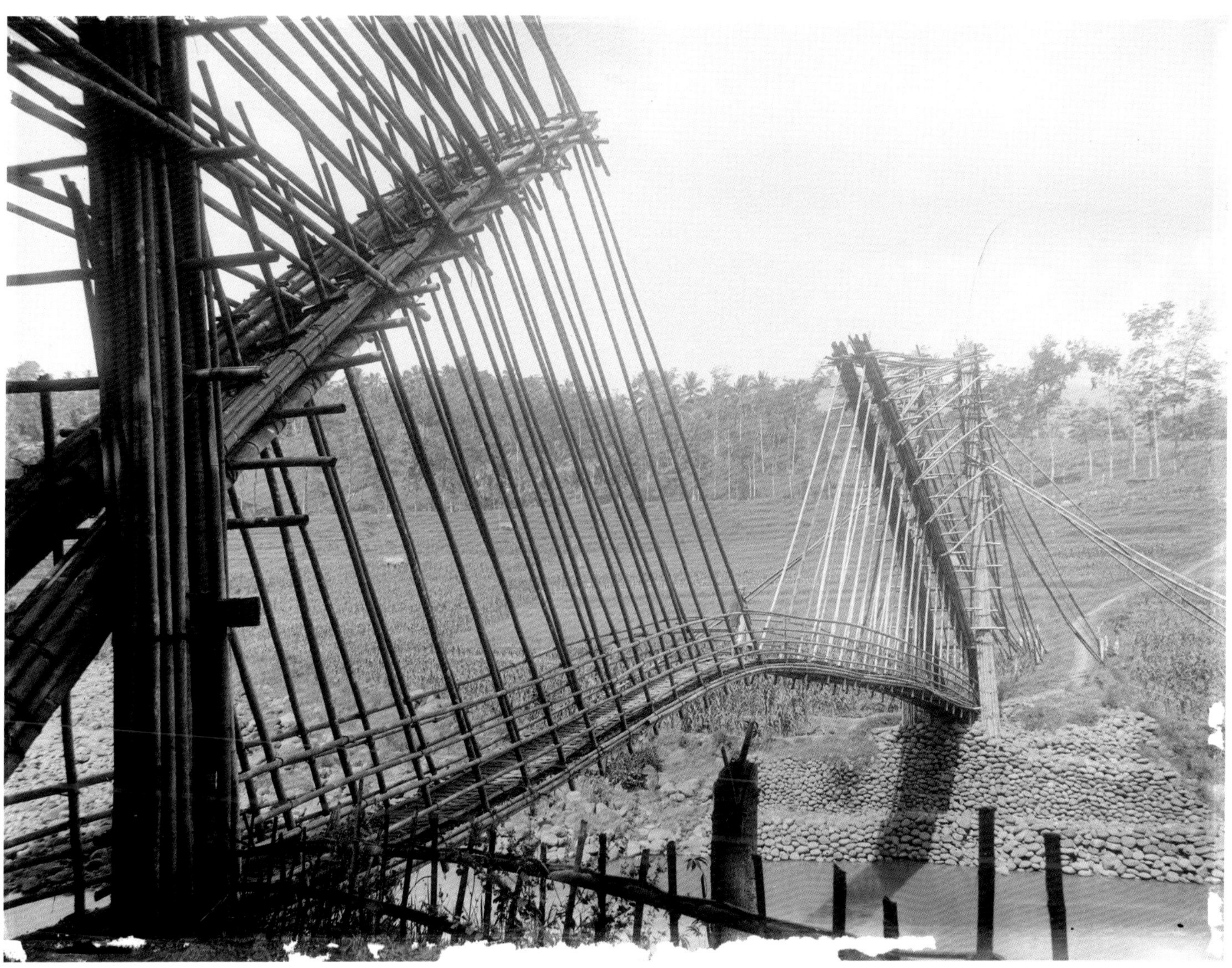

Different views

The way in which photographers portrayed the Netherlands East Indies, creating their own views of the Tropics, determined what people in the Netherlands saw and knew of the colony. The photographic studio that played a pre-eminent role in this belonged to the Armenian, Ohannes Kurkdjian (1851–1903). He opened a photographic studio in Surabaya in 1888, which continued operating until 1936. After his death the Englishman G.P. Lewis ran the studio. The Kurkdjian & Co photographic studio created carefully staged photographs in which the choice of subject, the composition, the framing, the use of light and the serene atmosphere were striking. Such images had a great influence on the ways the colony was perceived. Related to a painting genre at the time known as the 'Beautiful East Indies' ('Mooi-Indië') style, a romantic view was presented of a tropical paradise with vast rice paddies, volcanoes, rustling palm trees lining the seashore and a contented 'native' population enjoying life beneath the tropical sun. Kurkdjian & Co was a renowned and flourishing studio that was frequently asked to make corporate albums. Much of the work by the photographer Thilly Weissenborn (1889–1964) also has qualities of the 'Beautiful East Indies' style.

16
Bamboo bridge spanning the Serayu river at Wonosobo, Java
The angle of this image focuses the attention on the structure of the bridge, lending this photograph a more dynamic composition.
Photographer: Thilly Weissenborn (1889–1964), Lux Studio
gelatin glass negative
18 x 24 cm
1917–40
10026487. Gift: W. Viallé, 2004

THILLY WEISSENBORN (1889–1964)

Thilly Weissenborn's Lux Studio was located above Mr D.G. Mulder's 'NV Garoetsche Apotheek en Handelsonderneming' (a pharmacy and trade association) in Garut. From 1920 she was in charge of a small group of Sundanese employees. A woman who was a photographer and an independent entrepreneur was an exception at the time. The youngest of six children, she was born in 1889 in Kediri, but her family moved to Europe in 1892. Thilly's older sister Else studied photography in Paris and opened a photographic studio in The Hague in 1903. Thilly learned the initial tricks of the trade in Else's studio. Thilly Weissenborn travelled to Java in 1913 and continued learning about photography in the studio of O. Kurkdjian & Co., in Surabaya, where, under the supervision of G.P. Lewis, she was originally responsible for retouching negatives. She slowly developed into a photographer with her own style that displayed artistic similarities with the work of this famous studio. Garut was situated in the mountainous landscape of West Java and, thanks to the cooler climate and beautiful location, was a popular and busy holiday destination. Thilly Weissenborn made portraits on commission in her studio, but she was also adept in documenting the much sought after and more commercial subjects such as buildings, companies and interiors. In her 'free work' she concentrated on taking photographs of indigenous scenes, landscapes and photographs of 'ethnic types',[29] which were extremely popular with publishers and tourists at the time. Weissenborn's talents were not only in great demand in Priangan; she also received increasing numbers of commissions to take photographs elsewhere. She photographed Governor-General Fock's visit to Garut, producing the beautiful album that is preserved in Tropenmuseum collection. Governor-General van Limburg Stirum asked her to photograph Buitenzorg Palace and the Cipanas Estate near Sindanglaya. Weissenborn compiled many albums with selections from her own work, also for private individuals who were leaving Garut or Priangan or who wanted to send an album to their families in the Netherlands. Weissenborn was interned in a number of different camps during the Second World War, but she managed to survive. The Japanese surrender was followed by the chaotic Bersiap period,[30] and the havoc that befell Garut did not spare Weissenborn's Lux Studio and it was destroyed. The Dutch soldier and amateur photographer W. Viallé rescued 48 glass negatives (13 x 18 and 18 x 24 cm) from the rubble; these are now in the Tropenmuseum collection. In 1956 Weissenborn returned to the Netherlands for good. After her death in 1964 the Tropenmuseum received an album from her estate,[31] which is generally understood to be an album of stock photographs from her studio. A substantial portion of her oeuvre is contained in this rather plain looking album. Clients and publishers probably browsed it before placing an order at Lux Studio. With the contents – 149 daylight gelatine silver prints – Weissenborn made an important contribution to creating an idealised romantic image of the former Dutch colony. It is immediately apparent that Weissenborn composed her idyllic images with extreme care, and in doing so her work continued a style that had earlier been developed by the Kurkdjian photographic studio. AM

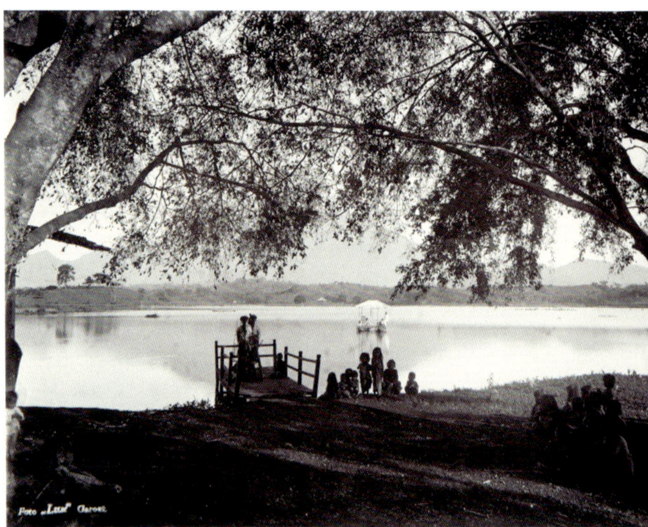

17
Angklung performers, children and a pleasure boat at Bagendit Lake, Java
Photographer: Thilly Weissenborn (1889–1964), Lux Studio
gelatin printing-out paper
17.4 x 23.5 cm
1917–40
60002464. Gift: Mrs A.P. van Duyn and Mrs A. Hetterschij-van Duyn, 1963

Images of an innocent, peaceful, hard-working Netherlands East Indies satisfied the political requirements of the colonial power and appealed to tourists' idyllic perceptions of the archipelago. Very few images portrayed the actual situation of the average population. Exceptions are the contrasting images by H.F. Tillema (1870–1952), who recorded his critical views of the colonial world in a substantial photographic archive that included his own images as well as those of others. He reproduced these in his many publications. One of the ways he did this was to use the picture story style (in which two contrasting photographs are placed side by side), but also by simply placing a caption beneath an official KPM photograph of a steamship in Humboldt Bay (see p. 79): 'Trade and traffic pave the way for cholera, even to the remotest corners'.[32] This undeniably gave this image other connotations than the client and the photographer had in mind when it was taken. Photography served to buttress the empire and create divisions between 'Europe' and the 'Others' with all the attendant hierarchies. The ethnographic institutes[33] in the Netherlands that collected photographs of the Netherlands East Indies organised and re-organised the images over the years in their repeated attempts to gain an overview of the diversity and complexity of the colonial society. The categories used at the time contribute to the way the images are interpreted now.

Some subjects are over-represented in a certain period and less so in others. For example, until 1900 and for a brief period thereafter the military aspect was emphasised, in particular the colonial wars in Aceh and Lombok. Anyone expecting live-action photographs of the military actions will be disappointed. The battlefield could not yet be captured photographically. Photographers were too busy fighting their own battles against long exposure times, heavy equipment and (in the early period) working with wet plate collodion glass negatives that had to be developed immediately after exposure. Military encampments, group portraits of soldiers, 'rebel' leaders who had surrendered, and the shattered possessions of the opponent were all that people got to see.

One shocking photograph (Fig. 19) shows a group of soldiers posing beside the butchered inhabitants of the fortified compound *(gampong)* Kuta Reh in 1904, after the Dutch army had overrun it during the notorious military expedition through the Gayo and Alas regions under the command of Lieutenant-Colonel Van Daalen. The triumphant military police (*Marechaussee*) stand on the top of a wall; the corpses of their victims are scattered below them on the ground. A child who survived the massacre sits in the middle of the carnage. This photograph provoked a great deal of discussion immediately after its publication, which occurred quite soon after the event. Since then, it has disappeared from the Dutch

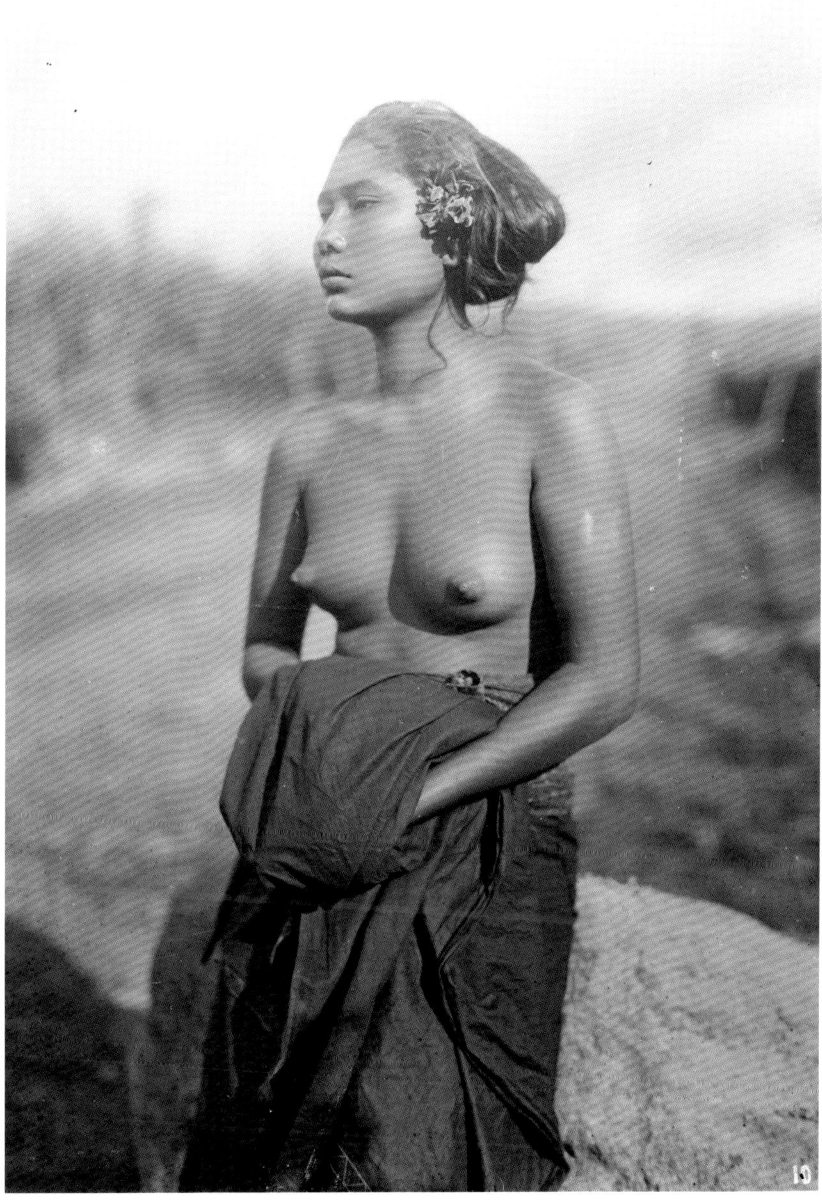

18
Portrait of a woman, Bali
Photographer: Thilly Weissenborn (1889–1964), Lux Studio
gelatin glass negative
18 x 24 cm
1917–40
10026475. Gift: W. Viallé, 2004

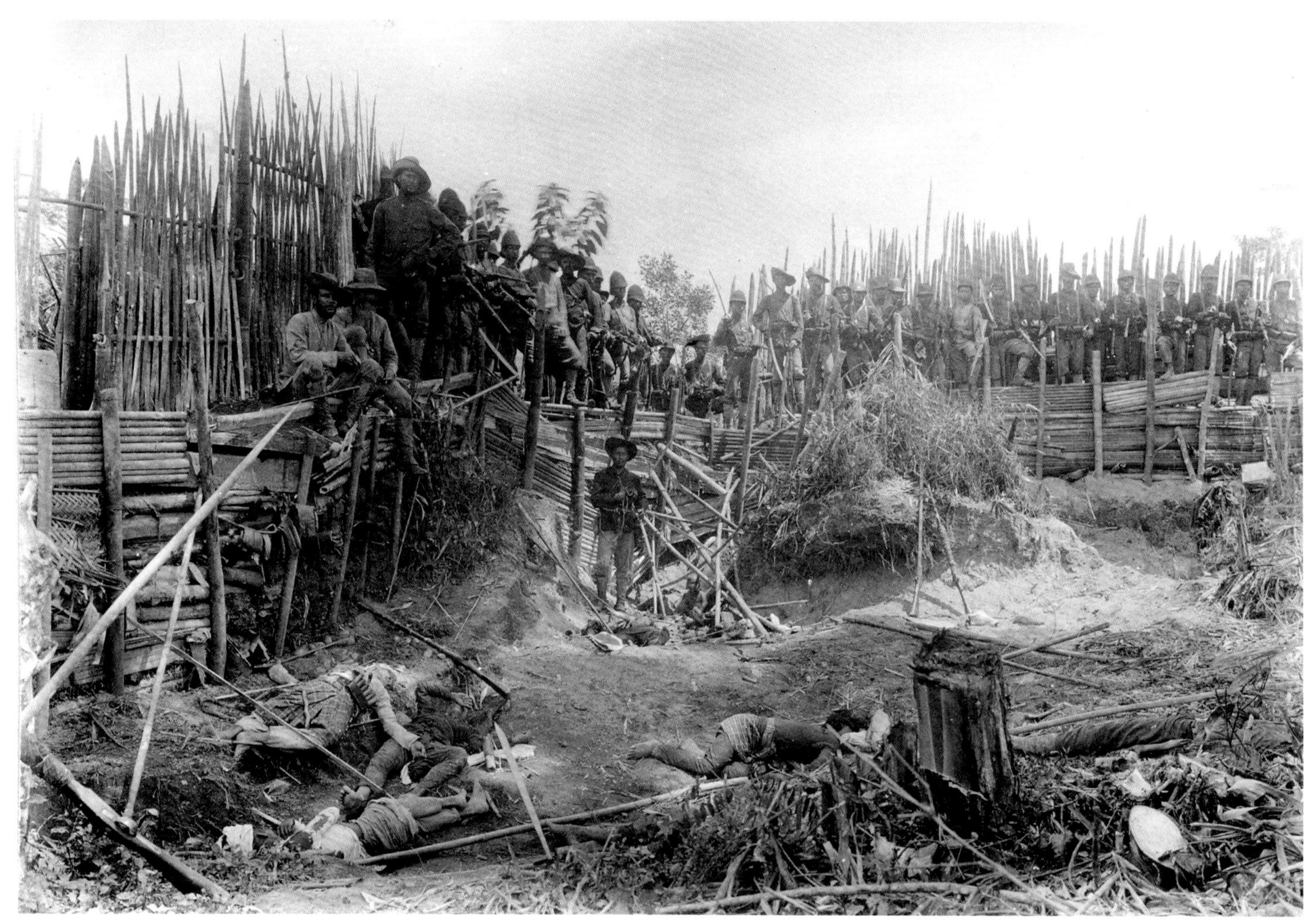

19
The military police ('Marechaussee'), including Lieutenant Colonel Van Daalen, with slaughtered inhabitants at the fortified Kuta Reh *gampong*
Photographer: H.M. Neeb
albumen print
11.6 x 17 cm
1904
60009090. Provenance: unknown

collective memory from time to time but it always resurfaces. For some it was an icon of the dark colonial era, for others a record of an unfortunate incident. The photograph was never suppressed but feelings of shame and discomfort have resulted in this photograph being covered up, much like a family secret.[34]

Beside the colonial wars, popular subjects less bound by time were also photographed, such as the landscape, 'ethnic types', people at work and images that portrayed an intimacy between the Europeans and the local population over whom they exerted control. This intimacy can be seen in family photographs, which show, for example, the relationship between the children's nanny (*babu anak*) and a European child (Fig. 2) and in the more erotic photographs (Figs. 18 and 26). Besides its obvious photogenic qualities, the fascination for the landscape was also related to an important goal of the colonial administration: mastery of the land itself, which required surveying the archipelago and creating maps so that more effective control could be wielded over it. The 'wild', 'untamed' natural environment was an obstacle to economic exploitation; it was almost as if the country was waiting for initiatives, vigour and knowledge to tame it and control the raw power of the rivers. Photographs of the virgin forests that frequently include a human to convey the superhuman scale (Fig. 20), landscape images of tree felling[35] and the clearing of the primeval forest (Fig. 21), resulting in cultivated lands (Fig. 7), served to emphasise the idea of the 'primitive' indigenous population relying on the 'modern', controlling, efficient Europeans as well as the contrast between these two groups. They legitimised the colonial undertaking as it was presented at, for example, the World Exhibition in 1883 in Amsterdam: the natural wealth of the Netherlands East Indies and the exotic primitiveness of the local population were appealing for the modernising and civilising entrepreneurship of the Dutch administration and private individuals.[36] These primitivising and frequently idyllic images of the indigenous population were also consciously constructed in studios, where photographers placed their subjects against a backcloth 'freely painted after nature'. Sometimes a uniform white backdrop was used, with selected attributes that alluded to a primitive state of being (Figs. 22 and 23).

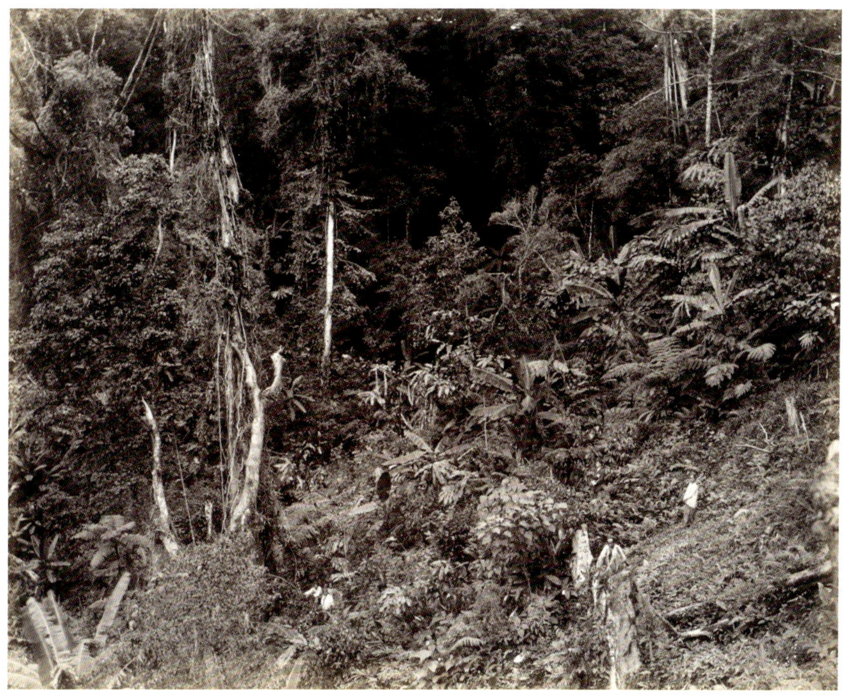

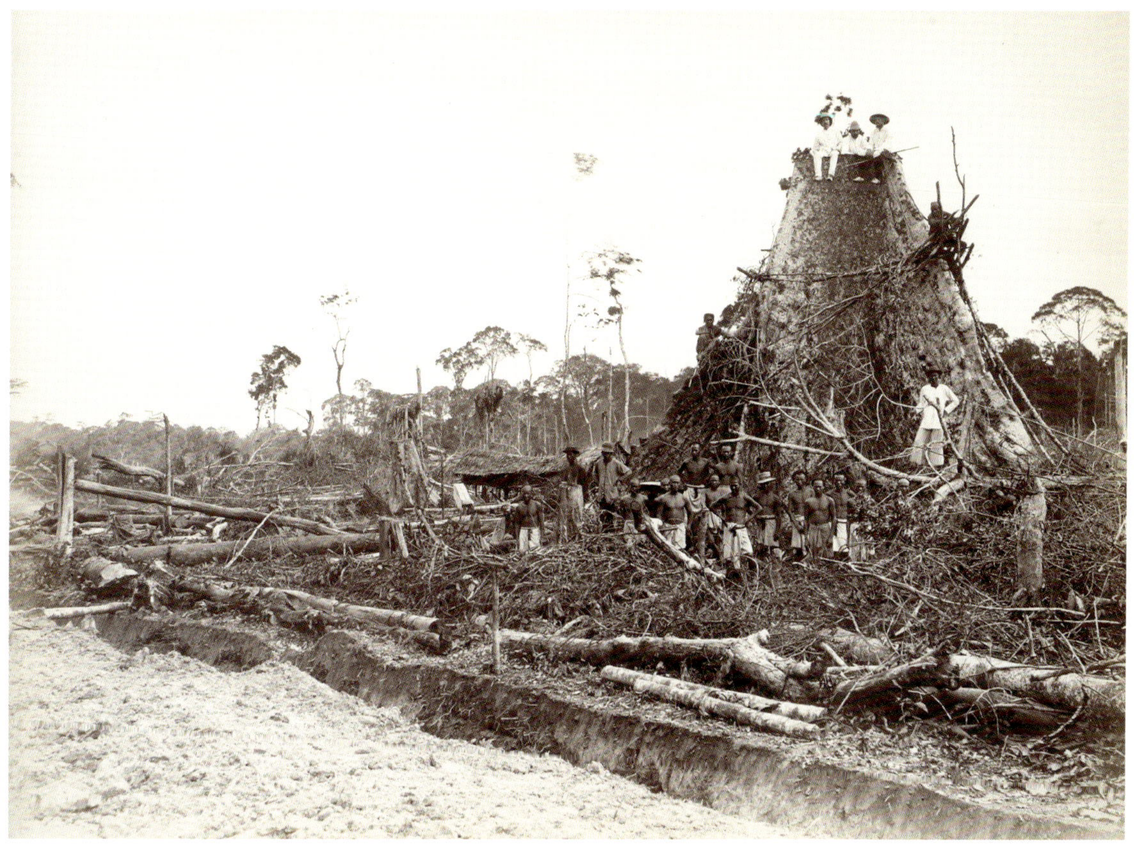

20
Primeval forest
Photographer: unknown
albumen print
22.2 x 28.2 cm
1870–92
60005111. Provenance: Prof Dr J.C. van Eerde, 1930

21
Group portrait by a felled woodland giant on area of deforested land on a tobacco plantation, Sumatra's east coast
Photographer: unknown
albumen print
25.3 x 35.4 cm
1888–90
60010558. Provenance: unknown

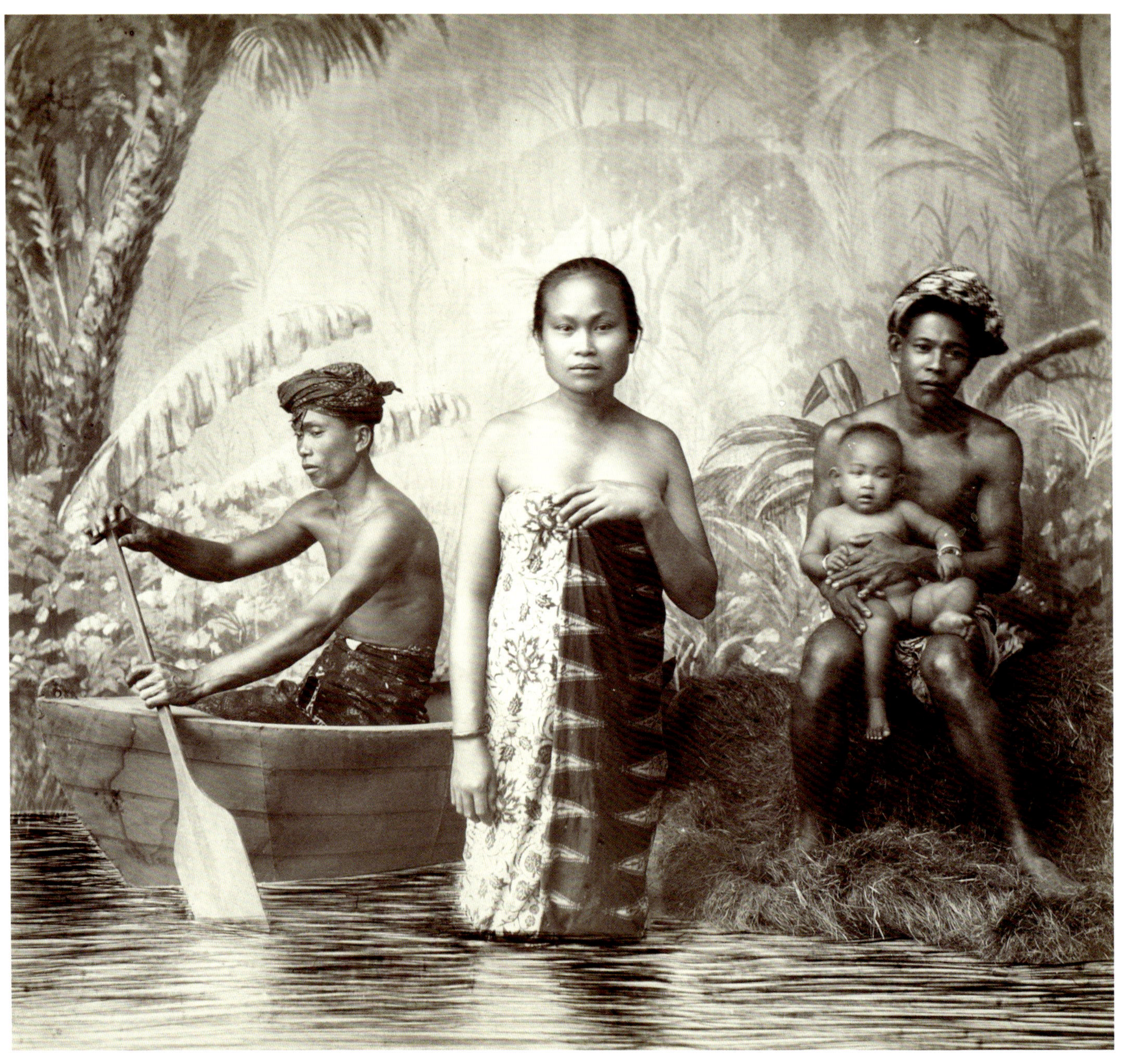

22
Studio portrait of two men, a woman and a child
Photographer: unknown
albumen print
22 x 24.2 cm
1870–1900
60039710. Provenance: Mr H.C. van der Wijck

'Ethnic types'

The frequently recurring and popular category 'ethnic types', part of this primitivising trope, was already in use from the 1850s. Ethnology – especially in the 19th century – was largely an armchair pursuit. At the request of anthropologists, photographs were made of objects in museums or private collections, and studio portraits were made of the local population, sometimes with the same objects that appeared in photographs of collections (Figs. 23 and 24).[37] These ethnographic images as well as photographs of people engaged in specific trades were also sold to the general public. From the middle to the end of the 19th century it was in the staged studio portraits that the photographer could best express himself artistically and create a characteristic rendering of the craft and its practitioner – and of the diversity of the local population as a whole. All the people in the photographs are nameless and are only identified by their trade or ethnic backgrounds. Such photographs of 'the Dayak' or 'the locksmith' (Fig. 121) remained in circulation for a long time because of their presumed timelessness and folklorist character. They could be purchased at commercial photographers and were later reproduced in large numbers as coloured picture postcards. As the number of Europeans taking their own photographs increased, the familiar studio portrait of an arbitrary salesperson or craftsman and his attributes was replaced by a portrait of 'Our Salesman', who proffered his wares to the lady of the house. The photographic genre of 'ethnic types' started coming to end when anthropologists began taking a camera with them on their expeditions and took photographs of the local population *in situ*. These portraits, made according to their own methodology, were purely for academic purposes and had no commercial function (see chapter on photography and science).

23-24
Studio portrait of a Dayak 'dressed as a warrior'; at right a variety of objects, some of which were used in the portrait
Photographer: unknown
albumen print, 22.2 x 18.5 cm / 23.8 x 18.6 cm
1870–1900
60005526 / 60005527.
Provenance: unknown

Salvage paradigm

The interventions in nature and the contacts between the local population and the European 'bringers of civilisation' raised the concern that many indigenous cultures were in danger of disappearing. For some photographers, including Tassilo Adam (1878–1955), this was the reason to take as many photographs as possible of these 'cultures that have been consigned to oblivion'.[38] Photography thus became a participant in a scientific imperative to capture evidence of dying traditions. Framed within an evolutionary or progressive taxonomic narrative with Europeans at the apex, capturing and systematically studying these 'primitive' traditions would not only save them from extinction but could also yield important scientific information about the development of humankind, thereby, it was believed, shedding light on the history that resulted in the Europeans being as advanced as they thought they were at the time.

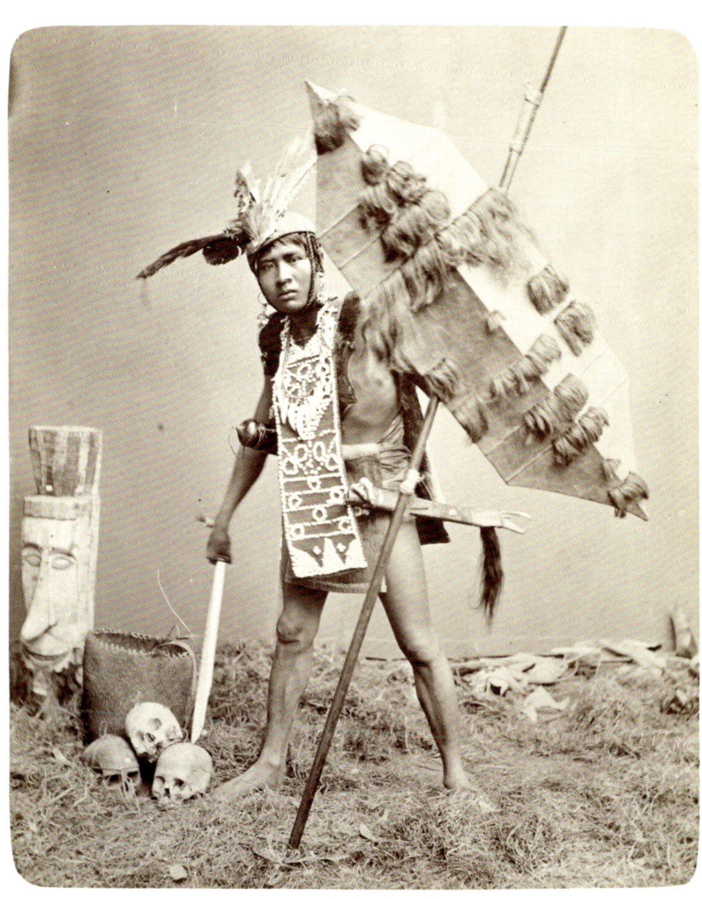

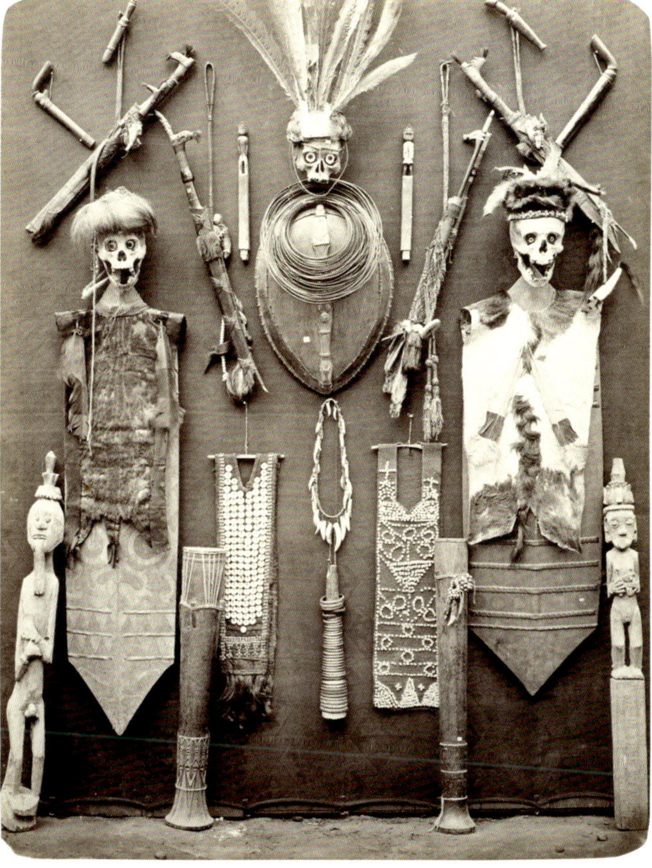

TASSILO ADAM (1878–1955)

He thought it was the most remarkable photograph he had ever made, a testament to true friendship and mutual trust: the portrait of *Sibayak* Pa Mbelgah and his family in Kabanjahe (Sumatra), with their ancestors' skulls arrayed before them. These had been specially taken out of the *geriten* (skull house) and arranged with the most valuable textiles and jewellery for the photographer. Gaining trust was not necessary to being a good photographer, as many other photographers would demonstrate, but it certainly helped. The German planter Tassilo Adam was a master at this, and it opened the way for him to document all facets of the Batak population. Later, as an established photographer in Yogyakarta, he would make a film, *Mataram*, for which he immersed himself fully in the local culture again. The film, presenting various cultural practices of the principalities ('Vorstenlanden') Yogyakarta and Surakarta on Central Java, took four years to make, and the Netherlands premiere was held at the Colonial Institute on 15 February 1927.[39] One scene is dedicated to the *wayang wong* performances that were held in the *kraton* at the beginning of September 1923 to mark Queen Wilhelmina's Silver Jubilee. After the event Sultan Hamengku Buwono VIII asked Tassilo Adam to compile an album of photographs that was presented to the Queen as a keepsake.[40] Back to Sumatra… The group portrait of Pa Mbelgah was displayed in February 1919 at an exhibition of the Deli Art Circle (Delische Kunstkring) in the 'Witte Sociëteit' club in Medan, which was also home to the Batak objects Tassilo Adam had collected.[41] Although Adam had been active as a planter on Sumatra's east coast since 1899, he much preferred documenting collections that were destined for museums. He started collecting from 1910, and devoted all his spare time to photography after 1914 when he lived in Pematang Siantar after a year of European leave. It is notable that he only took photographs of the Batak population; the world of the planters does not appear in his work. It is no surprise that he photographed with the eye of the systematic collector that he was, according him a unique position among the photographers who worked on Sumatra. Shortly after the almost 150 photographs and 700 objects were exhibited in Medan, they were added to the collection of the Ethnographic Department of the Colonial Institute's museum. They comprise one of the world's most representative collections relating to the Batak people.

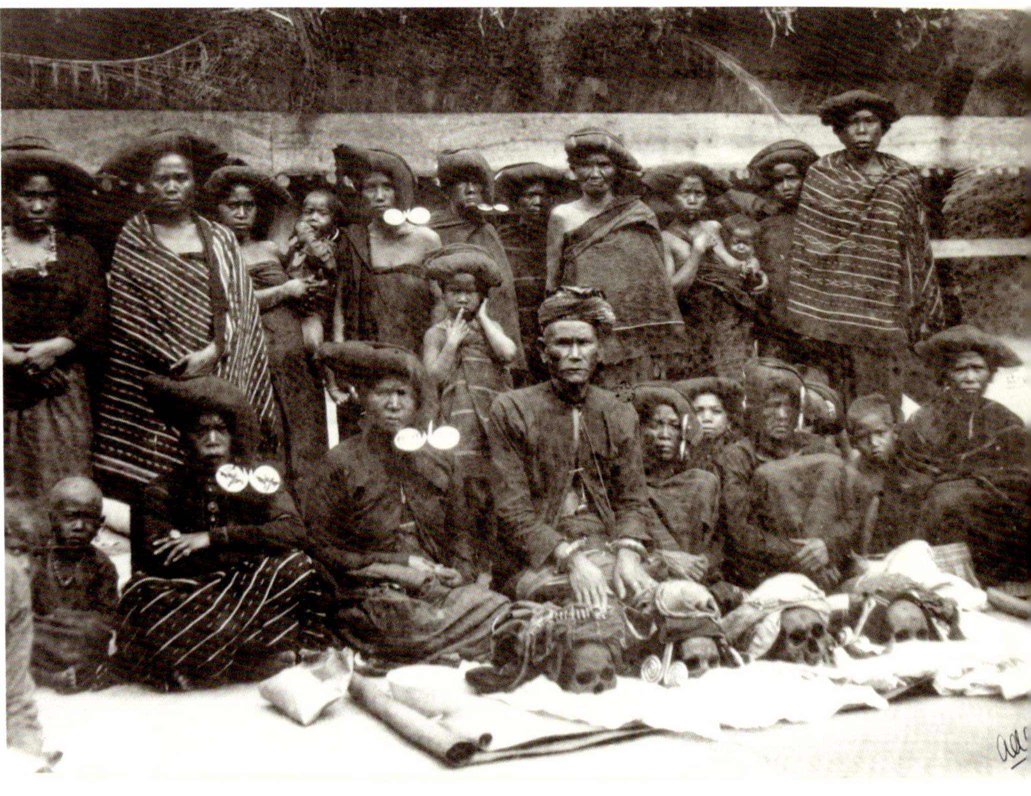

25
Group portrait of Sibayak Pa Mbelgah in Kabanjahe and his family, the skulls of his ancestors arrayed before them
Photographer: Tassilo Adam (1878–1955)
silver gelatin developing-out paper, card stock
35.5 x 50.7 cm (card stock: 50 x 65.1 cm)
1918
60052509. Purchase: Tassilo Adam, 1921

The photographs are enlargements he made himself that were glued to card stock as individual photographs, as collages or as panoramas. The cards are arranged by subject and several of them are signed. The original Ilford glass negatives, made with an Ica-Tropica camera (9 x 12 cm) and Tessar, Protar and Magnar Zeiss lenses, are also preserved in the Tropenmuseum collection. The photographs taken inside Pa Mbelgah's house are unique (Fig. 105). Adam used magnesium powder, which was not entirely safe because it exploded when ignited. RJ

The working body

Photographs in the category 'the working body' are somewhat ambiguous. On the one hand they show how hard the indigenous population worked to bring about the progressive modernisation of the (colonial) society, always, of course, under the watchful eyes of the ever-present Europeans. But on the other hand, the many photographs that portray traditional Indonesian craftsmanship rarely include a European, even if – or perhaps especially when – they were taken at trade fairs or exhibitions where handicrafts were promoted on a wide scale (Fig. 31). Consciously or not, was this a way to visualise the contrasts between old traditions and new developments, between the 'new' and folklore? Was it an acknowledgement of the knowledge, skills and deftness that are required to be a craftsman? Was it connected to authenticity? Was it to show that everyone had his own (work)place in the colonial society?

These are but a few of the many questions that emerge when first viewing the comprehensive photograph collections that have been collected by ethnographic museums in the Netherlands. It is to Rob Nieuwenhuys' credit that he published a great number of photographs of the former Netherlands East Indies that had been consigned to obscurity in his series of books of photographs titled *Tempo doeloe, fotografische documenten uit het oude Indië*.[42] He was himself a child of the country. The melancholic texts that accompany the photographs he selected are saturated with nostalgia for his youth in *tempo doeloe* ('days gone by').[43]

This later nostalgic (re-)appreciation is in itself an interesting (side-) development, but it should be remembered that in their time, these selfsame '*tempo doeloe* photographs' were modern, almost 'glossy' photographs.[44] The concept of 'colonial photography' is another subject currently under debate, and while the term has problematic connotations, it is generally used with ease in ethnographic museums. Perhaps it would be better to replace this emotionally charged concept by referring to 'photography from the colonies'. Purpose and function play a role, as do time and place, but it seems to be difficult to arrive at an unambiguous delineation and definition. Because of this, the term 'colonial photography' has primarily become a practical one that is used because everyone knows what it refers to, and insiders can relate to the nuances.[45]

In today's postcolonial and multicultural society, in which images of different complex colonial societies are available on the Internet, the issue is not so much about nostalgia and categorisation, but about questions such as those mentioned above. The challenge is to remove the Tropenmuseum photograph collection from its national context and work with other fellow institutes in other countries (the colonised and the colonisers at the time) on investigating the shared colonial representation and giving it a new international dimension.

PAUL SPIES (1904–63)

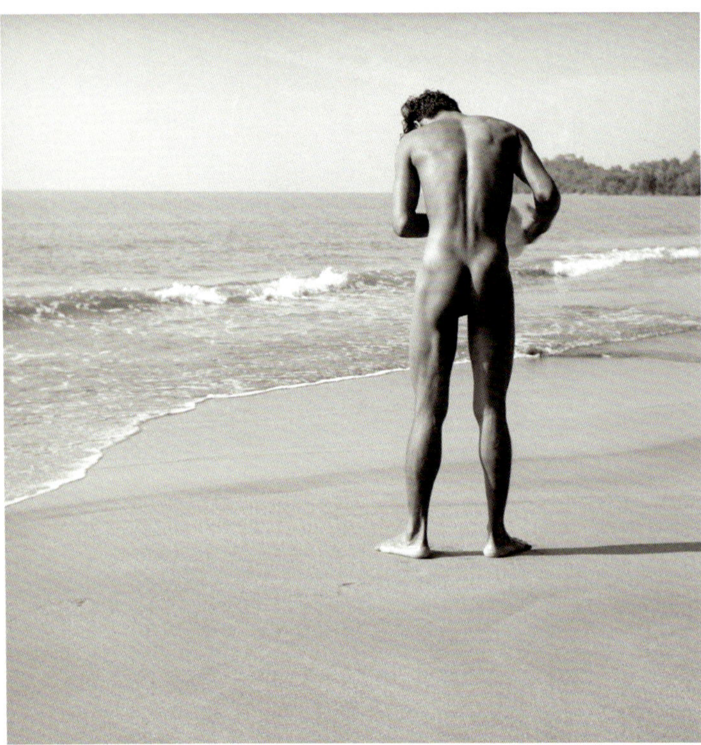

< 26
Nude portrait of Dewa Ketut Beng Gunarsa, partner of Paul Spies, on Gumpal Beach
Photographer: Paul Spies (1904–63)
Acetate negative
6 x 6 cm
1954
60030186. Gift: Dr. H. de Roever-Bonnet, 1970s. Former collection Rudolf Bonnet

> 27
Man near Iseh, after a painting by Walter Spies
Inspired by the artists working on Bali, Paul Spies experimented with composition and backlighting. The reverse of this photograph has a note by Spies: 'Near Iseh, Bali, Gerebeg. After a painting by Walter Spies †1942'. This refers to 'Iseh im Morgenlicht', a painting by Walter Spies in Paul Spies' collection.
Photographer: Paul Spies (1904–63)
silver gelatin developing-out paper
14.9 x 12.8 cm
1946
60033747. Gift: Dr H. de Roever-Bonnet, 1970s. Former collection Rudolf Bonnet

Paul Spies was already employed by the Java Bank (Rotterdam) when he left for the Netherlands East Indies in the 1920s. He worked at several of the bank's branches and was eventually appointed general director in Jakarta in 1949, where he remained as a member of the Board after Indonesia's independence, until 1954.
He travelled and took photographs his entire life. He used a Hasselblad but did not have his own darkroom. He had his photographs developed and printed during his annual leave at Capi Lux in Amsterdam, where he would sit in the darkroom for days supervising the quality of his prints.
In the 1930s Spies was one of a circle of Europeans living on Bali; he had a house built where he regularly withdrew from his workaday routine. He was a good friend with the artists Rudolf Bonnet and Walter Spies,[46] both of whom greatly influenced the modern art scene on Bali.
A patron of the arts, Paul Spies bought works by Balinese artists, and even had several of President Soekarno's much-coveted works in his collection.
Besides landscapes, Spies also made portraits of artists who were working on Bali. These artists were personal friends, hence the intimacy evident in the photographs. In addition to portraits of Rudolf Bonnet and Walter Spies, he took photographs of artists chatting in studios and many portraits of Balinese artists. In this way Spies documented the artistic life on Bali between 1930 and 1955.
His landscape photographs, some of which are directly related to paintings and drawings, resonate with the mystical atmosphere of life on Bali.
It seems as if photography was purely a hobby, which enabled him to study and photograph his surroundings. In all probability he also used photography as a front for political ends. In 1963 he visited a number of places in Central Laos, which was in the throes of a civil war. He was killed there by a group of Communist soldiers on 5 February 1963. Spies was buried with full American military honours in Laos. It is quite possible that besides his photography he also worked for the American Central Intelligence Agency (CIA) . AM

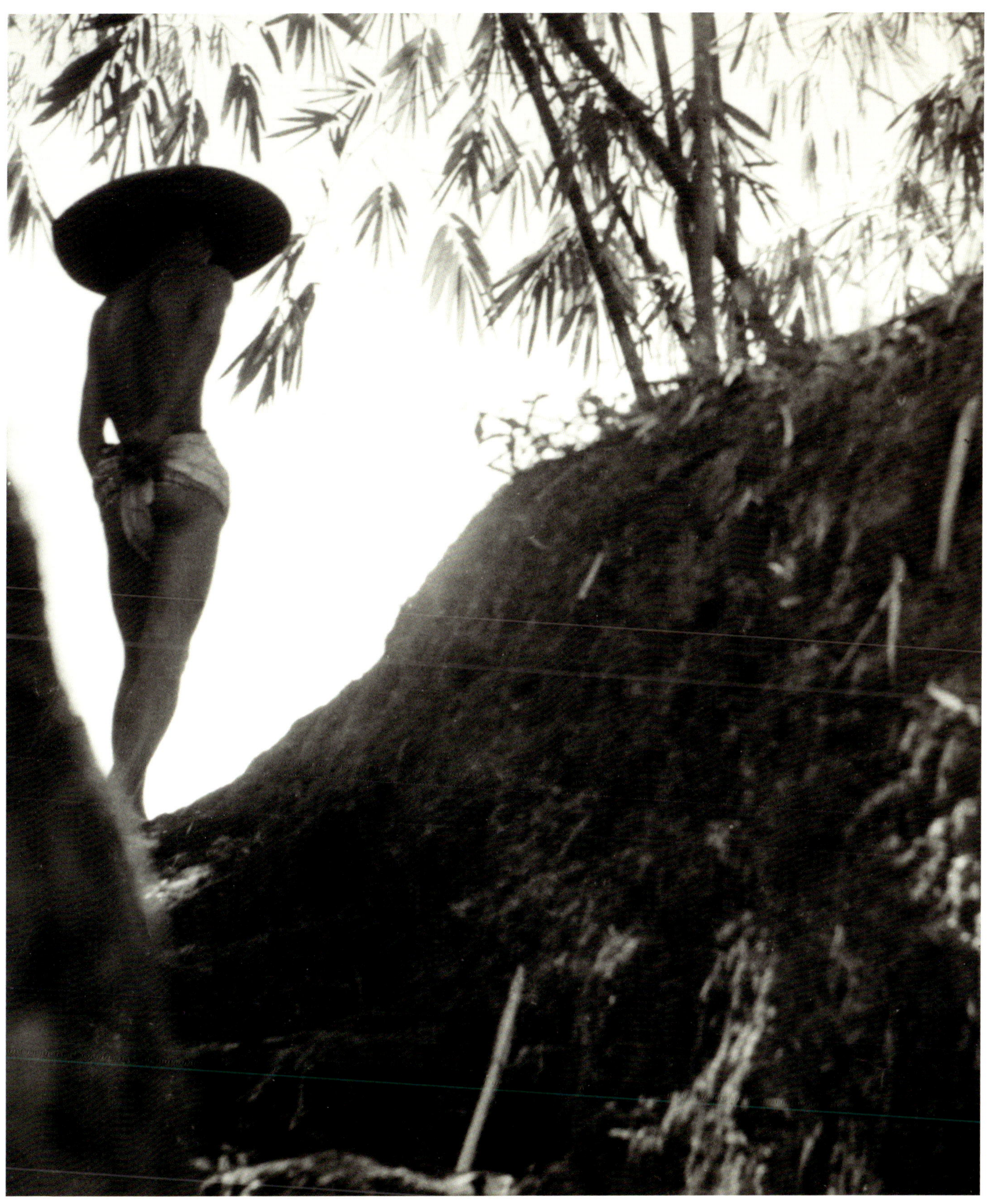

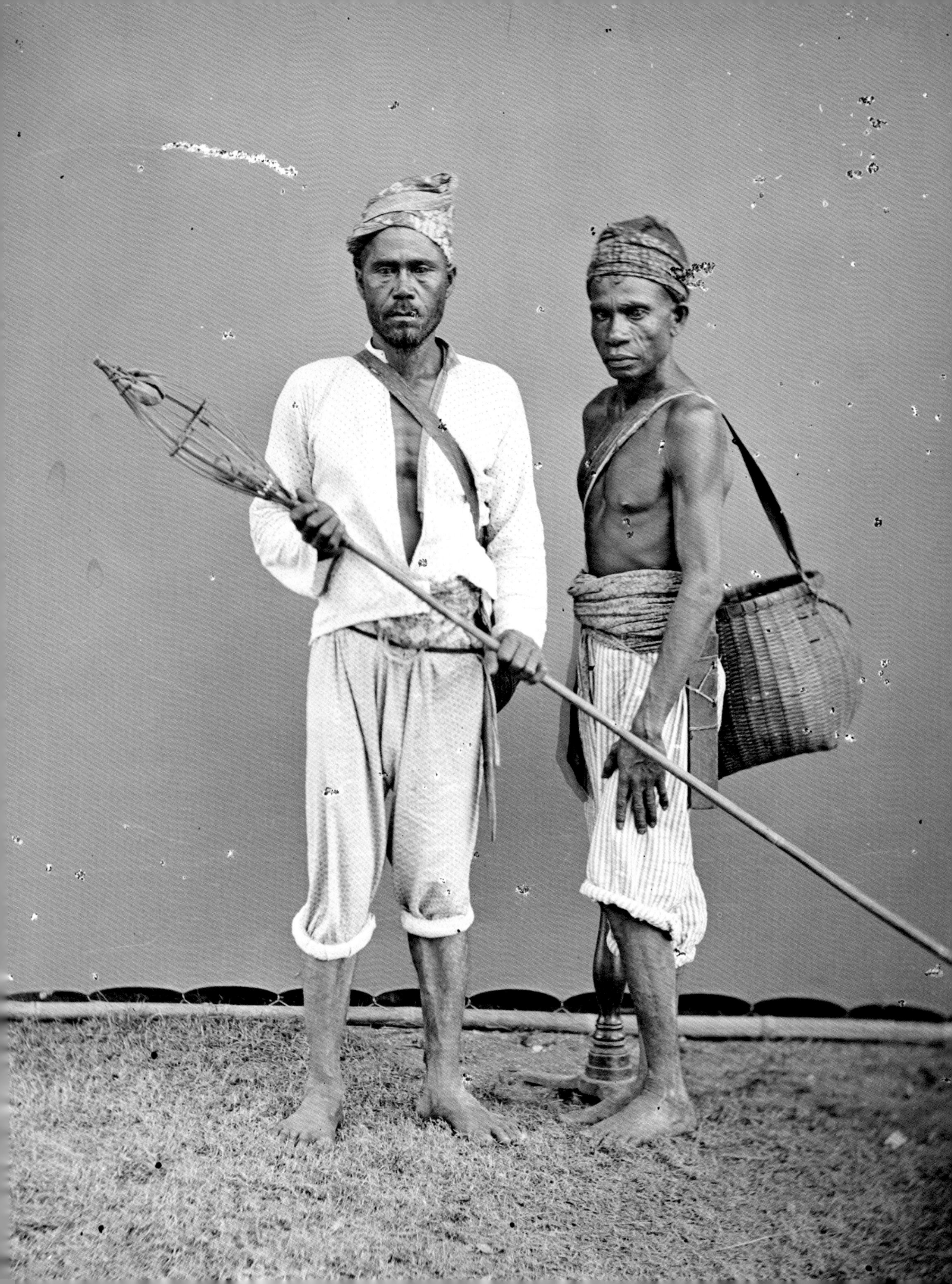

FROM COLONIAL TOPICALITY TO CULTURAL HERITAGE:

the history of the photograph collection

STEVEN VINK AND JANNEKE VAN DIJK

28
Portrait of two nutmeg pickers, Banda (Moluccas)
Photographer: H. Veen (1823–1905)
collodion glass negative
9 x 11.4 cm
1865–75
10012346. Purchase: D. Veen, 1913

The first time a photograph was included on the acquisition list of the Colonial Museum in Haarlem was in 1873: it was a portrait of the late Professor C.L. Blume (1796–1862) donated by his widow.[47] Blume was an exemplary researcher of Javanese flora. In the approximately 140 years that followed, the Tropenmuseum amassed a collection comprising roughly 200,000 photographs of Indonesia. For the first 70 years – as the Colonial Institute – the focus was on images that provided as broad an impression as possible of developments in the Netherlands East Indies. The Tropenmuseum continued collecting after the Second World War – and after Indonesia's independence. This resulted in a collection of historical photographs of the Netherlands East Indies, which is one of the most extensive and diverse of its type in the world. The history of the collection, its purpose and the way the photographs were used, reflect the course of colonial history and the role that the current Tropenmuseum and its predecessors played in that history.

Colonial Museum Haarlem

The botanist Frederik Willem van Eeden founded, and was the first director of, the Museum of Raw Materials, Natural Products and Human Crafts from the Netherlands' Overseas Territories and Colonies (Museum van Grondstoffen, Natuurvoortbrengselen en Volksvlijt uit de Nederlandsche Overzeesche Bezittingen en Koloniën) that opened in 1871 in the Paviljoen Welgelegen in Haarlem. The purpose of the Colonial Museum, as it came to be called, was to underscore the importance of the colonies for the Dutch economy. The focus was on collecting, inventorying and studying tropical products such as wood, plants, fibres, crops, minerals, and medicinal plants and herbs; not much attention was paid to ethnology.
Photographs were not explicitly discussed in 1871. There was no clear policy about how this relatively new medium could be employed, or which of the images were useable. Nonetheless, photographs were considered valuable objects and acquisitions continued. The 1883 annual report stated that it would be good to accompany the objects displayed in the museum 'with explanatory descriptions, and also to mount the many images and photographs in appropriate places on the walls'.[48]
Photographs received as gifts mostly related to indigenous natural and agricultural products such as cinchona, nutmeg, bamboo, cane sugar, *guttapercha* (a type of rubber), landscapes and the population.

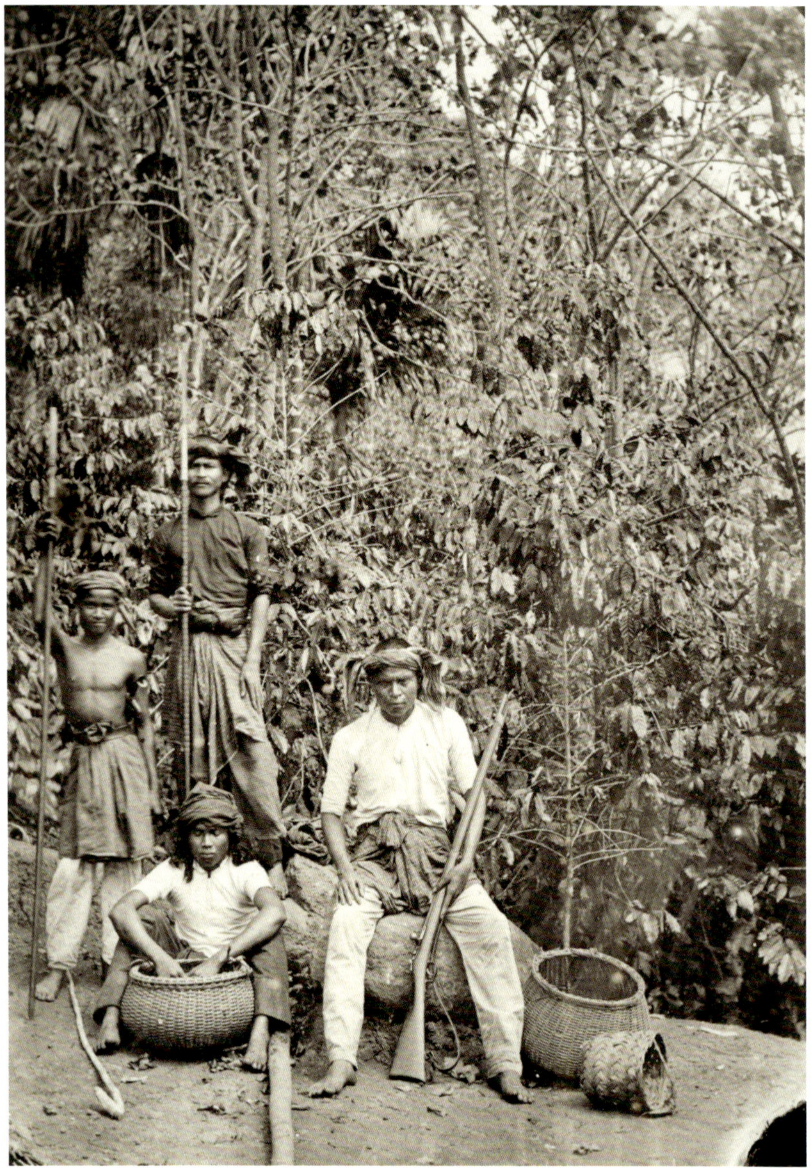

29
Armed men, including Teuku Umar, on a coffee plantation in Aceh
In all likelihood, this is not the renowned Teuku Umar, one of the most famous resistance heroes in Indonesian history. In the publication about his journey in 1880–81, Xavier Brau de Saint-Pol Lias wrote about a warning issued by the Dutch administration on Aceh advising people to avoid visiting the area because of the presence of Teuku Umar and his 'pack of thieves', but he says nothing about an actual encounter.
Photographer: Xavier Brau de Saint-Pol Lias (1840–1914)
albumen print
11.4 x 8.1 cm
1881
60039175. Gift: Karel van der Heyden, 1886

A series of 78 photographs was received in 1886:[49] 'a large acquisition (...) a collection of photographs of Aceh and Deli, presented by Mr Lieutenant General K. van der Heijden'.

The photographs, glued on cardboard and with French captions, were made by the French ethnologist, botanist and explorer Xavier Brau de Saint-Pol Lias,[50] who had travelled to Malaysia and Sumatra in 1880 to look for a suitable domicile for French colonists. During his stay in Aceh he met General Karel van der Heyden (Heijden), the governor and commander of Aceh. Van der Heyden was a lieutenant colonel in the Royal Netherlands Indies Army (KNIL) and took part in the military operations against the Sultan of Aceh's *dalam* in 1873–74 at the onset of the protracted war against the people of Aceh, who were fighting for their freedom (see the first chapter).

Another important acquisition of the early period is a beautiful album with portraits of the Sultan of Yogyakarta, Hamengku Buwono VII, and his family, which were made by the court photographer Kassian Céphas and were donated to the museum by the government official J. Mullemeister (see pp. 122-123).

With the arrival, in 1888, of Kodak's easy-to-use camera, marketed with the effective slogan 'You press the button, we do the rest', a significant change occurred in the number and kind of photographs being produced and therefore collected by the museum. This was itself an important moment in the development of photography, making the medium available to a broader non-specialised group who could afford these cameras. Photography became a hobby for scientists, planters, industrialists and government officials.

The number of gifts to the museum continued to increase. When the collection was transferred to the Colonial Institute in Amsterdam in 1915, 170 donations had been received.

Photographs were used to augment exhibitions of Indonesian products, and special photograph exhibitions were organised occasionally.

HENDRIK VEEN (1823–1905)

The oldest glass negatives in the collection

Hendrik Veen's name was nothing more than a footnote to the early history of photography in the Netherlands East Indies. The Tropenmuseum collection had several photographs with the designation 'coll. Veen Malang', or only the date '1913'. The subjects of these photographs are intriguing, as is the way they were photographed, their focus and depth, the near-palpability of the subjects and their obvious age. The date 1913 is misleading because it is not the year that the photographs were taken, but the year the collection was purchased. Veen's name is mentioned in the catalogue of the Dutch Colonial Section of the International Colonial and Export Exhibition (May–October 1883) in Amsterdam: '[...] we are indebted to Messrs Meessen, Veen, Woodbury and Page and several others for entire series of photographs, some of which are extremely beautiful landscapes'.[51] At least 280 (carbon print) reproductions of Veen's landscapes were exhibited along with 400 images of 'ethnic types'.[52] The individual and group portraits, landscapes and buildings were photographed in Semarang, South Celebes (South Sulawesi), Ambon, Banda, Malang, Probolinggo and many other locations.

The 1913 Annual Report of the Colonial Museum in Haarlem includes a record of the purchase of negatives from a professional photographer from Malang. The photographs were bought from a certain D. Veen in Haarlem.[53] According to the annual report, a note accompanying the photographs states that they were taken sometime around 1880, but because the newspaper that was used to protect them was dated 1875 it meant that the negatives could have been taken before 1875. An examination of the digital newspaper archive of National Library in the Hague produced, among others, an advertisement promoting the 'Photographic Studio of H. Veen, located next to the Roman Catholic Orphanage in Semarang' in 1866.[54] Veen was probably active as a photographer in East Java from 1865 to c. 1880,[55] first in Surabaya and later in Semarang and Malang. He frequently closed his studio and worked on location in a mobile studio, something quite usual for photographers during the second half of the 19th century. Hendrik Veen's portrait photographs are rather sober. No painted backdrops were used; the subjects pose near a table and a chair before a stretched uniform backdrop of which the frame is sometimes visible. The subjects, seated or standing, are portrayed full-length. If the table and chair were not included, subjects are depicted leaning against a wooden pole, which helped to eliminate any movement on their part during the long exposure time. The collection also contains 99 of Hendrik Veen's glass negatives (sizes 9 x 12 cm and 13 x 18 cm) and two albums with photographs of Bali (Alb. 0387 and 0343 are still part of the collection). The negatives are the only ones made using the wet collodion technique and are among the oldest in the collection. JVD

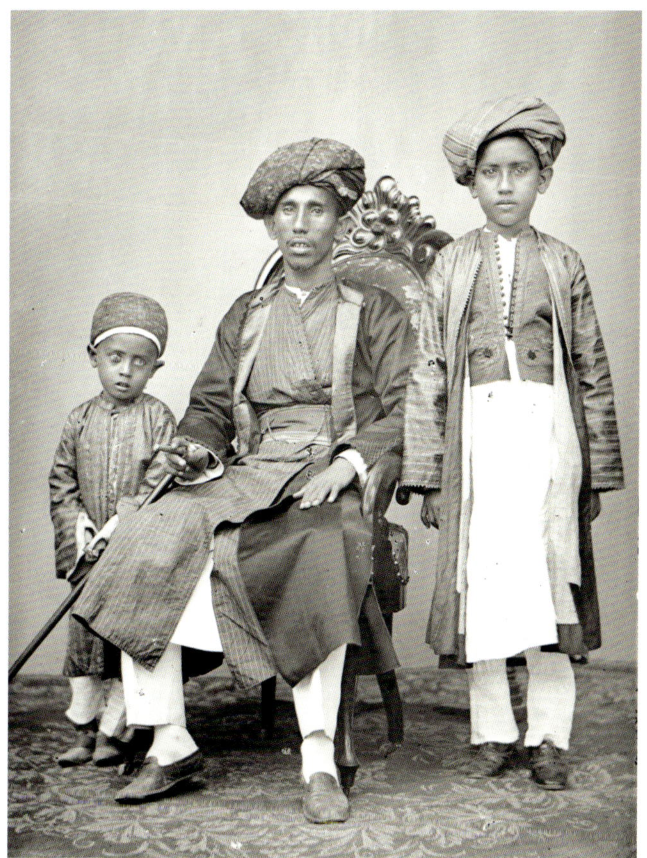

30
Portrait of the leader of the Arab community in Tegal, Java
Photographer: H. Veen (1823–1905)
collodion glass negative
13 x 18 cm
1865–75
10005286. Purchase: D. Veen, 1913

INDIGENOUS ARTS AND CRAFTS

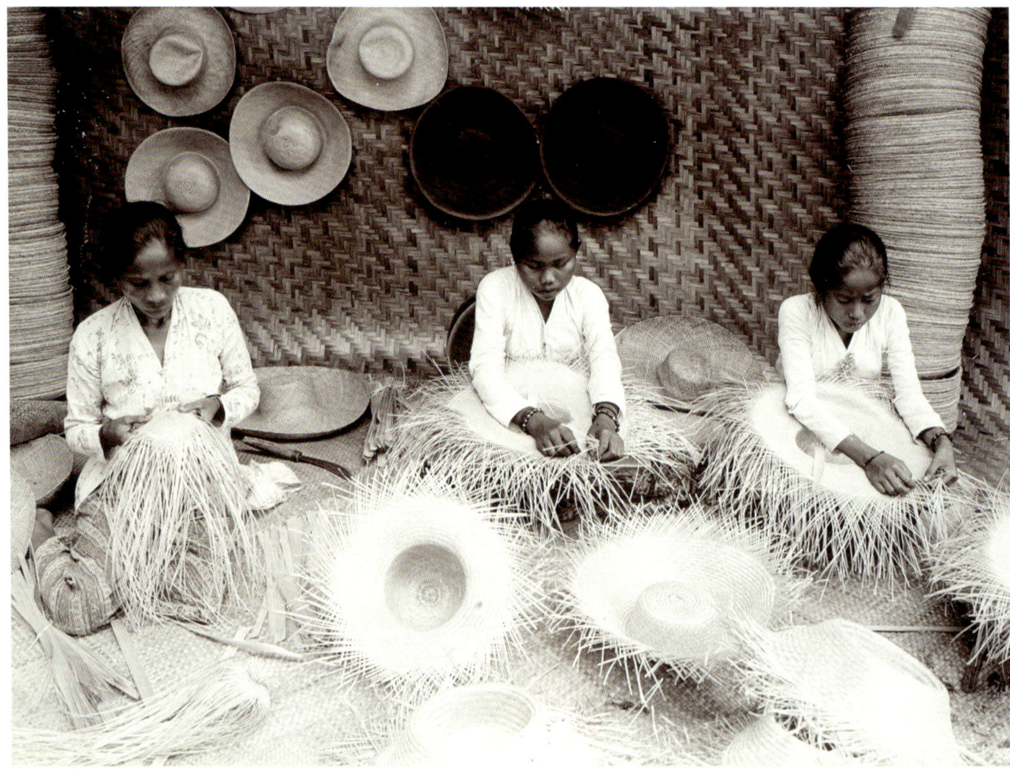

31
Plaiting bamboo hats
Photographer: unknown
gelatin printing-out paper
17 x 22.8 cm
c. 1910
60011604. Provenance: unknown

At first viewing this is a timeless image: three Sundanese hat plaiters engaged in a traditional craft, the finer points of which are handed down from generation to generation. Closer inspection reveals a date: circa 1910. The photograph does not seem to have been made in the natural working environment of the main subjects, a hat factory in Tangerang. Everything points to a corporate presentation in a special location. The prominence of the hats is noteworthy. The carefully composed setting suggests that this photograph was taken in a studio. This idea is reinforced by the fact that the photograph is part of a series that shows the various stages of bamboo hat production in exactly the same place. But the location in one of these high-quality images differs from the rest, indicating that in all likelihood this series was made *by* a professional photographer, but not *in* his studio.[56] The photographs were probably taken at a *pasar malam* (annual fair), which included arts and crafts demonstrations. Annual fairs were organised in Surabaya and other cities from 1905 by the District Commissioner (*controleur*) Johan Ernst Jasper (1874–1945) to create a larger market for indigenous arts and crafts.[57] Interest in indigenous arts and crafts blossomed around 1900 and gained momentum after the announcement of the Ethical Policy, by which the Netherlands had to assume greater responsibility for the welfare of the local population. Developing indigenous arts and crafts was one of the means to improve the locals' economic position. The photograph of the hat plaiters was reproduced in 1912 in the first volume of the five-volume series *De Inlandsche Kunstnijverheid in Nederlandsch Indië*, which resulted from the technical-artistic research conducted by Jasper and Mas Pirngadie (1875–1936) that had been commissioned by the colonial government.[58] At about the same time the image was published by the Haarlem firm Kleynenberg & Co. as a school poster with the caption: 'Plaiting hats for Europe, West Java'.[59] Steps were made to enter the European market. A few years earlier, wood carvers, mat and hat plaiters, weavers and batik makers from the Netherlands East Indies also demonstrated their crafts at the 1910 Brussels World Fair.[60] Photographs such as this appeared in school classrooms, as picture postcards and in Happy Families card games, in magazines and as reproductions in photograph albums. This broad distribution ensured the demonstrations reached a far wider audience than only the visitors to the annual fairs. For the first time the craftsmanship of the indigenous population was deliberately presented as an artform to the wider public.[61] RJ

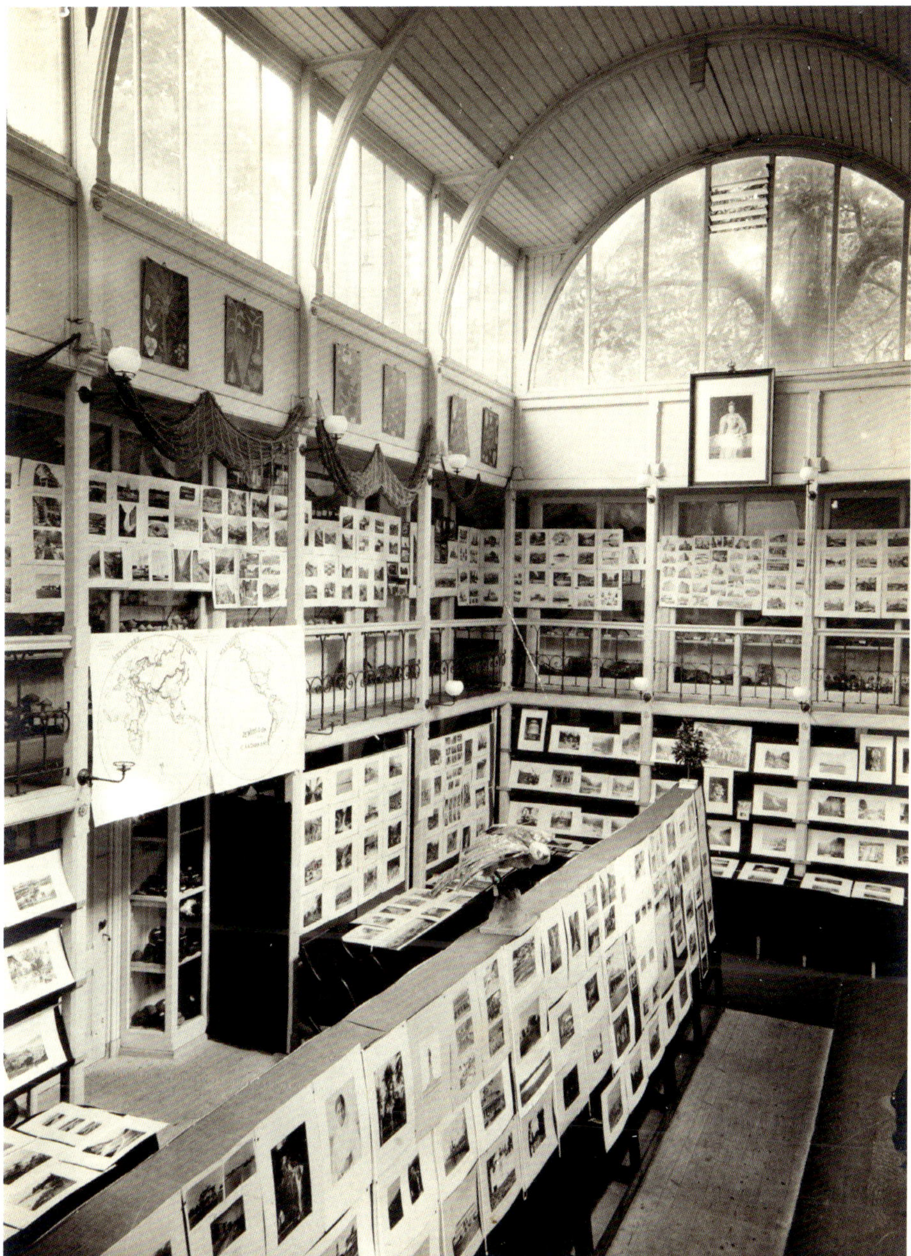

32
Photographic exhibition in the Colonial Museum in Haarlem after C.A.A. Dudok de Wit returned from his world trip
Photographer: M. Zwartjes
silver gelatin developing-out paper
22.9 x 16.8 cm
1905
60040378

A couple of photograph exhibitions held at the end of the 19th century displayed collotypes of Borobudur reliefs, views of Aceh and photographs of Suriname by Julius Muller.[62] The museum wanted more, but struggled continuously with a lack of staff and space:

The wider public – for whom the images are of particular value in forming overall impressions – cannot see the photographs and maps that are preserved on the top floor, because there are not enough supervisors to keep an eye on the visitors and there is also not enough space for people to move around.[63]

Photographs and lantern slides made from photographs were mostly used in lectures and publications.

The Amsterdam Colonial Institute

The Colonial Institute Association was founded in Amsterdam on 10 June 1910. During the inaugural meeting the initiator J.T. Cremer, former director of the Deli Company and former Minister of Colonial Affairs (among other positions), made an impassioned speech in which he defined the goal of the organisation: 'We want to set up an institute that will become the central colonial institute for trade and industry, education and science'.[64]
Among others, the ethnographic collections of the Amsterdam zoo, the Royal Zoological Society Natura Artis Magistra (Artis); and the Association for the Founding of a Museum for Geography and Ethnography (Vereeniging van de Stichting van een Museum voor Land- en Volkenkunde), both located in Amsterdam, were brought together in the Colonial Institute, along with the collection of the Colonial Museum in Haarlem.
The collections of photographs and negatives from Haarlem and Artis were stored at the General Secretariat of the newly formed Institute.[65]
Precisely how many photographs were involved is unclear. The Artis Geographical Society presented a gift of 95 photographs from the Artis collection in 1920. These are, almost without exception, 19th-century prints by famous photographers such as Woodbury & Page and Meessen.

33
The Sultan of Ternate's bodyguard
Photographic Studio: Woodbury & Page
albumen print
19 x 23.8 cm
1870–1900
60039372. Provenance: Natura Artis Magistra, 1920. Former collection Netherlands Colonial Association (NKV)

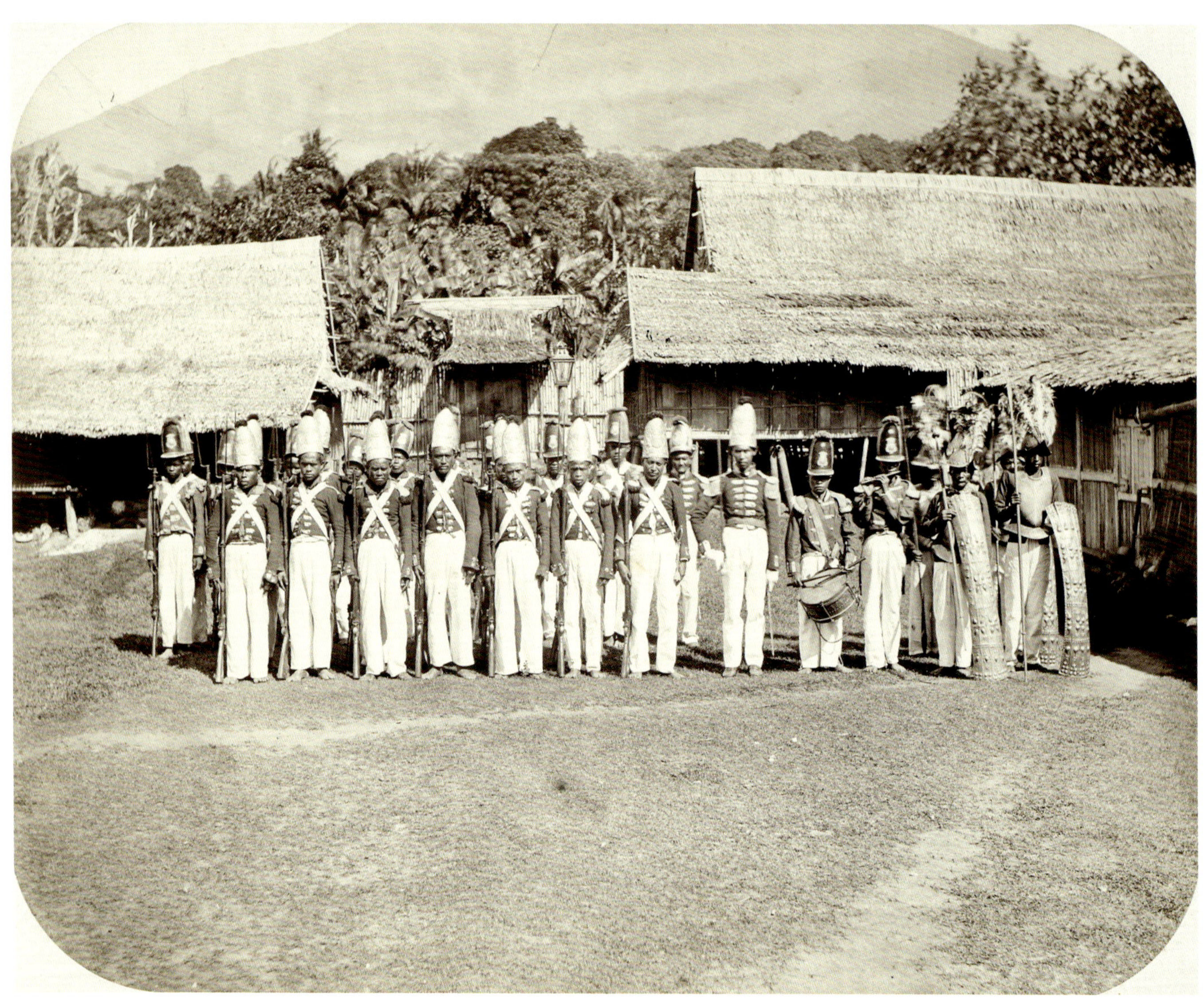

Like their predecessors in Haarlem, the Board of the Colonial Institute recognised the importance of using visual material to disseminate knowledge about the colonies.
The attitude towards the photographs being collected at the time was that these were contemporary images that were replaceable. That photographs became soiled through use or were lost was taken for granted. If possible, they were replaced by others. This is confirmed by the Colonial Museum's many requests for donations of photographs.

Films

The only time that the Colonial Institute Association awarded a paid commission for making visual material was immediately after its founding in 1910. The collection of slides at their disposal was not up to requirements, namely increasing knowledge about the colonies and stimulating interest among well-educated young people in a career in Indonesia. Readings, lectures and courses would have to be organised to achieve this goal. The Board of the Institute was of the opinion that the collection of slides was 'lacking in only one area, namely moving images. It is imperative that we complement these with cinematographic images'. Because the medium of film was still in its infancy, no request could be made to third parties asking them to donate films. The Institute did not want to assume the costs and wrote letter of request to the Ministry of Colonial Affairs for financial support. After all, the Institute's objectives were in keeping with the new colonial Ethical Policy, another reason why the film was considered of national importance. Minister De Waal Malefijt agreed to the funding request.
But who was going to make the film? The Institute insisted that it had to be someone who was 'familiar with the country and people of Indonesia, who would work with an academic approach, was absolutely reliable, and who was used to associating with the European as well as local communities. Above all, the filmmaker has to be able to cope with the climate and the fatigue associated with a life of travel'. These preconditions excluded the few Dutch filmmakers at the time, all the more so because their activities reeked of vulgar sideshow entertainment.
One of the supporters of the Colonial Institute, the former Aceh combatant and retired Governor-General, J.C. van Heutsz, drew the Institute's attention to a young officer in the Topographical Service of the Royal Netherlands Indies Army – Johann Lamster appeared to meet all the requirements and was on leave in the Netherlands at the time. There was one major drawback, however: he knew nothing about cinematography. Consequently, he spent a couple of weeks at the Société Pathé Frères studios in Paris learning film techniques and how to operate a 35 mm camera. Because he did not have enough time to learn everything, Pathé Frères provided an *opérateur* for a few months. The Institute had compiled a list of subjects to film. Lamster spent a year on Java, Madura and Bali making films according to the list supplied by the commissioners: the daily life of the Europeans and of the indigenous population, the most important agricultural products, and the new infrastructure.
Over the years these films were used regularly with great success, and they are still a unique historical document of a colonial past.[66]

A delayed photographic exhibition

Films might have added another dimension, but photographs were still important. In 1913 (amateur) photographers were asked to donate their negatives and prints to the Colonial Institute:

Amateur photographers can help us with the results of their work (...). We are primarily interested in photographs of plants and animals (preferably photographed separately), landscapes, city views, photographs of agriculture, mining, 'ethnic types', local customs, etc.[67]

This call was repeated many times, referring to:

Our ambition to make the Colonial Institute a central archive where negatives from the Netherlands East Indies are properly preserved, safely stored, catalogued, and protected and better cared for than is possible in the Tropics or by private individuals (...) [68]

Autumn 1915. The Colonial Institute – still lacking its own dedicated building – organised a successful exhibition in the Stedelijk Museum in Amsterdam, titled 'Old Javanese and Contemporary Balinese Hinduism' ('Oud-Javaansch en hedendaagsch Balisch Hindoeïsme').[69] More than 10,000 visitors attended the exhibition over a two-month period. This was followed in December by a lecture series in the Stedelijk Museum's auditorium, presented by, among others, the director of the Ethnographic Department J.C. van Eerde and the author Augusta de Wit. Abundant use was made of the photographs and lantern slides in the exhibition and at the lectures. This success inspired the Board of the Colonial Institute to enthusiastically take steps to expand the collection of photographs and lantern slides.

A plan had been devised that will make a lasting impact, namely to hold an exhibition of photographs of the Netherlands East Indies by amateurs and professional photographers in the Spring of 1917 (...), for which we shall specifically ask for images of subjects that are under-represented in our collections.[70]

Submissions could also be made by colonial governmental institutes that were taking photographs for their own uses, such as the Topographical Service, the Botanical Gardens ('s Lands Plantentuin, Kebun Raya Bogor) in Buitenzorg (Bogor) and a number of agricultural research institutions (see chapter on photography and science). The submitted photographs would become the property of the Colonial Institute. The aim of the exhibition was to disseminate knowledge about the colony. A jury would judge the works. Criteria included the subject of the photograph; the technical quality; the documentary value resulting from it's rareness (i.e., if it was taken during an expedition or in a remote place); and if the entire subject was included in the image. Amateur photographers were asked to document their daily lives: the interiors of their homes, their places of work, street views and schools. Submissions from specialists in the areas of agriculture, zoology ('e.g., crop pests, poisonous animals'), tropical hygiene ('improving national health'), and geology were welcome. Officials and soldiers who were stationed in the Outer Regions were asked to document the daily life of the indigenous population as much as possible. The pursuit of completeness gained full expression here.

The year 1915 did not seem to be a good time to organise a photography exhibition about the colonies due to several factors. The Netherlands East Indies suffered from a dearth of materials because of the First World War. Unemployment increased dramatically and communication between the colony and the Netherlands almost came to a standstill. These were among the reasons that prompted the Institute to delay the exhibition in 1916, and in 1919 the exhibition was cancelled altogether 'with great regret'.

Twenty-six submissions were received: seven from companies and nineteen from private individuals who resided in the Netherlands East Indies and in the Netherlands. As far as can be determined only one professional photographer submitted a photograph, Thio Piek from Buitenzorg. It is impossible to determine now if the companies hired professional photographers. In total 383 negatives and 843 photographs were submitted, the greater part by the Botanical Gardens. Also noteworthy are the 162 glass negatives sent in from The Hague headquarters of the Singkep Tin Company (Singkep Tin Maatschappij, see p. 126).

This wide-ranging expansion of the collection eventually resulted in an exhibition. Some of the photographs were displayed in 1923 at an exhibition marking Queen Wilhelmina's Silver Jubilee. The museum had not yet opened officially, but the organisers in Amsterdam considered it the perfect location for a jubilee exhibition. The exhibition was intended to provide an overview of the development and growth of Amsterdam as a trading and residential city and to provide impressions of the so-called overseas territories. The organising committee was of the opinion that there was a paucity of knowledge about the countries and peoples in the colonies, of the farming and mining, the many scientific expeditions, the local languages, traditions and customs, the flora and fauna, disease control, and art and craftsmanship.[71] The part of the exhibition devoted to Amsterdam was located in the Light Hall; the colonies were dealt with on the first floor. The top floor housed the exhibition 'Photographs from the Dutch Colonies' ('Fotografiën uit de Nederlandsche Koloniën') in addition to an overview of Christian philanthropy in the Netherlands.

The material received in 1917 was augmented with new gifts that were specially donated for this jubilee

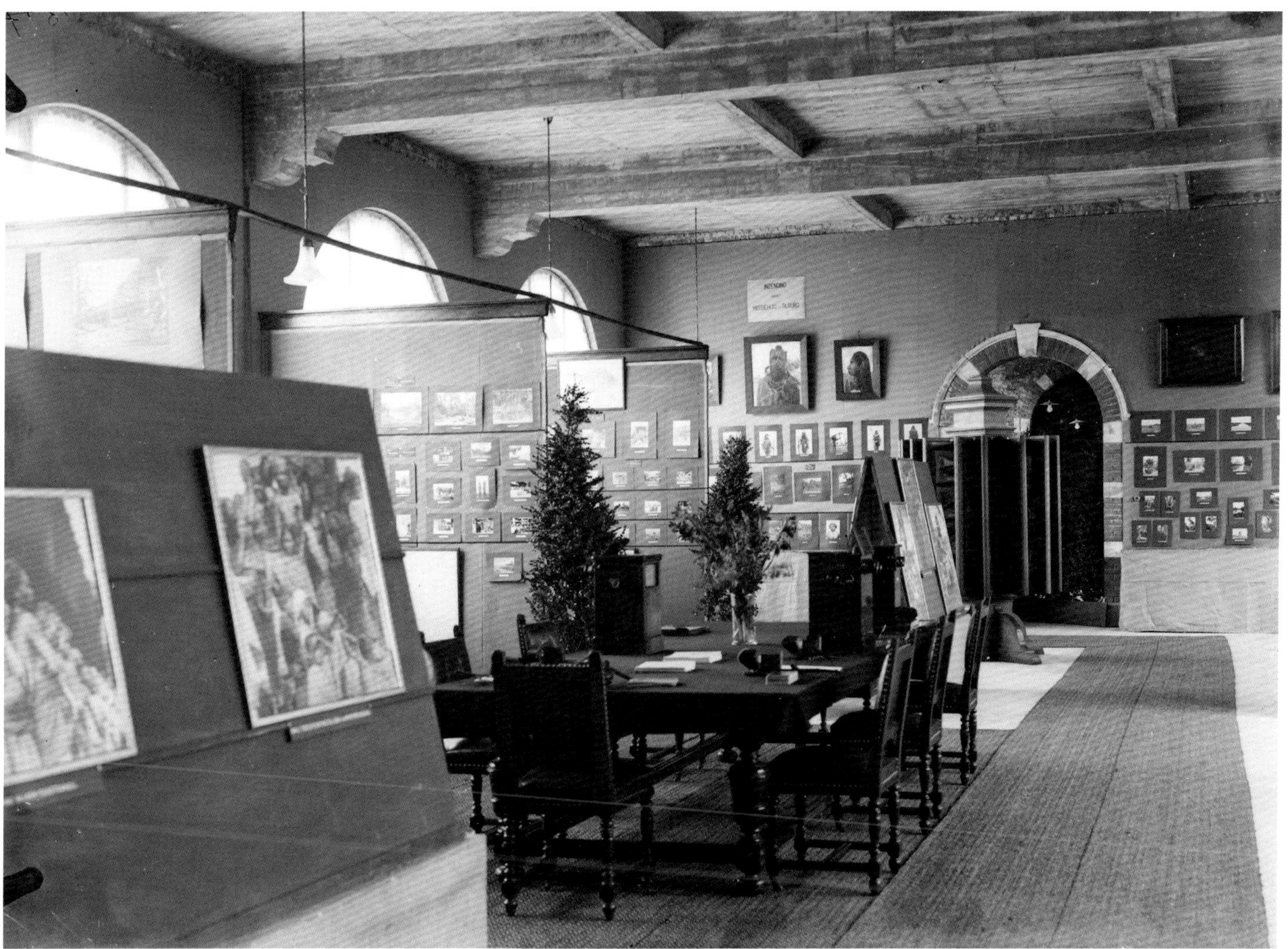

34
Photographic exhibition, part of the Anniversary Exhibition celebrating Queen Wilhelmina's Silver Jubilee in the Colonial Institute's museum
Photographer: unknown
gelatin glass negative
13 x 18 cm
1923
10000389

exhibition. Eighteen other institutes sent photographs and negatives, with the Bandung, Semarang, Surabaya and Makassar city councils being among the most notable contributors. The exhibition was accompanied by a catalogue that expounded on the objects that conveyed impressions of the colonies, and photographs were exhibited alongside the objects.[72]

The 'Batak on Sumatra' display acknowledged the services of Tassilo Adam, his collection of ethnographic objects and his photographs (see pp. 34-35).

Other departments in the Colonial Institute also used the photographs to show the progress that had been made in the colony over the past 25 years. For example, the Department of Tropical Hygiene used them to illustrate the fight against *framboesia tropica*: '[...] photogravures, which show how the severe symptoms disappear after an injection of neosalvarsan'. The Trade Museum (Handelsmuseum) used a series of photographs of the Association of Javanese Timber Companies (Vereenigde Javasche Houthandel Maatschappijen, VJHM) to provide an idea of forestry on the island Simaloer (Pulau Simeuleu). Unfortunately nothing can be found about this special photography exhibition in the catalogue.

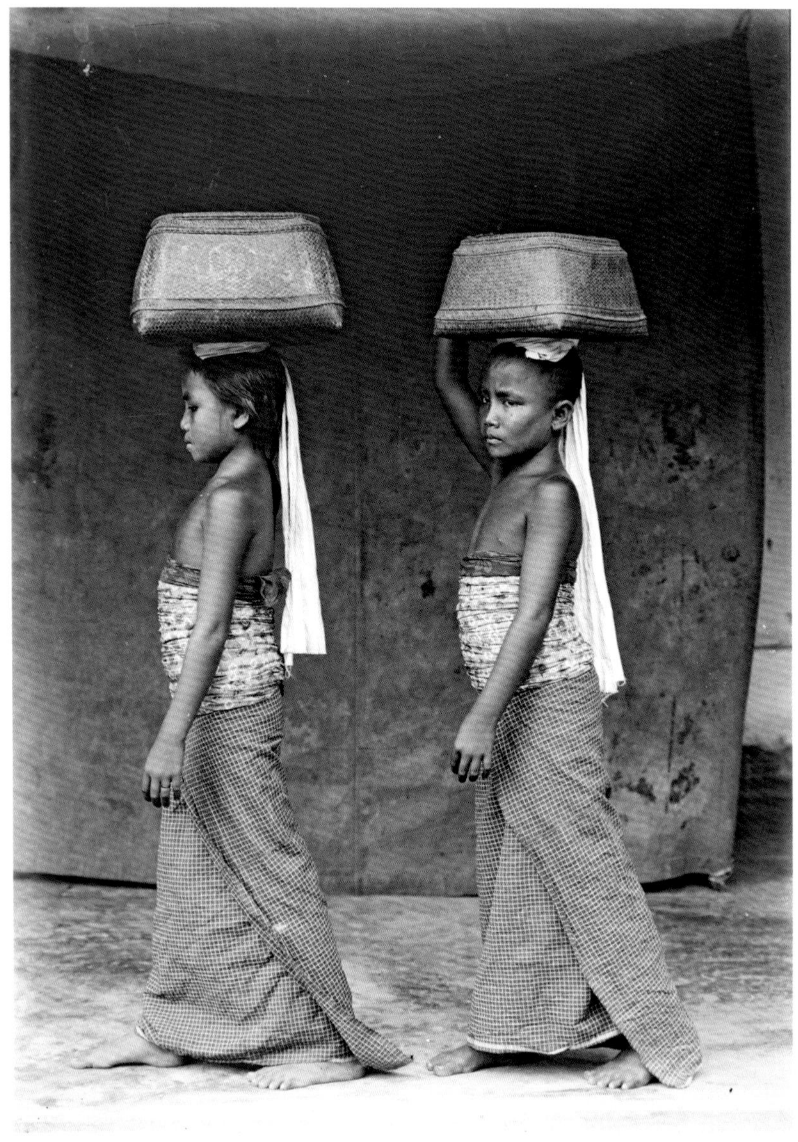

35
Studio portrait: Girls on their way to the market in Karangasem, Bali
Photographer: C. Gründler
gelatin glass negative
13 x 18 cm
1910–14
10013948. Gift: Augusta de Wit, 1917

The growth of the collection: 1915–40

The photograph collection expanded enormously between 1915 and 1940; a total of 498 gifts comprising thousands of photographs and negatives were received. The photographs were used to benefit the then prevailing colonial politics, i.e., making visible the results of the Ethical Policy (see the first chapter). Developing cities and the countryside, creating infrastructure, improving accessibility to healthcare and education for the local population, the rapid rise of industry and industrial processing of agricultural produce – all of these changes were happening at breakneck speed and the Colonial Institute had an almost insatiable demand for photographs portraying them. This material was used in a propagandistic way in publications, lectures and courses, exhibitions and annual fairs, both nationally and internationally.

Included in the gifts were important sub-collections from various expeditions; the Veen collection; the Jan Dinger collection – consisting of C. Nieuwenhuys' complete collection of photographs; donations from the Archaeological Service (Oudheidkundige Dienst) (see chapter on photography and science); and the collections of the author Augusta de Wit (1864–1939), Tassilo Adam and G.F.J. Bley. Institutes and private individuals all had their own reasons for donating their material. Bley, for example, hoped that his photographs would be 'a contribution, however small, to making beautiful Indonesia a little better known in Holland'.[73]

With the medium of photography already popularised by the introduction of the handy Kodak camera, photographs were now used to bring the Netherlands East Indies to the attention of a wider public. For example, lantern slides (the precursor to film slides) were made of existing photographs for lectures. Books that proved popular appeared, such as *Indië in Beeld*, which was published by the Royal Dutch Touring Club (Toeristenbond voor Nederland, ANWB).[74] This publication, with an introduction and an informative text, included 100 collotype photographs of 'the most beautiful natural scenes and everything else in colonial society that can be considered outstanding'.[75] At the initiative of H.F. Wagenaar Reisiger, J. Demmenie, photographer of the Topographical Service in the Netherlands East Indies, was dispatched for six months to take photographs on Java and Sumatra. The results were donated to the Colonial Institute; several were made into school posters later.[76]

The Colonial Museum, which opened in October 1926, also made extensive use of photographs, sometimes in a traditional way as prints, but they were also used in new ways. One of these new ways was the large transparent photographs measuring 35 x 40 centimetres that were placed in the windows of the Trade Museum and Ethnographic Department, between the display cases dedicated to indigenous trade and industry, weaving and weaving techniques.

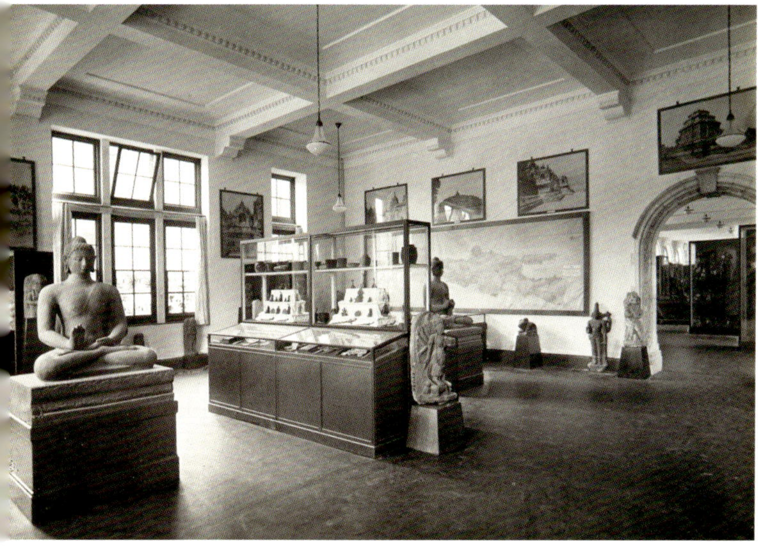

36
Indo-Javanese objects from and photographs of temple complexes and sanctuaries displayed in the 'Hindu Hall' of the Colonial Institute's museum
Photographer: C.A. Schouten
16.4 x 22.6 cm
silver gelatin developing-out paper
1926
60056182

For example, a light box with 20 transparencies that depicted ore processing on the island Nias was placed alongside objects from the island.[77] The 1926 annual report stated it as follows:

[...] transparent photographs with a matt glass background, representing Hindu–Javanese antiquities, temples, statues, architectonic decorations, etc., have been placed in the windows. Thanks to the kind assistance of Mr Th. van Erp, the Ethnographic Department now has twelve beautiful photographs of the Borobodur at its disposal, which will be used to create a separate window with transparent photographs of the Borobudur.

The use of transparencies frequently piqued the interest of other museums. The many stereoscopic viewing boxes were another innovation. The use of visual material for their own publications and the loans to many well-read magazines such as *De Prins, De katholieke Illustratie, Morks's Magazijn, Indië,* and *Nederlandsch-Indië Oud en Nieuw* increased annually until the mid-1930s. Before the Second World War, the Colonial Institute's photograph collection was the most important global source of visual material relating to the Netherlands East Indies.

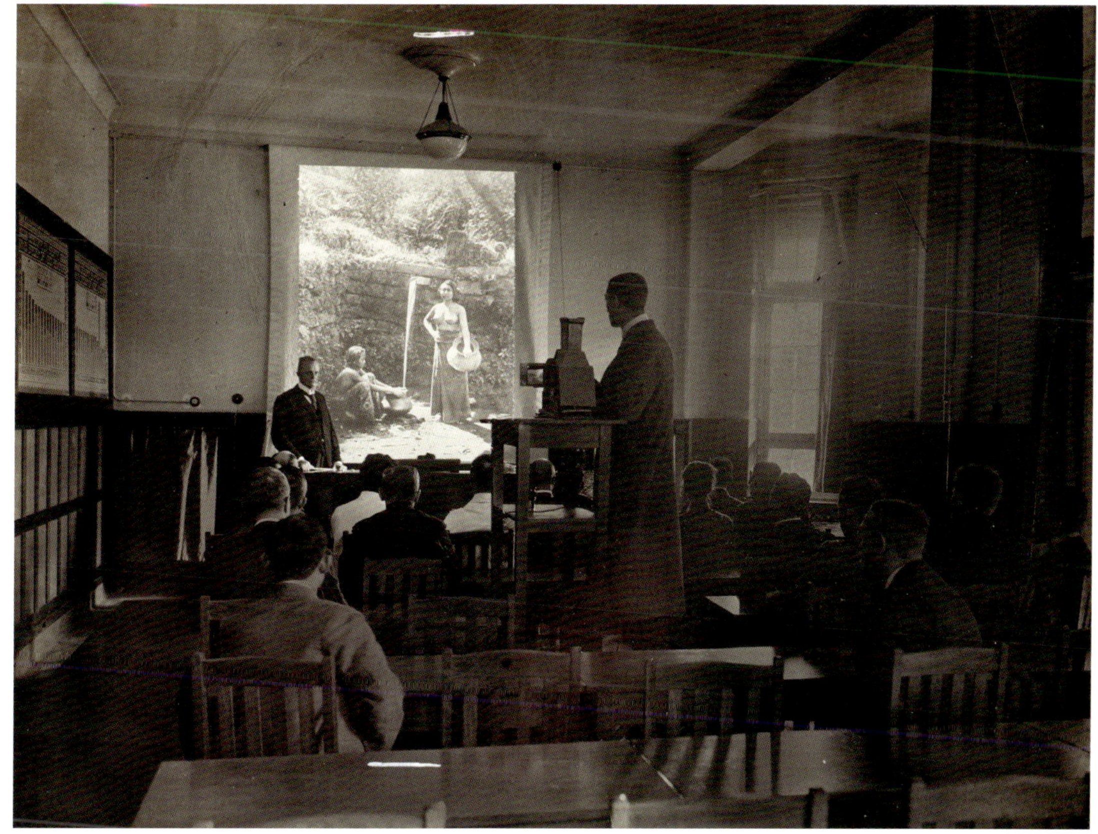

37
Slide projection at the laboratory of the Colonial Institute's Tropical Hygiene Department
It 'appears' that a transparency from the Colonial Institute collection, made by Kurkdjian Photographic Studio (1888–1936) in Surabaya, titled: 'Two Balinese woman at a well', is being projected on a screen. We use 'appears' here because if we examine the photograph, it is clear that Kurkdjian's photograph has been pasted onto this photograph.
Photographer: unknown
silver gelatin developing-out paper
17.4 x 23.7 cm
1920–40
60036893. Provenance: KIT Tropical Hygiene Department, 1995

THE COLOURS OF BLEY (1855–1944): AMATEUR PHOTOGRAPHER

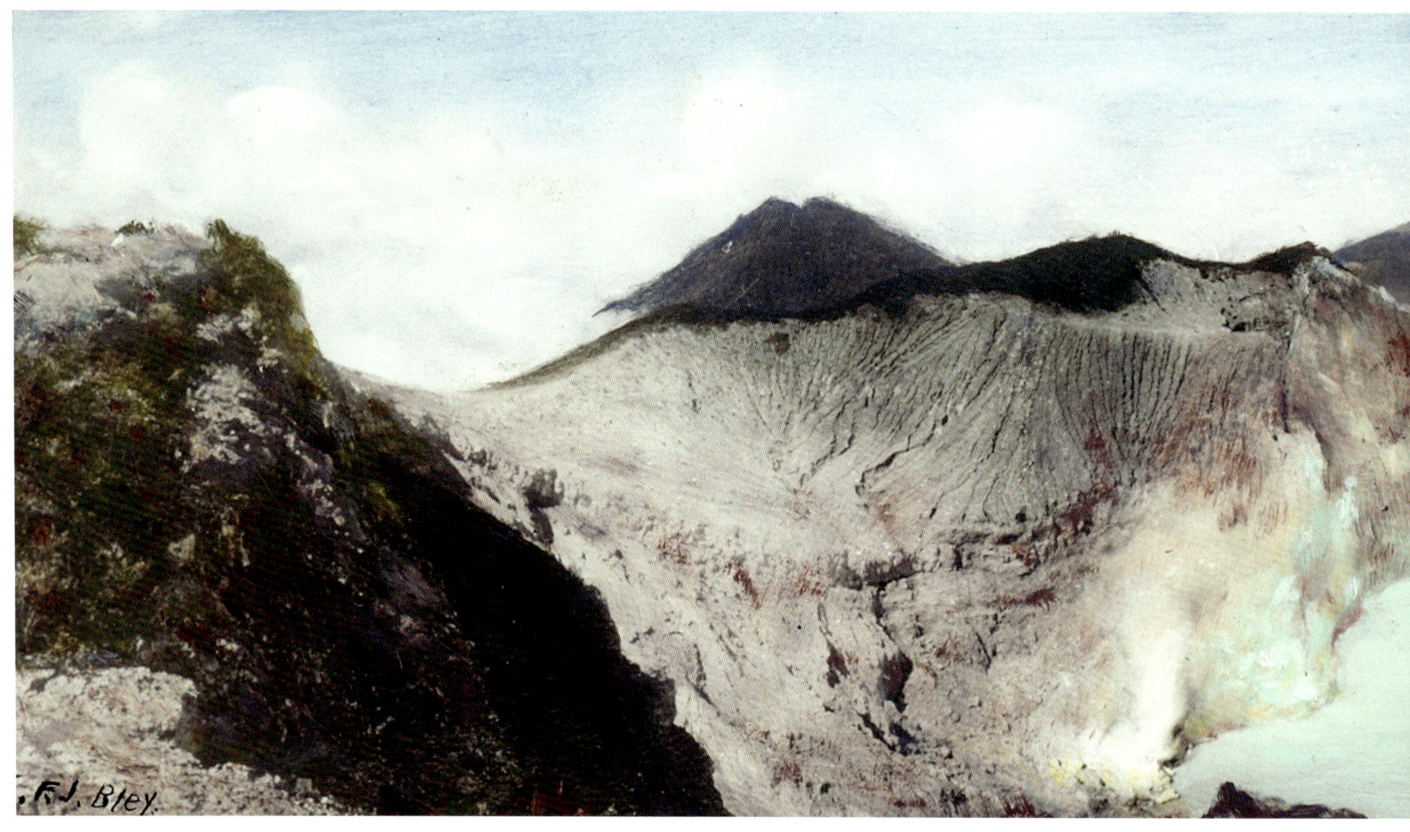

G.F.J. Bley was born in Jever (Germany), and attended the Mittweida Technical Academy. He arrived on Java in 1878, where he began a career as a machinist in a sugar factory. After several peregrinations he was appointed general manager (*administrateur*) of the Selokaton plantation in 1890, which was only growing Arabica coffee at the time. At Bley's initiative this became Robusta coffee, cinchona, kapok, cacao and especially tea. After returning from leave in Europe (1900) he also started a tea factory and was the chairman of the Semarang-Kedu Planters Association for a number of years. He already recognised the importance of advertising while he was a planter. Operating on behalf of the Planters Association, he devoted his energies to the International Fibre Congress in Surabaya (1911) and oversaw the successful submission of products and samples to the Colonial Exhibition in Semarang (1914). Later, as part of his preparations for the Tea Congress at the Annual Fair in Bandung (1924), he took photographs for the stands of the Sukabumi Agricultural Association (Soekaboemische Landbouw Vereeniging) and the Tea Research Station (Theeproefstation) in Buitenzorg. After retiring in 1916, he devoted himself to photography and researching fibrous crops, in particular kapok. He settled in Buitenzorg around 1918, where he was given his own space in the Treub Laboratory, where he could continue honing his photographic skills. G.F.J. Bley, who invariably added the words 'Amateur Photographer' after his name, was a praiseworthy photographer

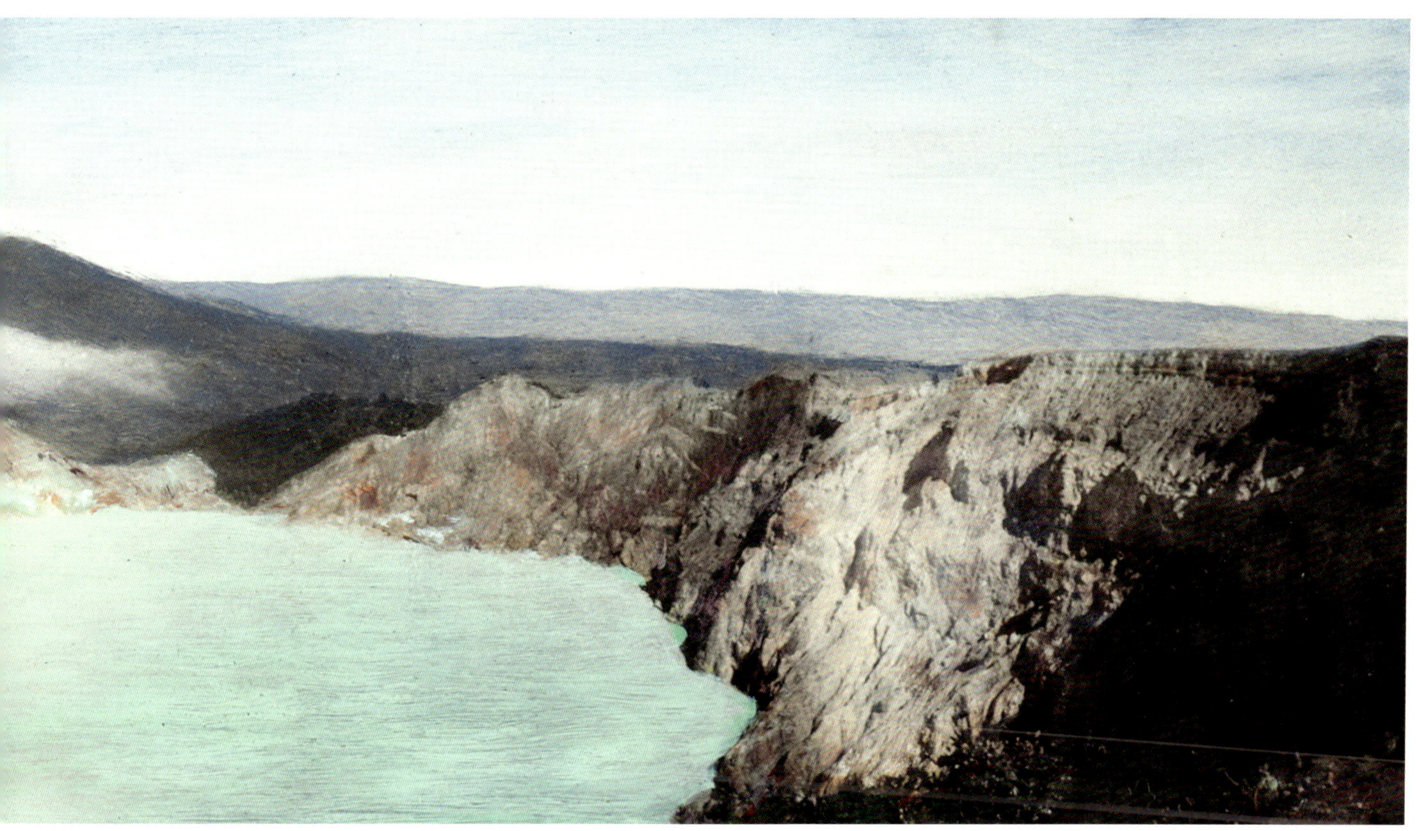

vith artistic aspirations and a keen ·ye for Java's sublime landscape, ›f which he took many panoramic ›hotographs. His use of colour luring the final processing of ıis photographs is especially ıoteworthy. Indeed, colour is rare ı the Tropenmuseum's pre-war ·ollection, although this should ›e qualified. Early photographs vere never pure black, grey ›r white: albumen prints, for ·xample, are a standard red or ·ellowish-brown or, after gold ·oning, sepia to purplish-brown. 3ut Bley went even further. ·Ie used baths that changed the colour of his silver gelatin developing-out-papers, causing his photographs of Wijnkoops Bay (now Teluk Pelabuhan Ratu) to frequently be blue and his panoramic photographs of mountainous landscapes to be green. Other photographs were carefully hand-coloured with watercolours, using painters' brushes. This was usually done by his apprentice Soekardi.

A number of photograph albums also include small paintings that on closer inspection appear to be painted photographic prints. Sometimes part of the photograph can still be seen, as in the image of the volcanic lake on the Ijen Plateau. Take note of the photographer's signature at bottom left. All his years spent in the Tropics seem to have not taken their toll on him, and Bley died when he was very old in 1944 in Buitenzorg. RJ

38
The volcanic lake in the Ijen crater
Photographer: G.F.J. Bley (1855–1944)
silver gelatin developing-out paper, painted
11.4 x 43 cm
1915–26
60055697. Gift: G.F.J. Bley, 1926

The Second World War – the Indies Institute: 1940–50

The Colonial Institute did not escape the consequences of the global economic crisis during the 1930s, and its subsidies were greatly reduced. An Advisory Commission was set up, which advised on technical equipment, and spent a great deal of time on the film collection. They decided that much of the film material had to be discarded because of its poor technical condition and because the substance of the subjects it covered had aged.[78]

The commission also dedicated itself to the photograph and negatives collections. They advised reclassifying and re-describing the photographs and negatives. The international Universal Decimal Classification System (UDC) was chosen. The entire collection was processed from 1941 to 1948. Prints were made from the negatives and negatives were made of the existing photographs and were reprinted. The resulting prints were glued to cardboard, filed, classified and described according to the UDC system. Some of the photographs and negatives were rejected because they were regarded as too dated and no longer relevant. A number of especially 19th-century prints are marked on the reverse with the comment 'rejected'. The rejected originals were stored elsewhere. In total almost 35,000 photographs and negatives were reclassified and re-documented.

In August 1944 the Colonial Institute was ordered to close by the German occupier – the 'Grüne Polizei' (Order Police) had started using the building.

The war ended in West Europe in May 1945, and peace followed a few months later in South East Asia in August. Indonesia's declaration of independence on 17 August 1945 changed the situation completely. The Netherlands refused to acknowledge the declaration and responded with military force. Because of international pressure the Dutch government could do nothing else than recognise the Republic of Indonesia, but this was only in 1949. The Colonial Institute had to re-orientate its content. Renamed the Indies Institute in November 1945, [79] its name was changed again in 1950 into the Royal Tropical Institute.

KIT – Tropenmuseum: old collection – new paths

After the change of name in 1950 from the Indies Institute into the Royal Tropical Institute (KIT), the sphere of activity was expanded to include the entire tropical and subtropical worlds, and considerably more attention was paid to extending 'technical assistance to countries undergoing rapid development'.[80] The photograph collection was included in this re-evaluation; photographic material – in particular from India, the Middle East, Africa and South and Central America – was acquired by appealing in writing to embassies, consulates and private individuals. By 1960 another 522 gifts had been received.

The re-evaluation also affected other departments in the KIT – the Departments of Tropical Products (formerly the Trade Museum), Tropical Hygiene, and Cultural and Physical Anthropology also had to change course. Among the consequences was that they disposed of their own photograph collections, which were subsequently added to the other photographs of the Netherlands East Indies, in the meantime already known as the 'historical photograph collection'.

Private individuals also continued donating their photographs and negatives of the former Netherlands East Indies, probably inspired by the notion that traditionally, the KIT was the ideal place for such material. Until about the 1980s, the KIT/Tropenmuseum paid scant attention to the by now historical photographs. A policy of collecting these images did not exist. The colonial past was no longer an issue in the public debate; at most it was discussed in the family circle.

In subsequent decades (1975–90) the KIT/Tropenmuseum's collecting policy focused on topical documentary photography from and about the Tropics: material that could also be used in exhibitions in the museum. The idea was that this 'contemporary' collection would grow to become a national photographic documentation centre in the area of development cooperation.

However, the 1960s saw the onset of a discreet change in the mindset relating to the colonial past. This period was too deeply embedded and had lasted too long to be cast aside. Part of the population of the Netherlands had been born in the Netherlands East

THE HILLERSTRÖM COLLECTION

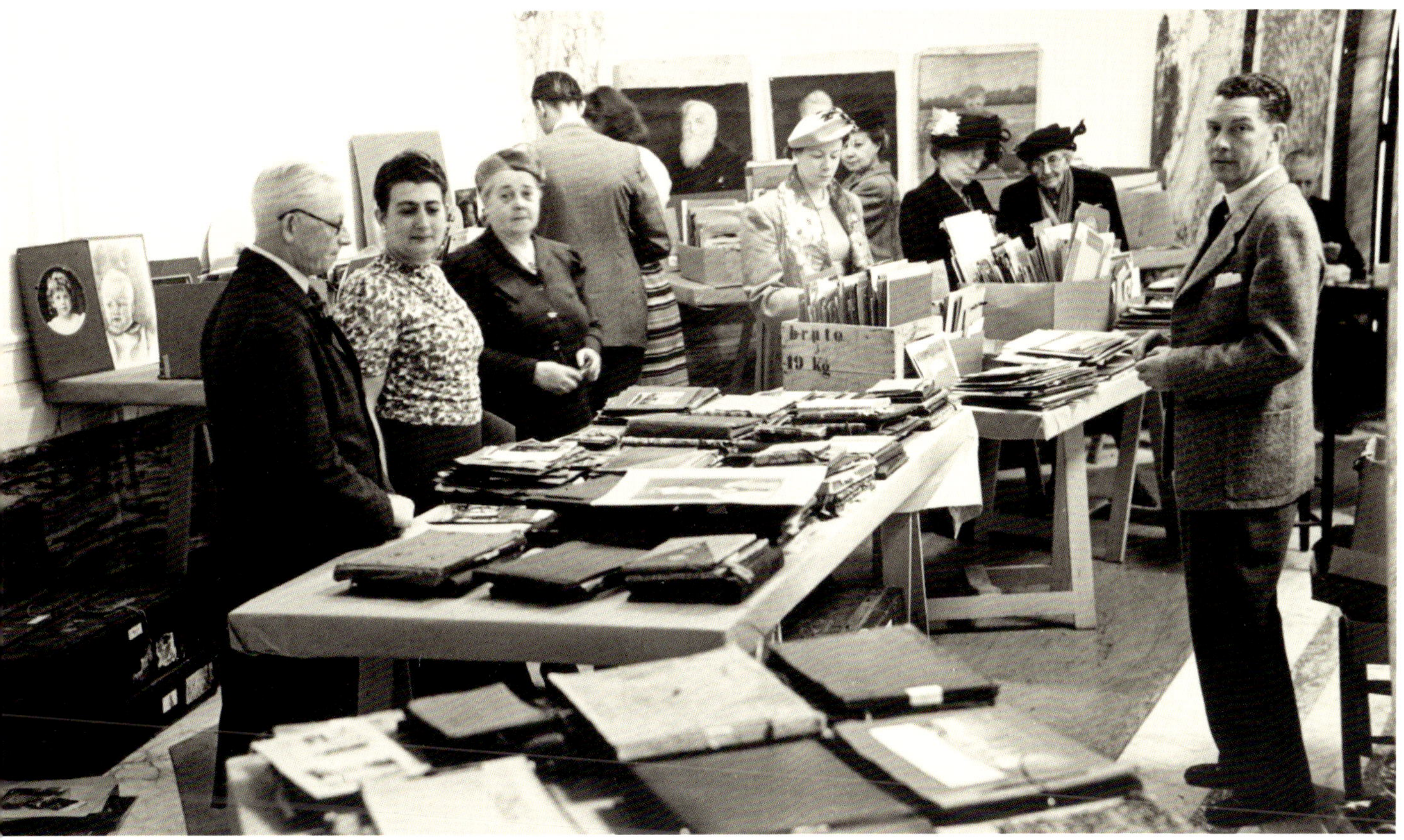

39
Browsing the Hillerström Collection at the Indies Institute
Photographer: unknown
silver gelatin developing-out paper
8.9 x 13.8 cm
July 1949
60043955

In 1948, 30 crates containing personal photographs arrived from Indonesia.[81] Dutch soldiers found these photographs while searching houses abandoned by Europeans on Java and Sumatra. They were brought to the Netherlands at the initiative of various organisations,[82] and the Ministry of Overseas Territories (Ministerie van Overzeese Gebiedsdelen). A year later another shipment of albums and portraits that had been found in Japanese refuse depots arrived in the Netherlands.[83] All this material was made available to interested parties in the Institute and in several other locations in the Netherlands. A search was begun that was overseen by the Indies Institute's Press and Publicity Department, and a total of 613 albums, 4996 separate photographs, eighteen baby books, 30 poetry albums, 84 separate album pages, six signed and 20 painted portraits and 1055 negatives were returned to approximately 2000 of their rightful owners before 1951. After the Ministry was discontinued in 1959, Mrs M.J. Hillerström took custody of the remaining photographs and continued searching for their rightful owners until her death in 1978.[84] After her passing, the 300 or so remaining albums were transferred to the Tropical Institute's Photography Department. Later, in 1980, the albums that had earlier been given to the magazine *Moesson* were also added to the historical photograph collection.[85]
As a result of the exhibition 'Family Photographs from the Netherlands East Indies: 1880–1942' the Photography Department made a final attempt in November 1999 to trace the rightful owners of the albums by organising viewing days, and a few more photographs and albums were returned to their owners. SV

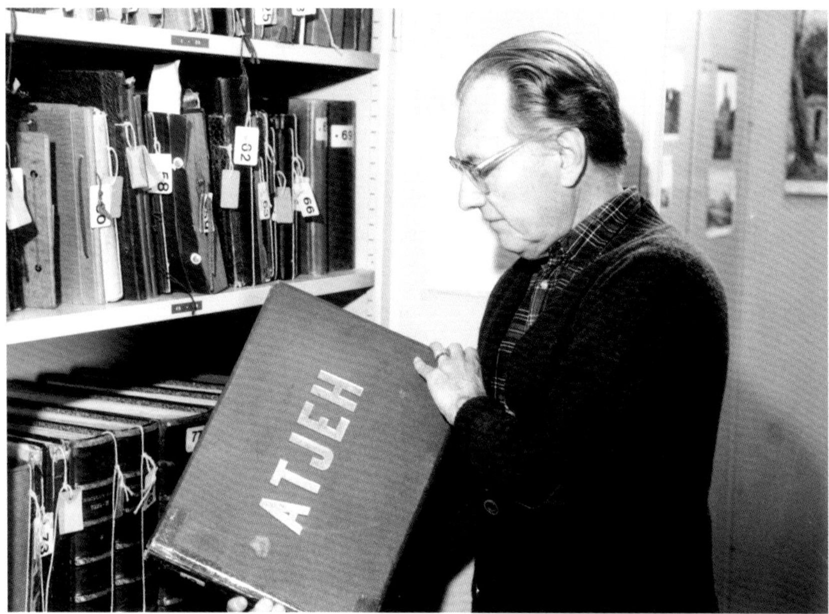

40
E.G. Spruyt (1922–2011) with several albums from the Tropenmuseum's historical photograph collection
Photographer: unknown
silver gelatin developing-out paper
12 x 16.6 cm
1986
60059791

Indies, had worked or lived there or had other personal ties. The activities of the Tong Tong Foundation were much discussed. This foundation had organised the annual Pasar Malam in The Hague from the end of the 1950s and had published the popular magazine *Tong Tong* since 1958 (it was renamed *Moesson* in 1978). It also published the photography books about the Netherlands East Indies by Rob Nieuwenhuys, of which the first, *Tempo Doeloe, fotografische documenten uit het oude Indie, 1870–1914*, appeared in 1961.[86] Photography seemed to be the medium of choice to keep these memories of 'days gone by' alive.

The demand for colonial photographs gradually increased and to deal with this, the meanwhile somewhat neglected collection was once again re-catalogued. This task was assigned to E.G. Spruyt in 1975.[87] Albums were numbered and separate photographs were classified by subject and stored in folders. These activities provided greater insights into the collection and in 1977 the Institute started duplicating photographs in collaboration with Arsip Nasional, Indonesia's national archive in Jakarta.[88] Partly because of Spruyts' efforts, the colonial photograph collection gained ever more repute, resulting in yet more gifts.

From a resource to a museum collection

On 1 August 1980 the Photography Department was assigned a new status in the KIT organisation. From this date the collection became the responsibility of the Tropenmuseum and the museum's director was responsible for the day-to-day management. The photograph collection actually consisted of two components: (1) 'contemporary' photographs and slides (1960–present) of various tropical and subtropical countries, many of which were made by the department's staff, and (2) a historical collection. The *contemporary collection* was regarded as the most important for the activities within the Institute, but the appreciation of the significance of the historical photograph collection grew. The steadily increasing demand for photographs of the colonial past for research and publications was mostly from outside the Museum. Many private individuals donated their photographs, and the collection continued to expand, becoming the central location where Holland's colonial past, especially that of the Netherlands East Indies, could be preserved and studied.

An internal memorandum of 1986 reported on the state of affairs of the history and composition of the collection.[89] By 1988 the demand for historical material had grown to such proportions that it outstripped the demand for contemporary photographic material.[90] The historical colonial photograph collection had meanwhile come to be seen as being of great national cultural-historical importance. Time and effort was spent on thoroughly documenting, preserving and digitising this substantial collection.

The upsurge of interest in old photographs at home and abroad has led to a new level of appreciation of the Tropenmuseum's historical collection. Space and time was made available to create exhibitions with this material. An important impetus to this was a large Amsterdam photographic event.

125 years of photography in the Tropics

An important photographic event, 'Photo '84 Amsterdam, the First International Photographic Exhibition', had been held a few years previously (1984).[91] Recognising the opportunity, the Tropenmuseum organised the exhibition '125 Years of Photography in the Tropics' ('125 Jaar Fotografie in de Tropen'), the first photography exhibition to feature its own collection since 1923. Although historical photographs were displayed, emphasis was placed on contemporary photographs and slides depicting numerous tropical and subtropical countries. It was a visual statement that affirmed the Tropenmuseum's position at the very core of society. This exhibition was thus a direct successor to the exhibition 60 years earlier that had provided insights into the colonial society at the time. The difference was that the older material – which was contemporary in 1923 – was now historical. The '125 years' in the title was actually misleading – at the time none of the photographs in the collection were dated before 1859.[92] The '125 Years of Photography in the Tropics' exhibition included old original prints as well as the highlights from the collection's richly decorated and substantively interesting albums.[93]
It was the first time that historical photographs and albums were accorded museal status, albeit somewhat hesitantly.
This re-evaluation led to a great number of exhibitions in the period 1990 to 2012 that featured material from the Institute's own collection, not only of the Netherlands East Indies (14), but also of Suriname (2), Curacao (1), Yemen (2), and India (1). This also resulted in substantial contributions to 'object exhibitions', in which historical photographs formed an ever-increasing supporting role or were even displayed as independent objects in themselves and were not exclusively used as background material: 'Batak in Images' ('Batak in Beeld'), 2006; and 'New Guinea > Irian-Jaya' ('Nieuw-Guinea > Irian-Jaya'), 1997. The information that had accompanied the exhibited photographs in the past was now seen as being insufficient. The photographers' names, previously regarded as inconsequential, were now important details, as was information about the photographic technique, the place and time the photograph was taken, and the reason and/or occasion. In brief, a photograph was increasingly being regarded as an object that deserved to be appreciated in context.
Requests to make exhibitions came from Indonesia (Erasmushuis, Historical Museum of Jakarta), Suriname, Yemen and Saudi Arabia.
Approaches to exhibiting changed – initially, the framed photographs were placed on partitions; later exhibitions became more conceptual and were realised in close consultation with exhibition makers and designers.

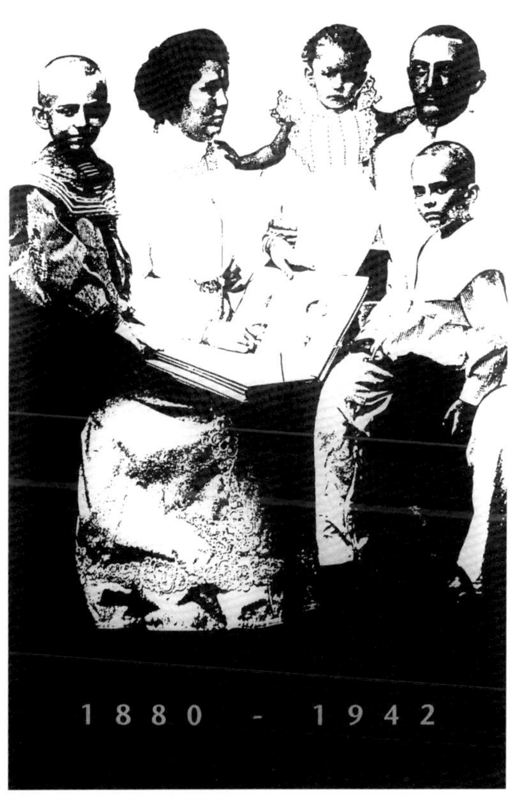

41
Banner that was hung at the 'Family photographs from the Netherlands East Indies' exhibition
It is designed after the photograph: 'Studio portrait of the Spruyt-Laurens family looking at a photograph album, Buitenzorg'.
Photographer: unknown
gelatin printing-out paper
27.1 x 22 cm
c. 1902
60027293. Gift: E.G. Spruyt

An example is the 2006 exhibition 'Batak in Images'. This exhibition was part of a dual exhibition with the 'Woven Worlds' ('Wereld van Weefsels') about four important collectors of Batak textiles, elsewhere in the museum. Photographs made by Tassilo Adam between 1914 and 1918 were central to the 'Batak in Images' exhibition. These were relatively early and unique images of the Batak community on Sumatra. Vintage prints by Tassilo Adam from 1918 that had been exhibited in Medan in 1919 were displayed alongside new prints made from the glass negatives.

Besides these two main visual threads the exhibition had two underlying themes. The automation and digitising of the photograph collection provided an insight into the entire archive of Tassilo Adam's photographs. Manual searches using the until-then usual categorisation of the photographs – by subject and region and not by photographer or donation – was an extremely time-consuming task. 'Batak in Images' was an opportunity to convey the overall picture, providing visitors with a glimpse of the archival procedures and automated work behind the scenes. The observations by the Batak themselves on the 90-year-old images provided a third level of interest. The villages and locations that Tassilo Adam had photographed were re-visited, the photographs were shown to the people there, and their reactions were recorded on film.

Conservation and collection management

The increased importance of the historical photograph collection went hand in hand with the development of a conservation strategy to ensure its preservation. First, special climate-controlled storage facilities were arranged. The large collection of albums was packed in acid-free boxes and stored in the depot. A second climate-controlled room was developed to house the original negatives. Furthermore, a distinction was no longer made between objects and photographs: from now on both were considered as complementary.

The Ministry of Development Cooperation, which had given financial support for the management and care of the collections, wanted more information about the actual status of the various Tropenmuseum collections. An international visitation commission was created.[94] Elizabeth Edwards, visual anthropologist and head of the Pitt Rivers Museum photograph collection at the time, was the consultant for the photograph collection. She stressed that, among other reasons, KIT's photograph collection is important because of the mutual relations between the photographs and the Tropenmuseum's object collection on the one hand, and the background information that could be accessed in the library, on the other.

The collection's potential lay in research and critical analyses of the relationships between ethnology and colonial history, and the history of photography and art.[95]

After this positive evaluation the Ministry decided to grant a subsidy to KIT so that it could improve its conservation methods and accessibility to the museum collection by digitising all its collections. This project was called 'Heritage Extra Project' ('Erfgoed-extra Project'). The most obvious component of this project was the preservation of the historical negatives. More than 50,000 negatives were processed and the basic data relating to these negatives were entered into the computer documentation system. At the same time the restoration of photograph albums began. Currently, 200,000 objects from the photographic collection have been entered into the database.[96] The greater part of these images is now available online. Interestingly, the Tropenmuseum also entered a partnership with Wikimedia, where the museum's images are available under a Creative Commons licence to be used free of charge by the Wikipedia community.

The importance of good public access became apparent when photographs from the series 'Indonesians in Holland' by Magnum photographer Leonard Freed (1929–2006)[97] were placed online in the framework of the 2010 exhibition 'One Way to Holland' ('Enkele reis Holland'). The museum received many reactions from people who identified some of the unknown people in the images as their family members. One respondent recognised her father in one of the images, of whom she had no photographs until that moment.

The Tropenmuseum continues to research and expand the collection of historical photographs

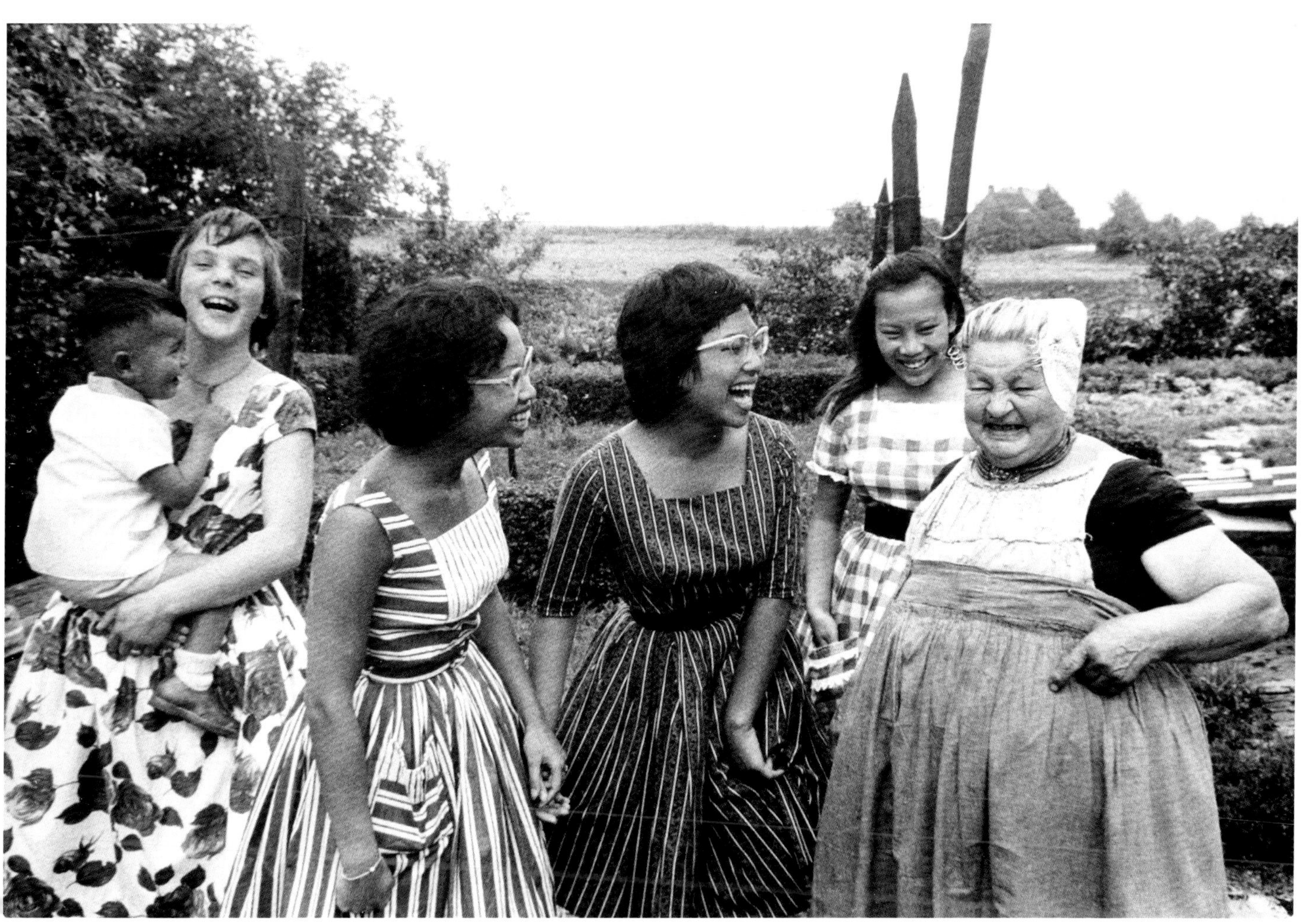

42
Girls of the Portier family enjoying the company of their aunt in law at Middelburg, Zeeland
Photographer: Leonard Freed (1929–2006)
silver gelatin developing-out paper
20.3 x 29.8 cm
1960
60059551. Purchase: B. Freed, 2010. With support of the BankGiro Loterij. © Leonard Freed, Magnum Photos Inc.

and albums, primarily, but not exclusively, for the museum's important Indonesian, Suriname and Caribbean sub-collections. The 2011 exhibition 'Netherlands-Indies Staged – Kurkdjian & Co. Photographic Studio (1888–1936)' ['Indië in scène – Fotostudio Kurkdjian & Co. (1888–1936)'[98]] is an example of this policy and it reveals the manifold and complex nuances of colonial history and representation embedded in this collection.

THE IWI COLLECTION

No other sub-collection in the Tropenmuseum's photograph collection is so deeply entwined with colonial society as the one that was transferred to the Tropenmuseum by the Indo Scientific Institute (Indisch Wetenschappelijk Instituut, IWI) in 2005.[99]

This collection originated with the founding of the Tong Tong Foundation in 1957 by Jan Boon (1911–74), a journalist and author who used the pen names Tjalie Robinson and Vincent Mahieu. Born in Nijmegen of an Indo-European mother and a Dutch KNIL officer, Jan Boon grew up in Indonesia. After Indonesia's independence, circumstances compelled him to move to the Netherlands in 1954, where he worked as a journalist and author. He was particularly interested in 'Tropical Hollanders' ('Tropen Nederlanders') for whom he founded the magazine *Tong Tong* in 1958, which he used as a platform for the Indo-European group in Dutch society. He asked his readers to send him personal stories, experiences and photographs, an appeal that met with a huge response. After Jan Boon died, his widow Lilian Ducelle continued the magazine; it was renamed *Moesson* in 1978. Most of the letters that were sent in were not preserved, but a lot of the visual material was, some of which formed the *Moesson* images archive. In 1984 another part was transferred to the Indies Scientific Institute, which was founded by Ducelle and Ralph Boekholt. The IWI would become an efficient scientific institute that collected and preserved photographs, films, books and other objects that were brought together by the Indo-European target group. Under director Edy Seriese and with the help of volunteers with an Indo-European background, the material was manually classified and made accessible from 1980 to 1990. Donations, correspondence and visitors were recorded, and queries about the collection and the history of the Netherlands East Indies were always answered. In 2005 the photograph collection was digitised and then transferred to the Tropenmuseum, where the almost 70,000 photographs form an important addition to the existing collection of family albums.

What makes the IWI photograph collection so special is its emphasis on material that was made from the 1910s to the mid-1950s by amateur photographers who frequently photographed their own, often domestic, environments. It mostly comprises Indo-European family albums with group portraits, children, parties, outings, offices, interiors, orchids and dogs. These often-cheerful photographs provide unique and intimate glimpses of Colonial society, but what they exclude also says a lot!

AM

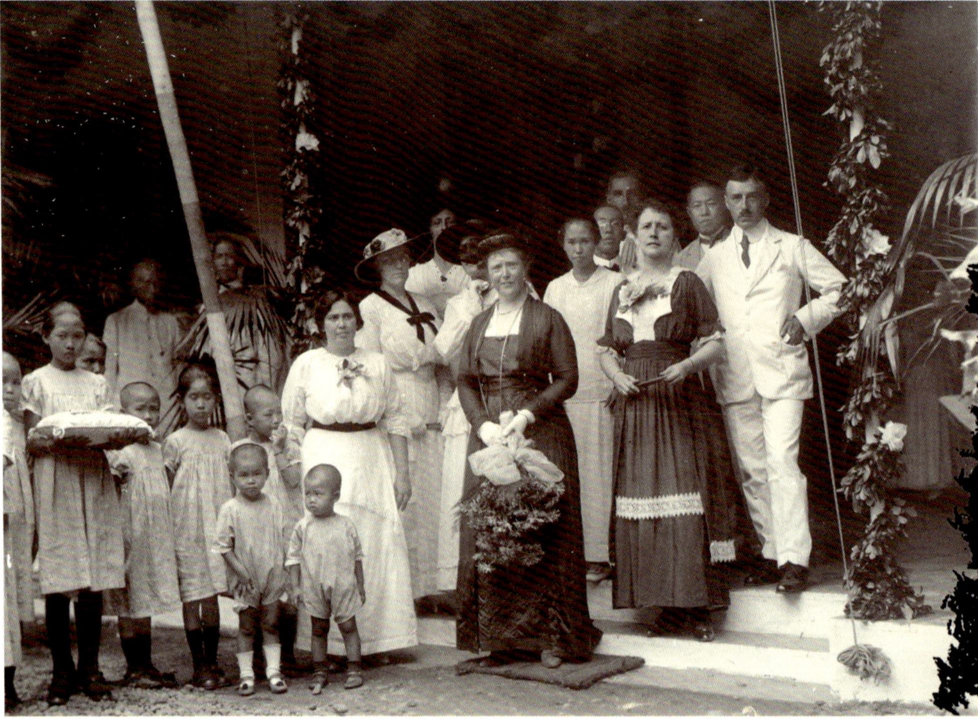

43

Opening a home for Chinese girls at Goenoeng Sari 41, Batavia, in the presence of Mrs Van Limburg Stirum (centre), the wife of the Governor-General

Photographer: unknown
gelatin printing-out paper
12.3 x 17.1 cm
17 October 1917
30003216. Gift: Indo Scientific Institute (IWI), 2006

CEES TAILLIE (1920–2005)

The preconditions attached to accepting a gift in the 1990s included ensuring that the photographs were of exhibition quality and were a significant addition to the collection. These two criteria were applied to a large negatives collection that the octogenarian Cees Taillie wanted to donate to the museum in 2004. He produced the material in Indonesia during the period 1946–49 while working as a military engineer, and later as one of the eight photographers of the Army Information Service (Legervoorlichtingsdienst, LVD), during the period when the Netherlands tried to restore the pre-war colonial status quo through police actions after Indonesia declared independence. He travelled through the eastern part of the archipelago from his post in Makassar on Celebes. Each week he sent his photographs to the Army Information Service in Jakarta, which chose the images that were suitable for publication in the Netherlands, where they appeared in numerous magazines, without the photographer's name, but with the note 'copyright LVD'. The LVD photographers were told to avoid as much as possible any images that would 'imply that a real war was being fought', so as not to upset the home front. After all, the Dutch were there to restore peace and order, so the images had to portray humane and peaceful activities. Taillie used two cameras and gradually created his own archive. This private archive consists of military photographs, and especially of photographs that express his curiosity for and fascination with the Indonesian population. Consciously or not, his photographs subtly record the gradual disappearance of the colonial relations evident in pre-war photographs. He carefully classified, documented and preserved these negatives for over 50 years. This 'living bequest' of historical material meant that it was possible to talk to Mr Taillie about his time and experiences in Indonesia – first hand information that provided the photographs with a much deeper context. Taillie had frequently come close to destroying the negatives in the 1950s (and thereafter). Prompted by the general mindset at the time that regarded 'Indië-gangers' (Dutch soldiers fighting against the Indonesian nationalists) as colonists and traitors, he was ashamed of having been in Indonesia. But he could not bring himself to do it: '…there is too much of me in those photographs'.[100] The gift resulted in the 2004 exhibition 'From Colony to Republic' ('Van Kolonie tot Republiek'). JVD

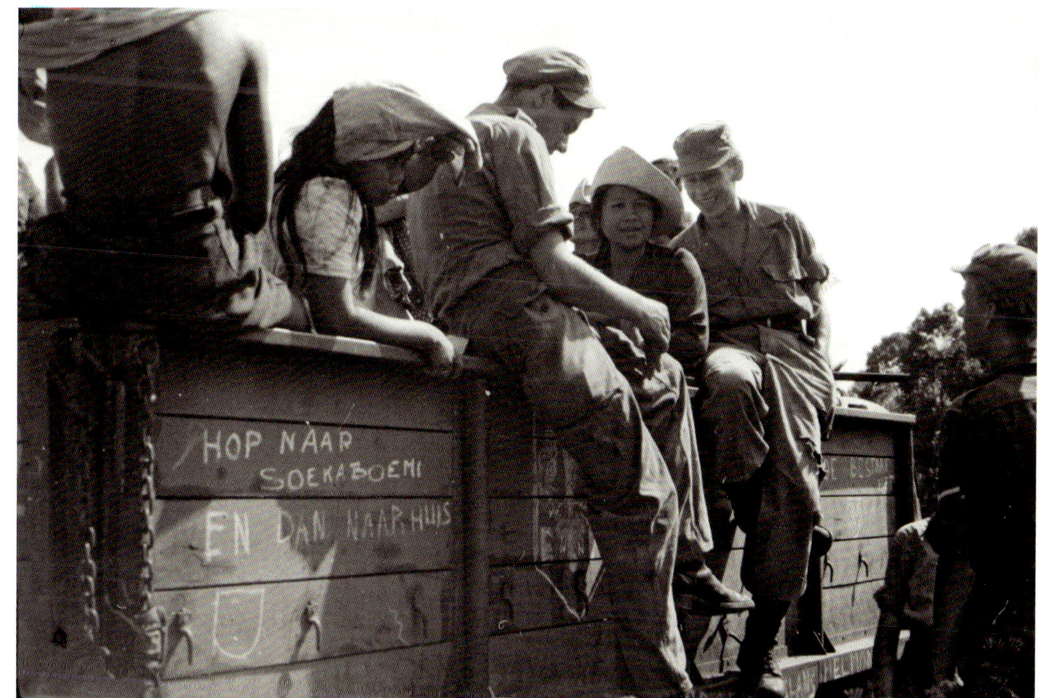

44
Dutch infantry with Indonesian women on their way to Sukabumi, during the first 'Police Action' ('Politionele Actie'), Java
Photographer: Cees Taillie (1920–2005)
acetate negative
2.4 x 3.6 cm
July/August 1947
10029186. Gift: Cees Taillie, 2004

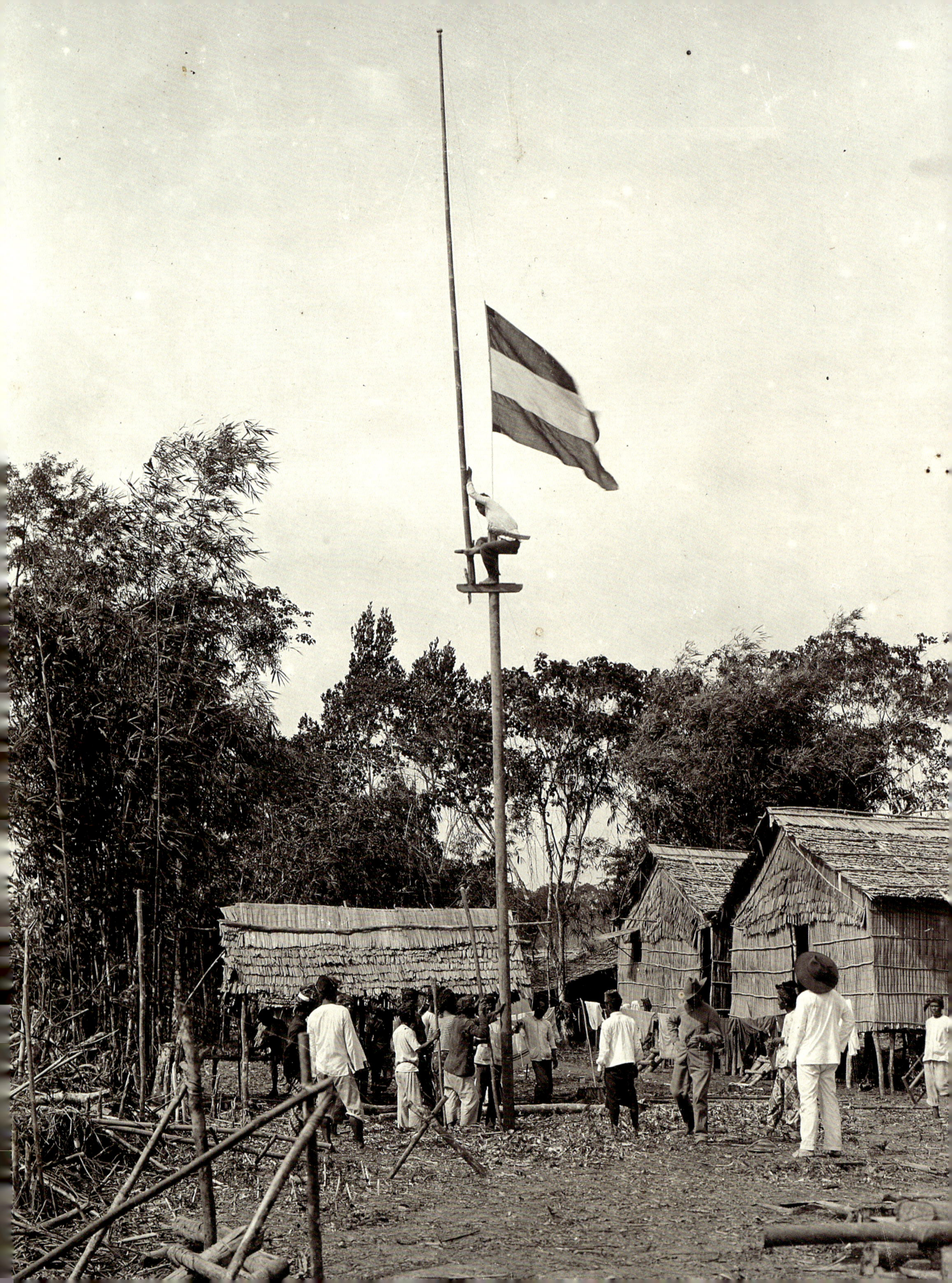

OFFICIAL AND SOCIAL LIFE

JANNEKE VAN DIJK

< 45
Raising the Dutch flag in Longiram (Borneo) during the establishment of the colonial administration on the Upper Mahakam
Photographer: unknown
collodion printing-out paper
16.1 x 11.4 cm
1900
60010383. Gift: B.M. Hupka-Barth, 1994. Former collection J.P.J. Barth

> 46
Portrait of the Regent of Tanette with her daughter, Celebes
Photographer: unknown
gelatin printing-out paper
13.4 x 9.5 cm
c. 1903
60001503. Gift: D.J. Oostenbroek, 1982

We Tanri Ollé, Regent of Tanette on the South West coast of Celebes since 1856, was decorated several times during her reign. One of these occasions was in 1898 when she was recognised for supplying the Dutch army command with information that had enabled the colonial government to restore peace during a punitive military expedition in her area one year earlier. From the time of her coronation in 1856 We Tanri Ollé had proven herself loyal to the Dutch authorities. She had already been named a Knight of the Order of the Netherlands Lion, had been awarded a gold medal for civic services, and in 1906 became a Commander of the Cross of Orange Nassau. When she died in November 1910 the *Sumatra Post* remembered her as a loyal subject and continued, 'The portrait of this, the oldest friend of the Dutch authority, has been published countless times in illustrated magazines'. The decorated Regent of tiny Tanette was seen as symbolising the assimilated society so desired by the colonisers.
The Tropenmuseum photograph collection has several photographs of We Tanri Ollé. Unfortunately, the photographer of only one of these images can be identified: Hendrik Veen had already photographed We Tanri Ollé and her royal household around 1865–70.

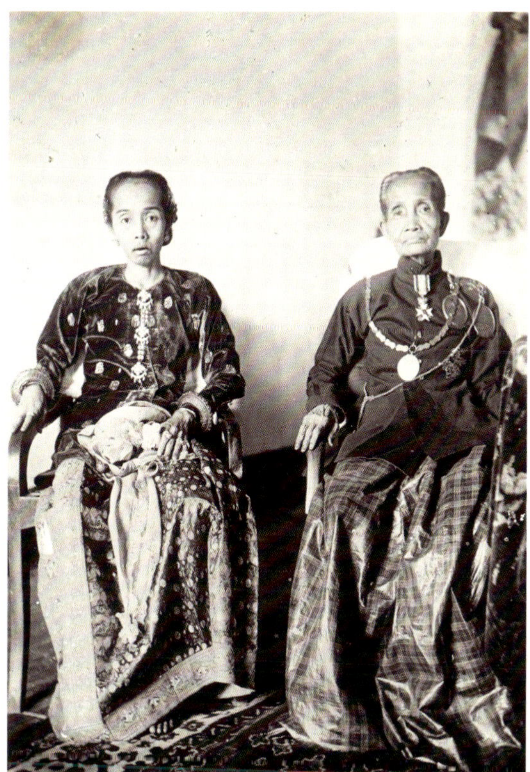

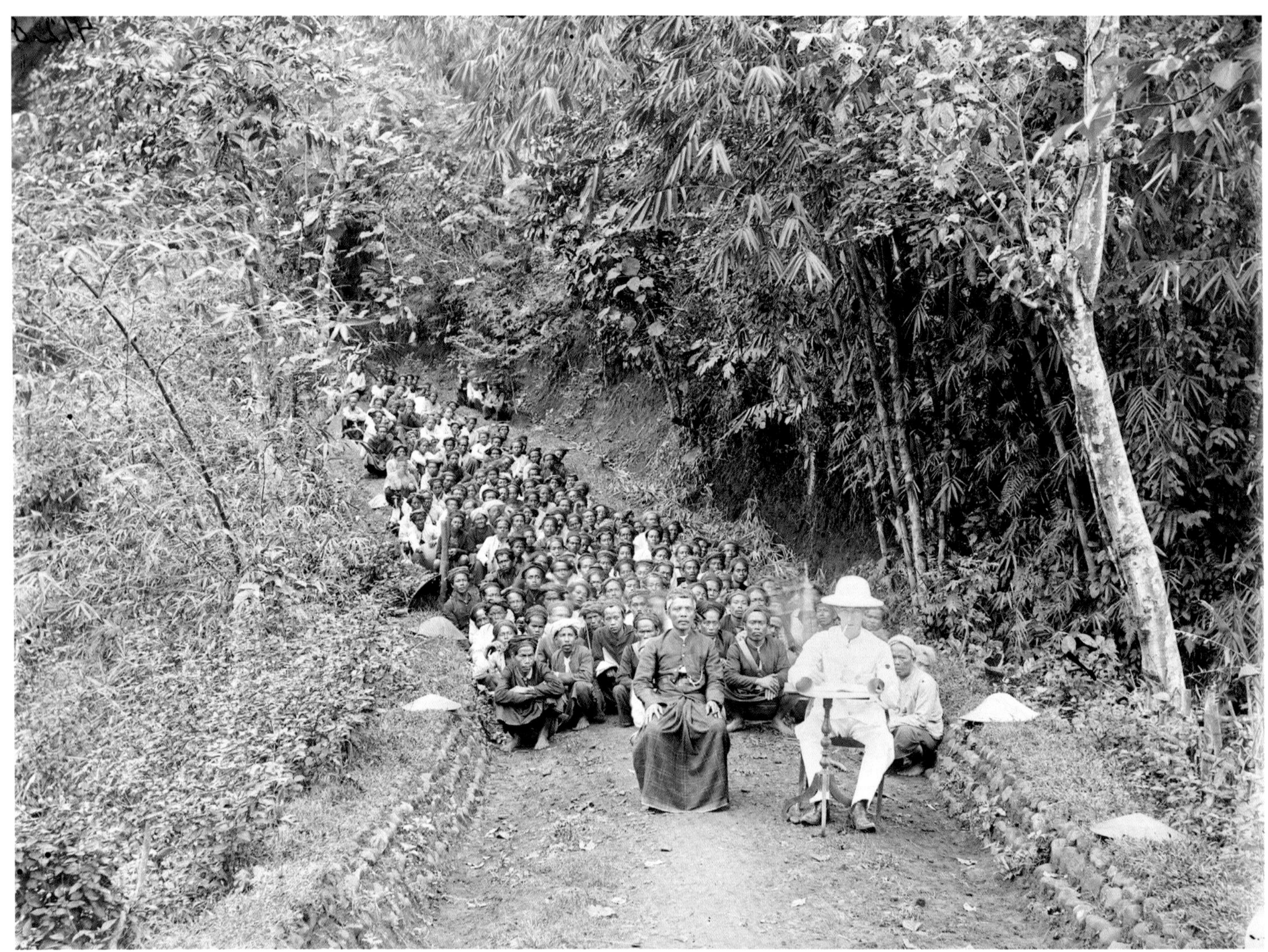

47
Land tax administration in Priangan, Java
Photographer: unknown
gelatin glass negative
13 x 18 cm
c. 1900
10001732. Gift: N. Scheltema, 1921

Cooperation with and support from loyal indigenous authorities formed the core of the Dutch colonial administration; to a degree it was a form of indirect government. From the beginning of the 20th century this reliance on local authorities became subtly visible in photographs. The signs and symbols of solidarity with the distant motherland were to be found from the northernmost point of Sumatra to the remotest corners of New Guinea (Papua). They could be seen in the images of people with a royal decoration, hoisting the flag in a Dayak village on Borneo (Fig. 45), a boundary marker nailed to a tree in New Guinea, and a portrait of Queen Wilhelmina on a triumphal arch.

The colonial government

At the beginning of the 20th century the entire archipelago – 55 times the size of the Netherlands with approximately 49 million inhabitants – was more-or-less under Dutch control. Roughly 168,000 Europeans lived in Indonesia, most of whom were officials in the Colonial Administration.[101] This was far too few to exert true authority, so use had to be made of the existing local administrative systems, and of an indigenous aristocracy that recognised and was loyal to the colonial authority. Besides the Internal Administration (Binnenlands Bestuur, BB), there was the Local Administration (Inlandsch Bestuur, IB), both of which reported to the government.

This initially did not amount to more than a type of symbolic authority in the Outer Regions (see the first chapter) and there was very little contact with the indigenous population. Young officials had to leave their government posts and regularly 'tour' their areas. These district commissioners, as they were called, had the most direct contact with the local population. They were the hands and feet, the ears and eyes of the Internal Administration, and had to gain the trust of local rulers, listen to grievances and negotiate according to instructions. This official attitude, even of this low-ranking government official, is clearly visible on photographs in which a local village chief or district head (*wedana*) is seen accompanying a young man in a white suit. They visited villages to collect taxes, monitor elections of a new village chief, or listen to complaints about the increases in the price of land leases or of forced labour. Both the village chief and the *wedana* frequently wore a white government jacket over their traditional attire or a white government hat, or carried a walking stick with a copper knob engraved with the letter 'W' (referring to King Willem III and/or Queen Wilhelmina) or the Dutch lion.

48
Group portrait with a regent on Buru, Moluccas
Photographer: unknown
gelatin glass negative
9 x 12 cm
c. 1920
10001634. Gift: J.H. Pieters, 1941

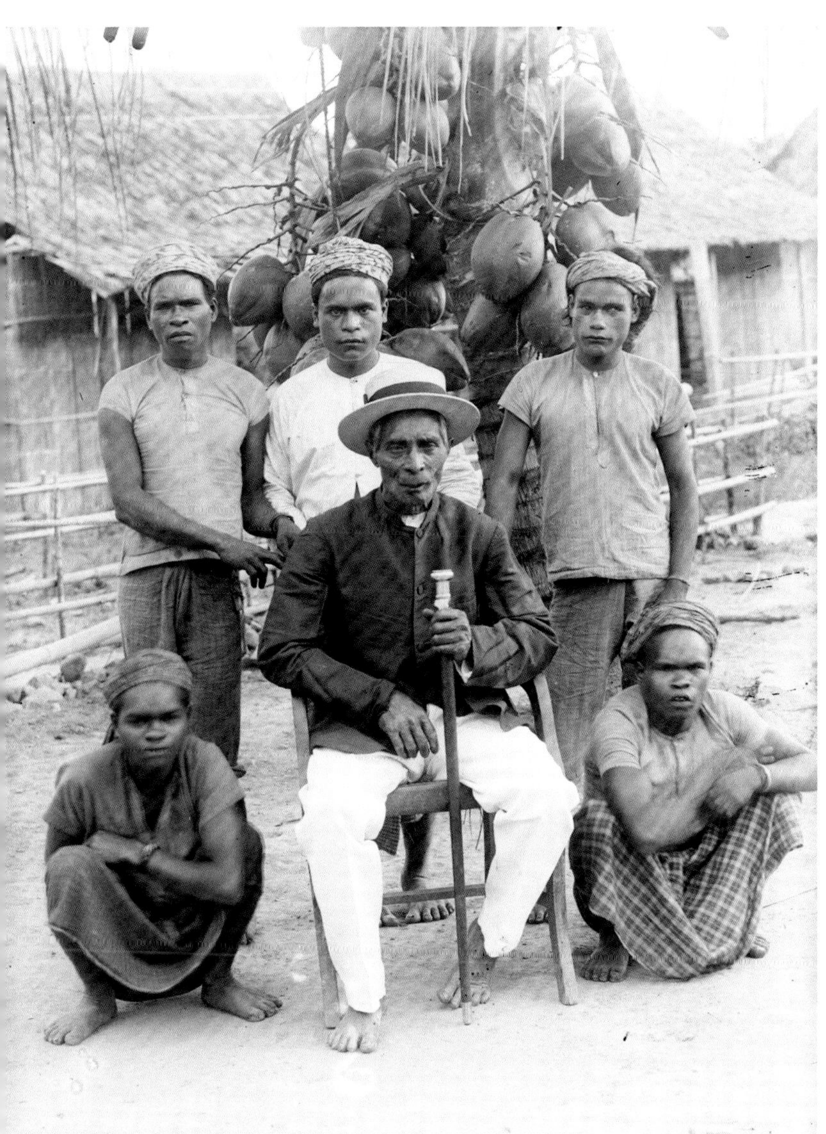

The district commissioners answered to the Assistant-Resident, who was outranked by a Resident and various other officials. The Resident was the head of a district and represented the Governor-General. The area the Resident had to oversee and his responsibilities were larger and broader than those of a district commissioner, and his place of residence was less remote. The Resident's house was often the most impressive in the city. He was also responsible for the Local Administration in his area and was therefore in close contact with his local counterpart, the Regent.

From the government's perspective the principalities on Java[102] and the self-governing areas in the Outer Regions were exceptions to the general rule. Local rulers (sultans), had direct authority over the inhabitants, but in turn had to strictly adhere to their agreements with the colonial government.[103] Contravening these agreements, of which acknowledging Dutch rule was pre-eminent, was seen as an act of resistance against the government and would provoke a military intervention in the form of a punitive expedition.

Official meetings between a Resident and a Regent were accompanied with a great deal of ceremony, in which displaying mutual respect for each other's status was paramount.

The Governor-General, the head of the colonial government, was recommended by the Netherlands Council of Ministers and appointed by the king (or queen). He was a deputy of the Crown and commander-in-chief of the armed forces. He ran the government of the Netherlands East Indies from his palaces in Batavia and Buitenzorg, and was surrounded by a staff of European officials and advisors. His direct contact with the local population was limited.

THE JAVANESE ARISTOCRACY

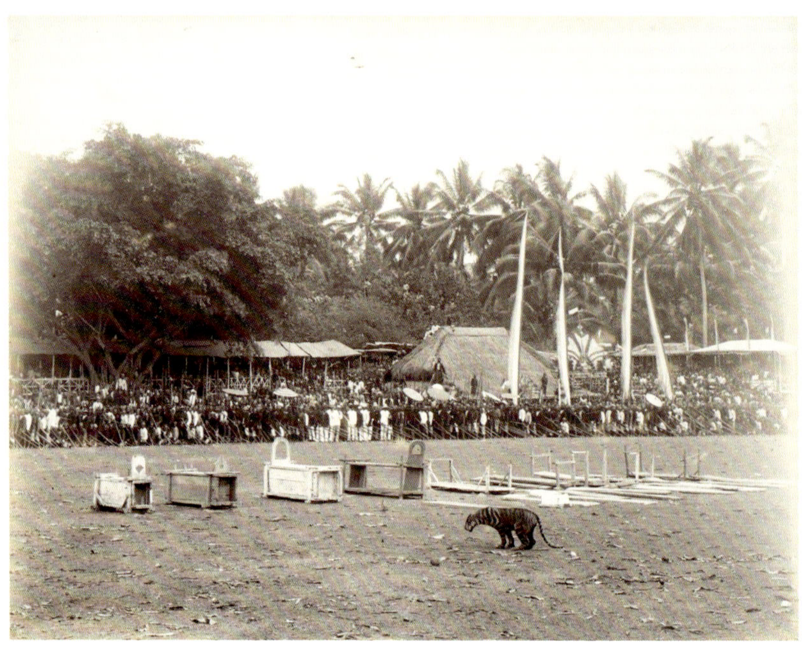

49
Tiger fighting in Blitar, Kediri residency
Photographic studio: H. Salzwedel
albumen print
21.1 x 27.3 cm
1877–92
60005106. Provenance: Prof Dr J.C. van Eerde, 1930

In the 19th century, Java was divided into administrative residencies that each consisted of different regencies. The Regents and their families formed the Javanese aristocracy, the hereditary local administrative corps (*pangreh praja*, 'the rulers of the realm'). They were at the top of the local administrative pyramid that also consisted of district heads and village chiefs. Considerably fewer European officials worked for the Local Administration, namely the Residents, Assistant-Residents and the district commissioners. Collectively, the local and European officials administered an area. The relationship between the Regent and the Resident or his representative, the Assistant-Resident, was one of a younger to an older 'brother'. This social convention subtly expressed the power relationship: each person respected the other's status, but authority was not unambiguous to say the least. Navigating these relationships required a sufficient degree of diplomatic skills on the part of European officials. There were incidents despite this: in 1856 Assistant-Resident Eduard Douwes Dekker (1820–87) accused the Regent of Lebak of abusing his power and extortion. It inspired one of the most important books in the history of Dutch literature, *Max Havelaar*, written by Douwes Dekker using his pseudonym Multatuli.

The Javanese population had always held their rulers in high regard. The Dutch used this to their advantage and gave the Regents crucial roles in the colonial administration, where they functioned as essential links between the Dutch colonial government and the local population. In return they received a salary that enabled them to maintain the lifestyle and appearance that was so important to perpetuating their rule over the population. 'The European has a bourgeois lifestyle; the Regent lives, or is assumed to live, as a lord', was Multatuli's analysis.[104] Regents always travelled with large retinues. They lived in small but magnificent palaces, steeped in ceremony and had an entourage that included gamelan orchestras and dance groups. They also organised tiger fights, the *rampok macan*. Tigers were released on the main square (*alun-alun*) that was encircled by rows of spear bearers. Regardless of how much the tiger tried it could not escape and the animals died cruel deaths. Tiger fights were originally part of the festivities celebrating the end of *Ramadan*, the Islamic month of fasting, in the courts of the principalities. They used to be preceded by a fight between a tiger and a water buffalo, in which the powerful water buffalo usually prevailed. Some believed that the tiger, a symbol of evil, represented the Dutch oppressor, while the triumphant buffalo represented the Indonesians.[105] By the 19th century the ritual was still practised in those regencies that still had tigers in their lands, but it had become a form of popular entertainment. RJ

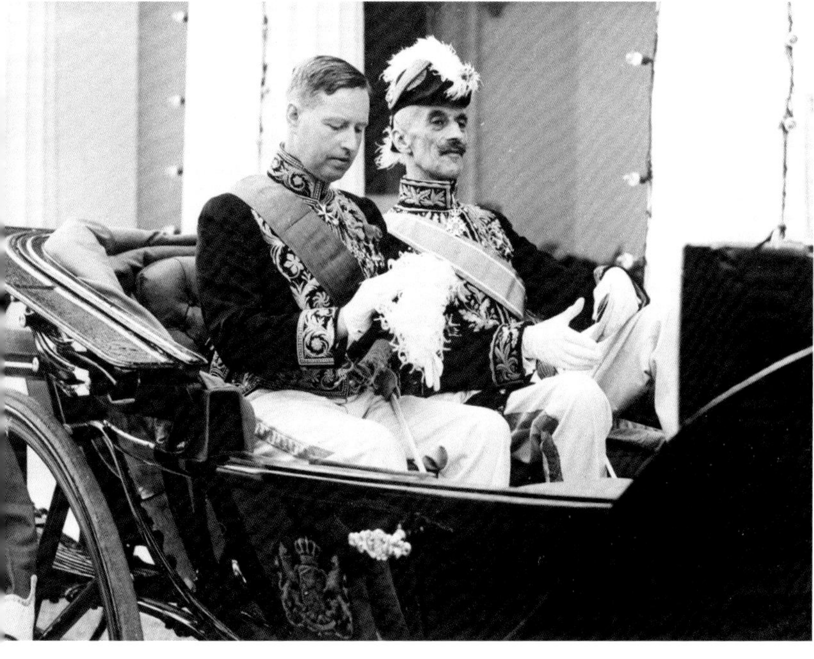

more pronounced, and how palpable the effectiveness of the Ethical Policy was. The government's tasks widened to include agricultural advice, poverty reduction, improving living conditions in the *kampong* (village) and introducing schooling at village level. Qualified people were needed for these tasks that required skills beyond those of the officials of the Internal Administration. During their working visits the Governors-General acquainted themselves with the activities of government institutions and private organisations. They could see how the Dutch presence continued to permeate into all sections of the society, and, in passing, became acquainted with traditional customs and practises of the local population. Dances were staged as a show of folkloric practices during such visits. Everything was carefully organised, and the locals were kept at an appropriate distance from the highest representative of the Crown.

50
The new Governor-General A.W.L. Tjarda van Starkenborgh Stachouwer (left) and the just-retired Governor-General B.C. de Jonge leaving the People's Council (Volksraad) building in Batavia where the transfer of power had just taken place
Photographer: unknown
gelatin glass negative
9 x 12 cm
16 September 1936
0018818. On loan: National Institute for War Documentation (NIOD), 1947

In the 1920s and 1930s, Governors-General went on annual tours of inspection, focusing on areas beyond Java. During these carefully prepared visits the Governor-General could see for himself how all facets of the government's influence were becoming

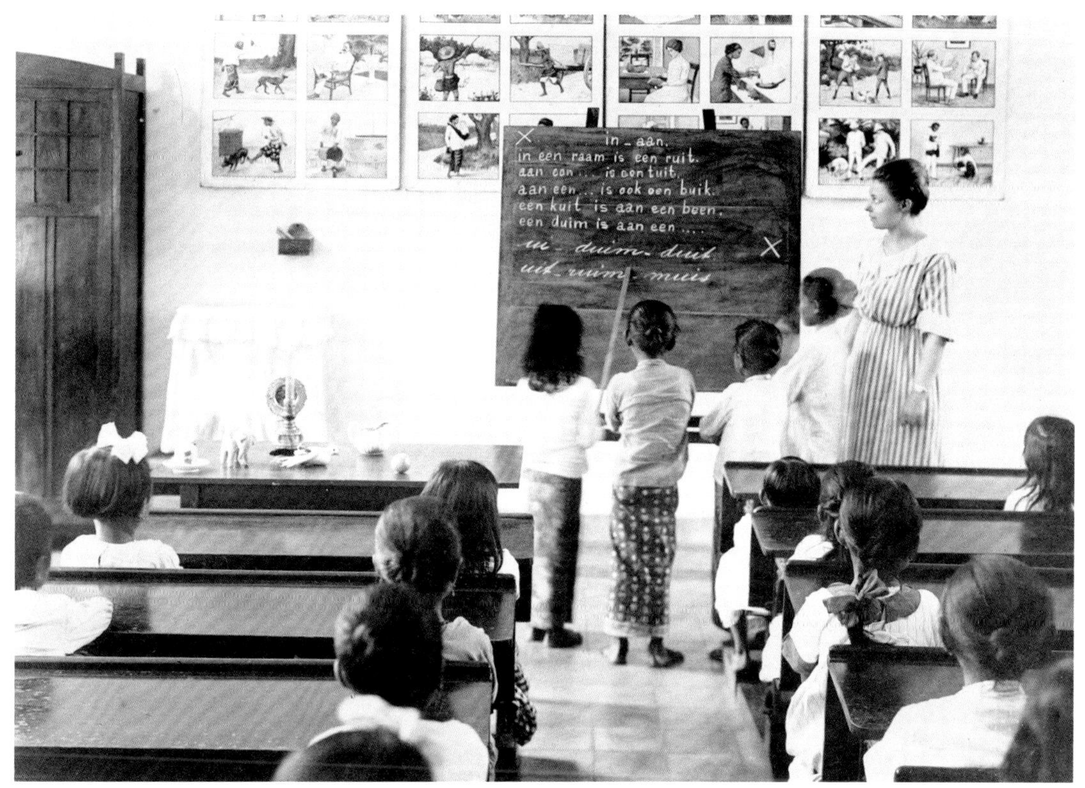

51
The teacher Hamer with first-year pupils at a blackboard during a Dutch lesson in the Kartini school at Buitenzorg
Photographer: unknown
gelatin printing-out paper
11.5 x 16.6 cm
c. 1920
60002667. Provenance: unknown

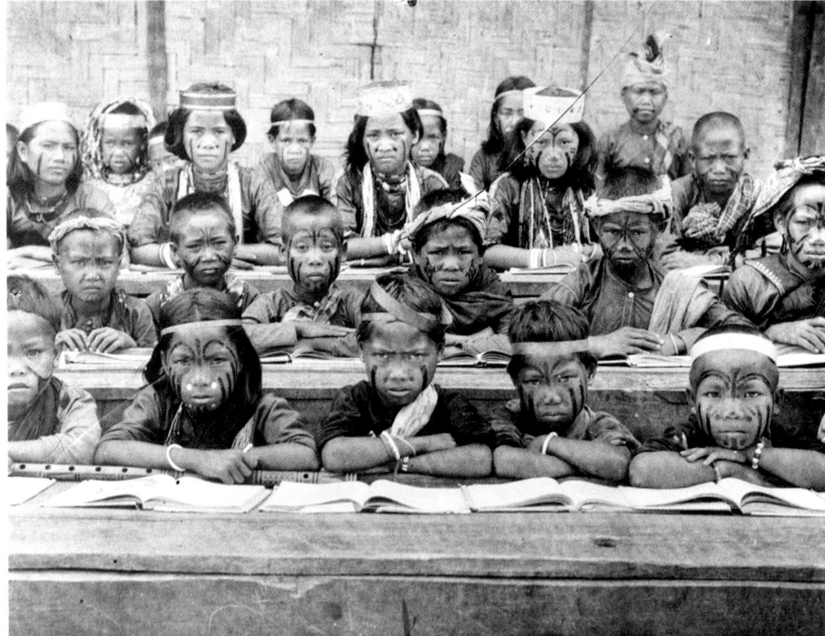

52
Pupils at a Protestant mission school in Poso, Sulawesi
Photographer: unknown
gelatin glass negative
9 x 12 cm
1915–35
10000810. On loan: Zendingsbureau (Oegstgeest), 1943

53
Portrait of an indigenous spiritual leader with the Dutch priest J.A.L. Nieuwenhuis, Missionary of the Sacred Heart (MSC), on Tanimbar Island (Moluccas)
Photographer: unknown
gelatin glass negative
9 x 12 cm
1911–25
10000699. On loan: Missiehuis (Tilburg), 1926

Missionaries

The Roman Catholic and Protestant missionaries occupied a unique role in the colonial society. The colonial administration, intent on maintaining peace and order, was concerned that their proselytising work would not be too influential and wanted to avoid at all costs a 'dual' mission that would result in Protestants and Catholics crossing paths. Confrontations also had to be avoided between Christians and Muslims, Islam being the religion to which the majority of the population subscribed. For these reasons, at the end of the 19th century the Roman Catholic and Protestant missionaries were allocated separate areas where they could pursue their activities. The 'untamed areas' of Borneo and New Guinea were allocated to the Catholics; Celebes, the Moluccas and the Batak uplands on Sumatra to the Protestants. In the case of the Batak, the road to heaven started in the school playgrounds.[106] Christian beliefs could be discussed in the classrooms. This pursuit of 'progress' also applied to other areas that could be used for conversions: medical care and social work were obvious mechanisms to achieve this. The missionaries, who often lived in extreme isolation, empathised with the indigenous population. They soon came into conflict with the strict dogmas dictated by the Netherlands and Rome. Their compassion for the indigenous cultures, especially after they started working with growing numbers of local teachers (*guru*), was not mirrored in Europe. Missionaries maintained close contacts with the Netherlands. The various magazines by and about missionaries frequently included reports of the weal and woes of missionary work and published appeals for financial support.

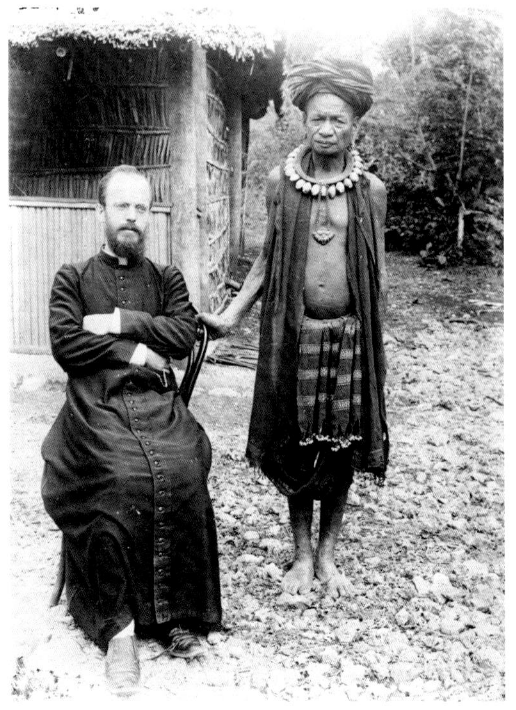

Officials and their cameras

Government officials frequently took photographs themselves and were photographed while performing their duties. Many of these photographs were donated or bequeathed to the Tropenmuseum later. There are no photographs taken by Governors-General in the collection, but they did donate albums they received during their visits. Governor-General Mr J.P. Count van Limburg Stirum (1916–21) and his successor Mr D. Fock (1921–26) are well represented in the collection. Fifty-three albums from Fock's estate were donated in 1941, and nine albums from Van Limburg Stirum's estate ended up in the museum's collection.

Governor-General D. Fock travelled to Sumatra's east coast from 9 to 21 September 1925. This was an important economic area because of the highly profitable rubber and tobacco plantations. In addition to visiting a number of plantations, and private and government institutes, he met with the semi-autonomous Sultans of Deli, Serdang, Langkat and Siak and with local and Chinese rulers.[107] The record of the journey, which has been preserved, reported that he was twice presented with albums of photographs: one by the director of the port on his arrival in Belawan (the harbour of Medan), 'which contained some information about the harbour', and another the following day in Kabanjahe by District Commissioner Brouwer during a viewing of the Batak exhibition.[108] The majority of the albums from Fock's estate could have resulted from the fact that Queen Wilhelmina celebrated her Silver Jubilee (1923) during his tenure.[109] This event was celebrated in great style throughout the Netherlands East Indies, and like all celebrations associated with the Royal House, enjoyed great popularity. A Silver Jubilee album was a perfect opportunity for many companies and institutes to demonstrate their loyalty to the Crown and underscore their ties with the motherland. The Queen's representative in the Netherlands East Indies gratefully accepted the tributes, including photograph albums specially made for this occasion.

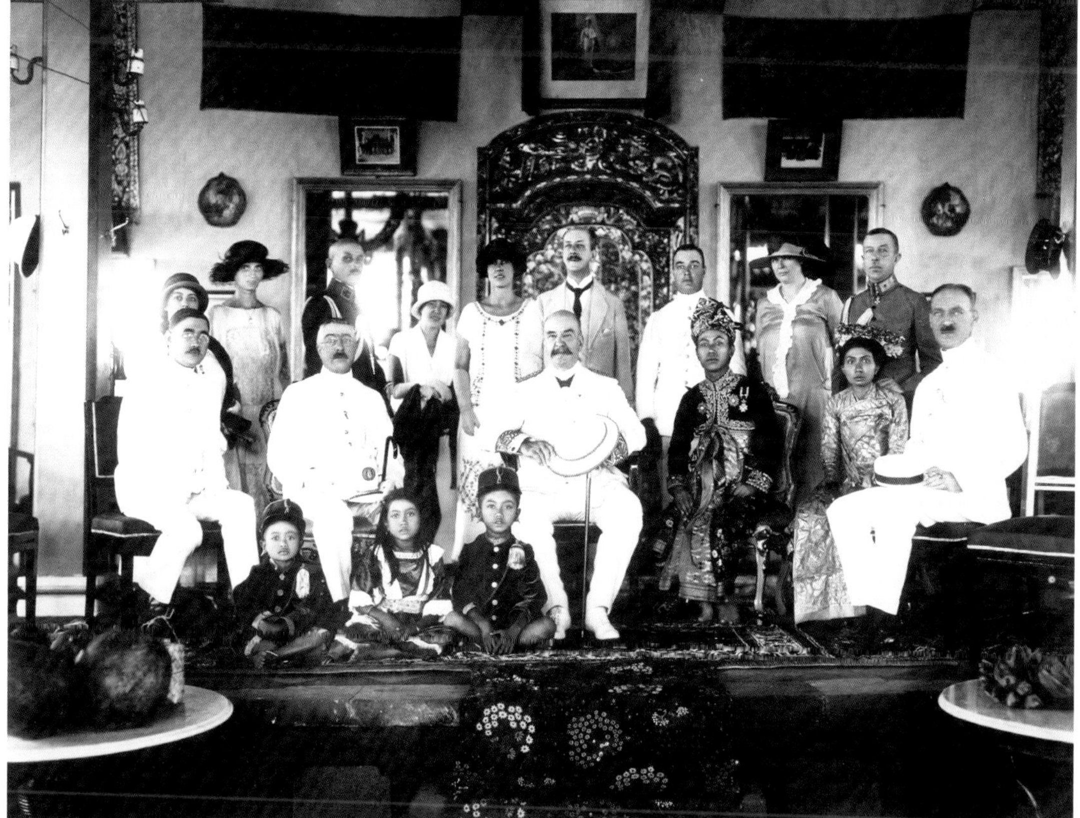

54
Group portrait during a visit by Governor-General Mr D. Fock to I Gusti Bagus Jelantik, the Regent of Karangasem, Bali
Photographer: unknown
gelatin printing-out paper
21.7 x 28.5 cm
April 1925
60017257. Gift: P.E.H. Moolenburgh (1872–1944), 1926

FATHER MARTIEN GLOUDEMANS (1904–79)

Martien Gloudemans was ordained in 1928. Barely a year later his congregation, the Missionaries of the Holy Family (MSF), sent him to Borneo (Kalimantan), where he travelled and preached a great deal between 1934 and 1938. For months at a time he would walk or use a proa to crisscross an area as large as France that was still mostly blanketed with tropical rainforest. He was assigned various official tasks on all these trips that ranged from seeking out new and especially better connecting roads, to visiting and inspecting the missionary stations.[110] After a decade spent in the Tropics – in Laham, Tering, Banjarmasin and Tarakan – Gloudemans returned on leave to the Netherlands in 1939, and assumed his duties again in 1946 in Balikpapan. His travels did not go unnoticed: accounts of his trips were published at the time in *De Koerier*, the *Soerabaiasch Handelsblad* and the *Koloniaal Missie Tijdschrift*. A book for young people recounting his adventurous journey from Samarinda to Pontianak in 1935 and titled *Tuan Glou* was published in 1962. *Volkskrant* journalist Cees Gloudemans wrote the book *Dwars door Borneo* (1997), recounting his own travels through Kalimantan, where he was hoping to retrace his uncle's footsteps. He recently donated five photograph albums documenting Father Martien Gloudemans' stay on Kalimantan to the Tropenmuseum.

In interviews he gave a few years before his death Gloudemans looked back quite extensively on his life as a missionary.[111] Besides the *adat* (local and traditional law) he emphasised 'loneliness' as the greatest difficulty the missionaries had to deal with. He tried to compensate for this by writing, which explains the many articles by his hand. However, the abovementioned photograph albums do not reveal this loneliness, documenting instead the social life of a group of missionaries on Kalimantan. The camera was used to record the rare moments that they came together. What makes this donation so valuable is that it was a unique addition to the Tropenmuseum collection, which contains many comparable photographs portraying the lives of planters or Indo-European families but not showing missionary life. Renewed interest by anthropologists in the life of missionaries makes these albums, which could be seen as ego documents, even more interesting.[112] The Roman Catholic home front in Europe might have bestowed heroic status on the missionaries, but anthropologists by contrast had an uneasy relationship with them. After all, they were a direct threat to the local culture. Despite this, anthropologists did seek out the company of missionaries because they knew their way around their areas, could arrange transport and spoke the local language. Furthermore, because some of them had lived among the locals for long periods, they had extensive knowledge of the local culture and the flora and fauna. The publications and personal archives documenting these aspects are now an important research source. RJ

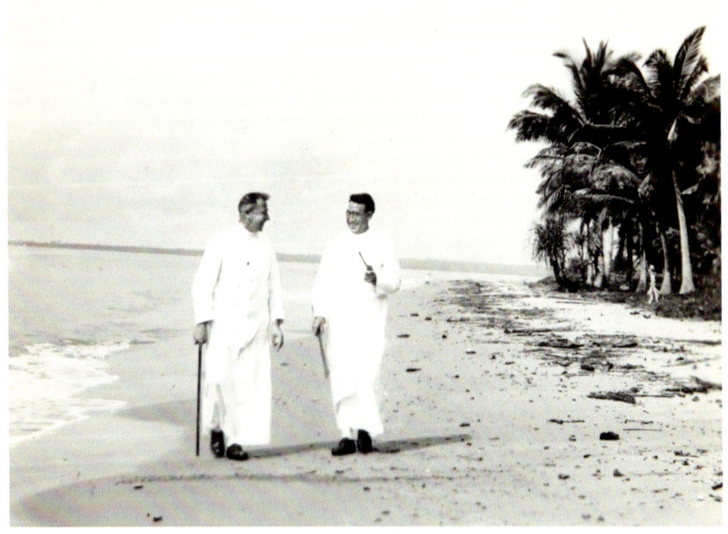

55
Two Missionaries of the Holy Family (MSF) strolling along the beach at Balikpapan
Photographer: unknown
silver gelatin developing-out paper
8.1 x 11 cm
c. 1938
60051424. Gift: Cees Gloudemans, 2007

BALI: AN IMMORTALISED PARADISE

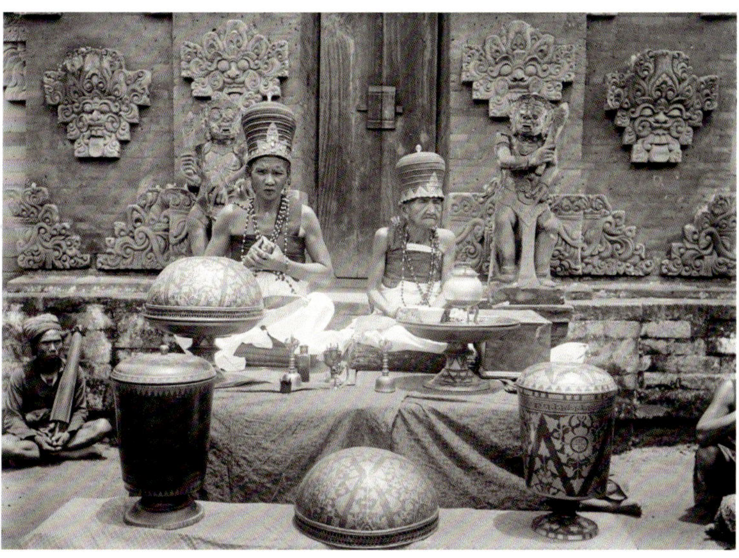

56
Balinese priests performing a ceremony
Photographer: unknown
gelatin glass negative
13 x 18 cm
1910–25
10001160. Gift: R.S. van Stenis-James, 1931. Former collection L.U. van Stenis

Bali came entirely under Dutch control after the *puputan* in Badung (1906) and Klungkung (1908),[113] later than most other islands in the Indonesian archipelago. Shortly thereafter, this island, with its picturesque landscape, vibrant cultural practices and specific form of Hinduism, was recommended as a holiday destination for the first time, and it has remained one ever since. Tourism to the island increased dramatically from the 1920s. Among international travellers were painters, photographers, musicians, film stars and anthropologists who stayed there for varying periods. They considered Bali a paradise that had hardly been affected by Western influence. Despite their contacts with the flood of tourists and the many modern developments, the Balinese would maintain many of their traditions, also in later years. Missionaries were forbidden from proselytising on Bali after one of their numbers was murdered in 1881 and because people were concerned that the unique Balinese culture would be tarnished. Islam did not manage to establish roots there during the colonial era either. The Balinese variant of Hinduism is still widely practised. Their beliefs focus on maintaining balance and harmony in their personal lives and in their society. The gods are appeased with daily offerings of rice, incense, flowers and fruit. There are many different types of ceremonies, and even Balinese dances are primarily intended to please the gods. Priests and traditional healers are frequently consulted to avert calamities and threats and thwart vengeful demons. The most important temple complex is at the foot of Agung volcano in Besakih, and there are at least three temple complexes in each village: a *Pura Puseh* (Temple of Origin), a *Pura Desa* (Village Temple) and a *Pura Dalem* (Temple of the Dead). The Balinese make small offerings to their ancestors in house temples located within their yards, seeking protection and prosperity. Steeped in religion and ritual, Balinese culture is replete with dazzling ceremonies, dances, *wayang* performances and gamelan music. Many of the images that immortalised this 'earthly paradise' through the years could be called 'beguiling' or 'enchanting'; that they are 'fascinating' is indisputable. They were used to underscore the idea of a Balinese idyll. For outsiders, attending a cremation is an undisputed highlight, and there are many photographs documenting cremations in the Tropenmuseum collection. Cremations are festive ceremonies, celebrating the release of the soul from its earthly bonds and its ascension to heaven, whence it returns to earth as a new life. The rites that precede a cremation can last for months. On the day of the cremation itself, exuberant crowds accompany the cremation tower in which the deceased are taken to the cremation site in a long procession, where they are placed in bull shaped coffins. After the cremation the ashes are cast onto the sea, and the souls float away on their long journey to the hereafter. RJ

THE GOVERNMENT OFFICIAL JAN JONGEJANS (1883–1939)

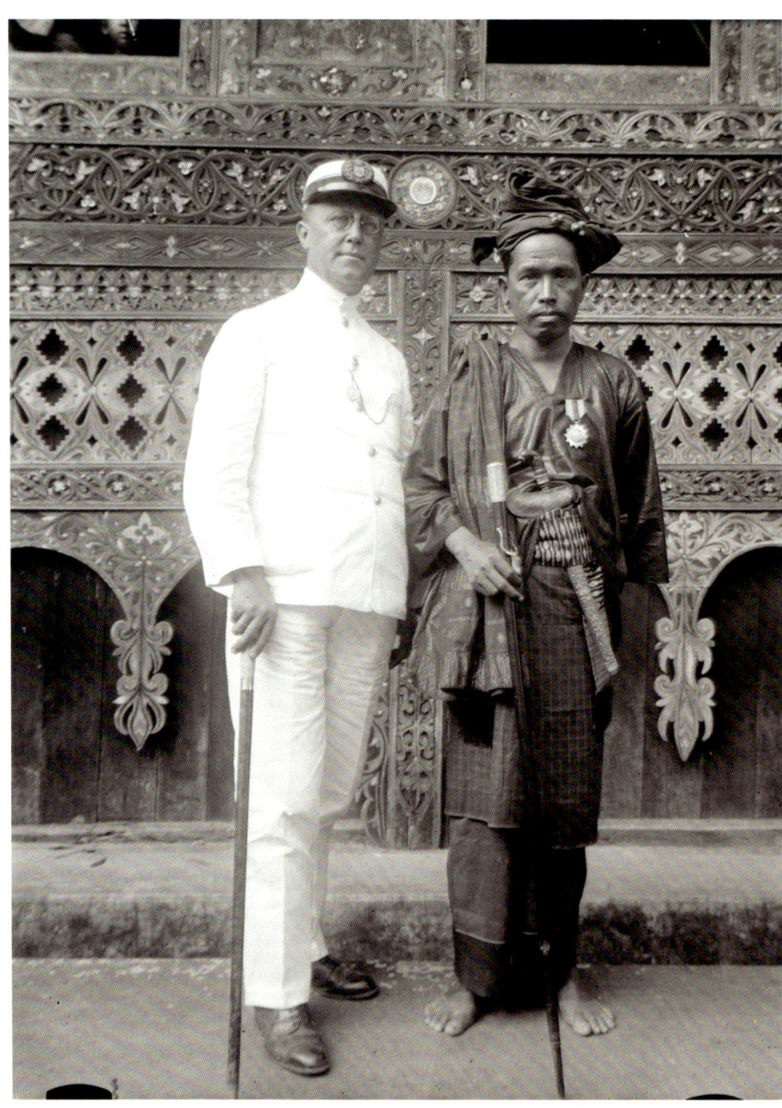

Jan Jongejans is one of the many officials who took photographs and donated their material to the Tropenmuseum. He had a successful, textbook career in the Netherlands East Indies. He was genuinely interested in the local population, as proven by the popular books he wrote later about his work.[114] He started on the lowest rung as an official in the Lampong residency in South Sumatra, and was appointed district commissioner of Central Borneo and Sumatra's western coast. He was next promoted to Assistant-Resident of Solok (Sumatra's western coast), where he had to deal with Communist insurrections in 1927. He later became Assistant-Resident of Pedir (Aceh), and finally, Resident of Menado and Aceh respectively.[115] He was also seconded to the East Indies Committee for Scientific Research (Indisch Comité voor Wetenschappelijke Onderzoekingen) to conduct research during the Central New Guinea Expedition (1920–21), where he was also responsible for the Dayak oarsmen and bearers. During the expedition Jongejans also had to research the ethnography of the population.[116] An article in the newspaper *Het Vaderland* remembered him as follows when he died in 1939: 'During his long and commendable career in Indonesia, Mr Jongejans made many friends, not least among the native population in the various regions […]. He was gifted in that he could associate with people of every ilk, which can only be attributed to his sound character, his good humour and his "honesty"'.[117] And that is how we perceive Jongejans in the many photographs of him posing in an immaculate white suit with the locals. He is clearly fascinated by his work and enjoyed his contacts with the local population who he portrayed in respectful and spontaneous ways. He set up his own camera, decided on the composition and had an assistant take the actual photograph. The museum did not receive any photographs of his family or his private circle.

57
Portrait of a Dutch civil servant (Assistant-Resident J. Jongejans) and a local ruler in Solok (Minangkabau, West Sumatra)
Photographer: unknown
gelatin glass negative
9 x 12 cm
1927–29
10001825. Gift: J. Jongejans, 1929

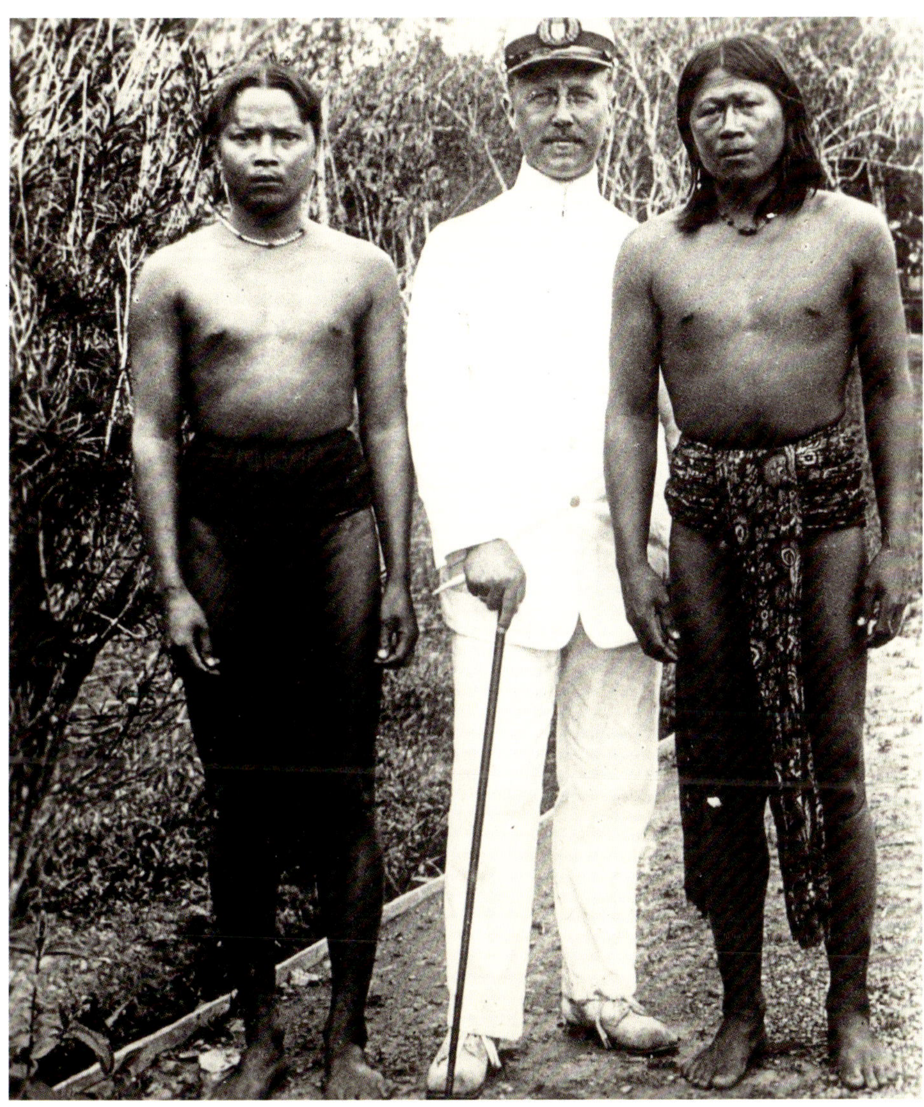

58
J. Jongejans when he was a District Commissioner, with two Dayak men in Tana Tidung, Borneo
Photographer: unknown
gelatin glass negative
9 x 12 cm
1917–19
10002947. Gift: J. Jongejans, 1929

Jongejans used his photographs in his book, *Uit Dajakland: kijkjes in het leven van den koppensneller en zijne omgeving*, in which he recounted his time in Borneo.[118] One of his recollections is of the events that unfolded while he was taking photographs in a remote *kampong*. He would travel for days, if not weeks, and visited places where the population rarely saw white people.

They did not seem to be afraid of the camera, so I immediately took some pictures of some of the ladies, but the fun ended that evening when they saw the plates developing and their ghostly figures appearing on the negatives. When I walked around the kampong *with my camera the next day, not a single woman would pose for me, and the children were nowhere to be seen, but fortunately the men were more sensible. Like the Papuans, they were afraid I would steal their souls.*[119]

He apparently recognised the value of his photographs while he was still alive. While on leave in the Netherlands in 1929, he donated 462 negatives and 250 lantern slides of Borneo (Kalimantan), Sumatra's western coast, and New Guinea. In November 1939, shortly after Jongejans' death, his widow donated another 155 negatives and 155 lantern slides of Aceh and Jambi. In March 2001 a daughter-in-law wrote that while she was reorganising a cupboard she found photographs of her in-laws that had been made by Jan Jongejans: '[...] They are of value to the Tropenmuseum [...] because they include several images of local inhabitants in traditional attire'.[120] JVD

A closed social life

From a contemporary perspective the photographs of officials are so much more than merely a visual document of the colonial government's attitudes. They are significant in that they show how the society became increasingly saturated with the presence of the colonists and how the colonists continually appropriated more space for themselves in the indigenous society.

This is nothing remarkable; after all, one of the consequences of the Ethical Policy was that the number of Europeans increased dramatically after 1910, and the professional European population continued to become more diverse. Now it not only included soldiers and officials, but also teachers, engineers, doctors, lawyers and missionaries, and women as well as men. Many were young newlyweds hoping to create a life for themselves in the Netherlands East Indies, and who, with all their insecurities, homesickness and need for company and entertainment, sought each other out. The Europeans only associated with their own kind and enthusiastically participated in events that reinforced their ties to the motherland. In albums or family photographs it appears that the feast of Saint Nicholas (Sinterklaas, 5 December) was an unbridled celebration, both at the school and among friends at the 'club'.

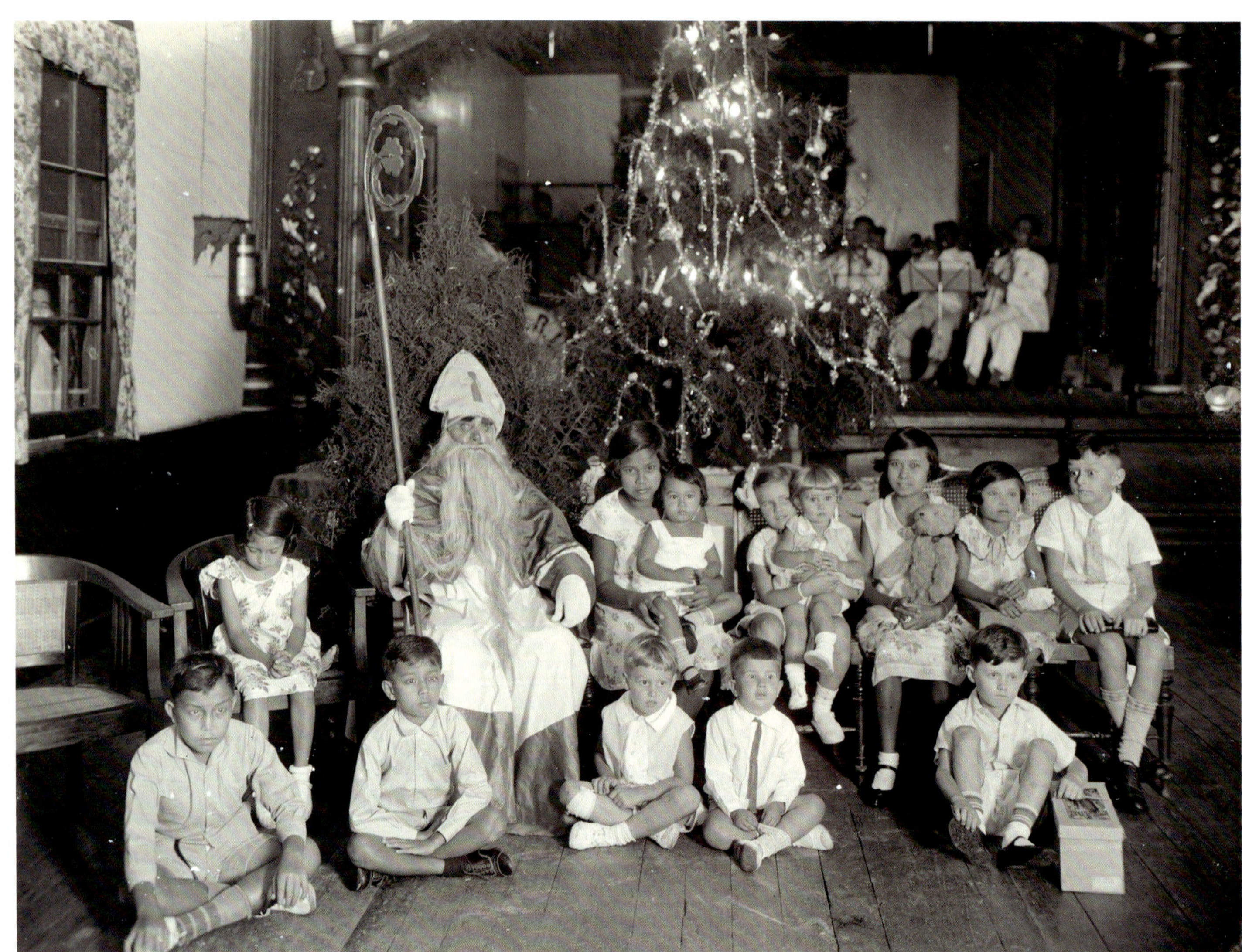

59
Saint Nicholas surrounded by children in front of a decorated Christmas tree in the Redjang Lebong Mining Company's club in Lebong Donok
Photographer: unknown
silver gelatin developing-out paper
14.1 x 19 cm
1925–32
60035614. Provenance: KIT ILS (Central Library), 1996. Former collection H.J.A. Sanders and W.M. Sanders-Hock

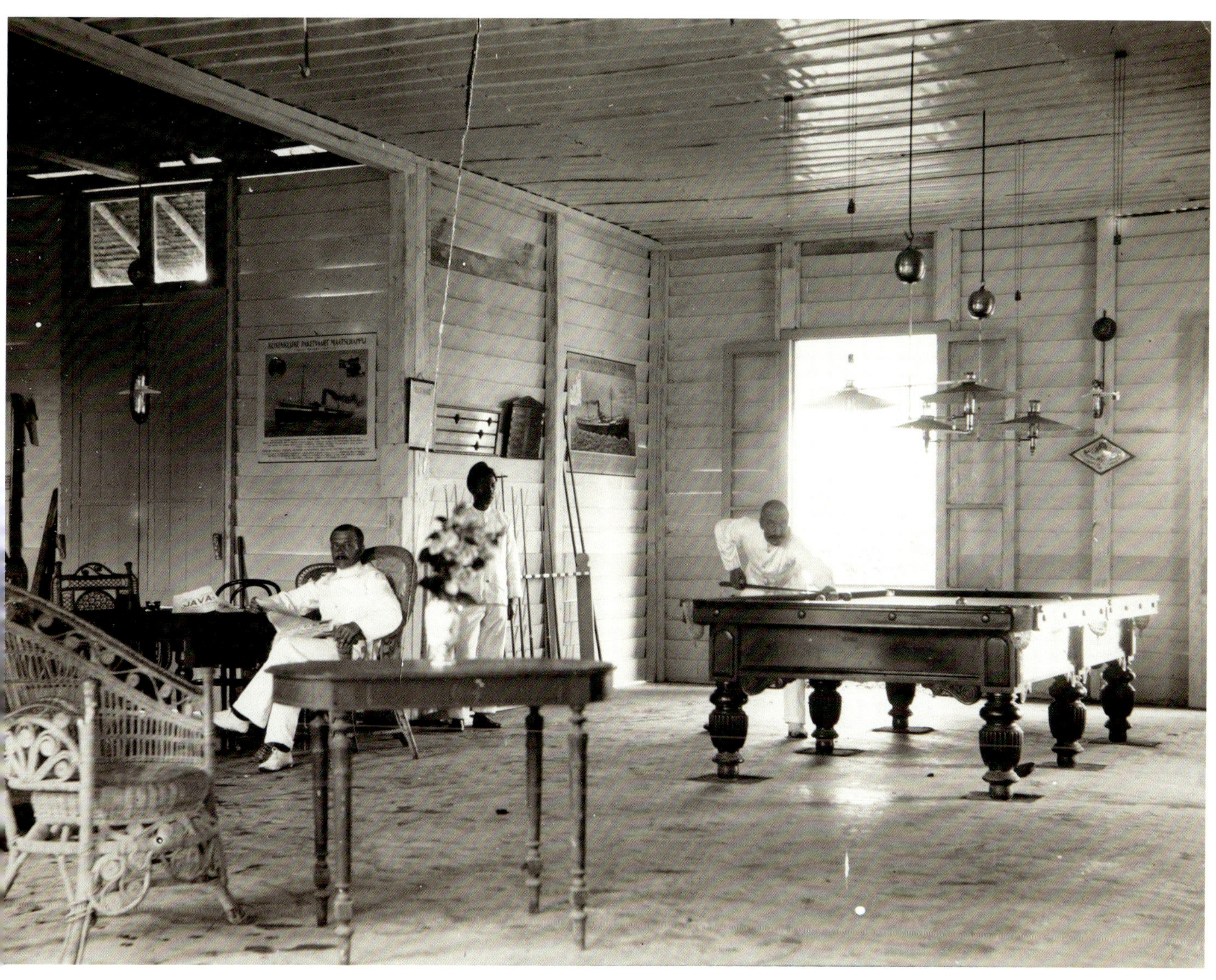

60
Billiard room in the Singkep Tin Company's club in Dabo (Riau, Sumatra)
Photographer: unknown
collodion printing-out paper
16.5 x 21.5 cm
1909
60055705. Gift: A. van der Winkel, 2008. Former collection W. van Schaïk and C.G.J. van der Winkel

The club was the heart of European social life in the Netherlands East Indies, almost a second home for many. Planters from far-flung plantations usually went to the closest city twice a month to buy provisions and suchlike and to meet each other in the club's sheltered environment, usually on Saturday nights. They danced, gossiped, drank and ate (European) food. The relaxed patriotic conviviality that prevailed was an informal counterpoint to the stuffiness of official life. Clubs in the cities balloted their members, and no women or Indo-Europeans could join. Such strict rules did not apply outside the large cities, and some companies even had their own clubs for their staff. The Royal House of Orange was a strong social binder and anything connected to Dutch royalty was an excuse for a celebration. It began in 1898 with the coronation of the young Queen Wilhelmina. The Queen's birthday on 31 August, her Silver Jubilee, and the marriage of Princess Juliana and Prince Bernhard, were celebrated in towns, villages and on plantations with songs, sack races, bobbing for apples and pole climbing for the children and the indigenous staff. The adults went out of their

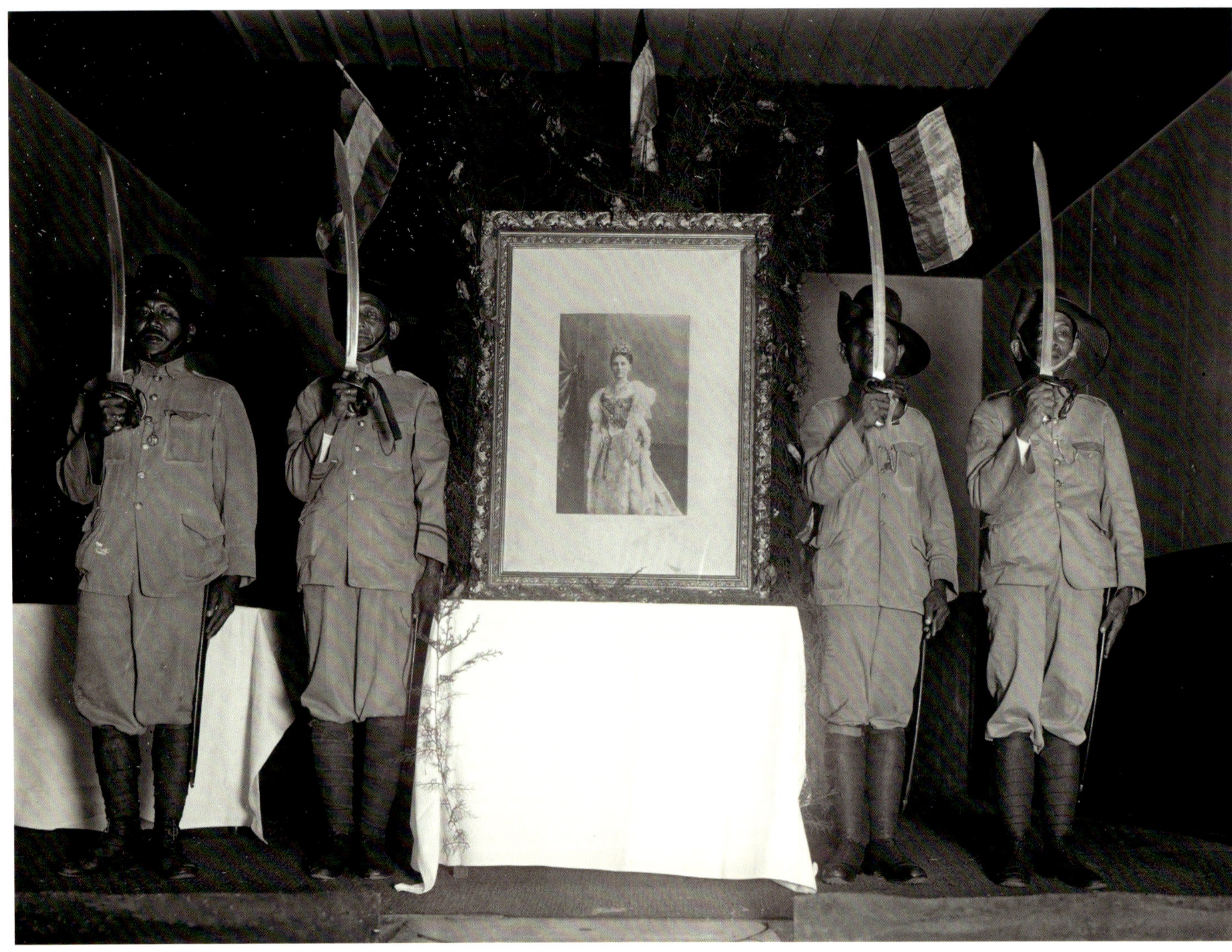

61
Police agents salute a portrait of Queen Wilhelmina during Queen's Day celebrations in the Redjang Lebong Mining Company's club in Lebong Donok
Photographer: unknown
silver gelatin developing-out paper
14.2 x 19.1 cm
1925–32
60035609. Provenance: KIT ILS (Central Library), 1996. Former collection H.J.A. Sanders and W.M. Sanders-Hock

way for fancy dress balls and processions with decorated floats. During these festivities the indigenous population invariably performed dances and *wayang* performances as part of the programme.
The Europeans in the Netherlands East Indies took many photographs. For many, particularly the *totok*, life in the Netherlands East Indies was full of adventure. They were young and had moved to a strange place and wanted to record their impressions of it for themselves and for their families in the Netherlands. Their houses, the surroundings, their places of work, the servants, their excursions, and not least the births of children were joyfully documented. For those back home in Holland these photographs were proof that they were prospering in the Tropics. Letters do mention misfortune, but this is only really seen in photographs as a gravestone.
The collection has countless examples of photographs such as these that portray the minutiae of the colonial world.
The growth in the European population also changed the appearances of the cities. Their new and large houses were located in spacious residential areas, the shops were stylish and well stocked and the streets bustled with cars, cyclists and horse-drawn carts. From the 1920s the photographs increasingly emphasised European society. The local population only appear in the photographs 'in passing'.
By withdrawing into their own social group and

62
Boy and girl with two Javanese domestic staff
Photographer: unknown
collodion printing-out paper
10.1 x 14.2 cm
1920–30
60019000. Provenance: via M.J. Hillerström, 1979

leading an inward-looking social life the Europeans lost more and more contact with the indigenous population, blinding themselves to the growing nationalism among the indigenous aristocracy that started taking shape around 1910 as political movements such as Budi Utomo, Sarekat Islam and the Indies Party (Indische Partij) emerged, all of which aspired to equality and more political participation. For many nationalists the installation of the People's Council ('Volksraad') in 1918, which could discuss colonial policies but take no decisions, was nowhere near enough; the Council had only an advisory role. It consisted of 60 members: 30 from the various indigenous population groups, 25 Dutch nationals, and five from the Chinese and other population groups. Some of the members were chosen indirectly, the rest were appointed by the Governor-General.

There was some resistance to the colonial administration at the local level – newspapers of the time frequently attributed this as the work of 'trouble-making Communists'. They were portrayed as naive supporters with nationalistic leaders who were not generally regarded as dangerous. The eyes of most Europeans remained closed to the reality of the changing political climate. The colonial lifestyle was brought to an abrupt – and for many, unexpected – end with the Japanese invasion of the Netherlands East Indies in 1942. The Japanese army occupied the colony without any significant resistance, aided by their slogan 'Greater Asia for the Asians', which ensured that many locals were won over to their side.

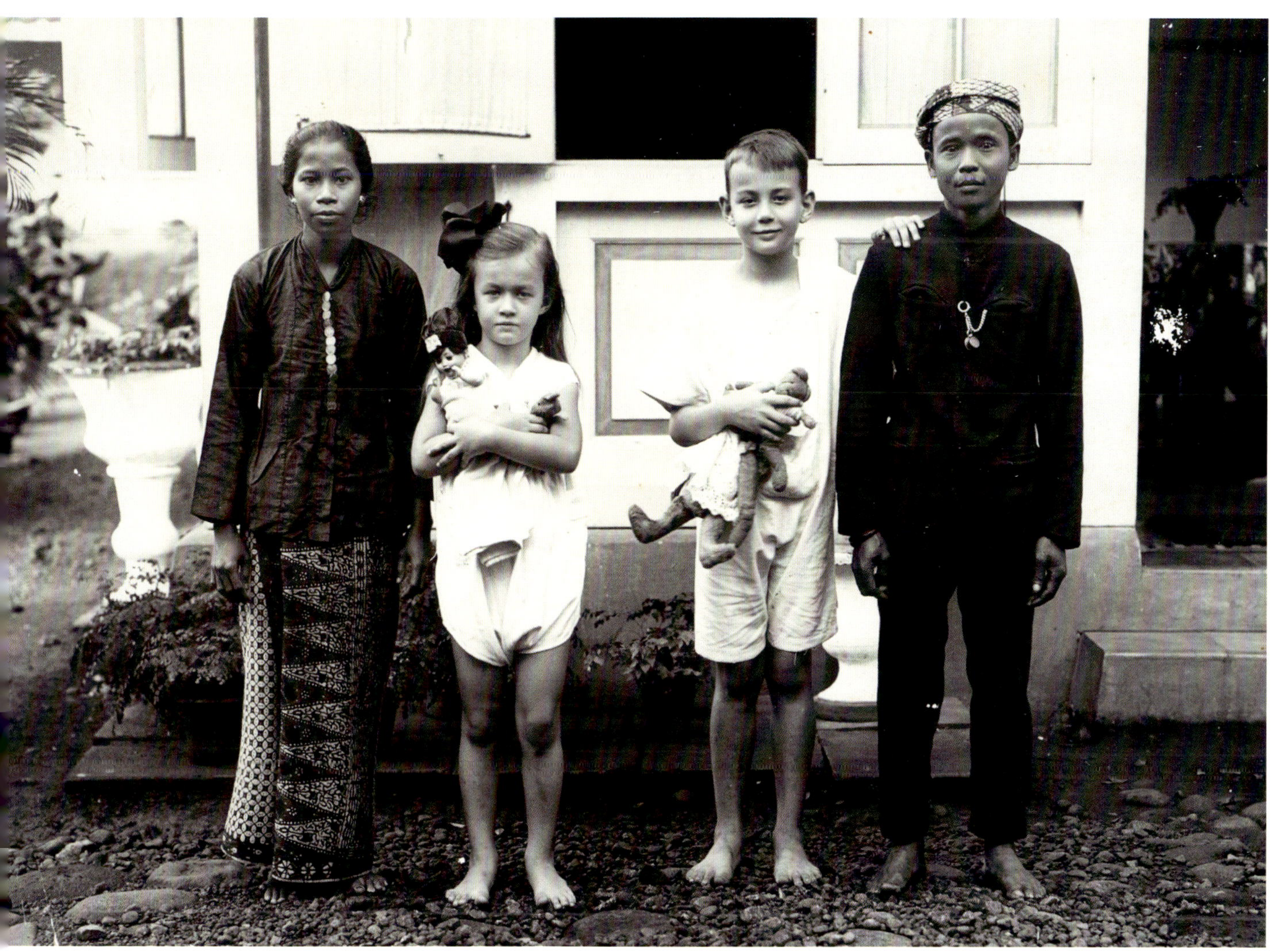

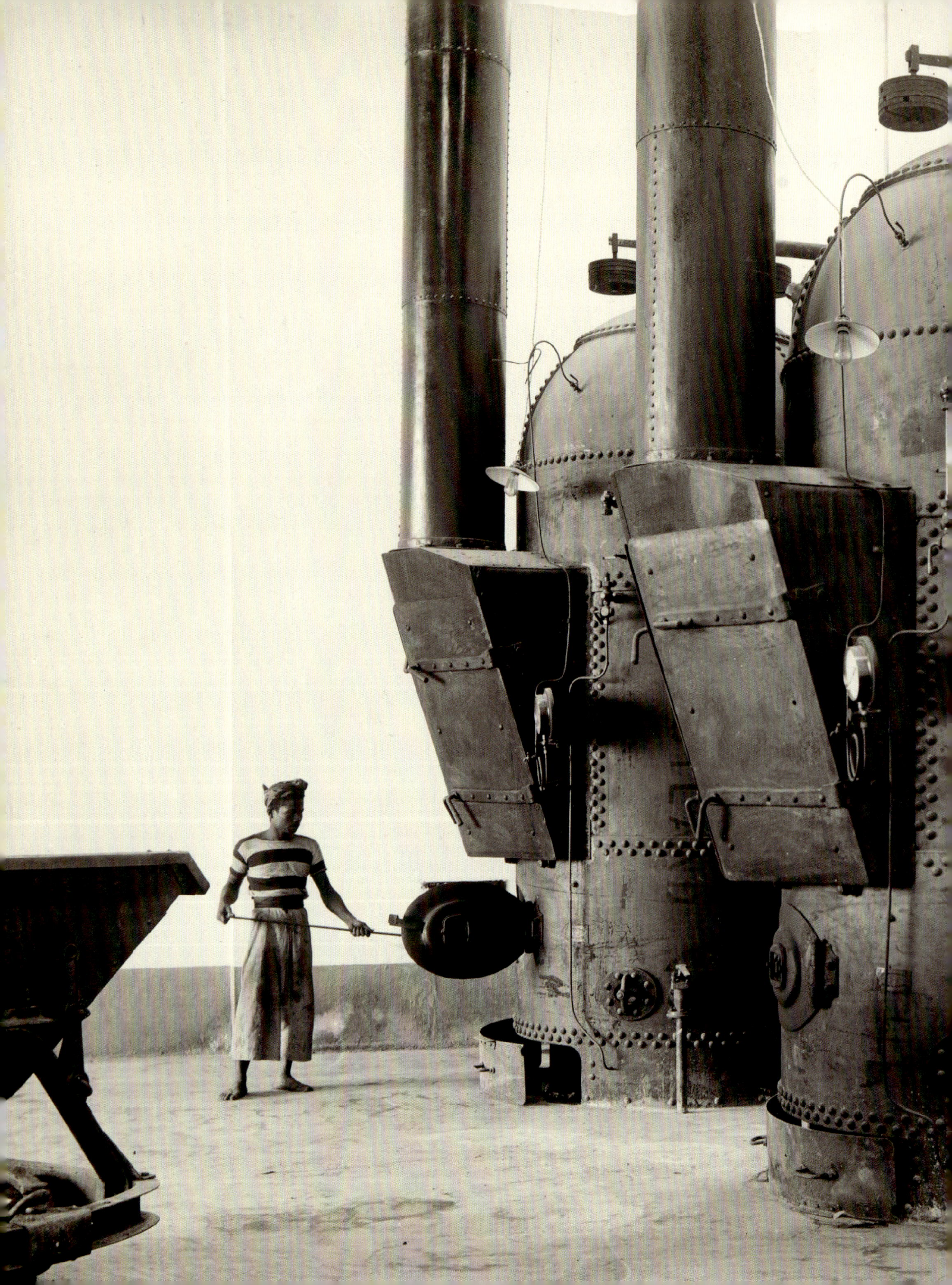

CORPORATE ALBUMS:
keepsakes, sentimentality and propaganda

JANNEKE VAN DIJK

63
Cochran boiler in the 'Keboemen' factory of NV Oliefabrieken Insulinde (detail)
Photographer: J.H. Austermühle
silver gelatin developing-out paper
17 x 23.2 cm
c. 1916
60022083. Provenance: unknown

The names of the 76 founders of the Royal Tropical Institute are engraved in gold letters on three marble panels in the entrance hall of its premises in Amsterdam. The Colonial Institute – as it was called at the time – was founded in 1910 thanks to donations from private individuals, companies and the government, all of whom had vested interests in an institute that provided the public with the most up-to-date information about the colonies. This applied especially to the Netherlands East Indies, where most of the benefactors had direct interests. A triptych also adorns the same entrance hall,[121] one panel of which is titled 'The West' ('Het Westen') and portrays two men at a drop hammer, surrounded by images depicting trade, science and industry. The second panel, 'The East' ('Het Oosten'), depicts a *sawa* landscape with a farmer ploughing a field with a team of caribou. The final panel, 'Cooperation' ('De Samenwerking'), shows a European and an Asian studying an irrigation plan. This triptych is a representation of the Ethical Policy that had become the guiding principles of the Dutch colonial government since the Queen's speech of 1901, which proposed improvements to the living conditions of the locals and to the infrastructure in the colony. The Colonial Institute was founded nine years later on these 'ethical' ideas, focusing on areas such as tropical trade products, ethnology and tropical hygiene. Departments for the first two of these were created in the Colonial Museum, which opened in 1926: the ethnographic collection was consigned to the Ethnographic Museum, the tropical products to the Trade Museum. In 1950 the Institute changed its name to the Royal Tropical Institute; this was accompanied by a complete reorientation of its objectives, resulting in the closure of the Trade Museum in the 1960s. In the 1960s part of the collection of tropical products and the entire photograph collection was subsumed into the museum's collection. This explains the enormous collection of photographs, negatives and photograph albums in the current Tropenmuseum collection that portray colonial trade and corporate life. Health care, education, infrastructure and economic development are recurring subjects in many albums.[122] All these were gifts: the Colonial Institute never paid photographers to work for it.[123]
The Board of the Colonial Institute actively solicited donations and asked companies to send photographic material documenting the latest developments. After all, this was the impression that the Colonial Institute wanted to share with the wider public in its exhibitions, publications and lectures: a modern and efficient administration of the overseas territories, in particular the Netherlands East Indies. What was once documentation of current events has become important historical records.

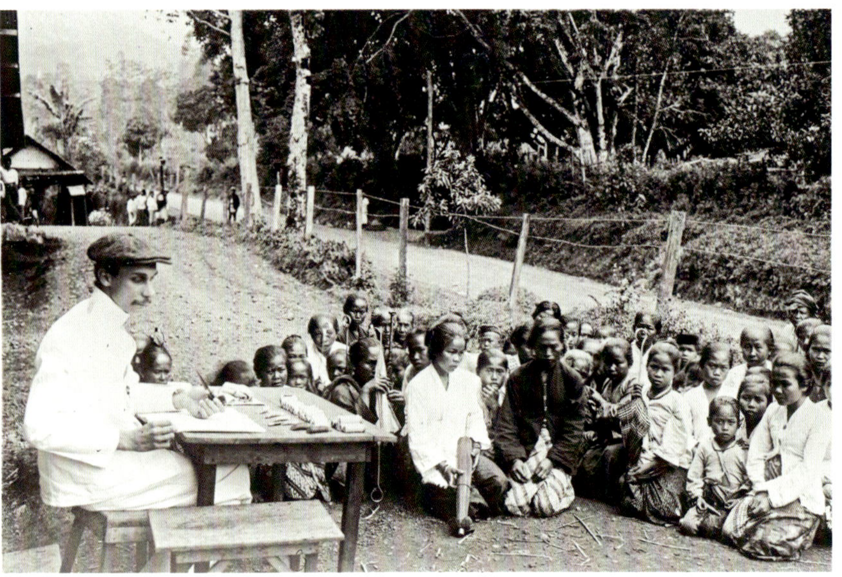

64
Paying wages to the tea pickers on the Tjiliwoeng plantation at Buitenzorg
Photographer: unknown
gelatin glass negative
9 x 12 cm
1910–30
10011962. Provenance: unknown

Development of trade and industry in the Netherlands East Indies

The abolition of the Cultivation System – which preceded the Ethical Policy – whereby peasants had to devote at least one-fifth of their land to cultivating government-designated export crops instead of rice, and a new ground lease regulation (see the first chapter) created great opportunities for private initiatives after 1870. Agriculture, largely geared towards export, was given a strong impetus. Traditional commercial crops, i.e., sugar, coffee, tea and cinchona, were supplemented with tobacco, cassava, oil palms, cacao, rubber and kapok. Roads, railways, irrigation systems, electricity and harbours were built. Private entrepreneurs were supported by the government and conducted research into crop improvement, the mechanisation of farming and the industrial processing of agricultural products. This resulted in the Netherlands East Indies enjoying an unprecedented position on world markets.
This economic growth, which started at the beginning of the 20th century, paralleled the ongoing developments of photography. Cameras and photographic techniques advanced rapidly and became accessible to amateurs. Many companies asked professional photographers to document the developments in their companies – and their new machines – in photograph albums.
Kurkdjian, Salzwedel, Herrmann, O. Hisgen & Co. Photographic Studio, and Lux Studio were much sought after professional studios on Java. On Sumatra it was primarily Stafhell & Kleingrothe and Lambert & Co who were active.

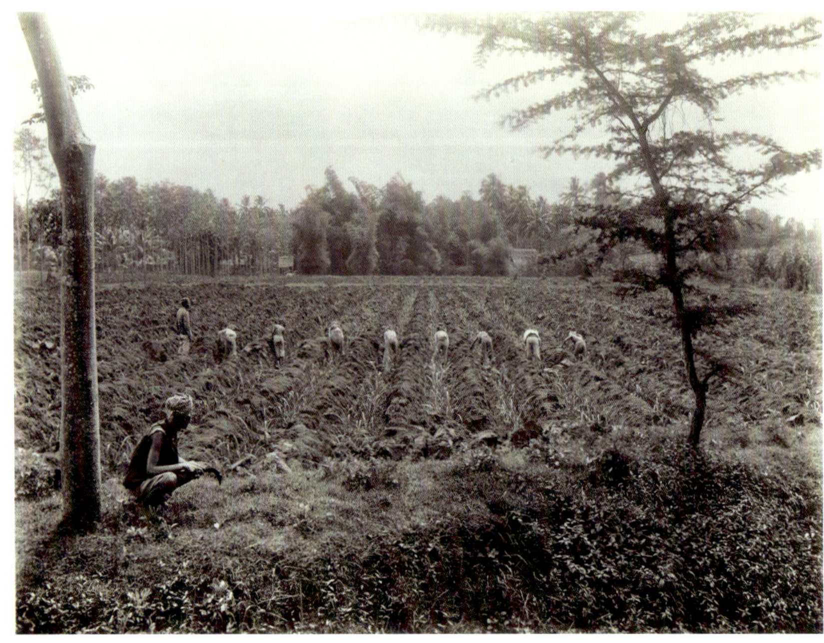

65
Weeding a field with recently planted sugar cane at the Ketegan Sugar Company, Surabaya
Photographic Studio: Kurkdjian (1888–1936)
gelatin printing-out paper
17.2 x 23 cm
c. 1912
60052495. Gift: W.F.H. van Aken-Bouricius, 2007. Former collection L.A. Bouricius

SAILING THE ARCHIPELAGO WITH KPM

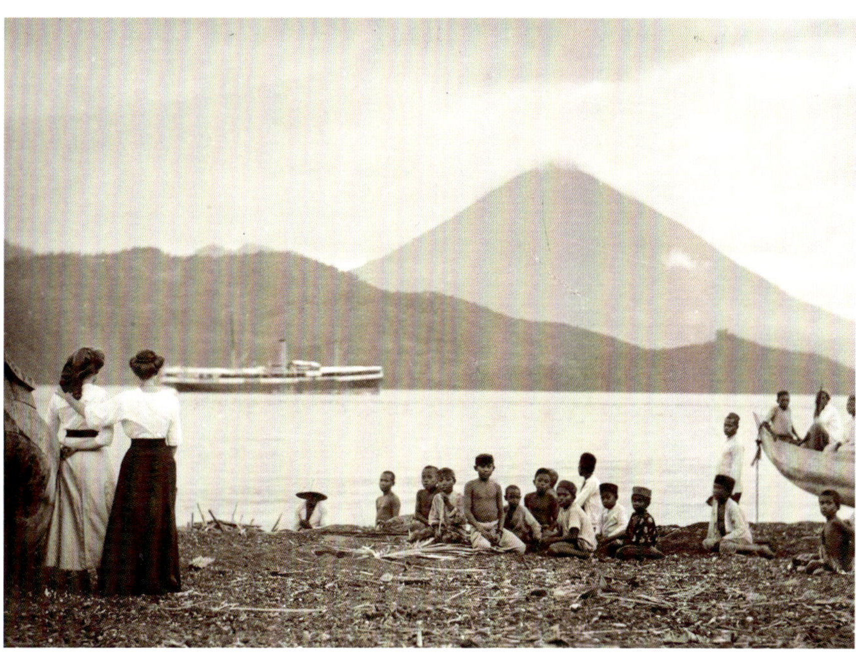

66
The KPM steamer *Camphuys* departs from Ternate
Photographer: A. Person
silver gelatin developing-out paper
11.9 x 16.4 cm
c. 1910
60018590. Gift: C.G.J. Rühl-van Swieten, 1965

In 1888 the Royal Packet Navigation Company (Koninklijke Paketvaart Maatschappij, KPM) was founded to provide scheduled services between the remote islands that make up the Indonesian archipelago. Twenty-five years later the shipping company had the situation firmly in hand. These were the heydays of modern Dutch imperialism, which saw sovereignty being established over the entire archipelago. The KPM performed so well in this period that it made itself indispensable. It had built up a closely-knit network of shipping lines and offices, and the government contracted it to transport men and munitions during military expeditions. This made it easier for the government to display its 'presence' in the Outer Regions and to exert its authority beyond Java. Showing the flag was an important sign of this control, and crews functioned as the government's informal eyes and ears.

They were certainly blazing new trails. Much had to be overcome, even in the far corners of the archipelago: difficult waters, sandbanks that shifted with the tides, treacherous reefs, inadequate nautical charts and a dearth of lighthouses. Most coastlines lacked port facilities and ships had to be on- and offloaded at a roadstead, which was sometime hindered by unfavourable winds. The cargo trade remained the most lucrative activity, despite the steady growth in passengers. The indigenous population also made increasing use of the ships, creating a market for their products in the region and beyond. Tourism throughout the archipelago increased because of the improved connections. To further stimulate this, in 1911 the *Guide through Netherlands India* was published by J.H. de Bussy in Amsterdam on behalf of the KPM. This guide was richly illustrated with photographs. The cover design seems to be based on photographs from three albums (Alb. 198–200) in the Tropen-museum collection. The shipping company presented them to Mrs A. Rühl-Van Swieten in Makassar on Celebes in 1914 as a keepsake of the trip her husband made in 1912 with L.J. Lambach. At the time, the latter was chairman of the Board and thus the most important KPM representative in the Netherlands East Indies. This explains the luxurious edition: more than 175 individual photographs glued to card stock in three separate cassettes. E.H. Rühl entered the service of the shipping company on 22 May 1891 as a warehouse master in Batavia. The German photographer A. Person took the photographs. The leitmotiv in the albums is the KPM steamship in the background of the photographs. They wait at the roadstead, in the bay, or alongside a pier or quay – a powerful symbol of Western presence. The indigenous population can be seen in the foreground. This image recurs repeatedly in the series, which also includes photographs that were usually taken during trips such as this. RJ

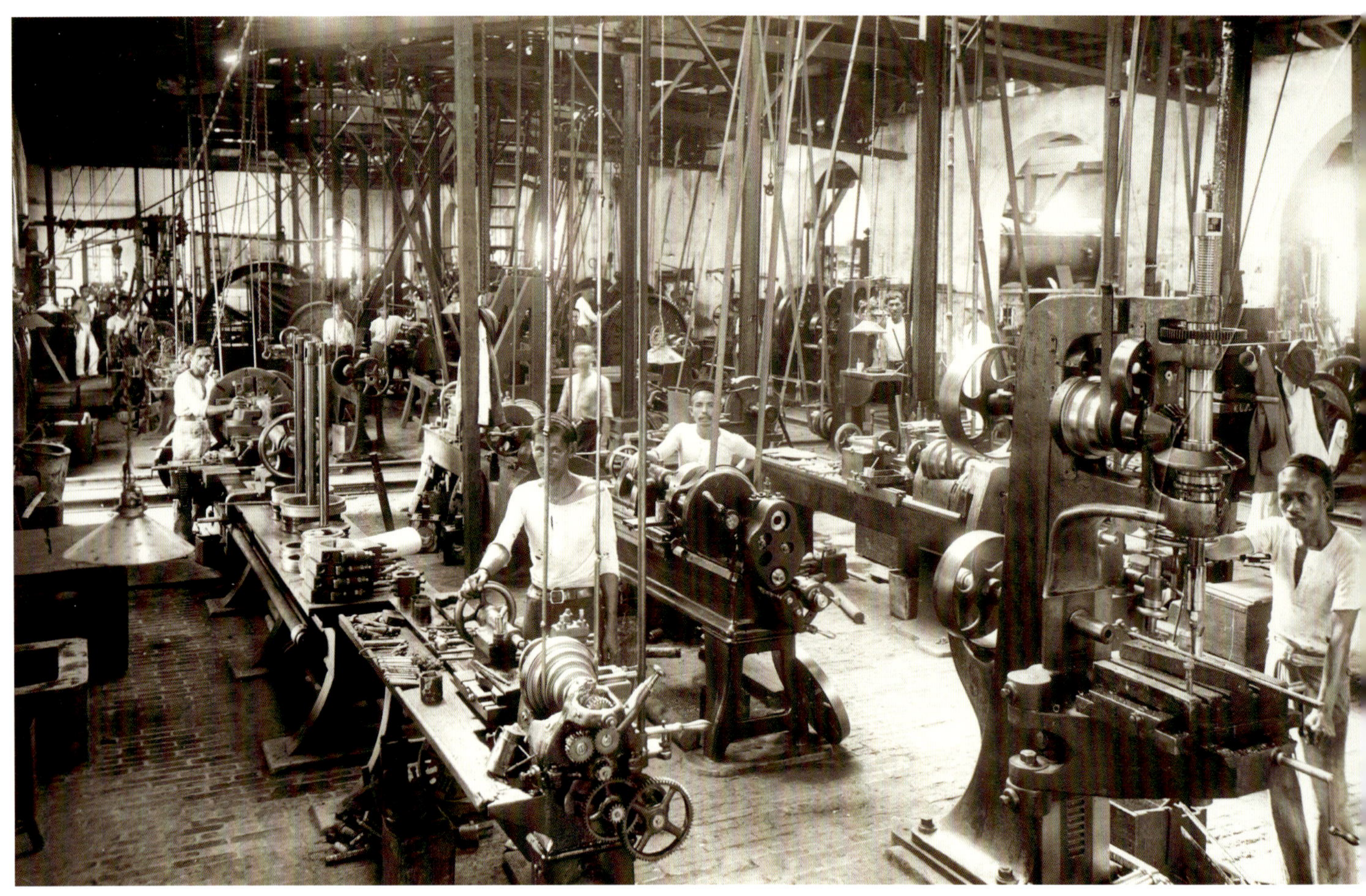

67
Workshop of the Deli Railway Company (DSM) in Medan
Photographer: C.J. Kleingrothe
gelatin printing-out paper
17.9 x 28.4 cm
c. 1915
60004423. Provenance: unknown

Corporate albums

Photograph albums that provide an impression of the economic and commercial activities in the Netherlands East Indies range from being extremely luxurious to having only a simple cover. A company celebration, the departure of an employee or a visit by a Governor-General was a perfect reason to have an album made. The occasion and the person's function determined their appearance and content. Their various functions seemed to have overlapped: they were souvenir and commemorative albums as well as tools of propaganda and promotional gifts. In addition to commercial enterprises, (semi-) governmental institutes such as hospitals, city councils, the prison system, and other bodies responsible for the roads, railways and ports also had occasion to commission a photograph album.

The Tropenmuseum photograph collection has more than 2600 albums,[124] approximately 200 of which can be classified as corporate albums.
Three quarters of these document the large agricultural undertakings, followed by mining and oil extraction. A number of 'industrial' albums were also produced by paper, leather and textile companies and engineering works.
The agricultural companies often owned several plantations where different crops were grown. They generally had a head office in the Netherlands, with a general manager who was responsible for the operational management in the Netherlands East Indies.
Albums depicting tobacco and sugar farming are among the oldest in the collection. Sugar farming was concentrated on East Java, and tobacco was cultivated on the east coast of Sumatra (Deli) and on a few plantations in the principalities of Central Java.

68
Photograph album commemorating the 25th year of tobacco cultivation on Deli, Sumatra (1863–88), presented to J. Nienhuys
Photographic Studio: G.R. Lambert & Co.
Leather, metal, wood, card stock
44.5 x 55 x 10 cm
1888
Alb. no. 1466. Provenance: unknown. Former collection J. Nienhuys (1836–1927)

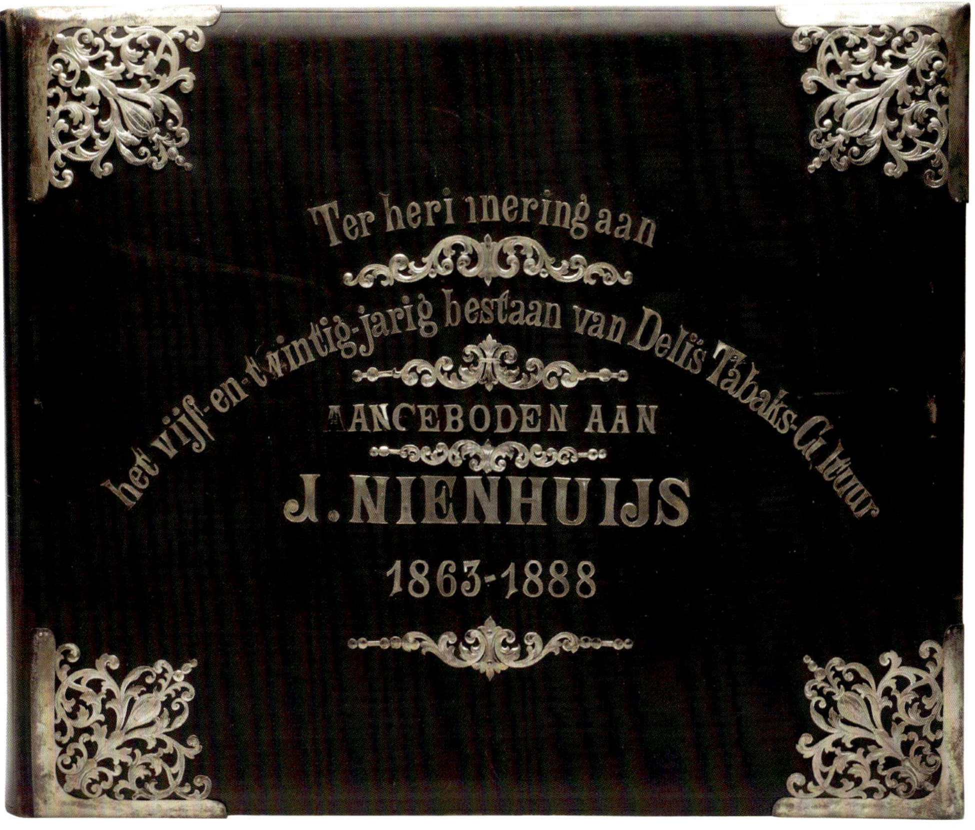

69
Group portrait with planters, including J. Nienhuys, on the Senembah Company's Tandjong Morawa tobacco plantation, Sumatra
Photographer: unknown
Silver gelatin developing-out paper
27.2 x 35.2 cm
1912
60022968. Provenance: unknown

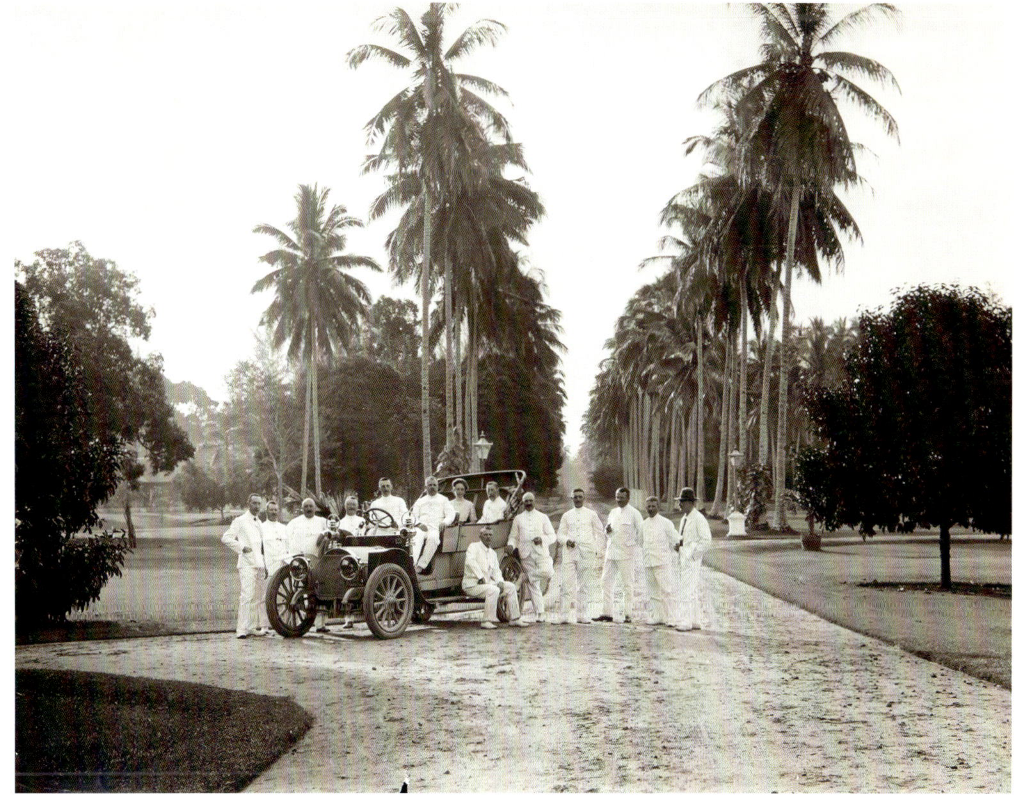

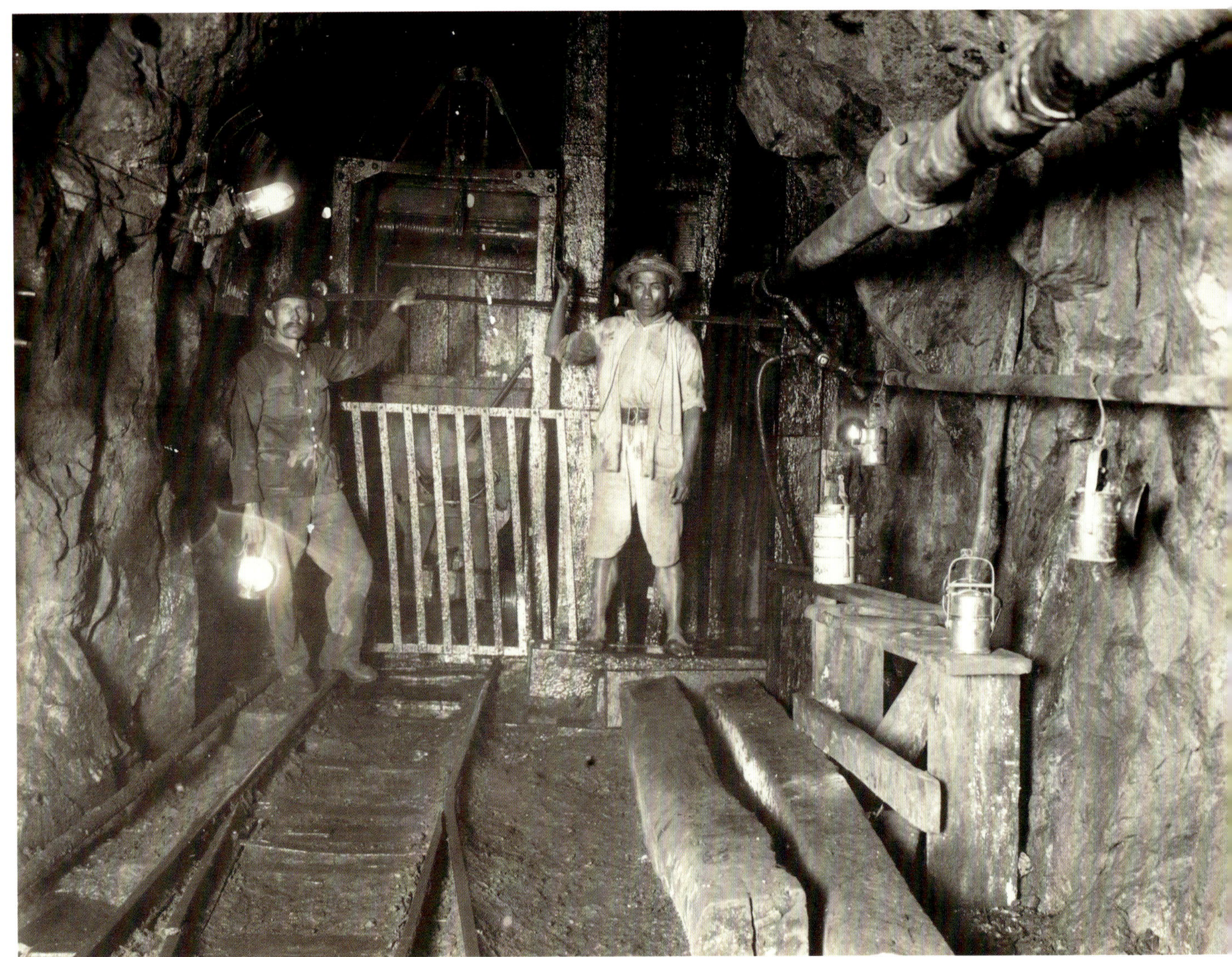

70
Miners with a lorry at the lift in a mineshaft in the Government's Gold and Silver Mines in Tambang-sawah (Bengkulu, Sumatra)
Photographer: unknown
silver gelatin developing-out paper
14.6 x 19.2 cm
1920–30
60043519. Gift: N.W. van Santen, 1980. Former collection H.J.A. Sanders and W.M. Sanders-Hock

Tea, cinchona and coffee mainly grew in the mountainous regions of Central Java; rubber, palm oil and copra mostly on Sumatra. Mining (coal, gold and silver) occurred on Sumatra's west coast, Bangka and Billiton were the source of tin, Borneo of petroleum.

Factories were primarily located in and around the cities on Java, with Surabaya as the centre of heavy industry. This was due to the increasing mechanisation of the surrounding sugar factories and the need for better infrastructure.

From felling to packing

Some of the albums are impressive objects: large and heavy, bound by hand in cowhide or snakeskin, with a decorative gold embossed design, and packed in a skilfully carved hardwood box. The photographs were all taken professionally, carefully printed as large images and provided with printed or handwritten captions.

71
Photograph album, front and back, presented by the staff of the Maron Sugar Company (Java) to general manager Douwe Feikema, commemorating his 25th year in the sugar business
Photographic Studio:
A. Herrmann (Surabaya)
leather, parchment, card stock
30.3 x 38.5 x 7.5 cm
19 May 1917
Alb. no. 1803. Gift: T.T. Feikema, 2001. Former collection D. Feikema

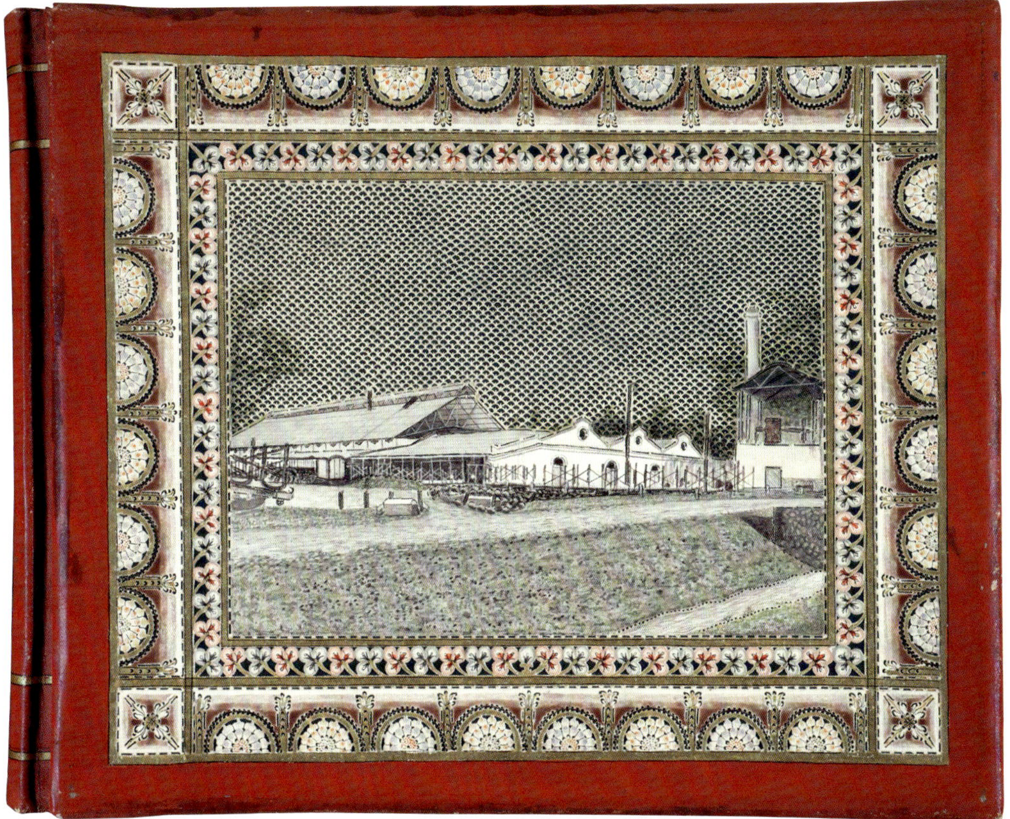

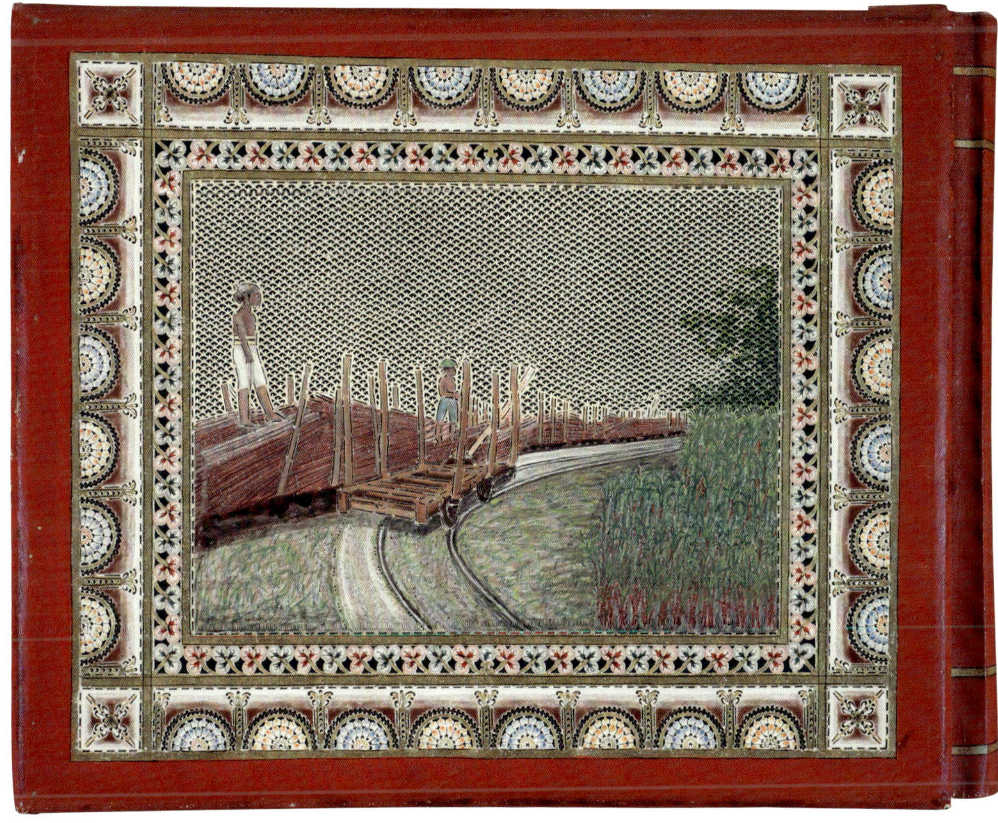

To create an overall impression with memories the recipient would cherish, the photographs of the company itself are usually interspersed with images of the social life associated with the company. The collection also includes albums with unappealing covers with, at the most, the words 'Photograph Album' written on them. Their contents sometime comprise surprising series of photographs that are often less formal than those in official commemorative albums.

The belief and pride in progress is evident in corporate albums that depict the entire story of a company's work, from stripping uncultivated land of the primeval forest to the final product, neatly packed in bales. Particularly albums depicting tobacco cultivation in Deli show the complete process from beginning to end.

A handful of Europeans, impeccably dressed in white clothing supervise the tree felling, the clearing of the land, the planting and harvesting, the selection of tobacco leafs, and the compressing of the bales. Finally, the name of the plantation was stippled in crate letters on the packaging. The labour of hundreds of anonymous workers was now ready for shipping to European markets. The photographs in the albums showing the work on the plantations all seem to try to provide an overview of the activities and capture the vastness of the fields, the enormity of the sheds, the mass of labourers.

72
Group portrait taken during the construction of a dike on the Hessa tobacco plantation in Asahan, Sumatra
Photographer: P.J. Freni
silver gelatin developing-out paper
11.5 x 16.1 cm
c. 1900
60002375. Provenance: unknown

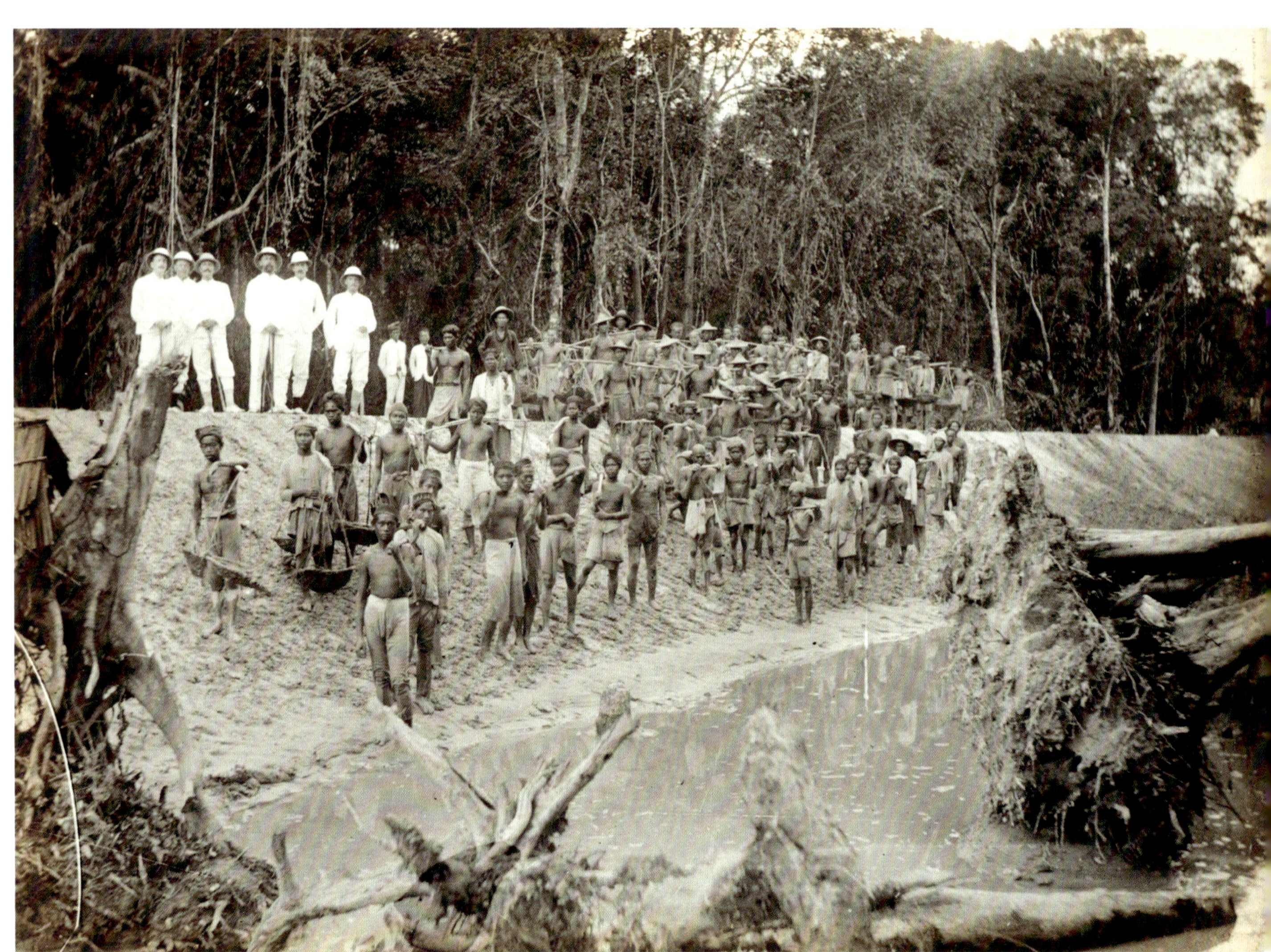

'ALL IS WELL IN THE COLONY'

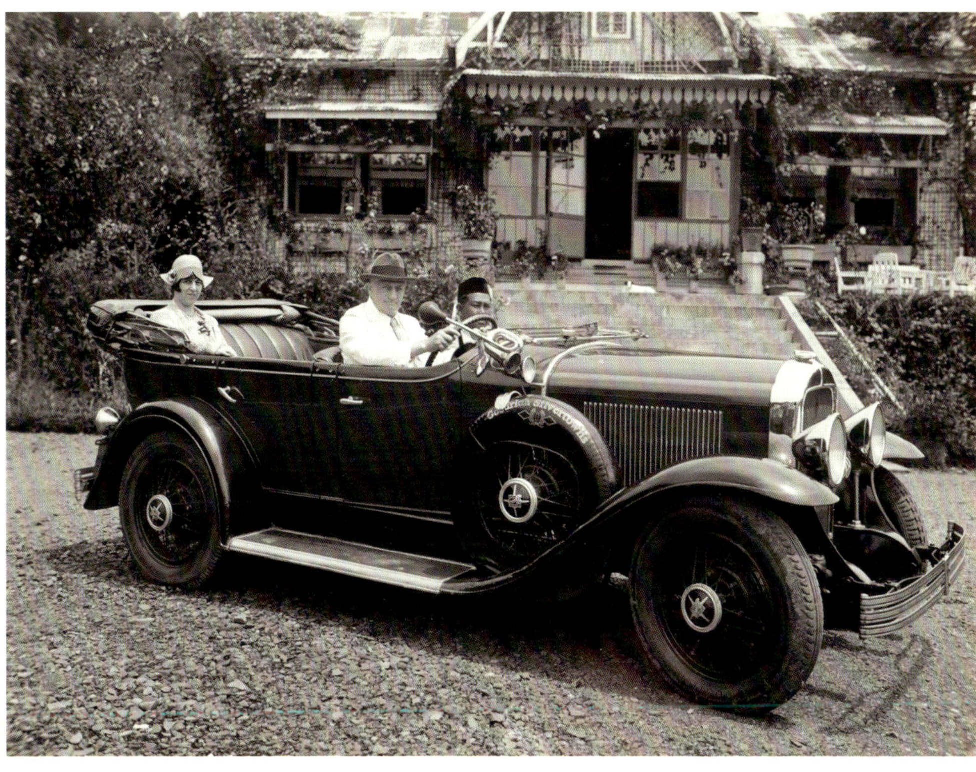

'The Sanders family leave with their Buick', reads the caption to one of the photographs in a commemorative album that was presented to the couple during their stay in the Netherlands East Indies. The photograph depicts Mr and Mrs Sanders around 1932 with their chauffeur in a Buick, a luxurious American car. In that year H.J.A. Sanders (1876–1939) grandly celebrated his 25 years of service in Lebong Donok, a village in the Bengkulu residency on south Sumatra. He had worked there since 1917 as a general manager of the gold mines belonging to the Redjang Lebong Mining Company. This company had been extremely profitable since it's founding in 1897.
The 1932 annual report mentions satisfactory operating profits, but the gold rush of its first years had long since disappeared. The ore was running out and mines were gradually becoming less profitable. At the end of December 1936 the ore extraction in the Lebong Donok mining concession was stopped and the grinding mills were decommissioned.[125] These events were reported in the mining company's annual reports, but were completely bypassed in the Sanders' family's photograph albums, which above all are pervaded with an atmosphere of 'All is well in the colony' ('Uit Indië niets dan goeds'). Outwardly, they appear to be valuable albums – one has a crocodile skin cover and is preserved in a wooden box; three albums are lacquered and decorated with Japanese and Dutch motifs, inlaid with mother-of-pearl; and one has a cover decorated with a pattern that is reminiscent of the work by the artistic couple Robert and Sonia Delaunay.
At first sight the Sanders family memorial albums appear to be neither corporate albums nor typical family albums. Yet we could still regard them as family albums, despite them providing an alternative view of family life, which usually involves raising children, family parties and suchlike. The photographs portray the social life of Mr and Mrs Sanders within a seemingly tightly knit, small colonial community in a remote place like Lebong Donok. Colleagues and friends appear to take the place of their closest family who were so far away in Europe.[126]
We see how they celebrated Saint Nicholas' day (Sinterklaas, December 5) and Christmas together, organised masked balls, paid each other visits, and enjoyed 'rice tables' at the club. The local mining staff was invited to attend more official occasions such as Queens Day (August 31), Sanders' anniversary celebrations in 1932, and the farewell party for the Sanders when they returned to Holland in 1937. RJ

73
H.J.A. Sanders and his wife in their Buick in front of their house in Lebong Donok
Photographer: unknown
silver gelatin developing-out paper
14.2 x 19 cm
c. 1932
60035602. Provenance: KIT ILS (Central Library), 1996. Former collection H.J.A. Sanders and W.M. Sanders-Hock

Albums as social documents

Besides their products, attention was also paid to the social aspects of a company. Because of their remoteness, many plantations had a close-knit, inward-looking community in which Europeans met each other on the tennis courts, in the club and at celebrations and parties. The photographs do not record any discord in their relationships, but the hierarchy is clearly evident – a few bosses and lots of employees. Unlike the hierarchy evident in corporate albums produced in the Netherlands, the hierarchy in Indonesia was based on colour and ethnicity.

The photographs were always made from a European perspective. Group portraits of managerial staff, white bosses in the fields or behind their desks – all these people are mentioned by name. The Chinese labourers who did the wide-scale felling, planting and harvesting, the Javanese labourers in the sugar factories, and the rows of gatherers in the tea plantations remain anonymous. Sometimes they are identified by the work they did, by ethnicity, or merely designated as 'native staff'. A few commemorative albums do mention local employees with a long record of service by name, usually when they were rewarded with a medal or a watch.[127]

For some unknown reason these photographs almost only appear in albums related to the sugar industry. The remote and largely self-reliant plantations recognised the importance of investing in their workers' wellbeing. The housing of the European employees was strictly regulated throughout the archipelago. The senior manager had the largest house, while lower-ranking employees had more modest houses that corresponded to their function. The labourers ('coolies') lived at the periphery of the complex in rows of *kampong* houses or sheds. These are never shown in detail; the photographs only depict the efficient organisation.[128]

These albums also show that almost every remote company had its own small clinic under the direction of a native '*Dokter Djawa*' (Fig. 89). Sometimes a ward is depicted, with a European doctor or nurse. The clinic, the fields, the company warehouses, the houses, everything is represented as favourably as possible in the photographs; everywhere has been tidied up and swept clean.

These types of images do not appear in industrial albums. These companies were based in or around the cities on Java and made use of public healthcare facilities. The workers lived in the surrounding *kampong*.

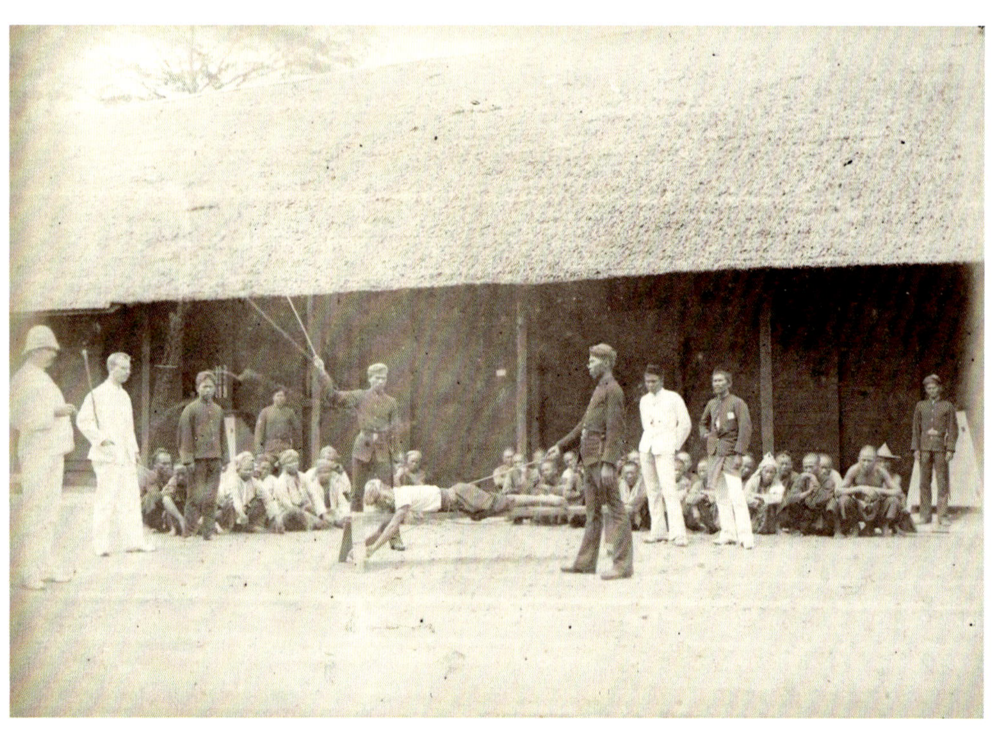

74
Administering corporal punishment, Binjai (Sumatra)
Photographer: unknown
albumen print
11.9 x 17 cm
1880–95
60007721. Gift: René Regendanz, 1994. Former collection Gustav Engelbrecht

If the photographs are to be believed, social disobedience did not happen, one exception being the photograph of a worker at a tobacco plantation on Sumatra being beaten as punishment (1875–1900).

The labourers were frequently subject to corporal punishment, certainly on the tobacco plantations in Sumatra where the managers had enforced their own justice for many years.[129] Of a later date are two photographs in an album with group portraits of workers at the Kalibagor Sugar Factory on East Java. The caption implicitly refers to social unrest: 'A group of Chinese strike-breakers', without further information or a date.[130]

On one photograph they are portrayed as a group, on the other between sugar cookers and laboratory assistants. A newspaper article of May 1920 provides the context.[131] A strike organised by the Union of Factory Workers (Personeel Fabrieks Bond, PFB), a union for indigenous workers, was declared on Kalibagor during the 'the grinding days' (*de maaltijd*), the period when the sugar cane is harvested, ground and processed in the factory, i.e., when the factory is at its busiest. The strikers were demanding that their union be recognised and wanted to settle wage disputes. The unrest continued despite a promised increase in wages. On 17 June, *De Nieuwe Rotterdamsche Courant* reported that the strike had been broken by hiring Chinese workers from the surrounding areas. All the striking workers were fired.

At the end of the 1920s and especially after 1930 the global crisis also impacted on the Netherlands East Indies. There were successive salary reductions for government employees, company employees were dismissed, and the rising nationalism resulted in strikes and disturbances. Nothing of this can be seen on the photographs. Life in the colony was still portrayed as calm and hopeful.

An example is the large, green album in a hardwood box (alb. no. 1786). The lid is decorated with peacocks, snakes and tropical flora. The reason for making this album is written in calligraphy: 'Presented to Mr J.J. Braat on the occasion of his departure from the Netherlands East Indies in November 1931 by the Braat Engineering Works N.V., Surabaya, Yogyakarta, Tegal, Sukabumi'.

Mr Braat was presented with a keepsake of the company of which he was a director for several years. It is a visual document containing 56 photographs that display a modern and efficient company.

The photographs were glued systematically into the album; first by branch, with a group portrait of the management, followed by images of the foundry, the turning department, the rolling mill and the offices. All the people in the photographs are hard at work. At the back of the album is a letter from the Secretary of the Association of Engineering Works (Vereeniging van Machinefabrieken in Nederlandsch-Indië) in the Netherlands East Indies, stating that Mr Braat '[...] notwithstanding recurring ups and downs, persevered in building up a company that can compete with similar companies in Europe'. The 'ups and downs' are revealed in the book commemorating the company's 20-year anniversary ten years earlier, in 1921. There were continual problems with the staff.

By nature the native is a farmer, not an artisan, he still has a limited degree of education, and the number of illiterates is still large, meaning there is a lot of dead wood, and as a result of the climate and other reasons the physical condition of the native lags behind that of Europeans. Their individual output is lower than in Europe, but this is compensated for with much lower wages. [...] In reality, the native labourer is basically a big child and can be easily thrown off balance, making him susceptible to work stoppages.[132]

The sugar workers' strikes in the early 1930s spread to other sectors. J.J. Braat Engineering Works was also affected – the company was brought to a standstill for three weeks.

Companies had to cope with other problems too. European managers increasingly had to deal with specialised Indonesian personnel in the middle and higher ranks. This also applied to the sugar industry. The Sugar Union (Suikerbond), founded in 1907, was a powerful trade union on Java that applied itself to settling wage disputes and attaining legal status, negotiated unemployment benefits and dismissals, monitored the level of education at the so-called Sugar Schools, and ran their own testing stations where they conducted research into crop improvement and new industrial processing techniques. The Sugar Union was a bulwark of European employees that faced a dilemma, as can be concluded from the end of the newspaper article *De Suikerbond in Indië en zijn streven*:[133]

People are afraid that the Sugar Union and associated trade unions will come under the control of educated Natives and Chinese, whose membership one cannot and will not refuse since they are employed in agricultural enterprises. We anticipate their numbers to increase significantly, something that for obvious reasons is viewed with a measure of distress. A peaceful infiltration that could eventually be a source of trouble.

The journalist must have had the growing nationalism in mind. The only thing that conveys the growing nationalism on album photographs is that more men are seen wearing the characteristic black Muslim cap (*kopiah*).

After the Second World War

The Tropenmuseum photograph collection has only a few albums that provide an idea of company activities in the years immediately after the Second World War.[134] Not surprisingly, the Japanese showed no scruples in the period 1942 to 1945, and left most of the companies without any staff or material after the war. This added to the political confusion that prevailed in Indonesia after its declaration of independence, and Dutch companies had to try to cope with this difficult and uncertain atmosphere. Nonetheless, a few companies did try to start up again, one example being the Netherlands-Indies Metalwork and Packaging Factory (Nederlandsch-Indische Metaalwaren en Emballage Fabriek, NIMEF).

The museum has three of this company's albums from the period 1949 to 1951 (Alb. nos. 0083, 0084, 0085). The company was founded in 1918,[135] and was reequipped and restarted after the war under the same name. NIMEF manufactured packing materials (tin, paper and cardboard) for numerous products. No pre-war albums or photographs of the company have been traced. The rebuilding is documented in 250 photographs in three albums. Only one caption mentions the situation during the war: 'the Japanese placed these printing presses in the tin factory'.[136]

The company had continued to operate under Japanese supervision during the war. The photograph shows a devastated factory hall with the carcasses of the printing presses, but whether this destruction occurred during or soon after the war ended is not mentioned. Photographs of the company's own armed security personnel imply that peace had not yet returned. The NIMEF resumed operations at full speed from 1949. The vastness of the factory hall featured less than in pre-war photographs; now the emphasis was on the machines that could be operated by only a handful of staff. More than in pre-war albums these three albums provide a view of the social life in a factory.

A housekeeping team of six women prepared coffee, tea and lunch for the 900 employees. Clerks hunch over their work, three ladies sit behind typewriters, and the administration is largely in the hands of Chinese employees. These employees remained loyal to the company after the war. In January 1950 a staff party was held with a badminton tournament, pole climbing, a bridge dive and a dinner for all the staff. Partly because of the loss of a large proportion of the Europeans, corporate photographs taken after 1945 have a pronounced 'Indonesian' atmosphere in comparison to pre-war photographs. The hierarchy is less evident, the atmosphere on the shop floor is less formal, the photographs seem to be less staged, and relationships have clearly changed. These post-war company photographs are more a portrayal of an Indonesian company than of a Western company in Indonesia.[137]

At the end of 1957 President Soekarno nationalised all remaining Dutch-owned companies in Indonesia.

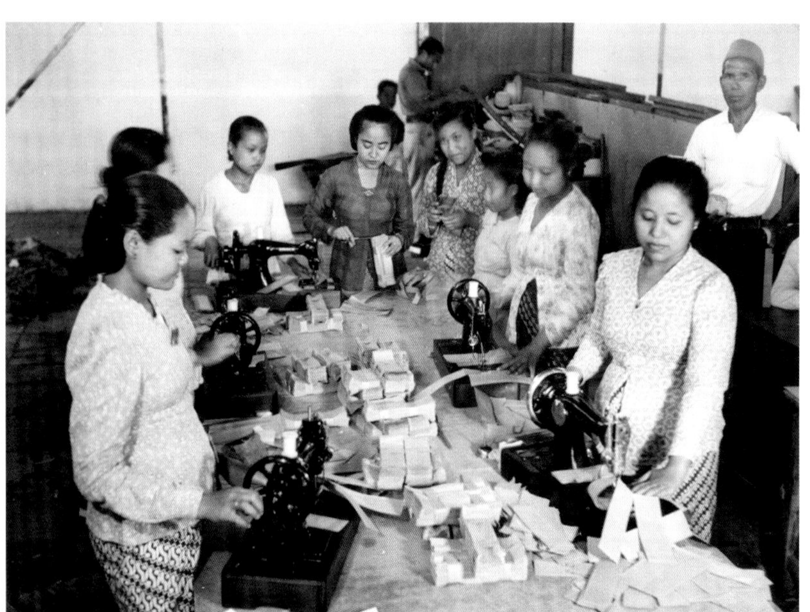

75
Workers at the NIMEF factory in Bandung
Photographer: unknown
silver gelatin developing-out paper
12.7 x 17.5 cm
c. 1950
60012095. Provenance: unknown

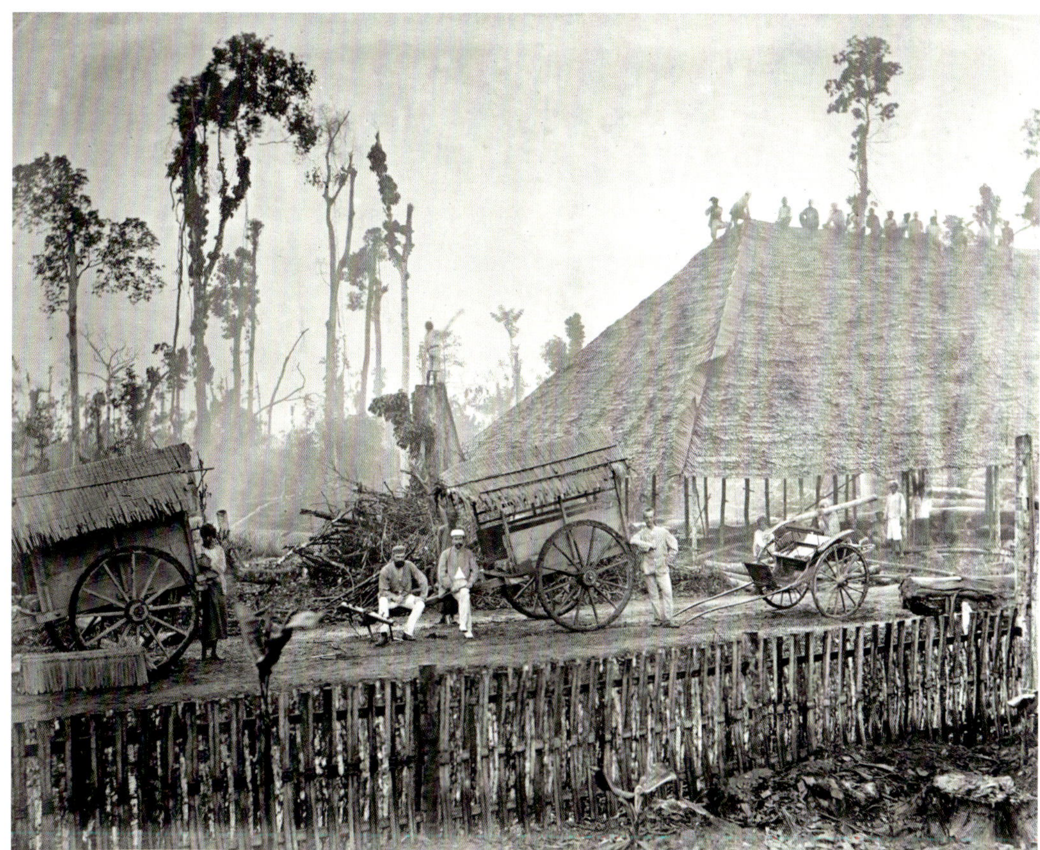

76
Constructing a fermentation shed on a tobacco plantation in Langkat, Sumatra
Photographer: unknown
albumen print
20.7 x 26.2 cm
c. 1879
60019110. Provenance: unknown

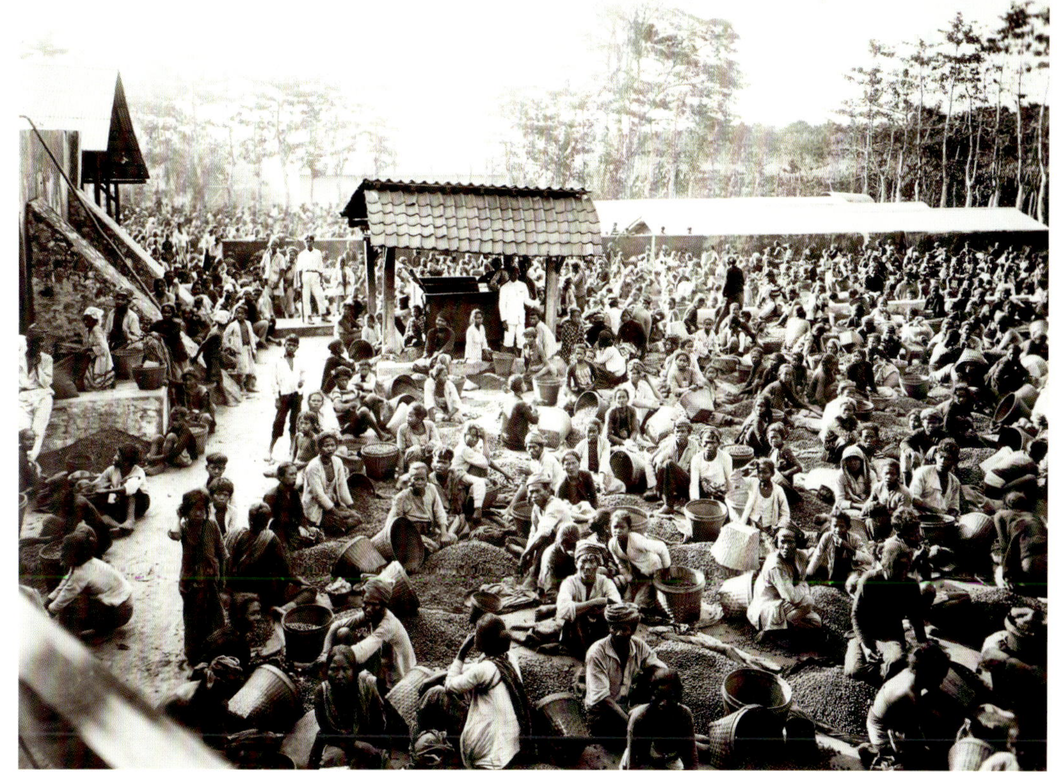

77
Sorting harvested coffee berries at the factory on the Satak plantation, East Java
Photographer: unknown
silver gelatin developing-out paper
15.5 x 20.5 cm
1929
60023155. Gift: Metzelaar, 1981

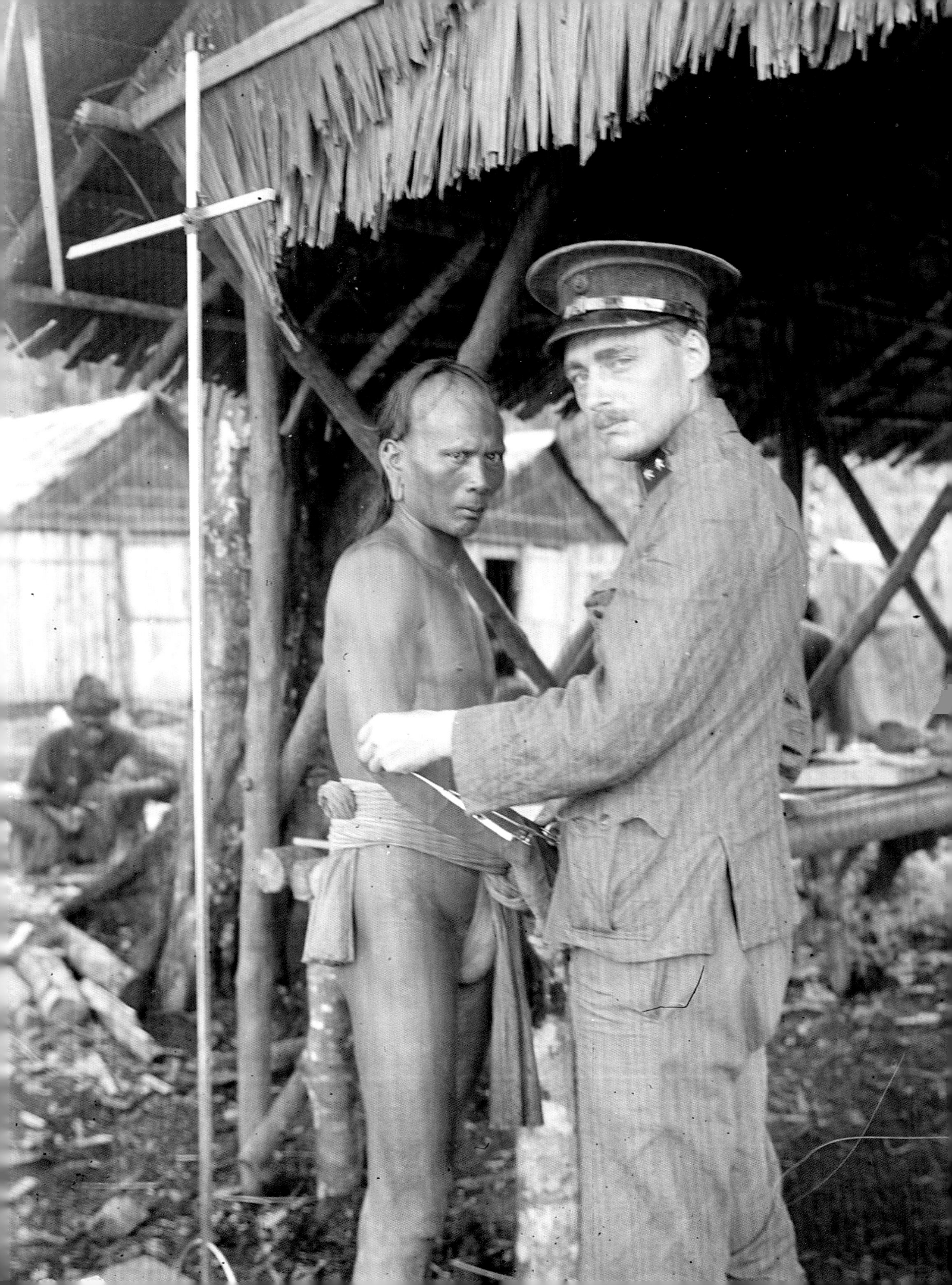

PHOTOGRAPHY AND SCIENCE

STEVEN VINK

78
The Officer of Health, Dr H.J.T. Bijlmer, physical anthropologist on the Central New Guinea Expedition, taking measurements of a Dayak porter
Photographer: unknown
gelatin glass negative
9 x 12 cm
1920
10009141. Gift: J. Jongejans, 1929

After the founding of the Kingdom of the Netherlands in 1815, a large number of overseas areas where the VOC had previously established its trading posts but which were taken over by the English during the Napoleonic era were rapidly 'returned' to the Netherlands. The greatest challenge facing the Netherlands was to further develop these territories as colonies. The economic development of these territories was prioritised for the motherland's own profit.

Nevertheless, the Netherlands East Indies was still largely unknown territory for the Dutch. The VOC had only been active along the coastlines of a number of islands, leaving their interiors undisturbed. Conducting scientific research throughout the entire colony was considered imperative. Attempts had been made earlier, the most famous of which is the work by the 17th-century botanist G.E. Rumphius with his collection and descriptions of plants and sea life in the Moluccas.

The Batavian Society of Arts and Sciences, founded in 1778, was an important initiative. Its initial activities focused on nature and culture, and it gradually started collecting and exhibiting antiquities from temples on Java and Bali. The Society had its own museum on the Koningsplein ('King's Square') in Batavia from the mid-1800s. The building is now part of the National Museum of Indonesia.

Most of the scientific research in the Netherlands East Indies was conducted during the 19th and early 20th century. Initial areas of focus were geology, the flora and fauna, and commercial crops. Later, more human aspects such as physical anthropology, ethnology and the history of the country and its people were included.

That the research focused on natural history was not that surprising, as it revolved around identifying crops suitable for commercial exploitation. For example, because its bark was the most important remedy for malaria at the time, the cinchona tree was imported from South America to the Netherlands East Indies in 1855 to be cultivated on a wide scale on the plantations. Within the space of a few years Indonesia became the largest cinchona producer in the world. One of the most famous natural scientists (and a cinchona planter), F.W. (Franz Wilhelm) Junghuhn (1809–64), also called 'the Alexander von Humboldt[138] of Indonesia', was partly responsible for the rise of cinchona culture on Java. Van Junghuhn was also a great advocate of the new medium of photography that was still in its infancy during his lifetime.[139] He is now especially known for the lithographs that

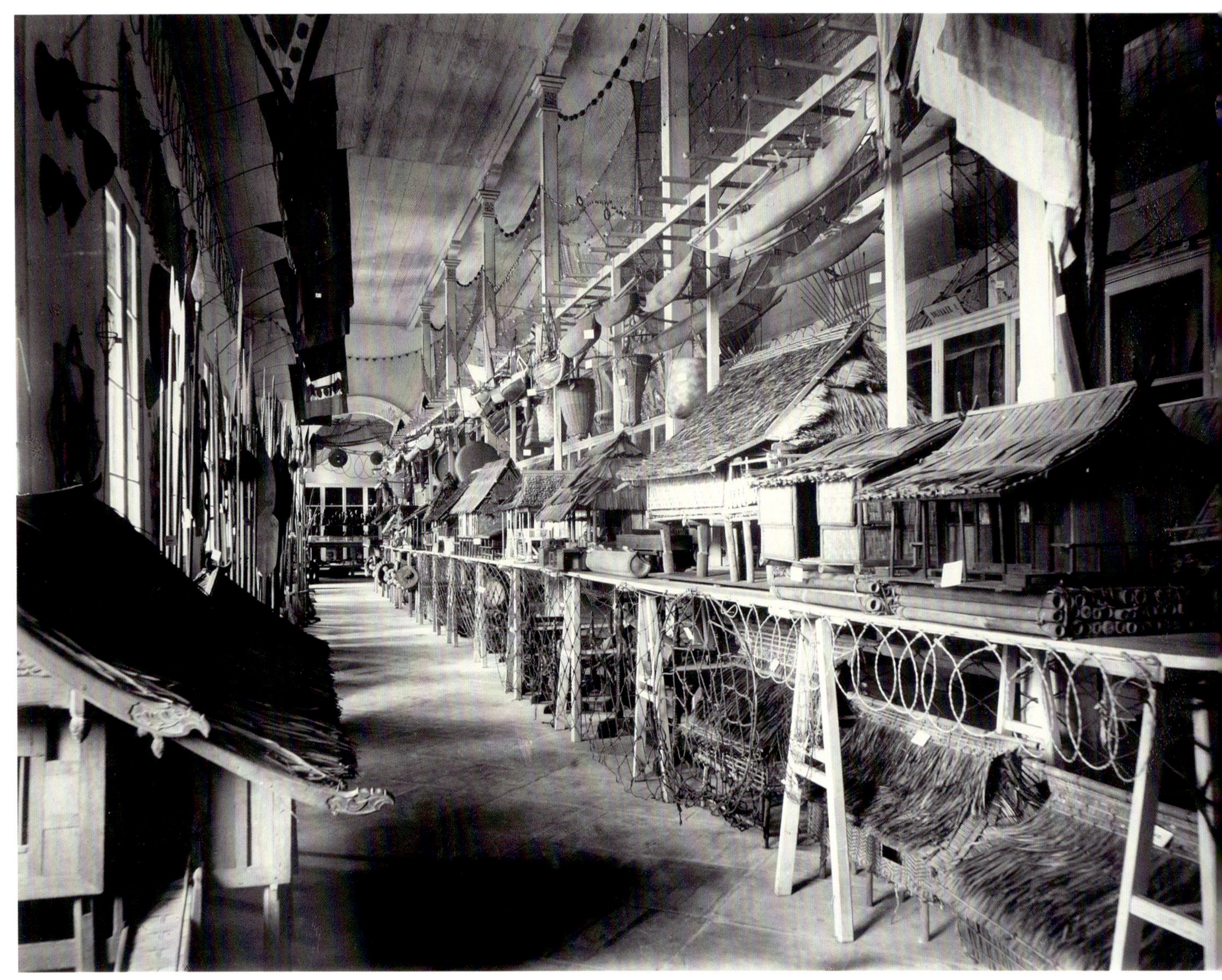

79
Museum of the Batavian Society of Arts and Sciences
Photographer: Tan Tjie Lan
gelatin printing-out paper
18.9 x 24.1 cm
c. 1896
60025179, Gift: Tan Tjie Lan, 1896

were made during his travels around Java. Although cinchona was vital to the burgeoning colonial economy, it was not the only crop that was grown; others soon followed, the most important being indigo, sugar, tea, coffee and tobacco.

's Lands Plantentuin, the Botanical Gardens

The Botanical Gardens were founded in Buitenzorg in 1817 at the initiative of C.G. Reinwardt to stimulate natural history research, especially into plant life. All the institutions conducting scientific research that fell under the auspices of the Department of Economic Affairs became part of this Institute.[140] The Botanical Gardens and the adjoining palaces of the Governor-General of the Netherlands East Indies (now the presidential palace) are the most well known, but the activities in the areas of collecting and researching indigenous plants from the entire archipelago were no less significant. This resulted in the (co-)organisation of scientific expeditions. The Colonial Museum in Haarlem and later in Amsterdam, maintained intensive contact with the Botanical Gardens, and exchanged information and collections, including the photography collection.

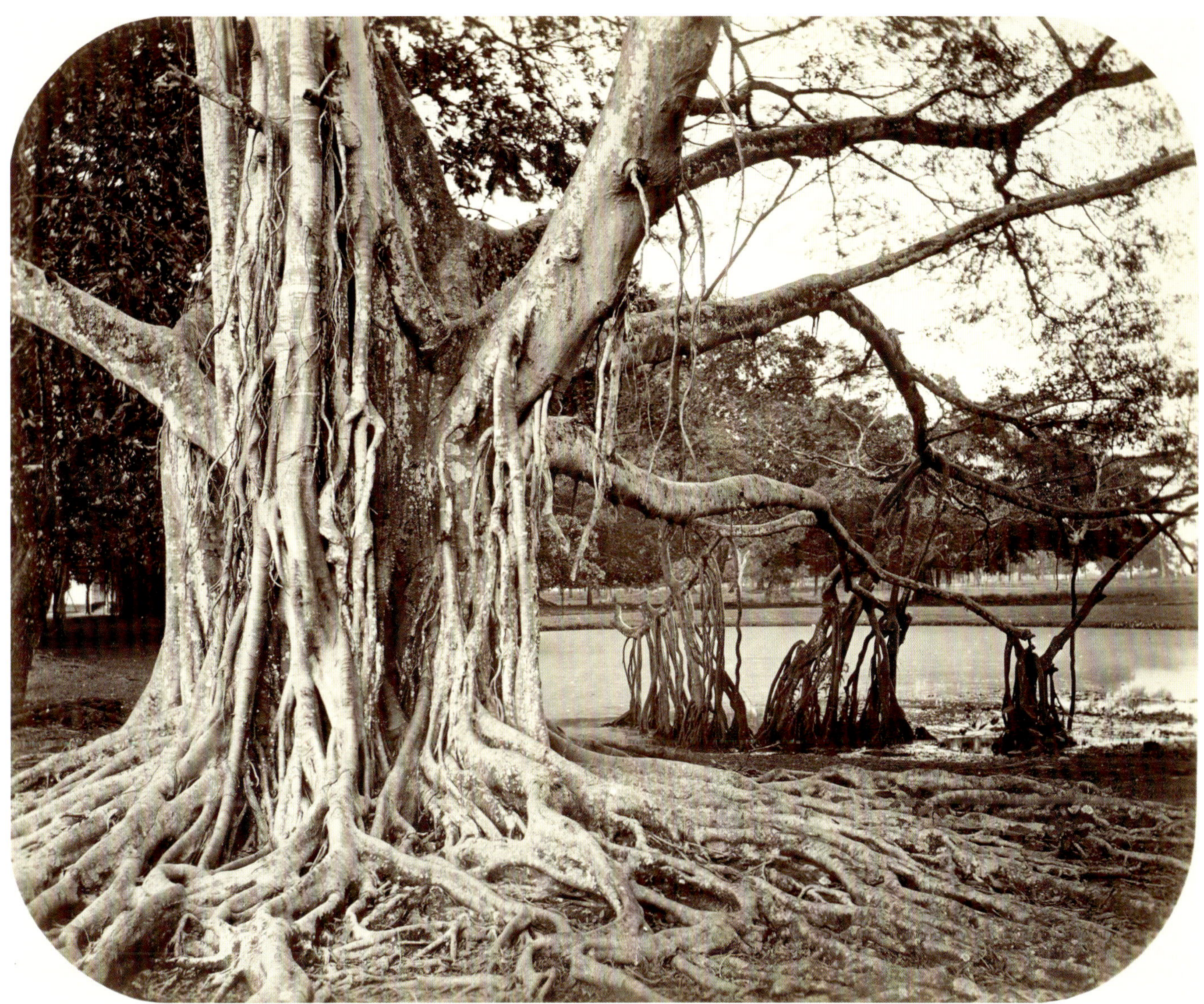

30
Waringin tree in the Botanical Gardens, Buitenzorg
Photographer: (attributed to) Woodbury & Page Photographic Studio
albumen print
19 x 23.5 cm
1857–1877
60019279. Gift: P. Altherr, via P.W. Osieck (1951). Former collection J. Altherr

Agricultural testing station

Plantation farming and the industrial processing of products became ever more important for the economy. A number of testing stations were established in several locations and were tasked with improving plants and seeds and farming techniques, with combating disease and conducting research into crop processing. These stations had their own experimental fields and well equipped laboratories. At the urgent request of the Colonial Museum plantations, factories and testing stations regularly supplied the Museum with photographs and negatives so that those back home could see how intensively people in the colony were busying themselves with agricultural research. In this way the Colonial Institute brought together a photograph collection that detailed all the stages involved in researching, cultivating and processing crops to a final product; these images were also widely used by many scientific journals.
An example of this is the work by the zoological botanist Louis Philibert Le Cosquino de Bussy (1879–1943). He moved to the Netherlands East Indies in 1905 where he worked for the Botanical Gardens and was stationed in Medan (Sumatra). In 1913 he became director of the Deli Research Station in Medan. He travelled throughout the

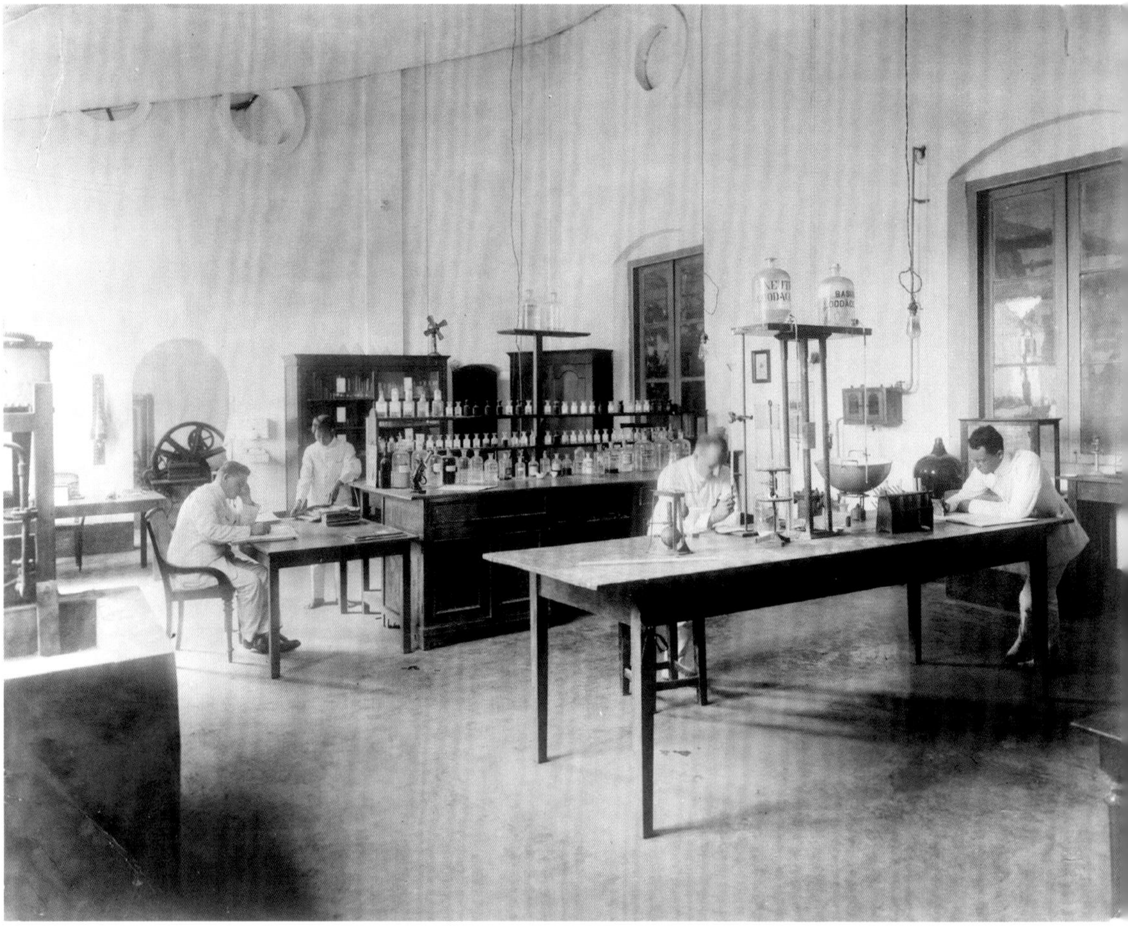

81
The laboratory of the Ketanen Sugar Factory, Java
Photographic studio: Kurkdjian
gelatin glass negative
9 x 12 cm
April 1916
10010744. Gift: Trade Museum, 1939

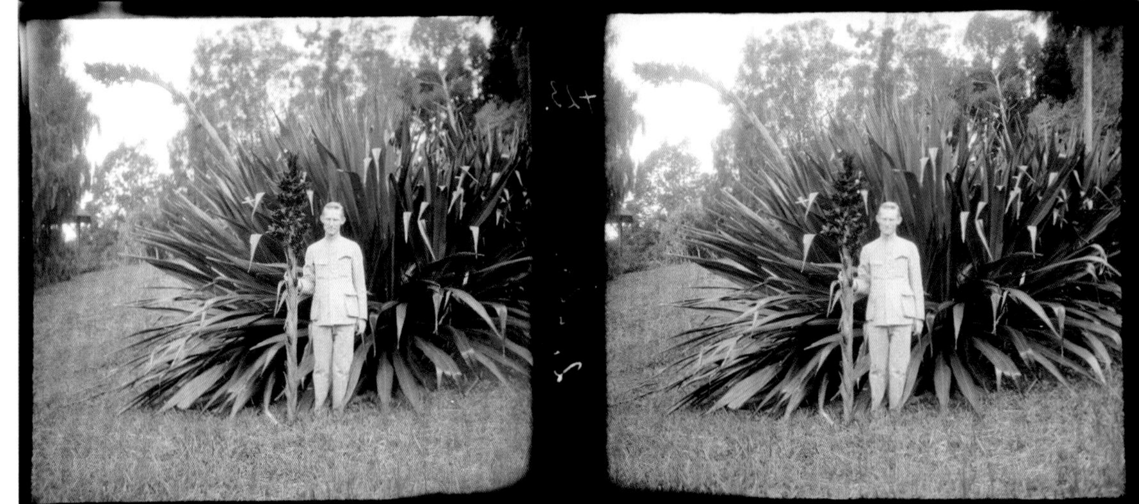

82
Stereoscopic photograph of Mr Bruggeman in front of a *Doryanthes excelsa*, at the Tjibodas Mountain Garden
Photographer: unknown
nitrate negative
6 x 12 cm
2 July 1927
10006019. Gift: Prof Dr L.Ph. le Cosquino de Bussy, 1929

Netherlands East Indies, visiting no less than 114 companies during his six-month trip. He created new departments of botany, zoology, chemistry, agriculture and soil research at the testing station in Medan. In 1916 he was appointed director of the Trade Museum Department in the Colonial Institute. During subsequent study trips to Indonesia (1916, 1927, 1936), he made hundreds of stereo negatives and lantern slides for the Colonial Institute's collection.[141]

Scientific Expeditions

Notwithstanding the importance of the natural history and agricultural research for the exploitation of the colony, these were not the only areas of scientific research. Geological research and the search for minerals were also of great importance. Gathering information about the population, their languages, customs and history was also necessary. To gain insights into all these aspects, the entire archipelago first had to be surveyed and mapped. The surveys were done by the Topographical Service, originally a military organisation, later a government service. By means of triangulation, surveying began throughout the archipelago, starting on Java and Madura, before moving to other islands. Conducting these surveys was a permanent fixture of military and scientific expeditions to the Outer Regions.

The word 'expedition' is usually understood to mean a journey to an unknown or remote area to conduct scientific research. Originally, the Royal Netherlands Indies Army (KNIL) busied themselves with this type of exploration of new areas, having the knowhow, the manpower and the organisation to undertake these tasks. While the KNIL could link these activities to military pacification operations or to taking possession of new areas, it also organised 'peaceful' military operations geared solely to surveying and mapping an area and describing it in detail for further exploitation. The military exploration of New Guinea, which lasted from 1907 to 1915, is the most well known example.[142] Geologists, botanists and anthropologists were also actively involved in exploring new areas. Organising an expedition was an undertaking that could not be taken lightly, and required precise preparation and

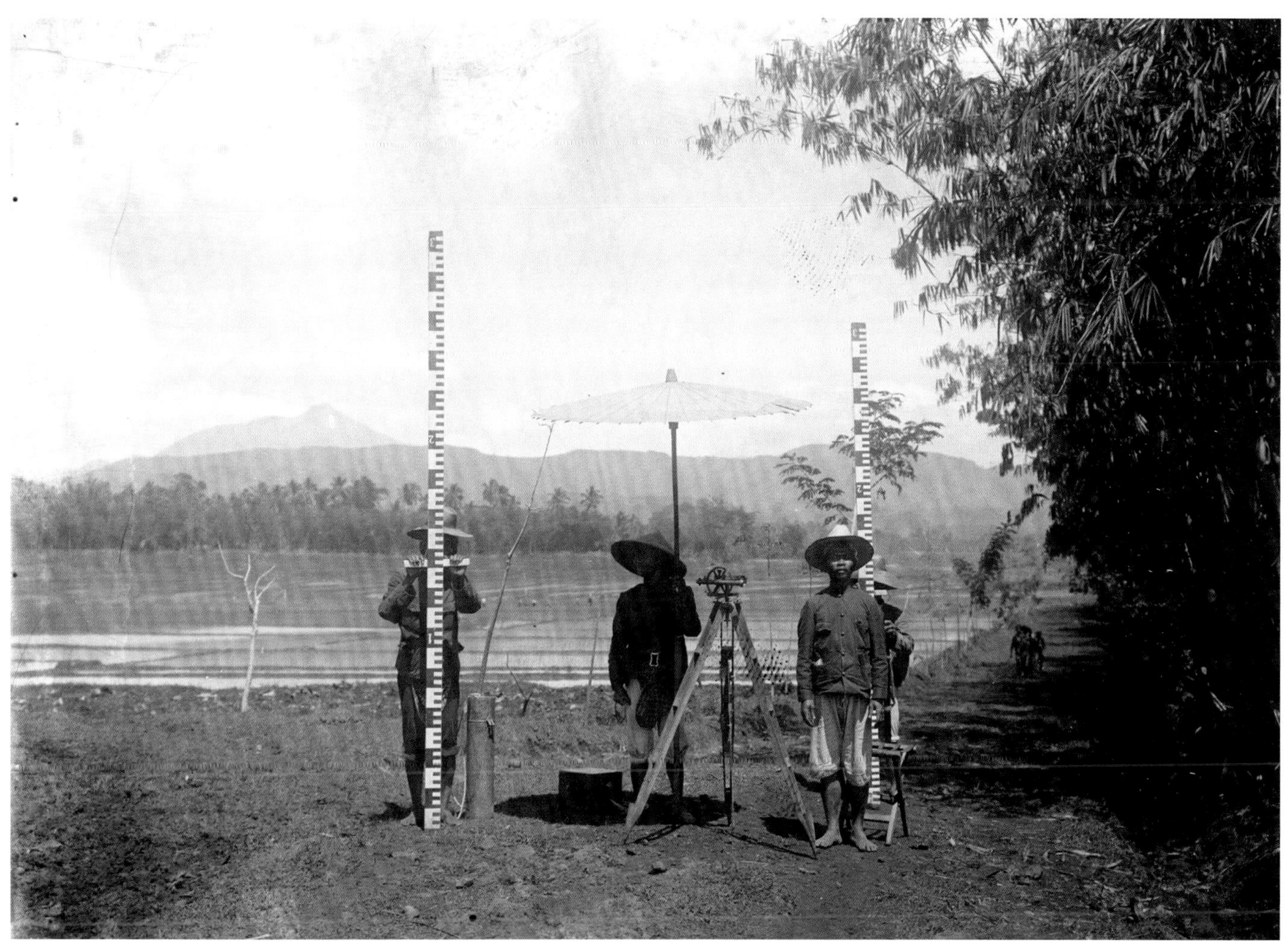

83
Employees of the Topographical Service in the field, Java
Photographer: unknown
glass negative
9 x 12 cm
c. 1910
10003964. Provenance: unknown

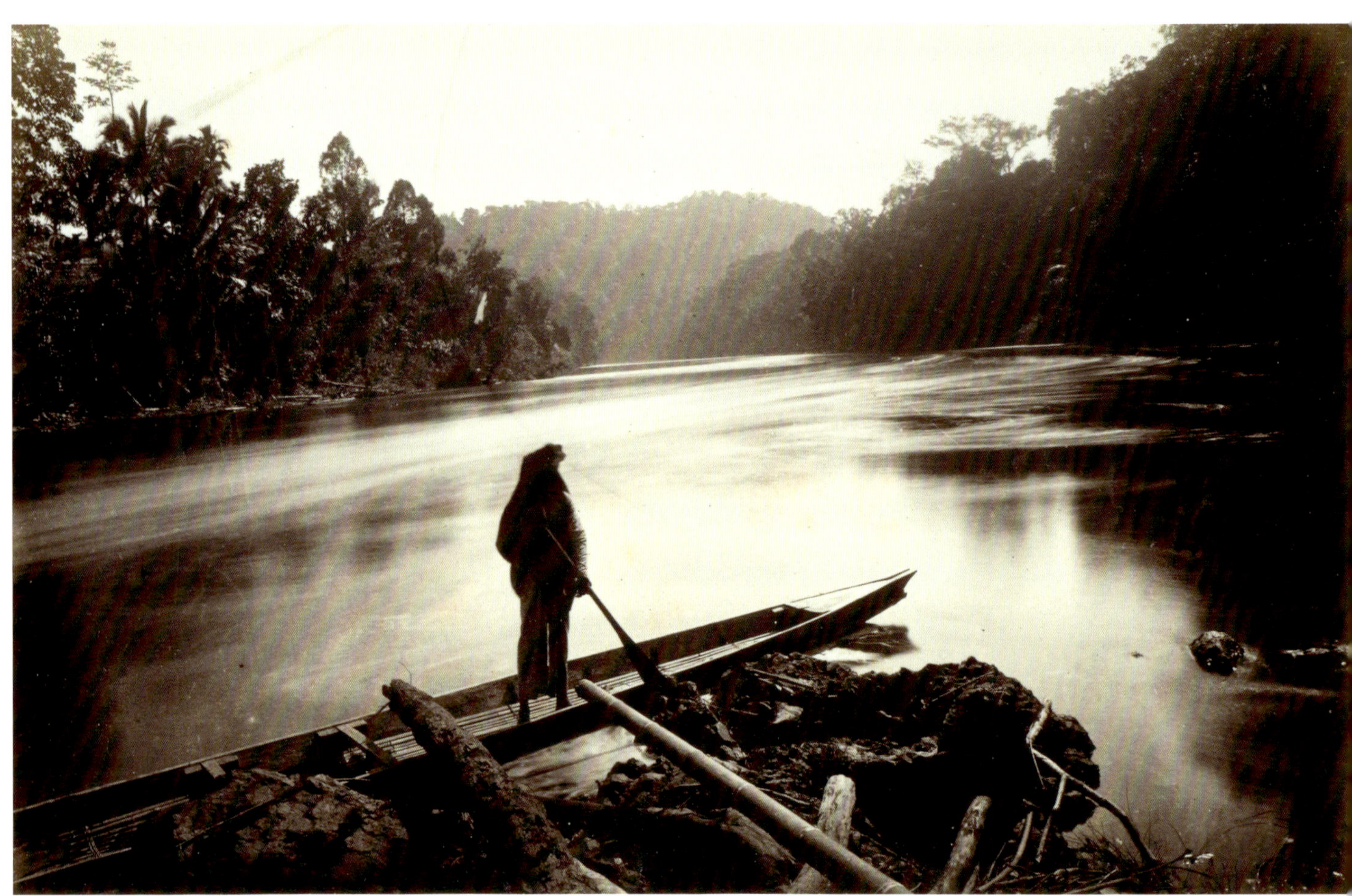

84
Batang Hari River near Gasing, Sumatra
Central Sumatra Expedition 1877–79
Photographer: Daniël Veth (1850–1885)
albumen print
9.5 x 15 cm
60003110. Provenance: unknown

organisation. A number of scientific organisations soon applied to conduct expeditions, one of which was the Royal Dutch Geographical Society (Koninklijk Nederlands Aardrijkskundig Genootschap, KNAG), founded in 1873 partly to contribute to scientific research in the Netherlands East Indies.[143] The society did this by organising expeditions to various regions and by publishing the results of the research in its famous journal: *Tijdschrift van het Koninklijk Nederlandsch Aardrijkskundig Genootschap 1884-1960.* The first truly large expedition set up by the KNAG in the Netherlands East Indies was to Central Sumatra in 1877/79 under the overall direction of Lieutenant-Commander J. Schouw Santvoort. Expedition member Daniel Veth was responsible for the photography, geology and geography. The purpose was to survey and map the catchment basin of the Hari River. Although the expedition was considered a failure it did result in a beautiful album of photographs (Alb. 0600; inv. nos. 60025158–60025185).[144] In total the KNAG organised around 40 expeditions in the Netherlands East Indies, including the final expedition, in 1959, to the Sterrengebergte (Pegunungan Bintang) on New Guinea.[145]

The Society for the Promotion of Research in the Natural Sciences in the Dutch Colonies (Maatschappij ter Bevordering van het Natuurkundig Onderzoek der Nederlandse Koloniën, MBNO) was founded in 1888 in Amsterdam. Melchior Treub, ex-director of the Botanical Gardens, was one of the founders, and because of its long and complicated name, the Institute was also known as the Treub Society. A subsidiary of sorts was established in 1890 in Batavia: the Indies Committee for Scientific Research (Indisch Comité voor Wetenschappelijke Onderzoekingen, ICWO). One of their most famous expeditions, the Siboga Expedition (1899–1900), was led by Professor Max Weber.

THE SIBOGA EXPEDITION OF 1899–1900

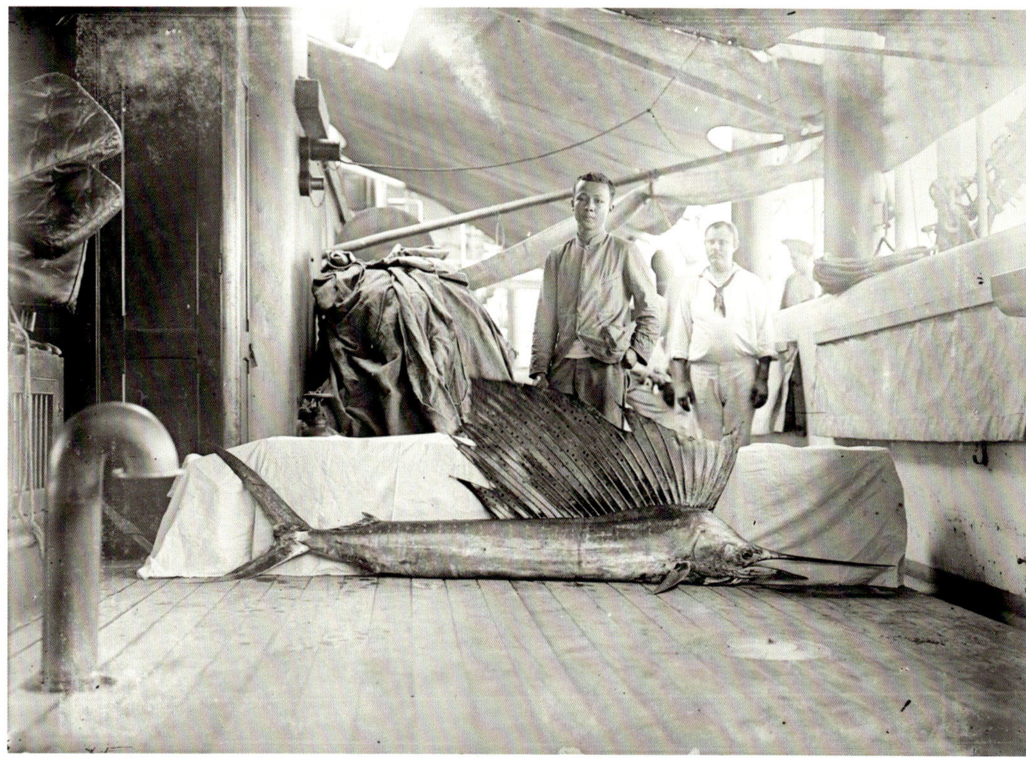

85
Sailfish aboard the
H.M. Siboga, Banda
Photographer: unknown
gelatin glass negative
13 x 18 cm
1899–1900
10006544. Gift: The Society for the Promotion of Research in the Natural Sciences in the Dutch Colonies (MBNO), 1915

In January 1916 a gift of 285 negatives was recorded in the photograph collection's benefactor's book that had come from the Society for the Promotion of Research in the Natural Sciences in the Dutch Colonies (the so-called Treub Society). The intermediary involved in this gift was the zoologist Professor H.F. Nierstrasz (1872–1935) from Utrecht, who participated as the second assistant in the Siboga Expedition in 1899–1900 to the eastern part of the Indonesian Archipelago. The zoologist Professor Max Wilhelm Carl Weber (1852–1937) led the expedition.

The Siboga Expedition was named after the huge, newly built military steamship, the *H.M. Siboga*. The Netherlands Indies Navy (Nederlands-Indische Marine) made the ship available for the duration of the expedition. The ship had to be modified: a laboratory was installed and several devices for use in deep-sea research were placed on board. During the expedition there were 63 passengers: 10 Dutch navy officers, 6 scientists, 45 Javanese sailors and 2 servants.

Of particular interest was the participation of the wife of the expedition leader, Anna Weber-Van Bosse. She was a marine biologist who, in addition to her scientific work on this expedition, published the report *Een jaar aan boord H.M. Siboga* (1904). This report contributed to the Siboga Expedition gaining wide repute among a broad public.

The purpose of the expedition was to conduct research into flora and fauna in Indonesian waters. This happened in the seas separating Borneo and Celebes, the North and South Moluccans Islands and the large and small Sunda Islands (Nusa Tenggara).

Marine animals and plants were collected from the shallow waters lining the coasts and from further out to sea. These were later analysed in reports. The scientific report of this expedition is one of the most extensive Dutch expedition reports in existence, and the negatives from it are still important examples of expedition photography in the Netherlands East Indies. SV

Expeditions were multi-disciplinary undertakings that involved contributions from a variety of experts: biologists, geologists, cartographers, anthropologists and ethnographers. Photography was an important aid in documenting expeditions, and because it was still a specialised pursuit in the mid-1800s, all the equipment had to be taken on the journey: heavy cameras and tripods, numerous glass plates, bottles of chemicals, distilled water and a portable darkroom, of course. Negatives had to be prepared and developed on site. The introduction of factory-made glass negatives at the end of the 19th century, and later, rolls of film, simplified expedition photography to such a degree that it no longer required specialised knowledge. Researchers could already begin their work during the expedition. Scientific journals published special guidelines on how to operate the equipment and take photographs during field research trips.

The Tropenmuseum has a large collection of photographs and negatives from military and scientific expeditions in the Netherlands East Indies. In particular the exploration of New Guinea is richly represented. The collections mostly come from the various participants in the expeditions. The collected objects were donated to the museum and the expedition reports were donated to the Colonial Institute's library.

Physical anthropology and ethnography

A bipartite division occurred within the field of ethnology between physical ethnology and cultural anthropology, which arose partly out of descriptive forms of ethnology. Physical anthropology is the study of physical characteristics of humans; cultural anthropology studies the activities and habits of people in their everyday surroundings.

At the end of the 19th and during the early 20th centuries physical anthropology involved collecting data relating to human physical characteristics such as body length, the shape of the skull, the colour of the skin, eyes and hair, weight and posture. Since Darwin published his theory of evolution, this discipline had been characterised by an approach in which various quantitative data were frequently linked to qualitative evaluation, with the implicit or explicit implication that the white race were at the top of the evolutionary ladder. To identify the differences between people, human remains were collected and people were measured during expeditions. Generally, the expedition doctor performed these tasks, but doctors and medical research institutes also took physical measurements in hospitals or laboratories. Despite this frenzied collecting of data about the physicality of humans and human remains, this research never yielded significant conclusions about differences between humans. In fact, in its 'statement on race', UNESCO scientists declared in 1950 that there are no clearly identifiable differences between the races.

Physical anthropological research in Europe was also politically discredited after the Second World War. In Europe human remains that had been collected from around the world were consigned to museums and university repositories. No further research was done into the measurements.

From 1915 the Colonial Institute also had a separate Physical Anthropology Department, with its own photography collection. The initiator and director for many years was Professor J.P. Kleiweg de Zwaan, assisted by Dr A.J. van Bork-Feltkamp; De Zwaan was succeeded by Professor R.A.M. Bergman.[146] The department was unstaffed from 1953 and was shut down in 1962. No photographs from its collection have been traced yet; they are thought to be lost.

Photography played an important role in physical anthropology: the measurements were photographed and used in further studies, as were the photographs of the different races. It was hoped that this approach would create as rational a classification of human beings as possible.

In the beginning, draughtsmen accompanied the expeditions to make onsite drawings of the locals, frequently resulting in personal interpretations instead of the desired 'objective' representations. What was needed was a method that would create objective portrayals of types of humans. The new medium of photography that became available from 1839 would hopefully satisfy this requirement. Soon, not only draughtsmen travelled with the expeditions but also people who had mastered photography. Early photography was complicated, expensive and time-consuming and draughtsmen were preferred. This changed when cameras and negatives became easier to work with, and by the end of the 19th

86
A Kayan Dayak man during a physical anthropological examination, Upper Mahakam, Borneo
Expedition to Central Borneo under the command of A.W. Nieuwenhuis
Photographer: Jean Demmeni (1866–1939)
gelatin printing-out paper
16.6 x 11.5 cm
1898–1900
60005457, Gift: Jean Demmeni

century photography could no longer be ignored as a way to create portraits of people.

At the time, photography was understood to be completely objective and thus extremely well suited for documenting physical characteristics. However, as we now know, this reputed objectivity was an illusion. People at the time grappled with this supposed objectivity too and sought out ways to ensure that photographs of 'ethnic types' were as true to reality as possible, also so that measurements could be obtained partly on the basis of images. Consequently, special demands were made of the photographers. Insofar as it was possible, they had to portray the subjects – human beings – frontally and in profile, in their natural state and standing alongside a measuring rod. Photographing the subjects without the context of their everyday surroundings was also important, so they were frequently portrayed standing in front of a sheet or a cloth to exclude subjective elements.

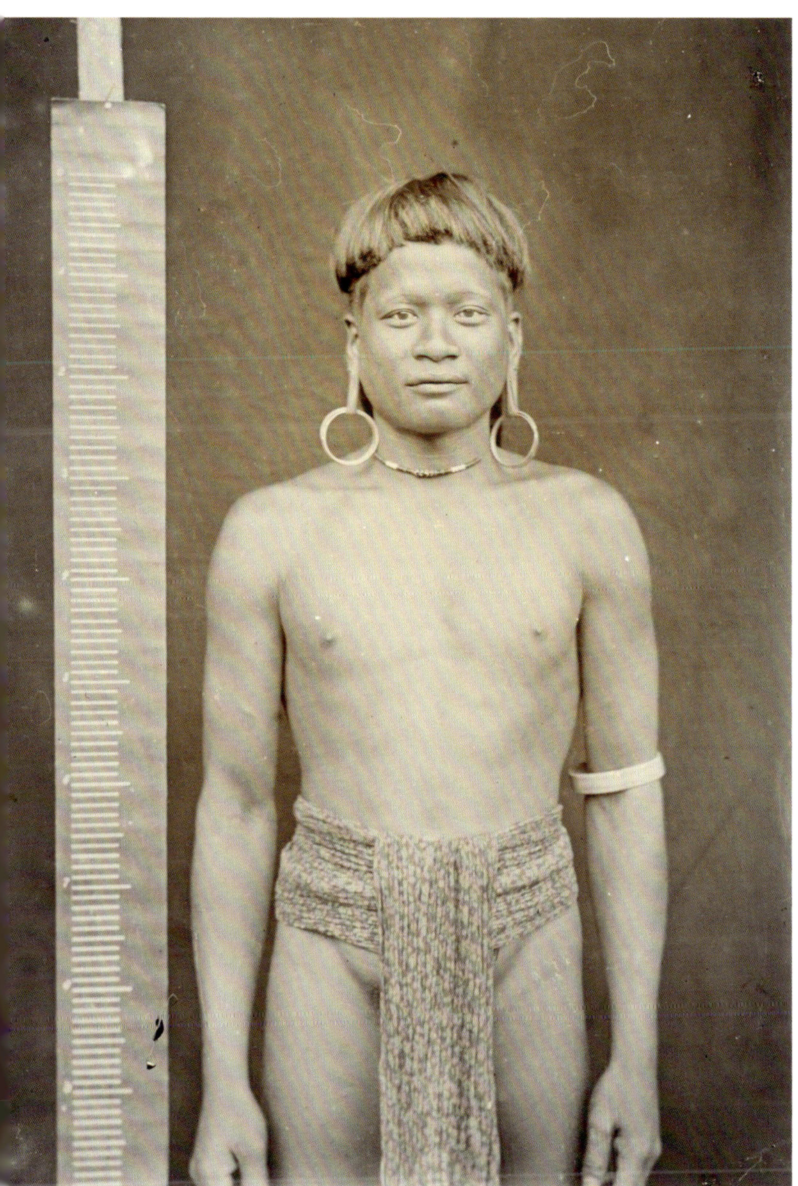

Actually complying with all these guidelines could only occur in a photographer's studio or in a laboratory. This precision was difficult to realise in the field where ultimately most of the photographs were made under difficult conditions. This is why we see all sorts of adjustments on field photographs, from which it can be concluded that although the technical aspects had been mastered, the complicated circumstances disqualified any attempt at spontaneity, compounding the difficulty of creating as objective an image as possible. If no measuring rod could be found, the locals were placed alongside a member of the expedition whose height was known. Anthropologists were continually confronted with human shortcomings when gathering data. They first had to gain the trust of the locals and then wait for as long as it took to receive permission from the community leaders. Photographing women was problematic because they were frequently kept away from the men in the expedition. Of course, the leaders and those who were measured and photographed had to be paid. Moreover, the subjects who were provided for the research were not always chosen by the anthropologist, but by the community. This also contributed to the subjective character of this ostensibly objective science.

Back in the Netherlands, further research was conducted based on the photographs and the records of human measurements. The intention was to use objective criteria to divide the human species into races and (frequently) to attribute a moral or intellectual status based on the alleged superiority of the white race. This smacks of racism now and is considered unscientific. This is also why nowadays this 'tainted' form of photography is looked at askance.

But what should be done with these photographs? That the photographs are of scientific and historical importance is indisputable, but in studying and making them publicly available do we not end up with the same problems that we have with human remains? Should such physical anthropological

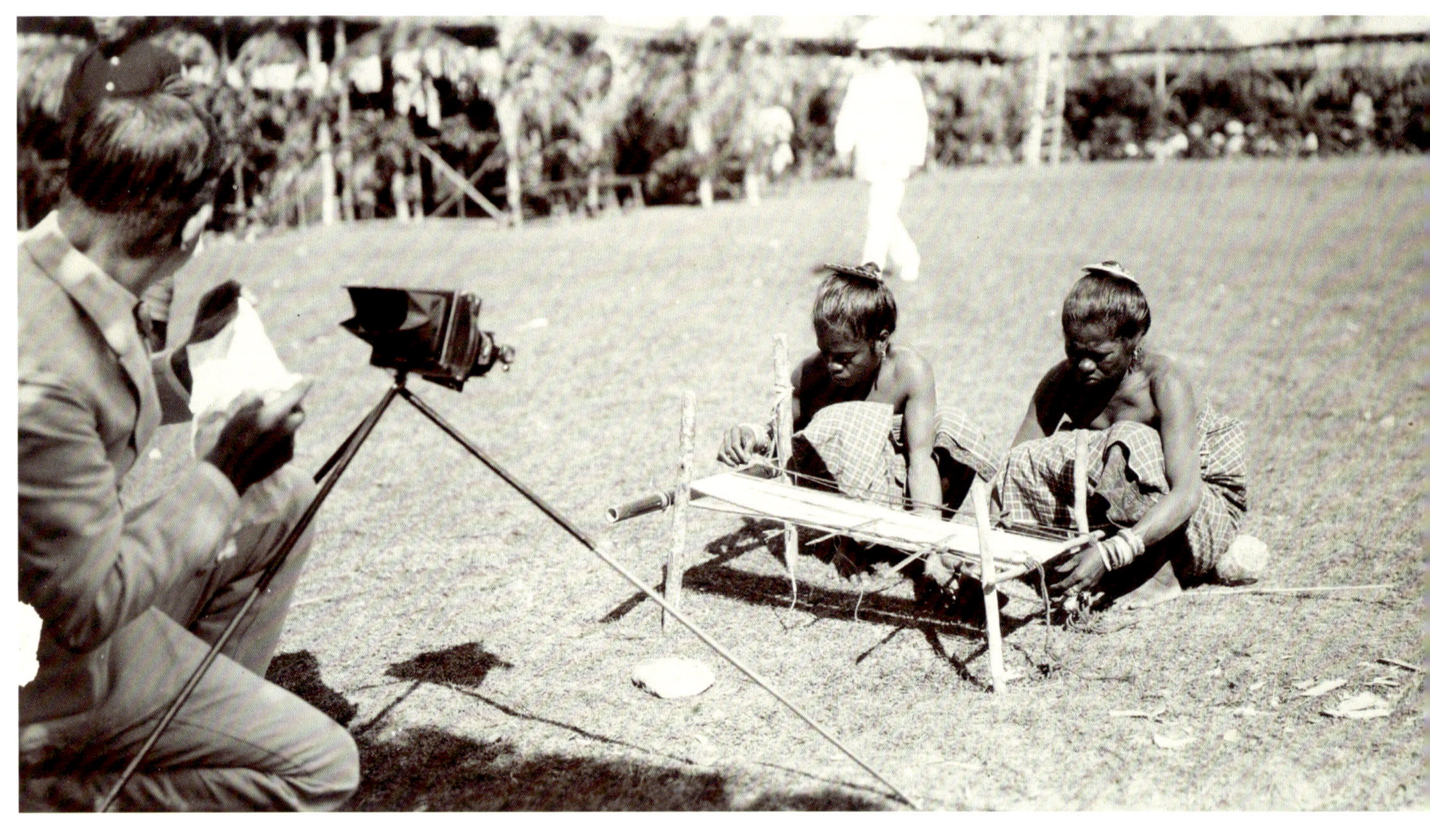

87
Photograph of a man who is making a photograph of two women and their weaving loom at Ende, Flores
Photographer: unknown
gelatin printing-out paper
7.5 x 13.5 cm
c. 1935
60028901. Provenance: via M.J. Hillerström, 1979

photographs, often obtained under dubious circumstances and collected with a specific purpose in mind, be made available online? Should they actually still be made available for research without first asking permission from the people who are portrayed? Perhaps they should be returned, but to whom and in what way? Some museums in Europe would like to remove from public circulation any photographs that 'typecast' people and place them in a research setting that classifies them according to physical characteristics. This is an ethical argument that requires further consideration. While the Tropenmuseum supports this in principle, the museum is still reviewing it's own policies regarding the use of such material. The problem of human remains in museum repositories is not an isolated one; photography plays an important role in this too. In addition to physical anthropological photography, ethnological research also involves photographing human beings in their living environments. During expeditions the cultural-anthropological and ethnographic research was sometimes done by a government official or by a member of the expedition, who conducted the research in addition to his own specialised tasks.

The short duration of an expedition meant that in-depth research was often not possible because a lot of time was needed to conduct observations. Such cultural-anthropological research actually requires living in an indigenous community so that the right contacts and structures can be established, the language can be learned, and most important, trust can be won. Missionaries who frequently lived for extended periods in one specific region engaged in ethnographic and anthropological research as an extension of their religious tasks. Photography was an important aid for the ethnographers; the photographs in many published studies confirm on the one hand that the author had 'been there himself', while on the other they visually augmented the ethnographic observations. Today these photographs are used to not only research the history of the relevant society, but also to understand the interaction and the perspective of the researcher and the camera.

Photography and tropical medicine

88
A member of the medical team of the Batak Institute's hospital (Kabanjahe) inoculating a five-month-old baby against smallpox in Deram, East coast of Sumatra
Photographer: unknown
silver gelatin developing-out paper
10.3 x 14.4 cm
26 June 1928
60017162. Gift: F.S. van Lonkhuijzen, 1966. Former collection J.J. van Lonkhuijzen

The Netherlands originally regarded the Netherlands East Indies as a conquered land that would enrich the Dutch treasury with the funds necessary to rebuild the country after the Napoleonic era. People gradually became aware that they had a moral responsibility (even if this was on their own terms) towards the indigenous population (see Ethical Policy, in the first chapter). This realisation was most evident in the medical sector. Originally, only military doctors were active in the Netherlands East Indies, but the rise of especially plantation farming and industry meant that civilian doctors also started working on location, in particular in the local clinics connected to the plantations. The missionary network also provided the world of colonial medicine with a new infrastructure. The government could not lag behind, and from the mid-1850s a training course was started for medical assistants and vaccinators (the so-called *Dokter Djawa*), which later became a training course for Indonesian doctors (Training School for Native Doctors [School tot opleiding van inlandsche artsen; STOVIA]), and in the 1930s was expanded to become a Medical Academy (Geneeskundige Hogeschool) in Batavia. Research into recurring diseases that exacted a great toll on the local and the European populations – cholera, the plague, typhus, malaria and beriberi – were among the priorities.

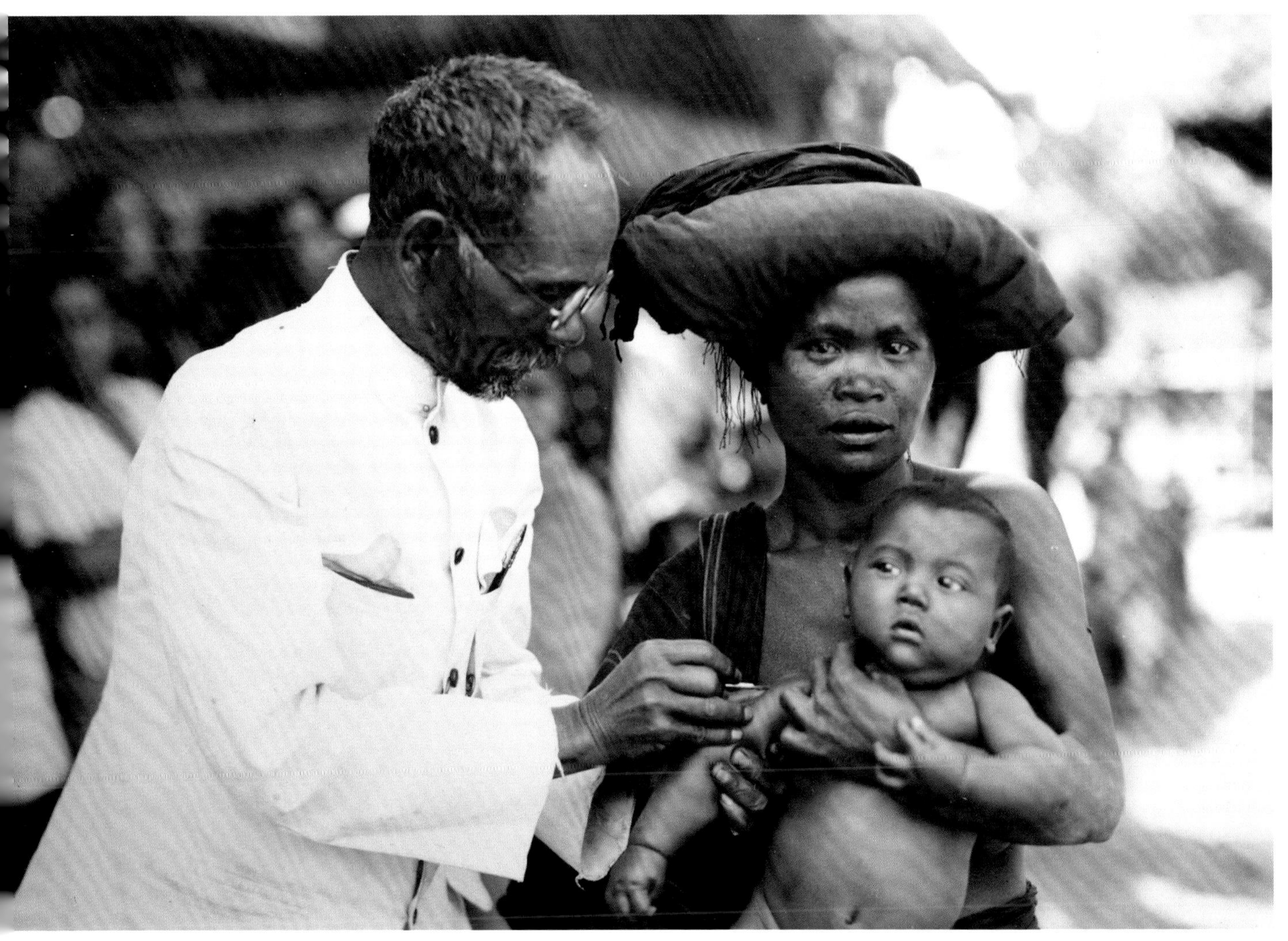

The Pathological Laboratory (later the Laboratory for Pathological Anatomy and Bacteriology) [Pathologisch Laboratorium; later Laboratorium voor Pathologische Anatomie en Bacteriologie] was founded in Batavia to research tropical diseases. Other institutes followed in Medan and Bandung. One of the most important researchers was Professor C. Eijkman (1858–1930) who focused on beriberi, and received the 1929 Nobel Prize for Medicine for his discovery of Vitamin B1. The Eijkman Institute in Batavia – an important research laboratory that still operates in the area of tropical diseases that also had a branch in Amsterdam – was named after him. The results of the research were used by the Civilian Health Service (Burgerlijke Geneeskundige Dienst), founded in 1911 (later the Public Health Service; Dienst Volksgezondheid), which was responsible for providing care and advice relating to tropical diseases and hygiene to the population.

Medical research in the Netherlands East Indies had repercussions in the Netherlands. The Netherlands Society for Tropical Medicine (Nederlandse Vereniging voor Tropische Geneeskunde, NVTG), a platform based in the Netherlands that was concerned with tropical diseases, was founded in 1907. This Society also initiated research into tropical diseases in the Netherlands. Their reasoning was that other Western countries were already busy with this, sometimes in cooperation with colonial partners, and the Netherlands could not trail behind the rest.

The concerns of the NVTG resulted in a research laboratory being set up within the Colonial Institute in Amsterdam. The focus was on disseminating information about tropical diseases and conducting scientific research into hygiene in the Tropics.

89
Anatomy lesson at the '*Dokter Djawa*' School in Weltevreden, Batavia
Photographer: unknown
gelatin glass negative
9 x 12 cm
c. 1915
10002345. Provenance: unknown

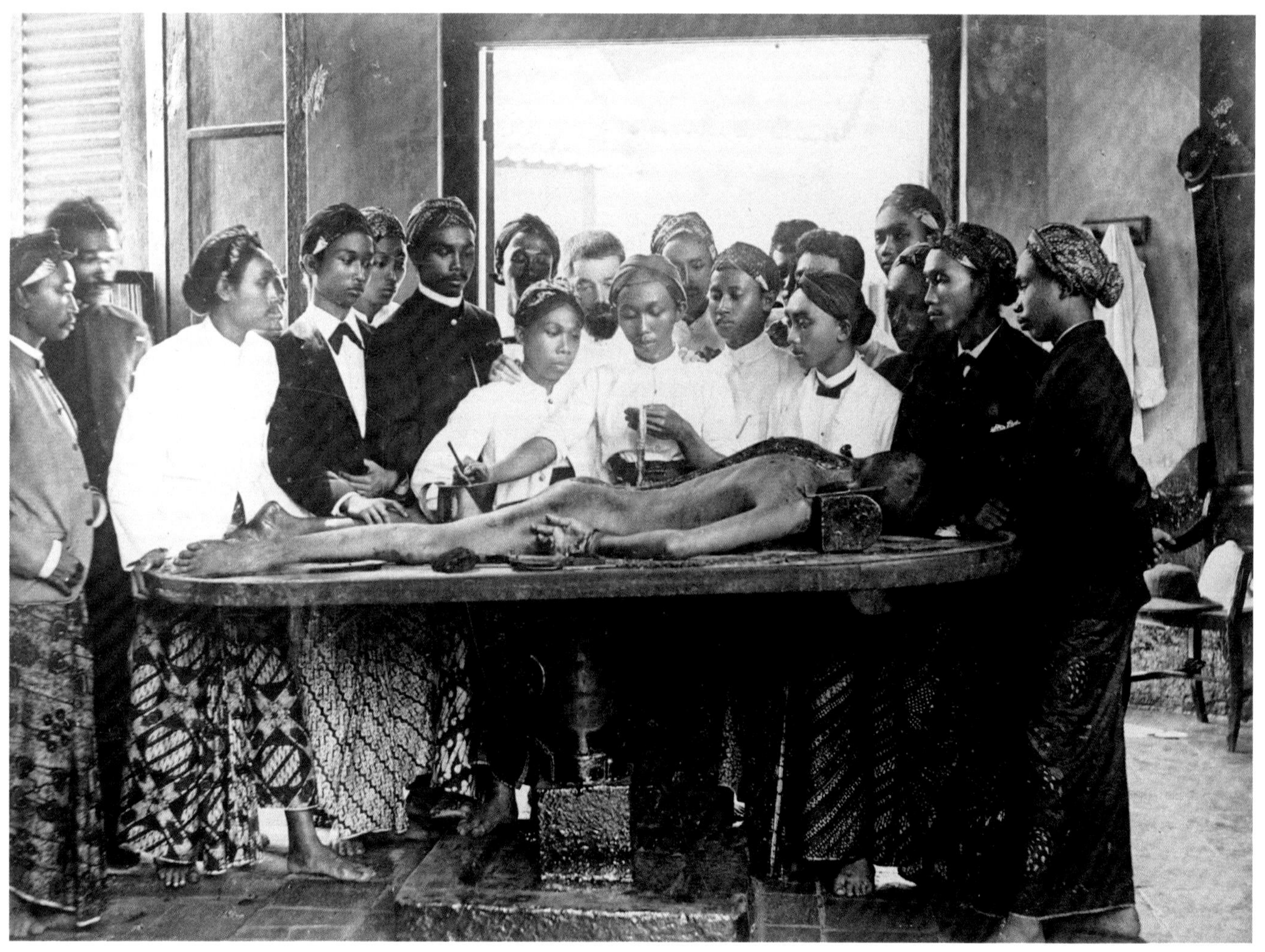

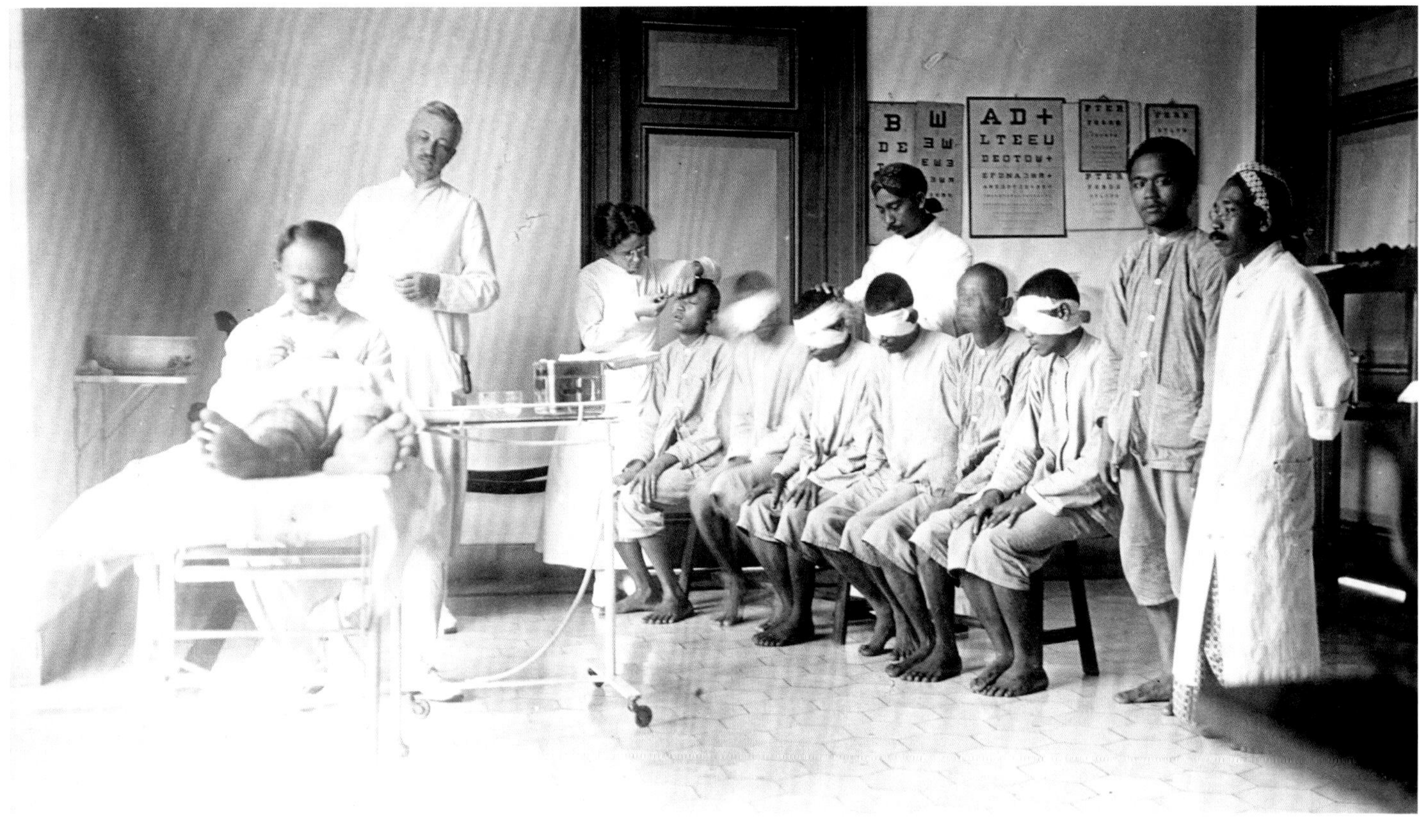

90
The operating room with ophthalmologists and patients in the Queen Wilhelmina Eye Hospital in Bandung
Photographer: unknown
gelatin printing-out paper
8.1 x 14 cm
c. 1920
60014723. Gift: F.S. van Lonkhuijzen, 1966. Former collection J.J. van Lonkhuijzen

Since its founding, this Tropical Hygiene Research Department (now the KIT Biomedical Research Department in the Amsterdam Medical Centre [AMC]) fell under the auspices of the Colonial Institute, but it already had its own building in 1917 on the Mauritskade in Amsterdam, not far from the place where the main building of the Institute was built.
The Department of Tropical Hygiene had its own photography section that was used for medical research and education; most of the visual material came from the Netherlands East Indies, including information about preventing tropical diseases. When the KIT's Biomedical Research Department relocated to the Amsterdam Medical Centre, the photographic collection of the Department of Tropical Hygiene was transferred to the Tropenmuseum photograph collection in the 1990s. It has yet to be categorised and made accessible.

Archaeological Society

For many years, the Batavian Society of Arts and Sciences, founded in 1778, was the 'guardian' of ancient Indonesian monuments such as temples, sanctuaries and statues on Java and Bali. These were overgrown and crumbling in the countryside. The government was completely disinterested, as maintaining them would only cost money. They gladly left the initiatives for research to the Batavian Society and private individuals. On the rare occasions that the government did help, their contribution never really amounted to anything significant. Scientific research into the past was still unimportant. One of the first initiatives, in 1845, was an attempt to photographically document the galleries of the Borobudur in Central Java with the best photographic process available at the time, namely daguerreotypes. The German photographer A. Schäfer was asked to do the work, but the results

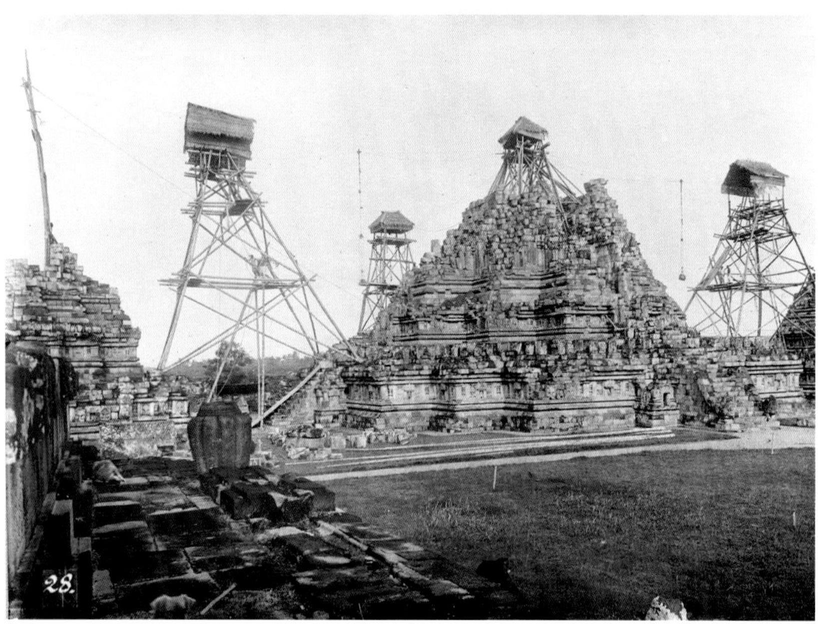

91
Restoration of the Shiva temple on the Candi Lara Jonggrang (or Prambanan temple) complex
Photographer: unknown
gelatin glass negative
9 x 12 cm
1917
10016164. Gift: Archaeological Service, 1921

were disappointing and the project produced only a handful of useable images.[147] Photographic techniques at the time were still too rudimentary to achieve good results, so recourse was made to the draughtsmen. A second attempt at photographically documenting a number of temple complexes was more successful. The photographer Isidore van Kinsbergen published his collection of photographs *Oudheden van Java* in 1872, followed a few years later by his images of the Borobudur. These two series were very successful, and helped to inform the wider public about the antiquities in the Netherlands East Indies. A third series of photographs dates from the 1880s. In 1885 the researcher J.W. IJzerman, chairman of the Archaeological Society in Yogyakarta, chanced upon the so-called hidden base of the Borobudur, a subterranean gallery with reliefs that forms the invisible foundation of the sanctuary. These reliefs were also photographed.

The increasing realisation of the significance of the Javanese and Balinese antiquities and their ongoing deterioration eventually convinced the government that they had to do something before it was too late. Hence, a Commission for Archaeological Research (Commissie tot Oudheidkundig Onderzoek) was created in 1901, which changed its name into the Archaeological Service (Oudheidkundige Dienst, OKD) in 1913. This service surveyed and photographed all the temples and antiquities.

The photographs were categorised and published regularly. The OKD also oversaw in-depth restorations of all the temple complexes and sanctuaries; after independence the Indonesian government continued this programme, with support from UNESCO. The resplendent temples and sanctuaries on Java and Bali are still among the most important tourist attractions.

The photograph collection of the Colonial Museum in Haarlem obtained its first collection of photographs of antiquities in 1894. That same year the Ministry of Colonial Affairs (Departement van Koloniën) in The Hague donated a set of photographs of the Borobudur, including albumen prints of the hidden base that were taken by Kassian Céphas.[148]

In 1900 the Ministry of Colonial Affairs donated a new set of prints made by the photographer Van Kinsbergen for his series *Oudheden van Java en de Borobudur*.[149]

Based in Amsterdam the Photography Department (Fotografisch Bureau) regularly received impressive donations of photographs (in 1915, 1920 and 1922) from the OKD in Batavia, amounting to more than 4500 images. The specially made new prints were glued to cardboard, documented and preserved in folders. They document the OKD period from 1914 to 1922.

Included in the Tropenmuseum's photograph collections, is yet another large set of prints from a later date, documenting the research undertaken at the large Prambanan temple complex in Central Java, led by the archaeologist P.J. Perquin of the Archaeological Service.

In 1921 the Archaeological Service donated a set of 347 photographs of the Borobudur reliefs, taken by N.J. Krom. This set formed the basis for the abovementioned important publication by N.J. Krom and Th. van Erp about the Borobudur reliefs.

THE HIDDEN BASE OF THE BOROBUDUR

In 1885, the engineer J.W. IJzerman, who was tasked with constructing the railway on Java and was an avid amateur archaeologist, unintentionally discovered the 'hidden base' of the Buddhist sanctuary, the Borobudur. Taking the degree of subsidence of the Borobudur into account, he calculated that roughly 300 reliefs were underground. He applied to the Archaeological Society in Yogyakarta for permission to conduct further research. He was not short of ideas when it came to the technical aspects of the investigation. A narrow ditch had to be dug first, so that a few of the reliefs would be exposed. These had to be photographed and then the ditch had to be filled in to prevent subsidence or the collapse of the Borobudur. All four sides could be dealt with in this way. The Archaeological Society in Yogyakarta referred the request to the colonial government, which rejected it. The Minister of Colonial Affairs eventually made 9000 guiders available in 1890. Kassian Céphas (1845–1912), a photographer active in Yogyakarta, received this technically complicated commission in 1890. He worked according to IJzerman's guidelines. There was very little distance between the camera and the reliefs; furthermore, the reliefs had to be cleaned. Céphas took 164 photographs between 1890 and 1891: 160 of the reliefs (one of each relief) and four photographs from each corner to create an overall impression of the hidden base. As agreed, he made fifteen prints of each photograph. Thirty years later the entire series was published in the large, standard work on the Borobudur, *Beschrijving van Barabudur*, by N.J. Krom and Th. van Erp (1920), where it was included as 'relief series O'. Unlike the original glass negatives, only the reliefs are reproduced in the book. Céphas' original photographs, now part of the Tropenmuseum collection,[150] show more of the surroundings.

The meanings of the representations became clear in the 1930s.[151] The reliefs of the hidden base represent passages from the *Mahakarmavibhangga*, a text that explains the doctrine of karma. The sermons are attributed to Buddha and are about the causes and consequences of human actions. Good deeds have good results, but bad deeds produce bad results.
Thanks to efforts of Th. van Erp the original glass negatives became part of the Colonial Institute collection in 1929. JVD

92
Borobudur relief, no. O 109, Java
This relief is located on the northern side of the Borobudur and according to N.J. Krom is derived from sutras 27 and 28 in the *Mahakarmavibhangga* (Great Exposition of the Law of Karma).
Photographer: Kassian Céphas
gelatin glass negative
18 x 24 cm
1890–91
10015846. Gift: KITLV via Th. van Erp, 1929

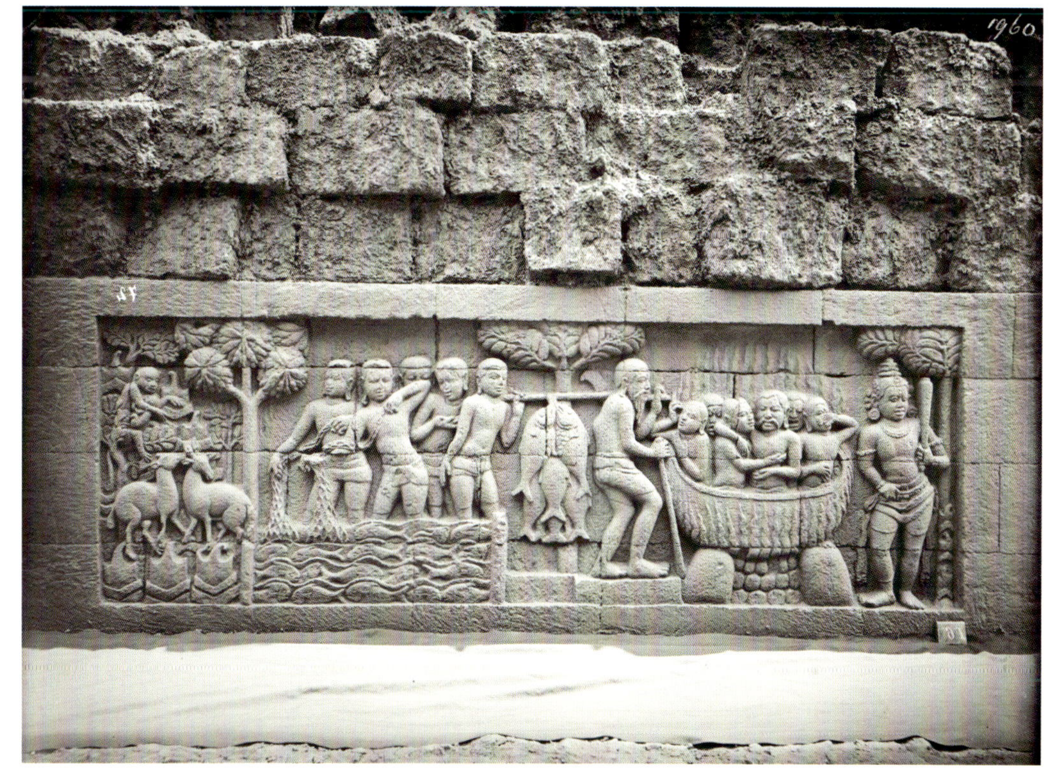

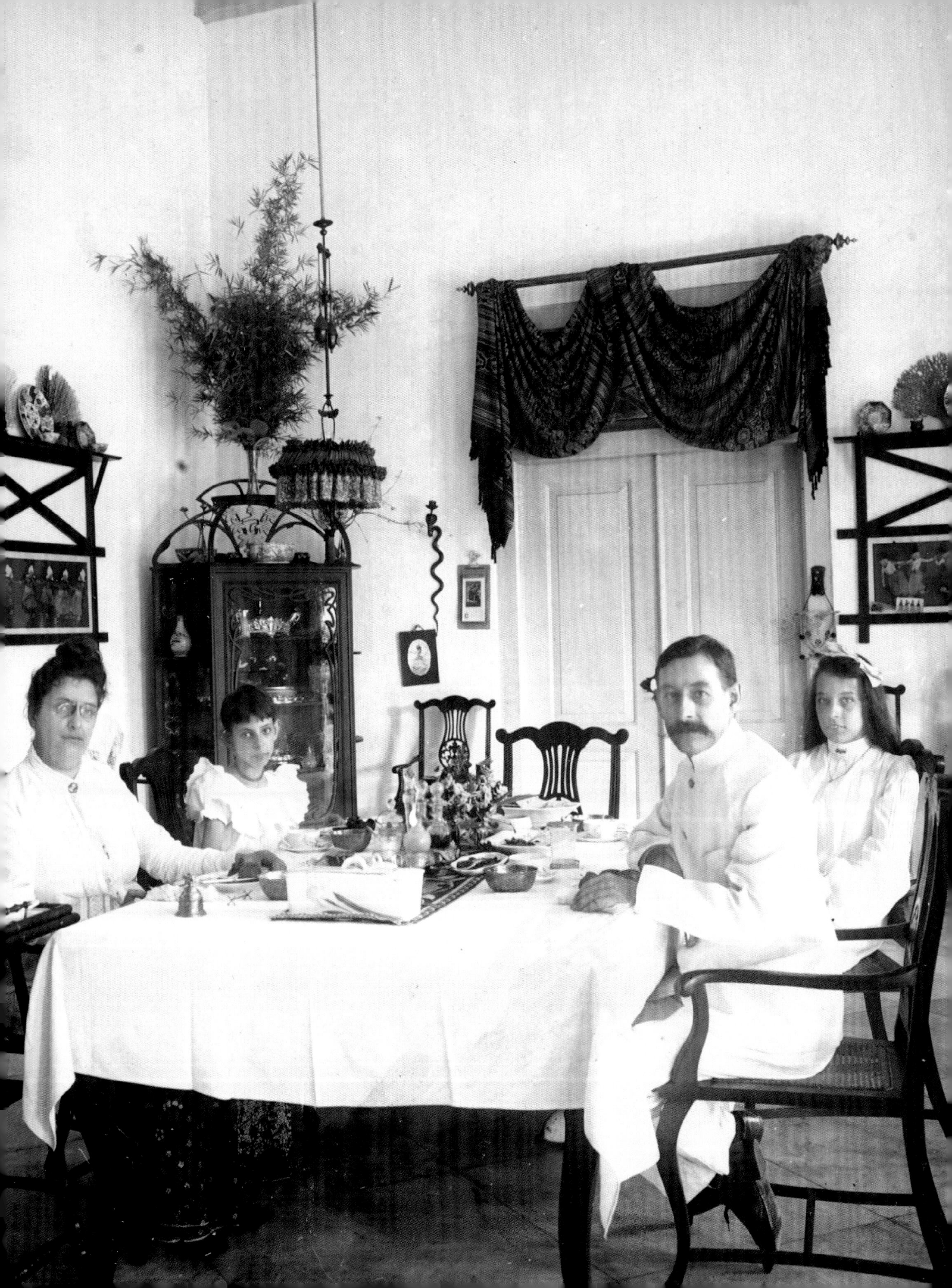

DOMESTIC LIFE

PIM WESTERKAMP

< 93
The Koning family at their dining table on the back veranda, Surabaya
Photographer: unknown
gelatin printing-out paper
13 x 7.8 cm
1902-08
60026752. Gift: S.F. van Musschenbroek, 1985

Introduction

The literature, the many photographic books about the Netherlands East Indies,[152] and the stories about the colonial past might create the impression that all the Europeans in the Netherlands East Indies lived in spacious, cool houses in the midst of large gardens with tall trees. This chapter critically explores this perception by examining the Tropenmuseum photograph collection. How and why were certain houses photographed and others not? What stories are conveyed by the interiors of the houses and the way people were portrayed within them? And what do the photographs tell us about relations between the Europeans and the Indonesians in the private sphere? A large quantity of photographs in the Tropenmuseum's collection depicts European houses, interiors and people in the Netherlands East Indies. These photographs differ markedly, because each period, and especially each island, city or environment, had its own dynamic, demographics and character. After all, the European community was not a clearly definable community,[153] consisting as it did of people who were born in Europe or in the Netherlands East Indies, and who were of European or Indo-European origins.

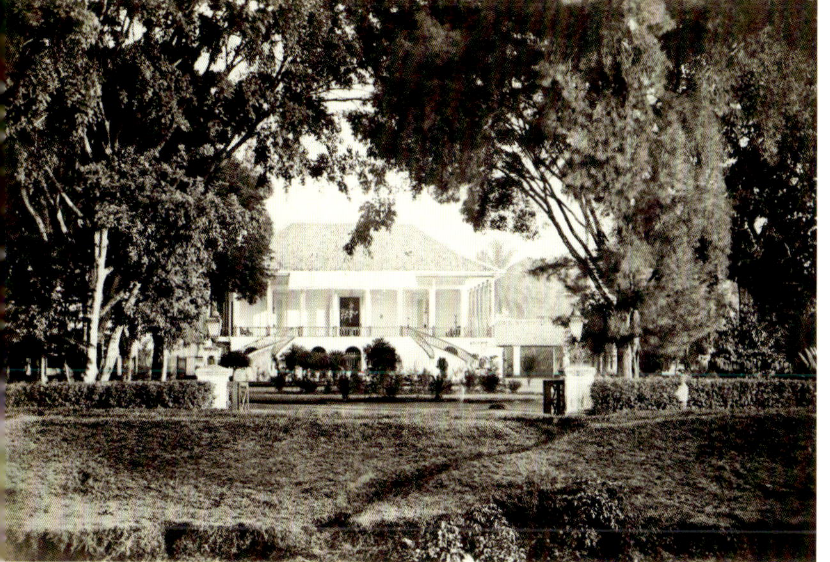

94
Residence of the director of the Health Service, Batavia
Photographer: (attributed to) J.A. Meessen (1836–85)
albumen print
13.5 x 19.8 cm
1867
60036620. Gift: A. Hondius-Crone, 1960

Houses of the elite

The earliest photographs in the Tropenmuseum collection that provides an idea of 19th-century European houses on Java date from around 1870. In that year 27,585 Europeans, 200,000 'Foreign Orientals',[154] and 16 million indigenous peoples lived on Java and Madura.[155] After the Suez Canal opened in 1869 and the Agrarian Act was adopted in 1870,[156] the number of Europeans steadily increased, as did the indigenous population, which meant that population ratios remained more or less equal until the Second World War. Most of the photographs of houses and interiors were originally made by professional photographers and later also by private individuals and were a reflection of how they saw the world around them.[157] Photography in itself was already status enhancing because it was originally an expensive and complicated process that could only be afforded by the elite, be it by hiring professionals or by acquiring the equipment themselves.[158] Most 19th-century photographs therefore portray the houses of the well to do, even though they only made up a very small percentage of the population. These houses appear to confirm the traditional *tempo doeloe* stories about houses in the Netherlands East Indies. The houses, their interiors and decorations, and their outward appearances reflected the status and positions of the occupants. Displaying this prosperity was vital in a society that often ranked education, class and money above ethnic differences.[159] This occurred not only in the outward display of daily life, but also by means of photographic proof. The photographs show the wellbeing of those portrayed, but rarely provide insights into the heat, the boredom, the hardships or other woes.[160] Houses of soldiers, poor Europeans or the indigenous population, do not seem to have been documented at the time. Most of the Asian residences that were photographed belonged to the aristocracy, local rulers or wealthy businessmen.[161] The limitations of 19th-century photography meant that photographing interiors was problematic because of the lack of light, so houses were mostly photographed from the outside.

One of the oldest photographs in the collection was taken in 1867 by the photographer J.A. Meesen and shows an enormous house on Kebon Sirih in Batavia (Fig. 94). It is an early 19th-century, two-storied house.[162] Other well-known studios, such as Woodbury & Page, and Van Charls & Van Es & Co., photographed European government buildings and the houses of the indigenous nobility. G.R. Lambert & Co. photographed plantation houses on Sumatra during the 19th century. With their photographs these studios recorded the prosperity, progress and status of the government, companies and planters. They could be used to attract new European investors and employers. The photographs of plantation houses show the exteriors and front verandas of the enormous stately homes of the general managers or the smaller dwellings where the employees lived. Young employees without a European wife frequently lived with an Asian woman. Because these partners almost never had official status, they were not included in most of these photographs, creating the impression that the community existed only of men.

The photograph on this page shows the impressive residence of the general manager of the Parakan Salak tea plantation in West Java in 1888. That year several photographs were taken of the residence, which Adriaan Holle built for his wife Jans van Motman[163] in 1871. The author Hella Haasse (1918–2011) accurately describes this residence in her book *De Heren van de Thee*,[164] as part of her chronicle of a couple of families who had just arrived from the Netherlands and who became part of a group that dominated West Javanese cultures in the second half of the 19th century.[165] Prior to this, major landowners came from old – especially Indo-European families,

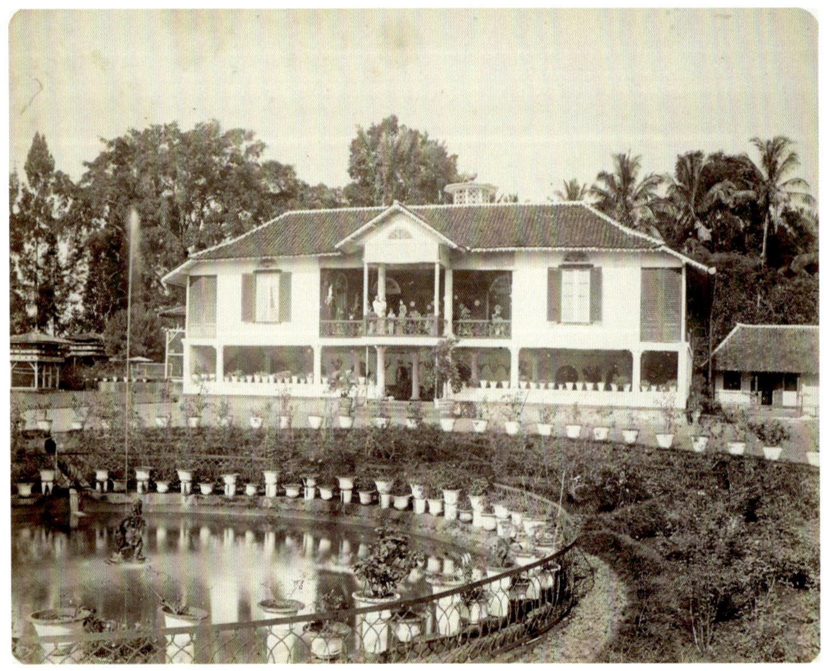

95
General manager's house at the Parakan Salak tea plantation, Sukabumi
Photographer: unknown
albumen print
18.1 x 23.3 cm
1888
60022661. Provenance: unknown

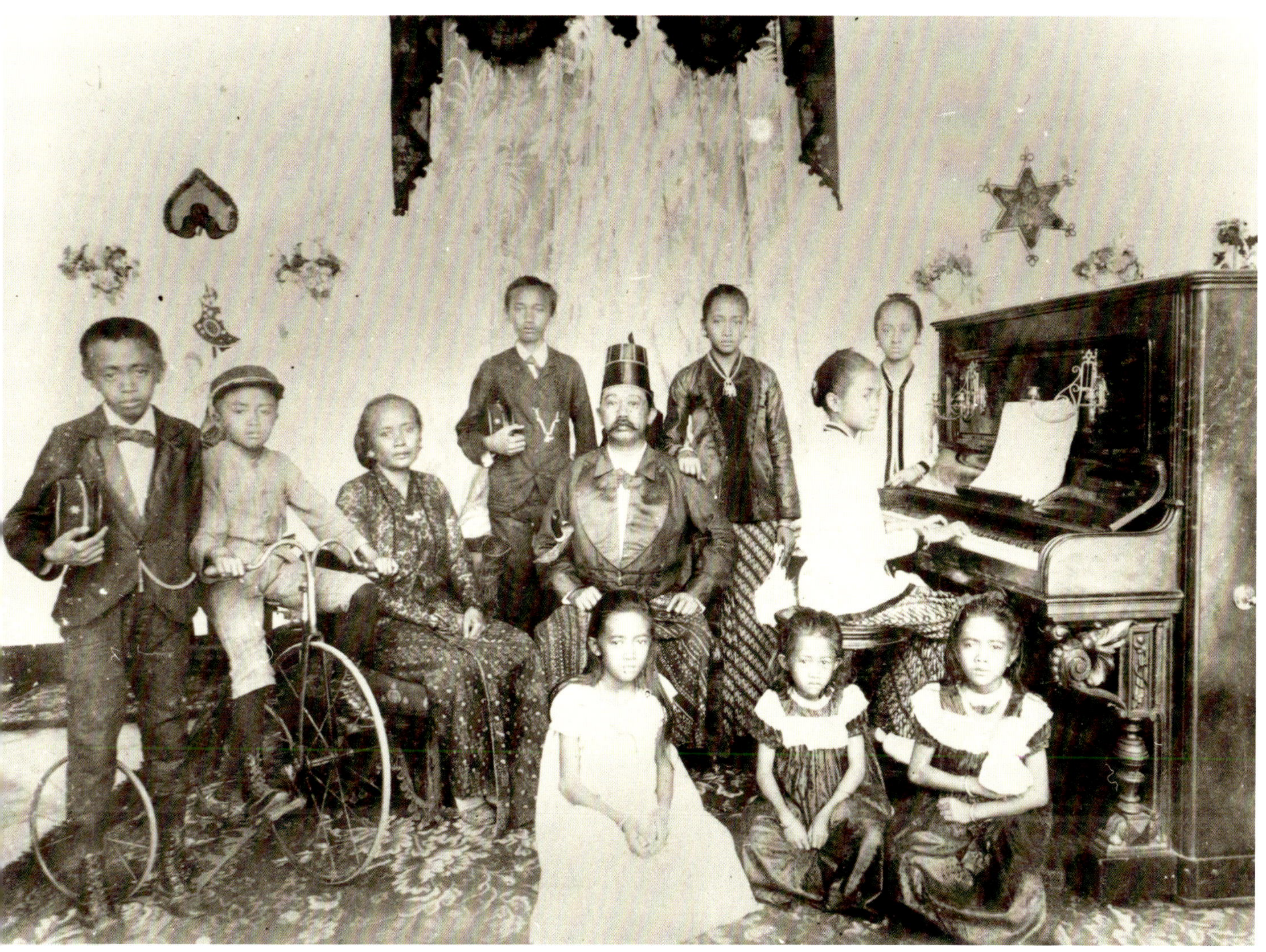

96
R.M.T. Tjokronegoro III, Regent of Blora, with his family, Central Java
Photographer: unknown
silver gelatin developing-out paper
10.7 x 14.7 cm
c. 1900
30999382. Gift: Indo Scientific Institute (IWI), 2006

such as Ament, Van Motman and Van Riemsdijk.[166] Some newcomers adopted aspects of the lifestyles of these old distinguished families, for example, in the architectural style of the houses and how they associated with their servants[167] and labourers. Others tried to preserve the interiors and diet they were used to in the Netherlands.[168] The previously mentioned Adriaan Holle was an exception to this. He played and composed music for the gamelan he kept in his house,[169] and was a close friend of the district chief, Raden Nata di Saga.[170] A photograph from 1888 reveals that he still played the gamelan and that he also had a large set of *wayang* puppets.[171] He was deeply involved with the Sundanese culture, but this could have been prompted by the need to safeguard his business interests, something that occurred frequently.[172] Planters, encouraged by the colonial government, partly emulated the lifestyles of Javanese nobility to gain the respect of the local population. Europeans had to have the same or even higher prestige than the local rulers, and ways to display this included a large house, a gamelan and *wayang* puppets.[173] Another possibly reason for photographing the houses and their interiors was to express this prestige to viewers in the Netherlands East Indies and in the Netherlands. Another obvious reason was recording the moment as a keepsake.

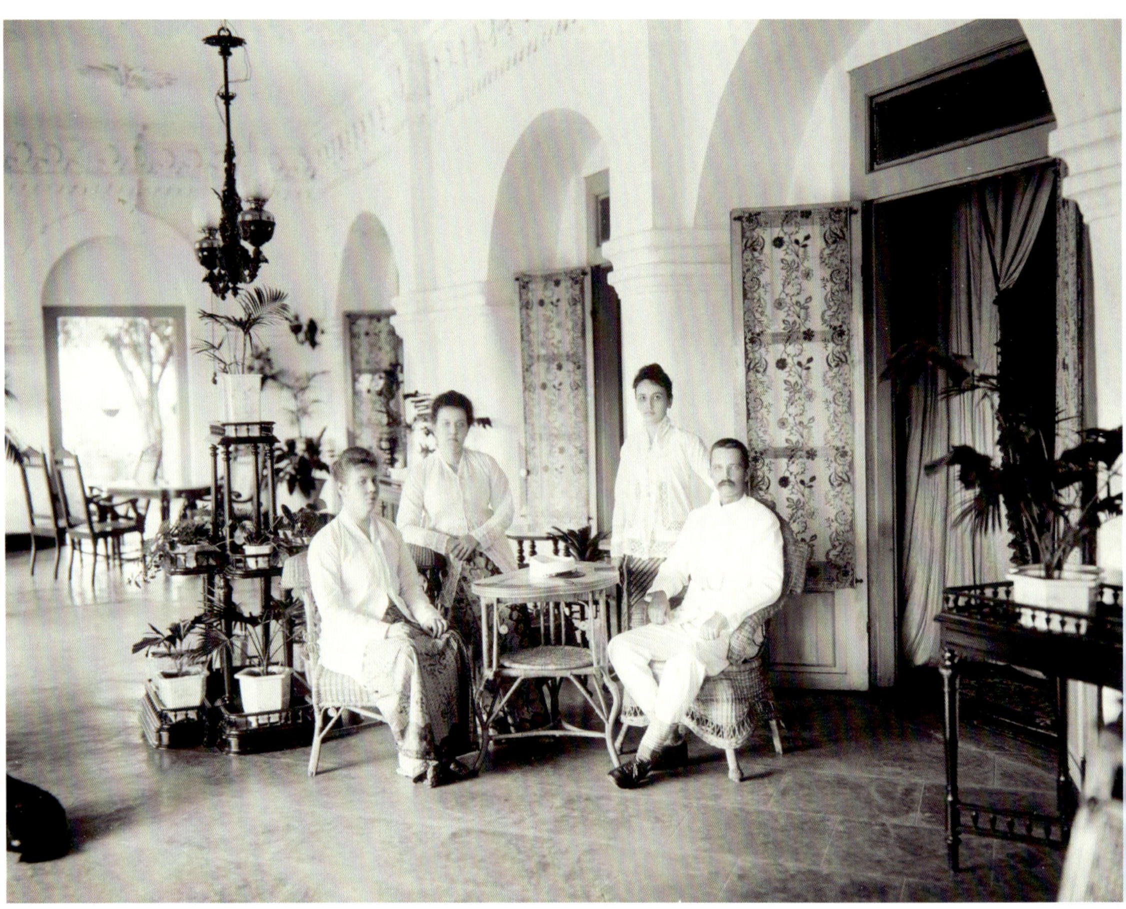

97
Mr and Mrs J.A. Pietermaat with the Boes Lutjens sisters on the front veranda of the house belonging to the general manager of the Kalibagor Sugar Factory
Photographer: unknown
gelatin printing-out paper
18 x 23.4 cm
1905
60004378. Gift: K. Pietermaat-Soesman, 1929

Javanese aristocrats had associated with Europeans since the 17th century, and members of these noble families were granted easier access to the European education system from the second half of the 19th century.[174] Partly as a result of this, they also introduced European elements into their homes, and adopted European clothing and lifestyles to display their 'progress' and modernity and to safeguard their interests as well.[175] The family of the Regent of Blora, Raden Mas Toemenggoeng Tjokronegoro III, is one such example. In the photograph of him with his family, his three oldest daughters are wearing Javanese clothing, one of them is playing the piano, all of his sons are wearing Western attire (one is sitting on a bicycle), and his three youngest daughters are all dressed in European clothes.[176] This shows that the lines of separation between the various ethnic groups were not always that clear-cut. Material differences between privileged Europeans and the well-to-do indigenous population were sometimes indiscernible.[177]

Lay out of the houses

In the second half of the 19th century European houses had roughly the same floor plan: a front veranda, an inner gallery and a back veranda.[178] This type of architecture, known as the *colonial style*, frequently included large classical pillars and huge verandas.[179] Many of the photographs depict these different spaces. The front veranda was large with tables and chairs placed to the left and right. This was a public space where the family received morning guests dressed in sarong and *kebaya*.[180] The front veranda usually had a doorway leading to the 'office', the domain of the master of the house, where he would work, study or receive business callers. This could be a throwback to the 18th-century custom when men socialised at the front of the house (public space), with the women at the back of the house (private space).[181] Another door, usually in the centre of the veranda, led to the inner gallery. This was the family's private space, with comfortable chairs, frequently a piano, display cabinets and sometimes a small desk for the lady of the house. The walls were decorated with paintings, prints, photographs and Chinese porcelain plates. Doors to the left and right led to the bedrooms, with the entranceway to the back veranda at the far end. Furniture there included a dining table and the ubiquitous sideboard. There was also a table and chairs where the family could relax during the evenings. This space was strictly private terrain, especially in older houses. There was a separate annex behind the house for the kitchen, the toilet, the bathroom and the servants' quarters.

The interiors

Most of the interior photographs discussed here date from the last decades of the 19th century and although the photographers are mostly unknown, it could be assumed from their composition and styling that the majority of the early images were made by professionals. Sometimes the massive and luxurious furnishings in the living rooms overwhelm the space. The occupants are not included in most of the photographs, and if they do appear, they are usually posing on or in front of the front veranda or at the dining table on the back veranda.

What impressions do the photographs convey regarding the interiors and design of these houses, many of which had a lot in common? Most photographs show a hybridisation of styles and objects. Some houses were organised and decorated in true 'Dutch' fashion, with nothing to suggest a life in the Netherlands East Indies.[182] Other houses incorporated elements from local cultures, with the familiar 'Beautiful Indies' ('Mooi Indië') style paintings,[183] Javanese batiks with *wayang* figures, Sumba cloths, a gong, copper Javanese bowls and indigenous weapons hanging on the walls, VOC furniture or small Javanese cupboards and side-tables.[184] These could share the space with Dutch paintings and memorabilia. The variety of interiors thus shows a blend of European, colonial and Indonesian furniture, utility wares and art.

98
The inner gallery of the D.A.P. Koning family villa, Surabaya
Photographer: unknown
gelatin printing-out paper
17.2 x 23.2 cm
1904–14
60025777. Gift: S.F. van Musschenbroek, 1985

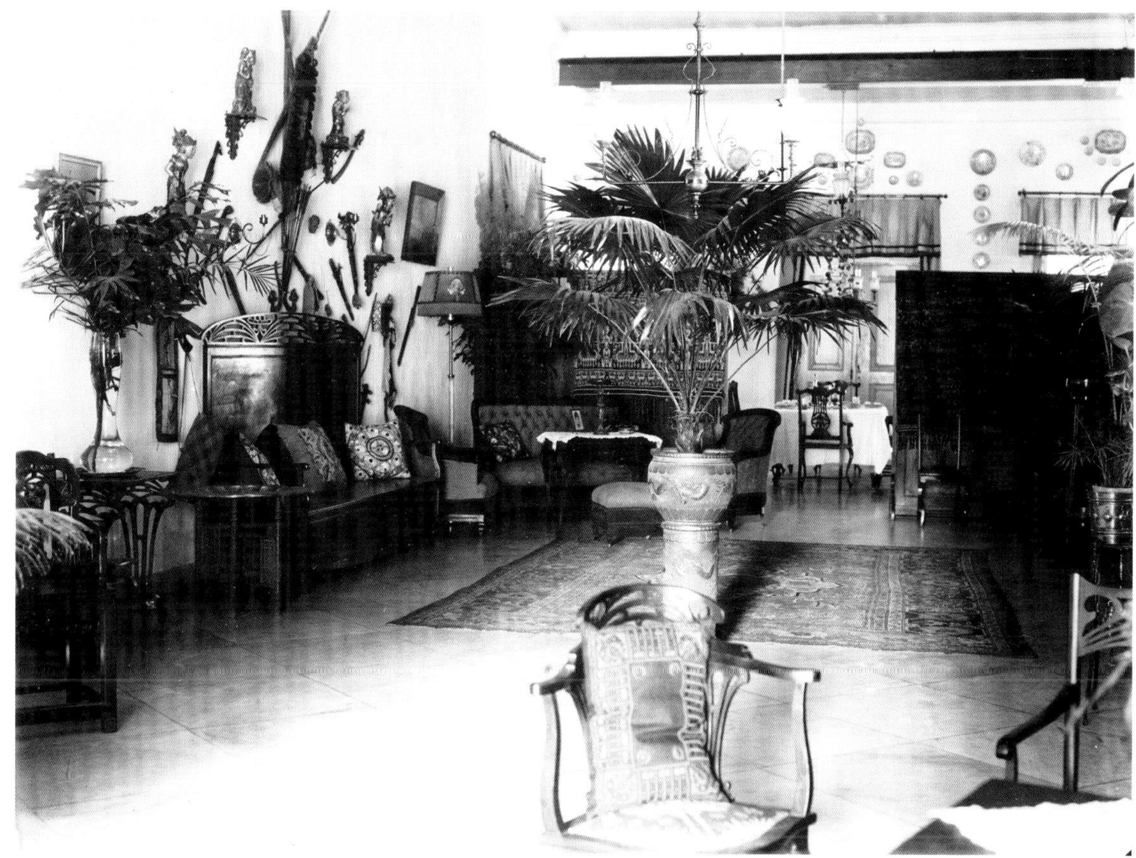

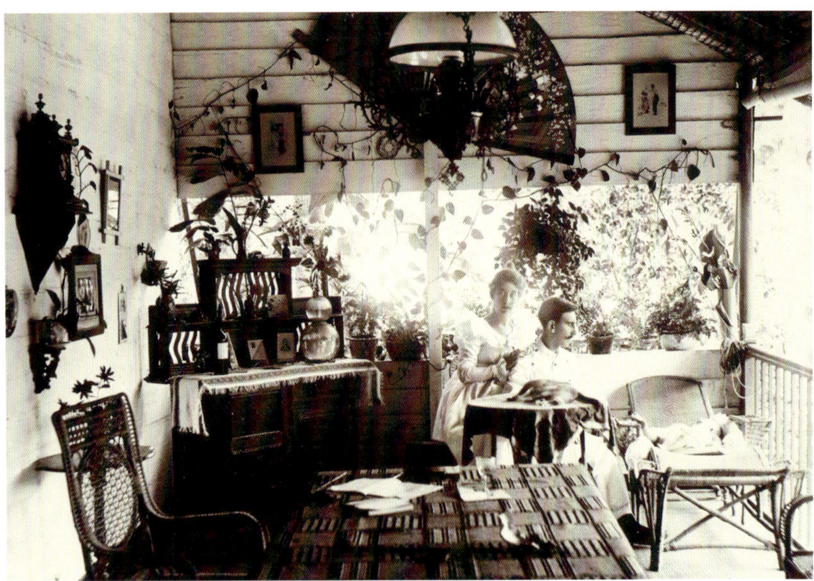

99
Johan Kunst and his family on (possibly) the back veranda of their house, Medan
Photographer: unknown
silver gelatin developing-out paper
11 x 15.8 cm
1899
60026520. Gift: M. Müller, 1984

The choice of furnishings depended on several factors: taste, status and family history – the higher the status, the larger the house. The longer a family had lived in the Netherlands East Indies, the more colonial their lifestyles could be. Because of the many transfers to other posts, only personal objects were taken along, and families sold their furniture and other household effects at public auctions, the so-called *lelang*.[185] Newcomers purchased their requirements at such auctions, resulting in interiors often becoming mish-mashes of different styles.
One thing is certain: houses of Indo-Europeans families did not always have 'hybrid' interiors and newcomers from Europe did not always arrange and decorate their houses in purely European style.
This is evident from, among others, the houses of the Vlissingen-born director of the Dutch Navy Institute (Marine Etablissement) in Surabaya, D.A.P. Koning, who lived in two residences at the beginning of the 20th century.[186] In all likelihood he hired a photographer to make pictures of his houses.[187] They contained elements that frequently recur on photographs of other interiors. On the one hand these are the little Dutch windmills, Frisian bracket clocks and spoon racks, and paintings of pastures with herds of sheep and prints of dancing farmers and their wives in the style of Rie Cramer, as seen in the Koning family's dining room (Fig. 93).

The same print of dancing farmers also appears in a photograph of at least one other interior.[188] However, Koning also collected an enormous quantity of Indonesian objects. Balinese statues on plinths lined the walls in the inner gallery, Sumba cloths were draped over folding screens, a copper Palembang lamp hung from the ceiling and he had a collection of swords from Borneo and elsewhere hanging on the wall. A collection of spears decorated the wall near the Bechstein grand piano.[189] Other interiors also have similar cloths, weapons and lamps. These types of objects appear to have been especially popular and were sold in shops and by travelling vendors.[190]
Not every house was lavishly furnished – people who were just embarking on their professional careers lived more modestly. The veranda of the house of Johan Kunst – who, as a young man, was just starting his career in 1899 – in Medan was simply decorated compared to those of the larger houses.

Houses and servants as status

As stated previously, photographing houses and their interiors had a status-enhancing effect.
The photographs imply that there was a specific 'traditional' way that well-to-do Europeans, as well as prominent and wealthy Asians, had themselves and their houses photographed.
An example is the very early photograph from 1858 of Mrs Johanna Junghuhn-Koch, who is depicted with some her female servants who are seated on the ground. The way the seated servants are arranged is reminiscent of an 1867 portrait of the wife of Raden Mas Toemenggoeng Tjondronegoro, the Regent of Kudus. She sits surrounded by the wives of lower-ranking local rulers and servants. As mentioned, Europeans borrowed some aspects of the etiquette (including with their domestic staff), lifestyles and houses from the examples set by Javanese nobility.[191] Later, the servants in the photographs no longer sit on the ground, but are placed behind the Europeans. Showing the owners in front of their house with their servants and sometimes a carriage had also been widespread among Asian families. Servants in the photograph are shown serving drinks or food, their presence enhancing the status of the Europeans.

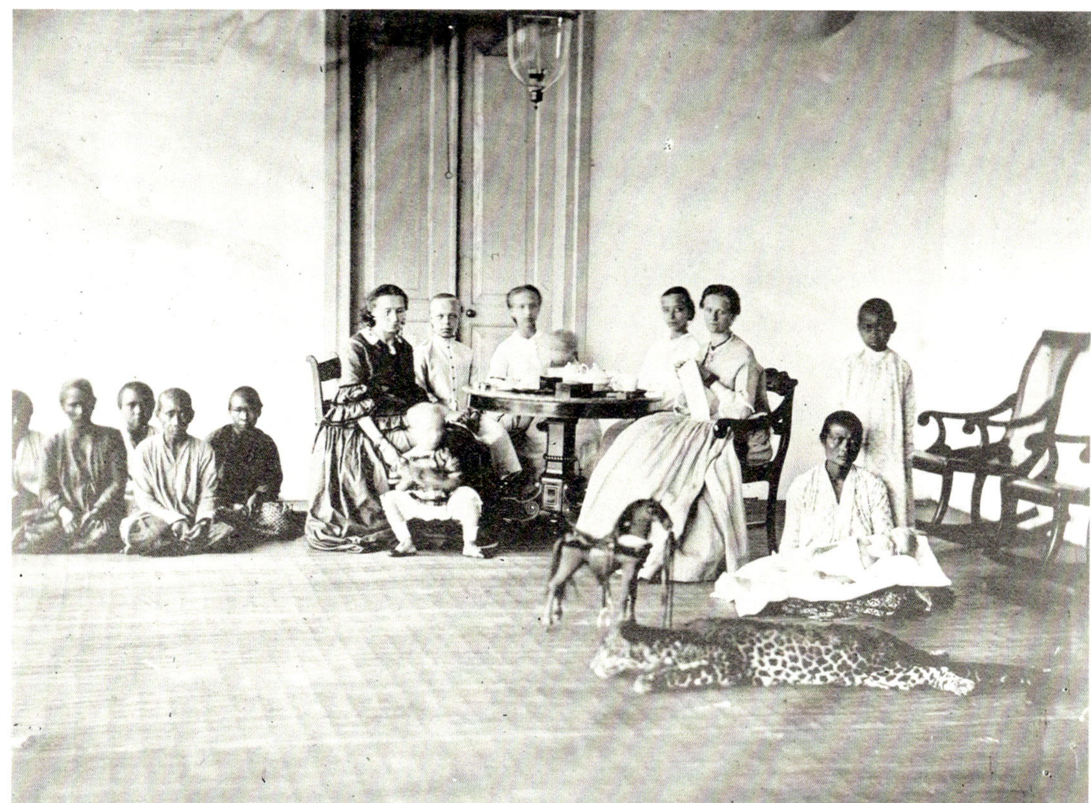

100
Junghuhn family, Lembang, Java
Photographer: unknown
gelatin glass negative
9 x 12 cm
c. 1858
10018738. Provenance: Junghuhn

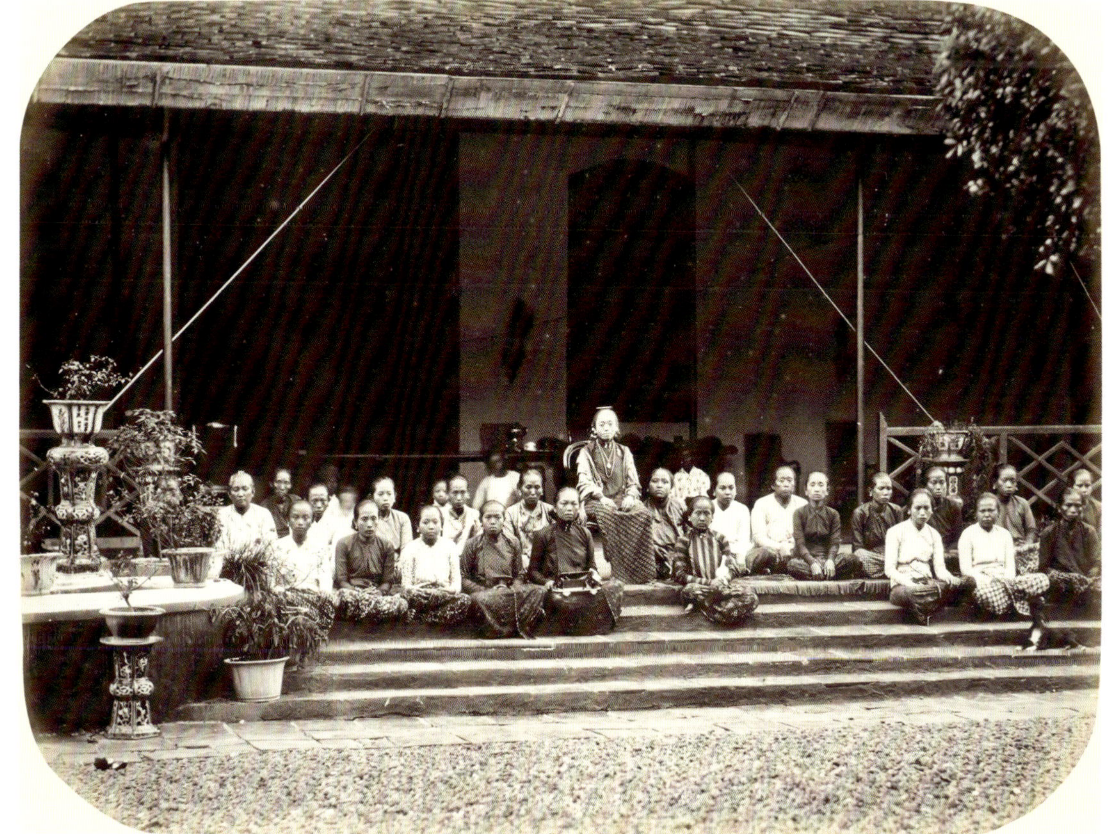

101
The wife of Raden Mas Toemenggoeng Tjondro-negoro, Regent of Kudus
Photographic Studio: Woodbury & Page
albumen print
17.8 x 23.7 cm
1867
60005224. Provenance: unknown

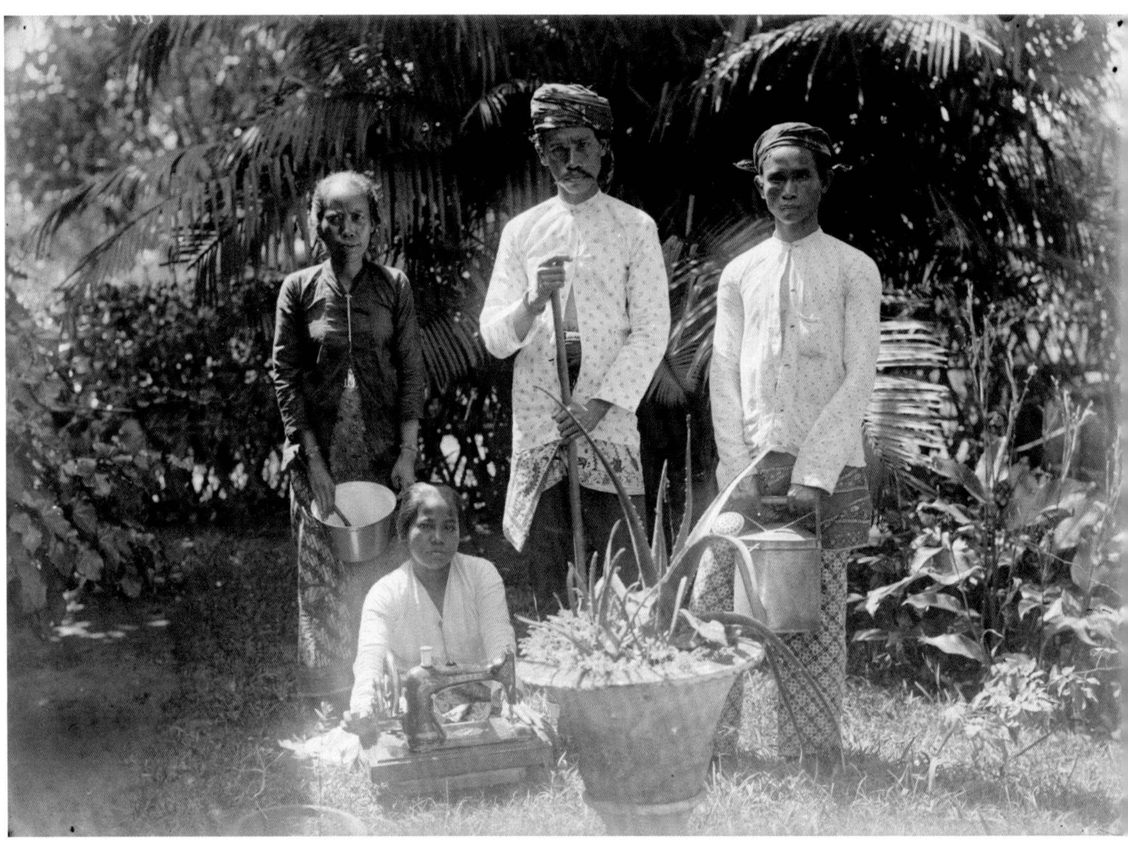

102
Four servants, West Java
Photographer: unknown
gelatin glass negative
13 x 18 cm
c. 1920
10013917. Gift: J.W. Hissink, 1927

103
Woman with a cook in the kitchen, Java
Photographer: unknown
gelatin printing-out paper
11 x 8.1 cm
c. 1925
60029842. Provenance: via M.J. Hillerström, 1979

Some Europeans had photographs taken of their servants either individually or in groups, a practise that affirmed status and prestige, as had happened earlier in paintings.[192]
To make their functions clearer, some were photographed holding objects that denoted their tasks in the household and indicated their rank: the cook, the seamstress, the house boy and the gardener.[193] The greater the number of servants, the more specialised their tasks. The most important among them were those closest to the family because of their work, such as the nanny, the cook and the houseboy. In the 17th and 18th centuries the lady of the house and the female slaves frequently had a close relationship.[194] This changed in the 19th-century colonial society, after slavery was officially abolished in 1860.[195] In the early 19th century most of the European women in the Netherlands East Indies were still being born there and could communicate in the local languages. After 1870 the number of people born in Europe increased rapidly and there were closer ties with the Netherlands. Households and lifestyles became increasingly European.[196]

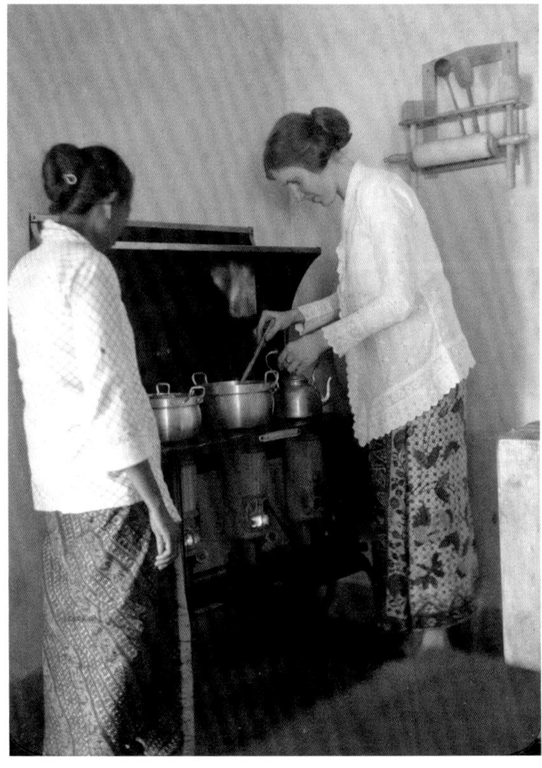

Housewives, especially those who had moved to the Netherlands East Indies after attending the special courses about life in the Tropics, were sometimes trained to educate their servants in Dutch standards of cleanliness.[197]

The lady of the house thus taught her staff how to cook Dutch food, and wash and iron clothes. Cleanliness was all-important and servants had to learn how to maintain it. Real involvement and familiar relationships with the servants were less widespread at this time.

Impoverished population

The photographs described and illustrated above especially reflect the lifestyles of the privileged upper class. The prosperity that these houses and their interiors evoke was not available to everyone. Some sections of the European population, 'pure-blood' Europeans or Indo-Europeans, were also poor and had to live in tiny, inadequate houses.

The only photographs in the collection that depict the wretched circumstances of a number of Europeans were taken by the pharmacist Hendrik Tillema (1870–1952) in Semarang. Their houses were comparable to those of poor Indonesians, something that damaged the prestige of the Europeans that the government wanted to project. A report on this poverty appeared in 1902.[198] That only very few photographs are known that depict these circumstances confirms the assumption that photographs of houses were primarily made for the elite and that they mainly had to affirm the prestige of the Europeans.

This is not that exceptional, because the domestic life of Indonesians was likewise rarely photographed. Most photographs are of the houses of rulers or rajas, with the occupants dressed in traditional attire and holding weapons. These photographs were made to record the culture: houses, clothing, jewellery, weapons and an occasional musical instrument. Such photographs were not made for the benefit of the local people, but were primarily intended

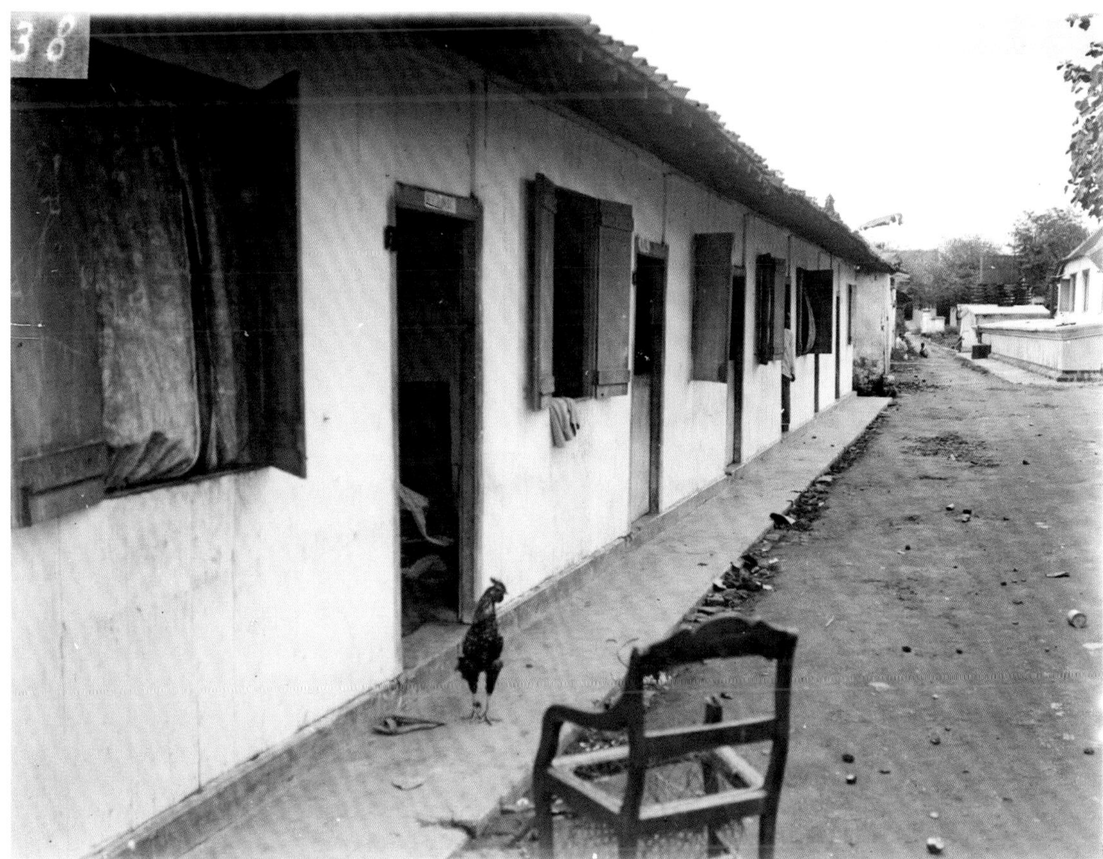

104
Terraced houses for Europeans in Semarang
Photographer: Dr H.F. Tillema (1870–1952)
gelatin glass negative
9 x 12 cm
1905–15
10014777. Gift: Dr H.F. Tillema, 1916

105
Interior of a Karo Batak house, the house of *Sibayak* Pa Mbelgah at Kabanjahe
Photographer: Tassilo Adam (1878–1955)
gelatin glass negative
9 x 12 cm
1914–18
10013608. Gift: Tassilo Adam via Dr. Hamberisser, 1921

to document ethnographic and ethnic differences. The locals lived in wooden or bamboo houses, which were simple compared to European standards. The dark interiors of their houses were much more difficult to photograph so additional equipment had to be used when photographing them. Because photographs in these local houses were made with very brightly burning magnesium flash powder, people in the photographs often have tightly shut or wide open eyes. The photographs rarely provide a spontaneous impression of domestic life. They confirm the distance between the presumed 'simple, underdeveloped and primitive' Indonesians and the 'prosperous, developed, orderly and clean' Europeans. Furthermore, the photographs of the local population confirmed for the European elite their own prosperity, modernity and superiority.

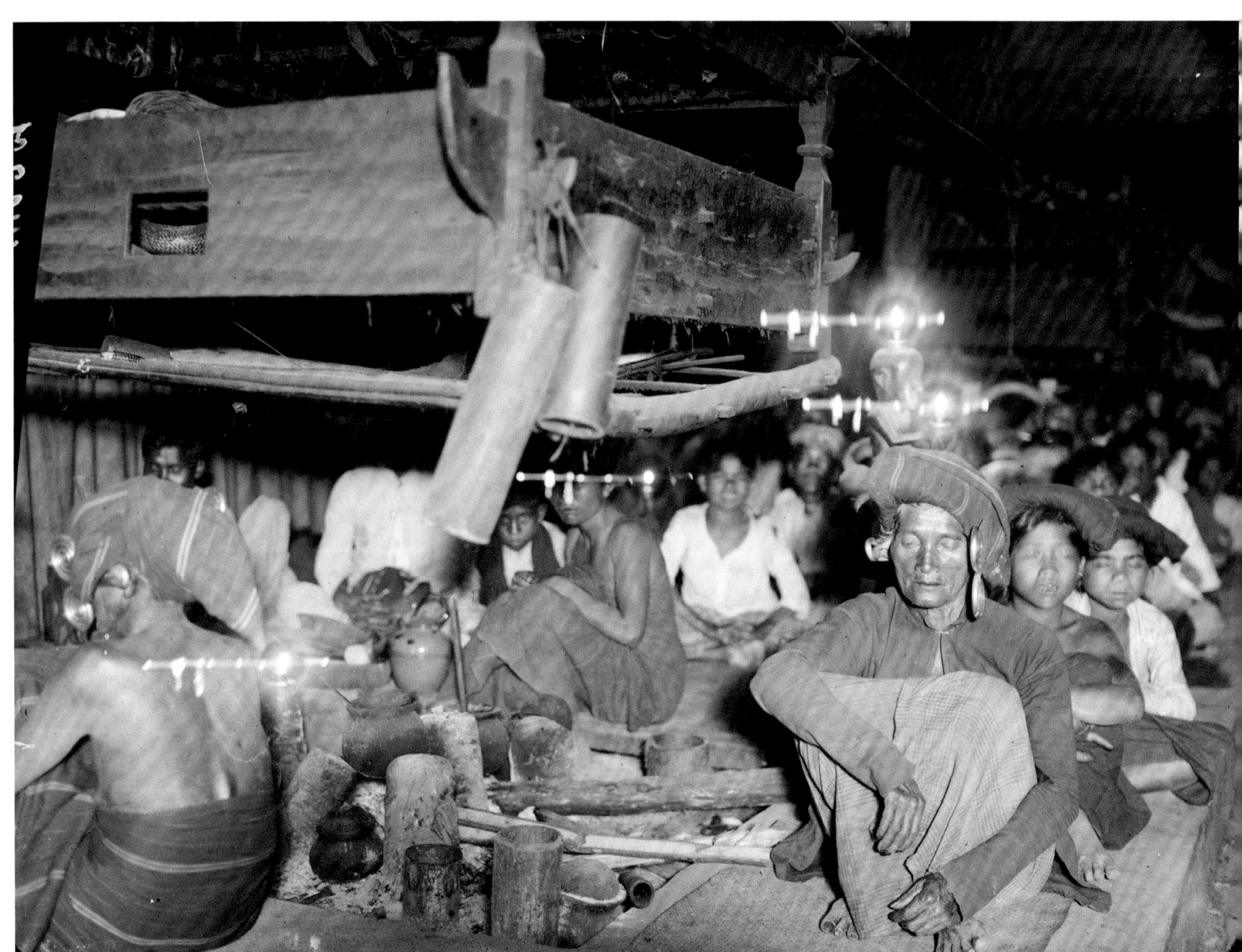

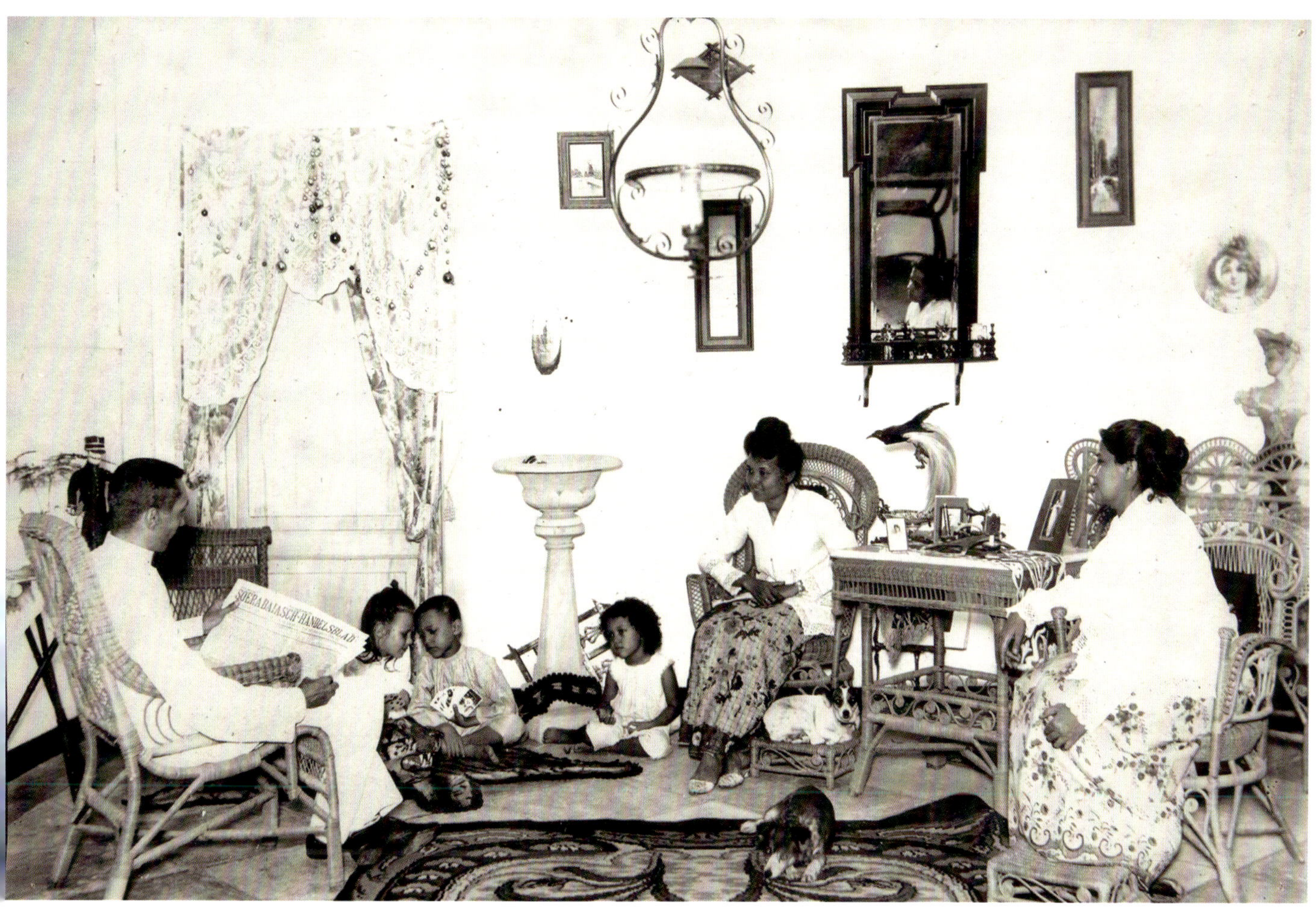

106
Family snapshot, Surabaya
Photographer: unknown
silver gelatin developing-out paper
25.2 x 38 cm
1915–40
30054421. Gift: Indo Scientific Institute (IWI), 2006

20th-century photography

The 19th-century photographs in the collection mainly provide impressions of the life of the European upper class, which appears to be predominately white. This is a distorted image, because there are very few photographs in the collection of Indo-European families from that earlier period.[199] Where they are present in the collection, these photographs show a 'Dutch' man with an Indo-European or Asian woman.
Once photography became available to the wider public after 1900, images also appeared of the middle class in more modest houses, and of indigenous houses in all corners of the archipelago.[200] Taking photographs became extremely popular, especially at parties, weddings and social occasions with family and friends. There are also a lot of photographs of Indo-European families from this period, especially from the IWI collection (see p. 58).
However, the bulk of these photographs mainly document the daily life and social activities of the European community. They provide an impression of people in and around their houses. Now that photographs and photography had lost their function as exclusive and status-enhancing pursuits, houses no longer had to be represented with such formality. Photographs were now being made of the intimacy of a relaxed domestic family life. The houses gradually changed too, becoming more compact – the front veranda became smaller and enclosed and the architecture displayed more European features. The houses were not as open as before, which seems to be reflected in the more closed and private character of the photographs depicting domestic life in the 20th century.

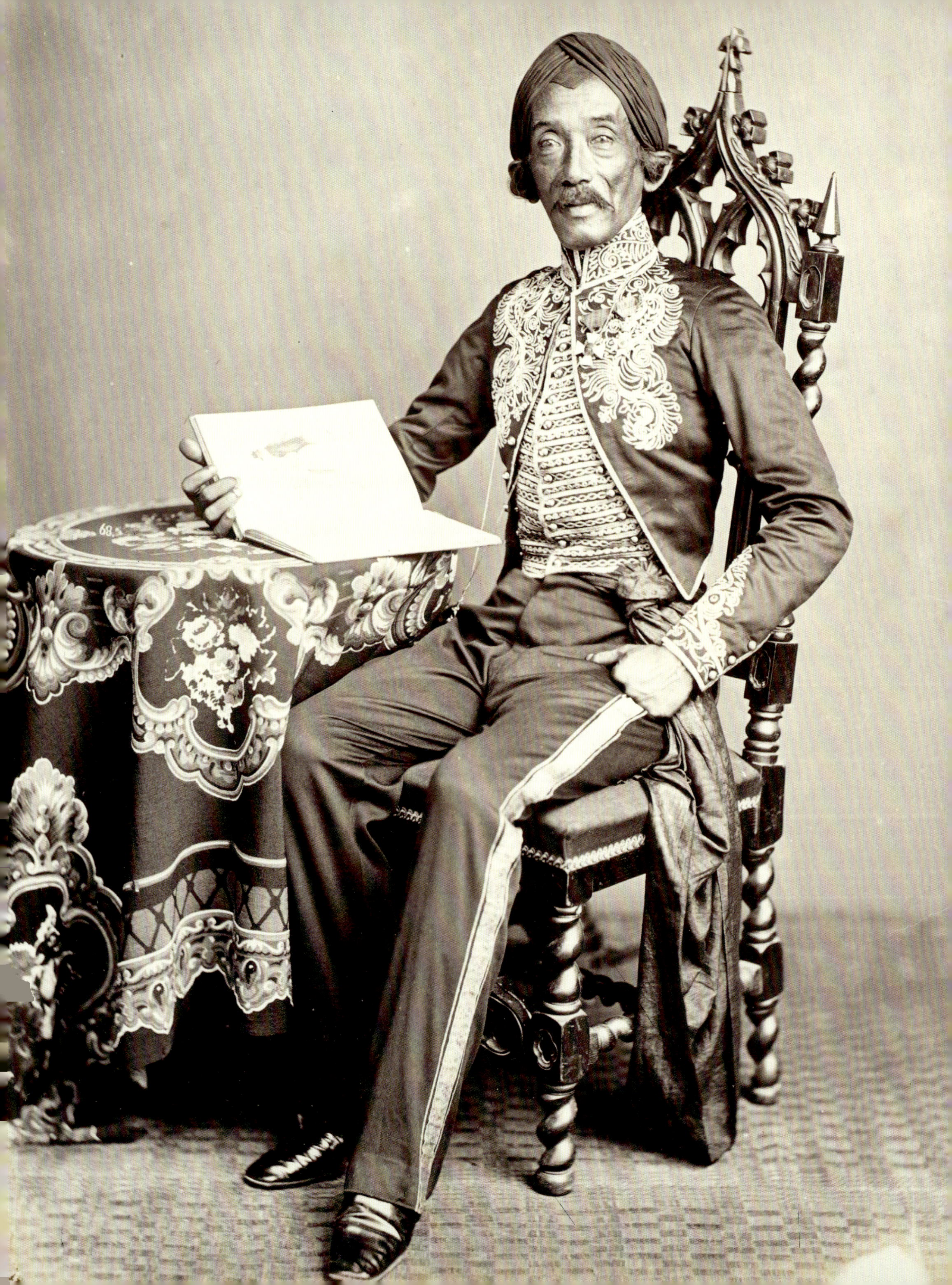
68

COLONIAL PORTRAIT PHOTOGRAPHY

ANOUK MANSFELD

107
Portrait of the painter Raden Saleh Syarif Bustaman, Batavia
Photographic Studio: Woodbury & Page
albumen print
24.1 x 18.2 cm
1860–72
60004954. Gift: J. Schijff, 1935

In a period in which photographs and digital images have become the norm, it is difficult to imagine that the invention of the earliest photographic techniques, more than 180 years ago, would have had the groundbreaking impact that it did.

In the second half of the 19th and at the beginning of the 20th century, the period in which photography indisputably conquered the market, a growing number of people had photographic portraits made of themselves. Initially, it was mostly intellectuals and artists who were photographed, but a wider group of people were rapidly attracted to the new phenomenon of photography.[201]

In the Netherlands East Indies photography was met with the same reaction as in the rest of the world; the way it was utilised typified relationships within the colonial society. This chapter deals with the portrait as a portrayal of one or more people whose identities are known. The person in the photograph is usually the commissioner. The many anonymous 'types' who were photographed in studios,[202] which can be considered as the photographers' 'free work', are excluded from this discussion, and are addressed elsewhere in this book.

Photographic portraits elaborated on a genre in painting in which one or more posing figures are the subject. The blossoming of the portrait genre can be explained by the fact that faces are immediately recognisable. A status-enhancing portrait is thus more than merely a representation of a person; the staging tells a story of its own. What is visible in the background conveys a great deal about identity: how the person lived, what he or she thought of him or herself, and especially the impression they wanted to create of themselves. Painters and photographers are aware of this, as are actors, and politicians and monarchs have been making use of this since time immemorial by commissioning portraits of themselves. Portraits have therefore always had a function as *memoria* and were a way for the subject to endure; it is no coincidence that the word 'immortalised' is usually used in conjunction with the word 'portrait'.[203]

The second reason for the flowering of the portrait genre is that it provided artists and photographers with an important – if not the most important – source of income. In the Netherlands East Indies it was predominately professional, and mostly Western, photographers who were believed to have mastered the complicated processes during the second half of the 19th century and in the early 20th century. At the time, the photographic profession was at the interface between handicrafts, trade and science, the European chemical formulas had to be

adapted to the tropical climate, and there was much experimentation.
Many professional photographic studios opened in the Netherlands East Indies in the second half of the 19th century. The abolition of the Cultivation System in 1870 and the arrival of European women in the colony during the last quarter of the 19th century exerted a powerful influence on the society. A well-to-do bourgeoisie developed, which – as in the Dutch Golden Age – were the most important clients for portrait commissions. With the increase in colonial affluence the demand for portraits and group portraits in the Netherlands East Indies increased significantly.

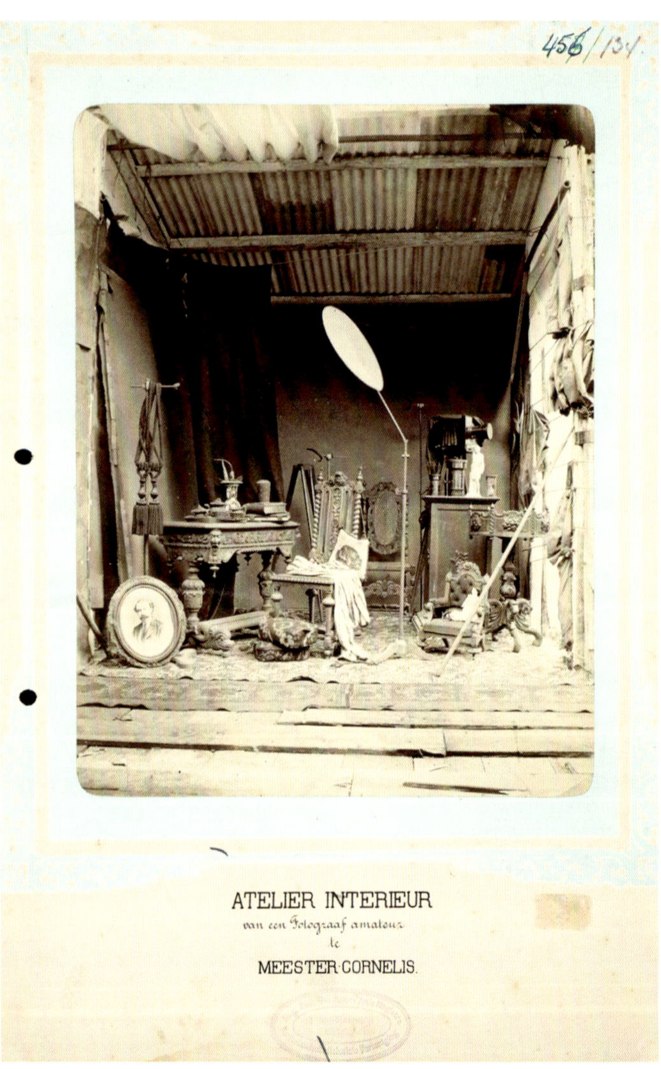

108
Amateur photographer's studio in Weltevreden, Batavia
Photographer: unknown
albumen print
24.4 x 17.9 cm
1870–1905
60032614. Provenance: Natura Artis Magistra, 1920. Former collection Netherlands Colonial Association (NKV)

To ensure that their portrait photographs could compete with painted portraits, photographers fitted out their studios with decors and a variety of objects they could use to 'dress' their photographs. These studio attributes created a link between the subject and the background, and the photographer's craftsmanship was demonstrated in his ability to merge all the elements into a harmonious whole. Even an amateur photographer's studio was filled with objects that were used for making portrait photographs.
The time it took to pose for a photograph in no way compared to that required for a drawn, let alone, painted portrait. This meant a significant reduction in time and cost for the client. The relatively fast and cheap portrayal of a person was thus the most important reason for photography becoming so popular.
The oldest object in the Tropenmuseum photograph collection is a daguerreotype with a portrait of a young boy (Fig. 109). The static character of early works such as this is due to the technical limitations associated with the relatively long exposure time. Subjects were usually placed in front of a uniform background and use was made of as much daylight as possible; sometimes mirrors were used to reflect it. To reduce the exposure time during this process, a person's face was sometimes dusted with flour to amplify the amount of light reflecting off it, but even then, he or she had to remain motionless in the sunlight when posing for the photographer. The complete lack of spontaneity in children's portraits is therefore not surprising.
This image may have had something to do with Charles Jacques Sayers (1844–93), who at a later age would become the general manager of the Poegoe Sugar Factory on Java. This would mean that the approximately 10-year-old child in this photograph would be the grandfather of the painter Charles Sayers (1901–43).[204]
The popularity of daguerreotypes in the mid-19th century primarily arose from the demand for relatively cheap portraits. Almost all early portraits in the colonial period were taken with daylight; magnesium flash bulbs only came into use around 1900. Decors, carpets and personal attributes were placed outside such that they created the illusion of an interior. Most photographs were made *in situ* from roughly 1870: the client-commissioner was

> 109
Portrait of C.J. Sayers, born in Batavia in 1844, Semarang
Photographic Studio: Grivel & Co
daguerreotype
image: 9.2 x 7 cm, complete: 18.4 x 15.3 cm
1852–57
10033229. Gift: N. Vonwiller Gerhard and S. Vonwiller Pert, 2002

photographed – with or without companions – in full regalia on the veranda or in the garden of his colonial villa. These static images provide an impression of the subject's way of life, which was displayed as an extension of his own identity. An important reason for making this type of portrait reportages was to give people back home in the Netherlands an idea of the prosperity in the colony. It was commonplace to compile an album from such images as a status symbol. Furthermore, albums were also made as visual keepsakes for people who returned to the Netherlands after their years in the Tropics. Portraits made during the second half of the 19th century were also given or sent to friends as so-called *cartes de visite*.

These smaller portraits (c. 11 x 6.5 cm) were glued to robust cardboard. Originally, the negatives for these were made using the wet collodion process. A special camera with multiple lenses was used to take twelve or more photographs that were captured on a negative. The entire negative was then printed on albumen paper and the individual images were cut

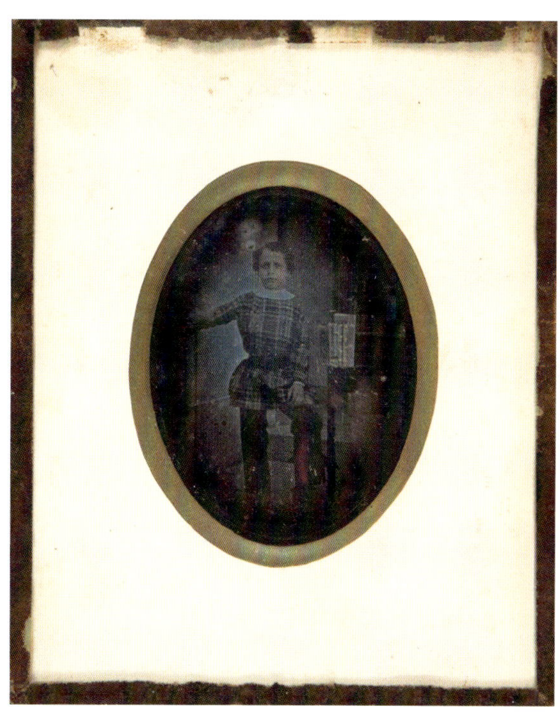

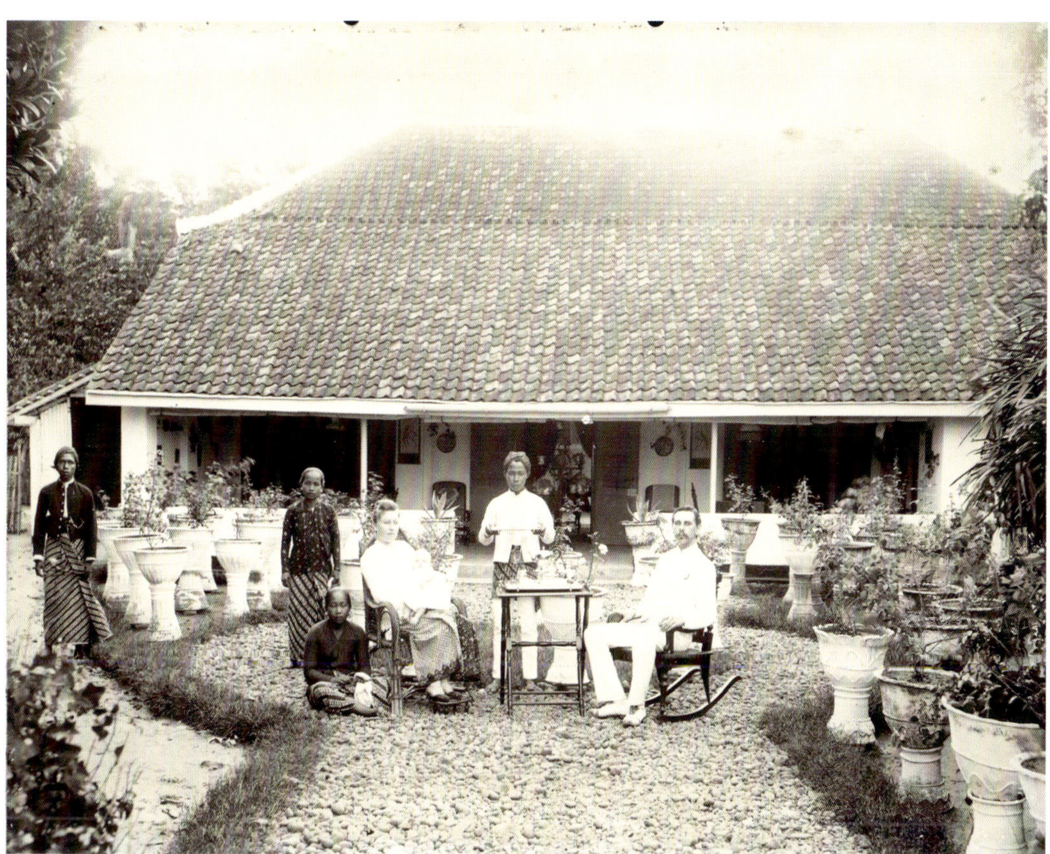

110
Group portrait of the Nienaber family, with servants, their villa in the background, Madiun
Photographic Studio: Charls & Van Es & Co
albumen print
21.5 x 27.5 cm
1899
60002225. Gift: J.C. Nienaber, 1983

TWO DIFFERENT WORLDS

Court life appeals to the imagination. The Tropenmuseum collection has a loose-leaf album with studio portraits of the Sultan of Yogyakarta and his family. Court albums such as this were presented as commemorative albums to government officials or other members of the local European elite who were leaving Yogya. This copy is from the civil servant J. Mullemeister (1838–1926), Resident from 1889 to 1891. The most important portrait in the series is that of Hamengku Buwono VII (1839–1921), the Sultan of Yogyakarta since 1877. He is wearing a very special garment: a copy of a jacket that according to Javanese tradition was gifted by the Prophet Muhammad himself at the end of the 15th century, and was preserved in the palace as a *pusaka* (holy heirloom). Its origin gave the power of the sultans over their subjects additional religious merit.[205] His status is also evident from the gigantic *parang rusak* (broken machete) motif on his *kain panjang* (hip wrapper). He is also wearing *sumping ron* ear jewellery and a *kuluk* (headgear). The sultan is seated on the *dampar kencana*, the golden throne with a footrest. A *sirih* (betel) set can be seen behind a cuspidor that has been placed on a low table. Everything in the portrait indicates that this is an official State portrait. Such portraits were primarily made to project status and prestige, not to reveal some personal aspect of the sultan's life. The pose is repeated on other photographs of this and other sultans. He was also frequently portrayed in military uniform, underscoring the European aspects of his status.
The Javanese court photographer Kassian Céphas (1845–1912) made this photograph.[206] He had a studio in Yogya, but brought all his decors to the *kraton* for this occasion. In strong contrast to other works by Céphas, the portraits have a formal character because the status and symbolism of the sultan and his family had to be accentuated. Céphas' aesthetic portraits of young Javanese women, in which his son and successor Sem probably assisted

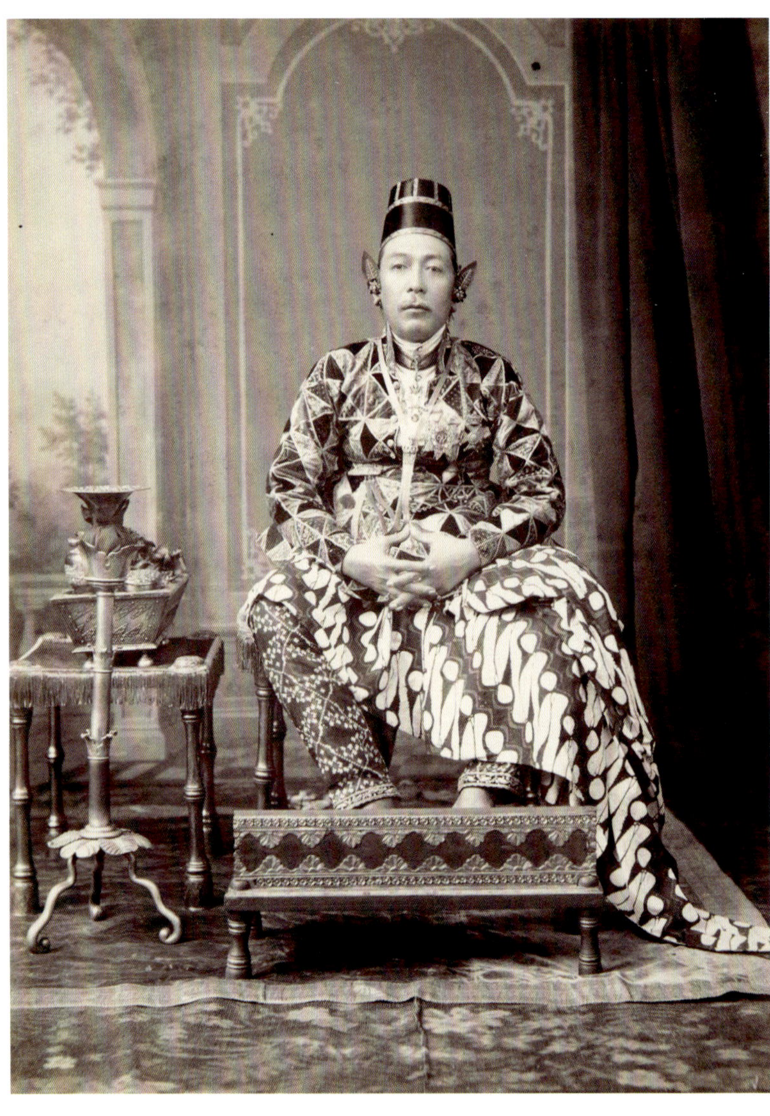

111
Studio portrait of Hamengku Buwono VII, Sultan of Yogyakarta
Photographer: Kassian Céphas (1845–1912)
albumen print
21.4 x 15.6 cm
1880–91
60001455. Gift: Heirs J. Mullemeister, 1941.
On loan from 1914–41.

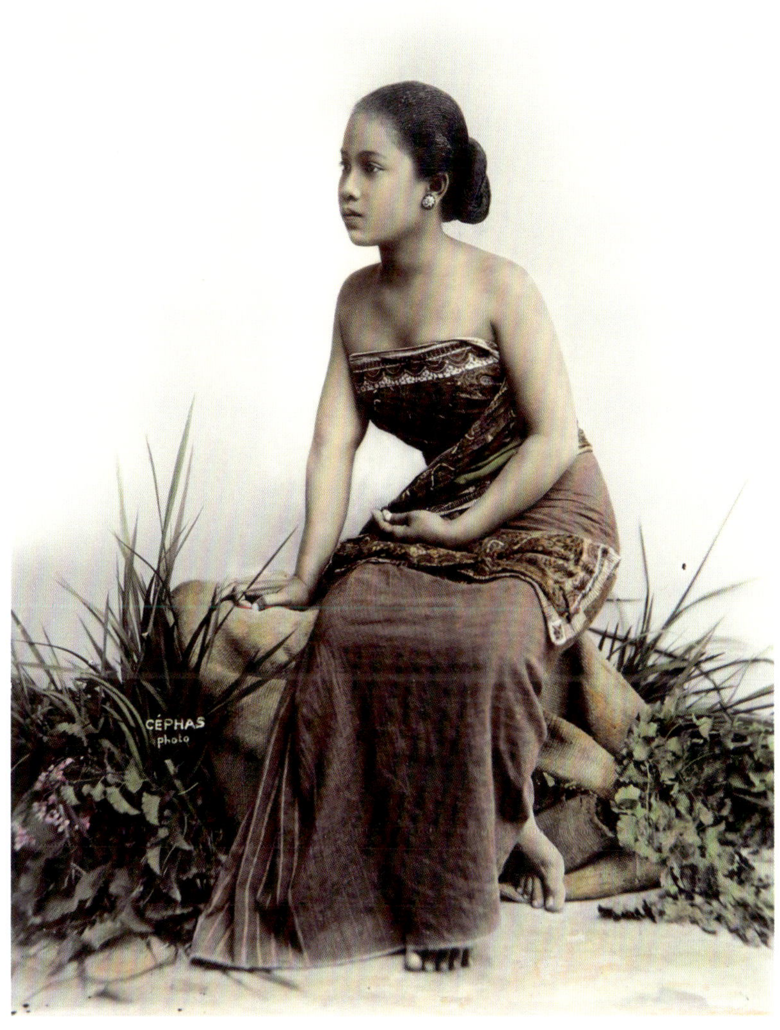

112
Studio portrait of a Javanese woman, possibly from Yogyakarta
Photographer: Kassian Céphas (1845–1912)
gelatin printing-out paper, coloured with water colours
22.7 x 16.3 cm
c. 1900
60027279. Provenance: unknown

him, portray a completely different world. The detachment between the photographer and his models appears to have disappeared in these portraits, and the atmosphere is more relaxed, casual and livelier. These photographs undeniably had another function. They were intended for a wider public of European immigrants and travellers, and were very popular, possibly because of their exotic and sensual character. They were also distributed as picture postcards, with a text reading: 'Javaansche schoone / Native beauty'.[207] The Tropenmuseum has a particularly beautiful photograph from this series, a gelatin printing-out-paper that was also hand coloured.[208] It was rumoured that this was a portrait of a princess who had been abducted from the *kraton*, a story that can be consigned to myth, but which emphasises the erotic charge attached to this photograph. RJ

from the larger sheet. They were then glued to pieces of cardboard that were slightly larger than the print. The name of the photographer's studio in decorative letters adorned the front or back of the cardboard as a simple form of advertising.

It was considered good form to exchange these *cartes de visite*, which were often provided with a short inscription and the signature of the person who was portrayed.[209] These signed portraits were collected in special, elegantly designed albums. One example is the album of S. Locker de Bruijne, Resident of Sumatra's East coast, who collected around 1877 portraits of people from his milieu in a luxurious album with gold-edged pages.

So-called cabinet portrait cards were also made for display, and measured roughly 17 x 11 centimetres, a suitable size for framing. These portraits, popular with Europeans and the local aristocracy, were frequently printed for special occasions such as a wedding or a jubilee and they also functioned as keepsakes of beloved people.

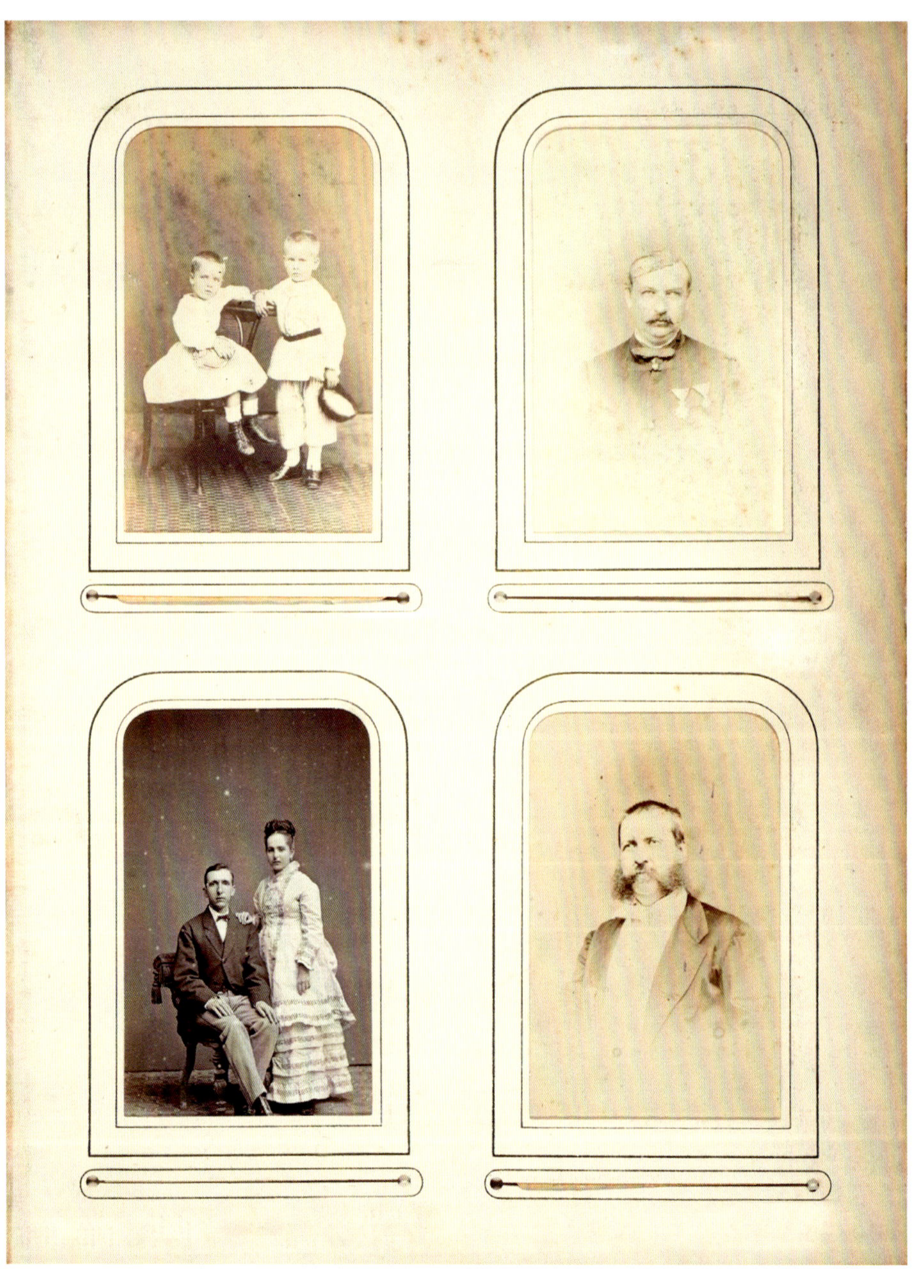

113
Album sheet with *cartes de visite* from the Netherlands East Indies
Photographer: Various, including Woodbury & Page
albumen prints
26.3 x 19.6 cm
c. 1870–77
Alb. no. 1472, p. 5. Gift: J.J. Locker de Bruyne-Knottenbelt, 1952

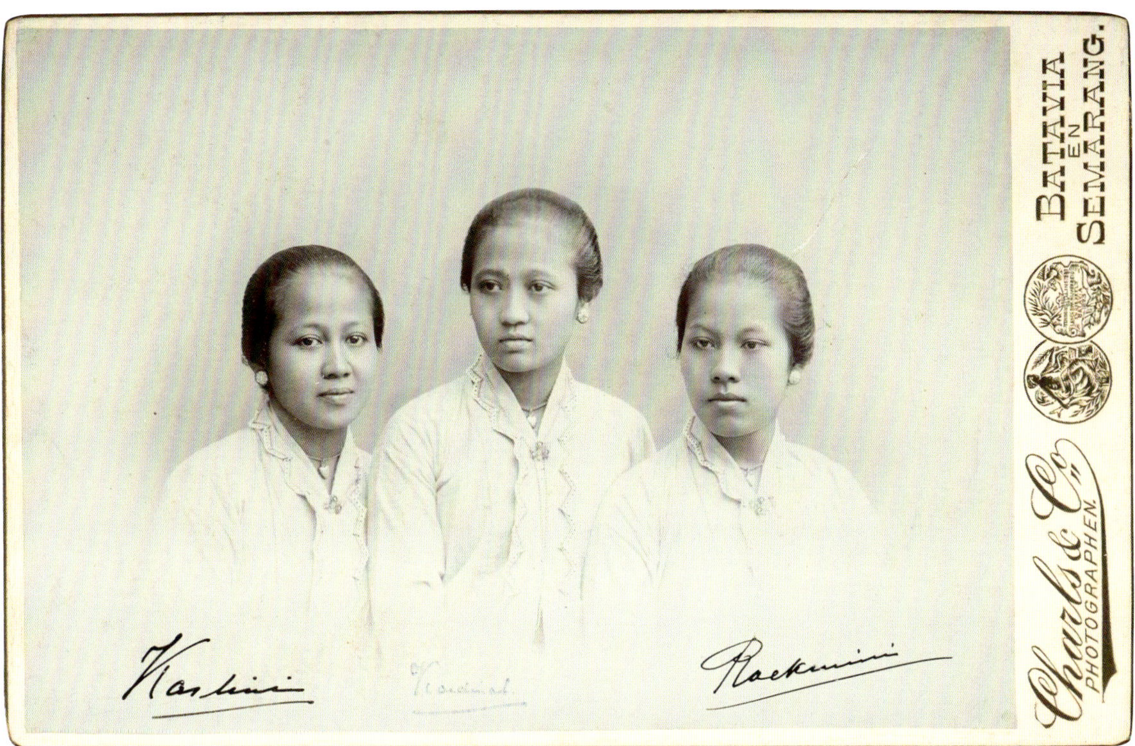

114
Cabinet card photograph with signed portraits of the three sisters Kartini, Kardinah and Roekmini
The reverse of the cardboard has a handwritten poem that refers to a 'three-leafed clover', as the three sisters were known:
'The dove descends from heaven, Down to Earth, As white as snow, and soft as silk, So swift on the wing, Clover stalk in its beak, Carefully held, With three clover leafs, That fit together. The dove drops the stalk on the Earth, In the gentlest motion, And immediately, with flapping wings, It returns to Heaven. Yet, contentment, contentment, Awaits those who find the clover, Here below, It represents Faith, Hope and Love, Together they are one. 1 May 1902.'
Photographic Studio: Charls & Van Es & Co
collodion printing-out paper
10 x 14.5 cm
c. 1900
60033327. Purchase: H.L. van der Kamp, 1999

The group portrait of Raden Ajeng Kartini (1879–1904) and her two sisters is a fine example of this. This group portrait, which was distributed after Kartini's death, proved incredibly popular and was collected by a great many people.
Kartini was born in Mayong, a village near Jepara. Her father was Regent Raden Mas Sosroningrat. She was very close to her sisters Kardinah and Roekmini. Their father allowed them to attend junior school, but refused all their entreaties to continue studying because they had to await a proposal of marriage, as tradition decreed. In these years Kartini read Dutch literature and was an avid letter-writer. Her letters recount details of her life, the fate of Indonesian women, the struggle against arranged marriages and the importance of education. Kartini, who was married off to the Regent of Rembang, died at the tender age of 25 while giving birth. Her letters were published after her death. She is still regarded as the first feminist in Indonesia and is celebrated each year on her birthday, 21 April, National Women's Day, named 'Hari Kartini' in her honour.

In emulation of the colonial upper class the Asian aristocracy (lords, regents) had portraits made of themselves to underscore and display their status. These portraits show a mix of traditional and Western influences, as can be seen in the studio portrait of the Regent of Wates (Fig. 116).
In this portrait the regent is depicted standing beside a small table with an attribute. He is wearing the official clothing that was widely used after 1870: a braided coat with a flat bow and European-looking shoes; a headdress, the stately *krisses* and a *kain* with a *parang* motif make up the indigenous elements. By being photographed in official costume the regent shows that he is part of the colonial government. Nonetheless, on the table beside him is a *kraton* headgear with the embroidered initials of Sultan Hamengku Buwono VIII. Men in the sultan's army also wore these caps, by which the regent indicated that his area fell under the authority of the Sultan of Yogyakarta and furthermore stressed his Javanese identity.

STUDIO PORTRAITS OF EMPLOYEES AT THE SINGKEP TIN COMPANY, RIAU ARCHIPELAGO

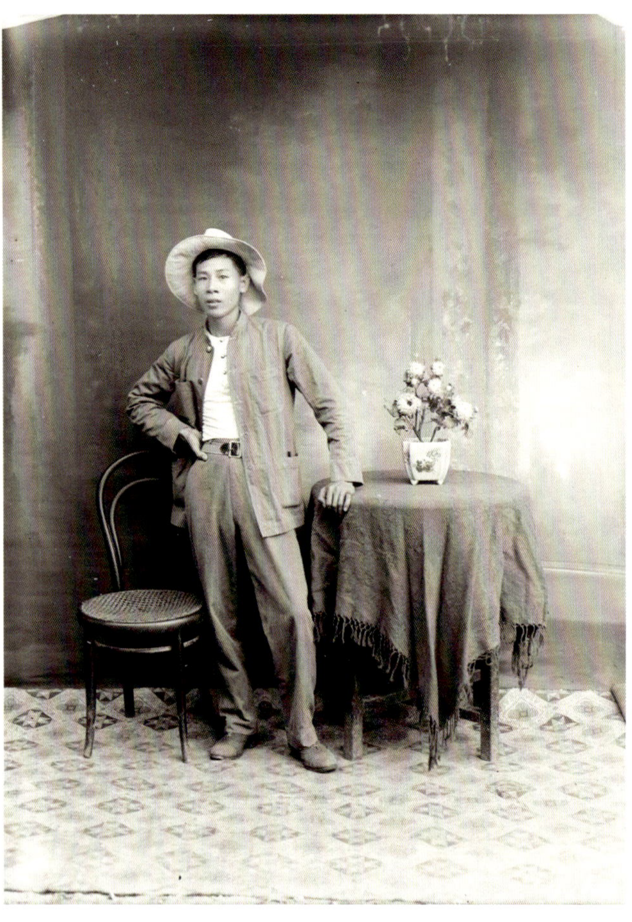

115
Portrait of a Chinese foreman at the Singkep Tin Company, Riau Archipelago
Photographer: unknown
gelatin glass negative
13 x 18 cm
1900–10
10005288. Gift: Singkep Tin Company, 1917

In 1915 the Colonial Institute Association in Amsterdam announced a competition for submissions of visual material of the Netherlands East Indies so that they could arrange an exhibition in the Netherlands about the colony. A large part of the submitted material was only used later, after the First World War, in the Colonial Institute's jubilee exhibition of 1923 (see p. 46).
Among the submissions in 1917 were a large number of original glass negatives depicting the Singkep Tin Company in the Riau Archipelago. This company was founded in 1889 and was taken over in 1933 by the large Billiton Company (NV Billiton Maatschappij). The negatives include images showing the activities in the mines, and studio portraits of the employees.
Around 1900 studio portraiture in the Netherlands East Indies was still the preserve of the colonial elite. The indigenous population were photographed as 'exotic types' but – exceptions such as the local rulers excluded – not as people with their own identities, and company photographs show labourers on the shop floor, not in a studio. However, employees at the more modernised Singkep Tin Company were photographed in a mobile studio that was set up outside and on the shop floor. The surroundings can be glimpsed behind and beside the painted backcloth that appears in all the images, leading to the conclusion that it was still technically necessary to take photographs by daylight.
The Singkep Tin Company thus made it possible for a significant number of its employees to have a professional photographer make a posed portrait of them. What is noteworthy about these photographs is that the employees, who are depicted with and without their families, are all shown with the same studio attributes. Probably supplied by the photographer himself, these attributes provide the viewer – in contrast to portraits in the painterly tradition – with no additional information about the status of the depicted person. The descriptions of the negatives that accompanied these photographs when they arrived in the Tropenmuseum collection only note a person's function and sometimes their ethnicity, but not their name – they were and are anonymous. What remains is a series of portraits of unknown but proud men and women. AM

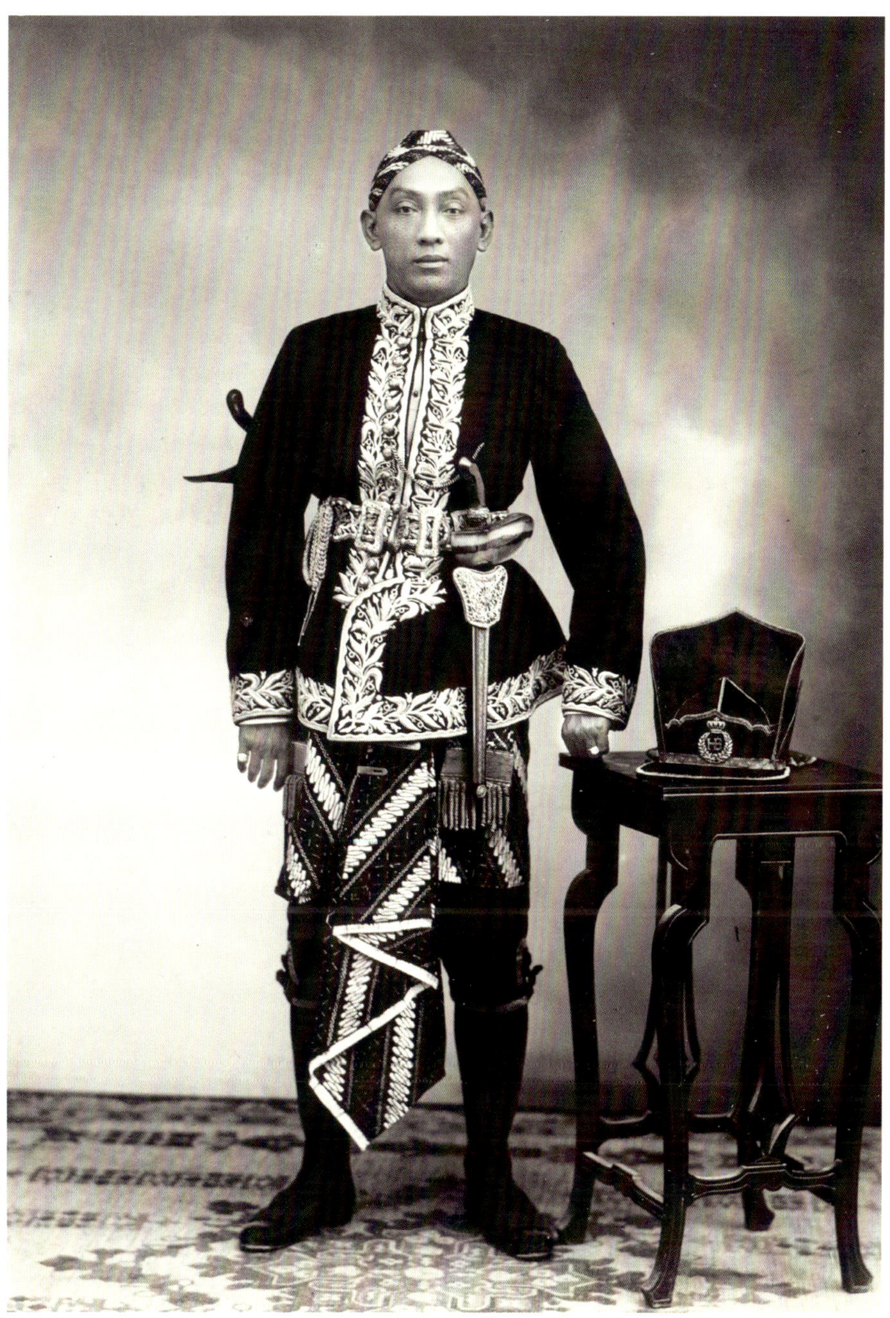

116
Studio portrait of the Regent of Wates, Java
Photographer: unknown, gelatin printing-out paper
13.6 x 9.5 cm
1921–25
60034670. Gift: F.E. Douwes Dekker, 1992

In the first decades of the 20th century it became even easier for people to take their own photographs. Eastman (Kodak) had resolved most of the technical issues, and photography in the Netherlands East Indies was no longer the exclusive preserve of the elite.

In addition to the professional photographers, growing numbers of amateur photographers were active in the archipelago, although the word 'amateur' in this regard does not do justice to their work. From around 1900 many so-called amateurs were actually highly proficient photographers who cooperated in well-organised associations and whose works in some cases cannot be distinguished from those of a professional photographer. It is noteworthy that these photographs have a more personal character and provided the first impressions of domestic life in the colony.

A good example is included in the albums that were compiled by the amateur photographer Jan Theodoor Ponse, who worked as a tobacco planter for the Deli Company on Sumatra. He made several fascinating photographs of his family in and around their house. From the moment that cameras became widespread people started taking intimate photographs of their world, and a growing group of people started photographing their own environments from the 1920s.

The photographs give an impression of life in households in all layers of the population; these (group) portraits no longer accentuated the status of those in the portrait but were, to an increasing degree, intended to capture a specific moment and place in time. Such snapshots were usually made spontaneously. Everyday objects or events are frequent subjects. Although many of the snapshots are not entirely perfect or are regarded as 'amateurish', they do document the 'real' life of people and were therefore objects of value for the photographer (and his or her family).

Happy and memorable occasions were photographed frequently: excursions on motorbikes and in cars, receiving visitors on the veranda or sharing intimate dinners, as seen in Fig. 118. These photographs emanate an atmosphere of boundless optimism and zest for life. A good example is the series of portraits

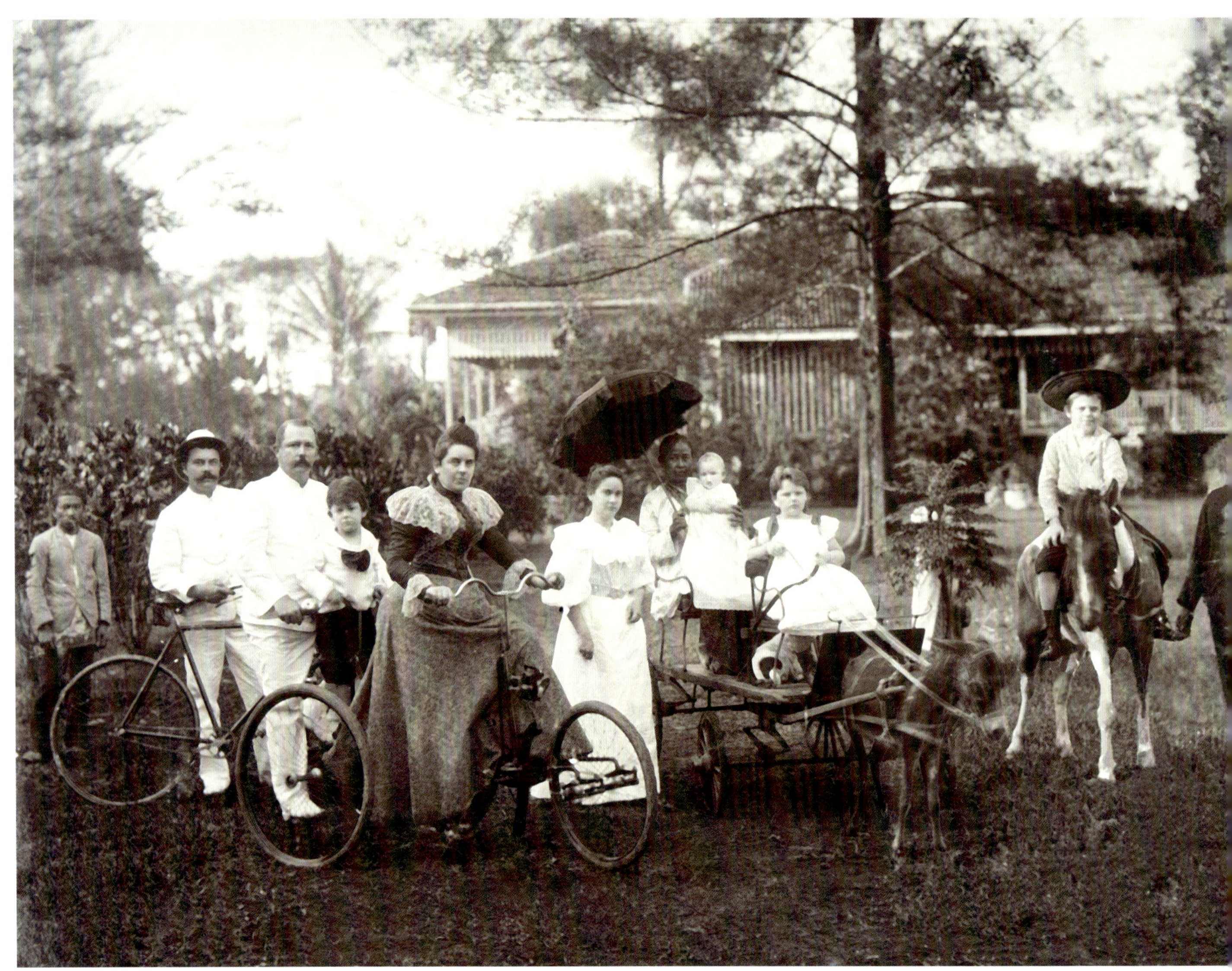

117
Group portrait of the Ponse family with servants in the garden, Sumatra
Photographer: J.Th. Ponse
gelatin printing-out paper
27.5 x 36.1 cm
c. 1895
60028999. Gift: A. Ponse-Smalt, 1998
digitally restored 2012

and group portraits made by Mr Vane who was a permanent tenant of the Haverkamp guesthouse in Batavia. These portraits have the character of a snapshot, see Fig. 119.

For contemporary viewers these images provide a far more realistic impression of daily life than the formal colonial portraits. However, the meaning of each portrait that is preserved in a museum collection is now completely different from its original meaning. Viewing historical portrait photographs thus remains a strange experience; the photographs show unknown places and, in most cases, deceased people. And while a lot of subjects can be identified, many cannot. Anonymous photographers sometimes wrote captions to their images, introducing a degree of confusion in some cases that will never be resolved. All the albums have blank spaces and empty photo corners. For whatever reason, someone wanted to have a specific photograph as a keepsake, or perhaps they wanted to erase it from memory. This has resulted in these types of images being alienated from their original context; they have been eliminated from the story. These individual photographs have gained a new life because the viewer involuntarily fills in what he or she wants to see. Even if the viewer is familiar with a portrait's history, he or she always looks at the photograph from a different perspective from that of the person who is portrayed.

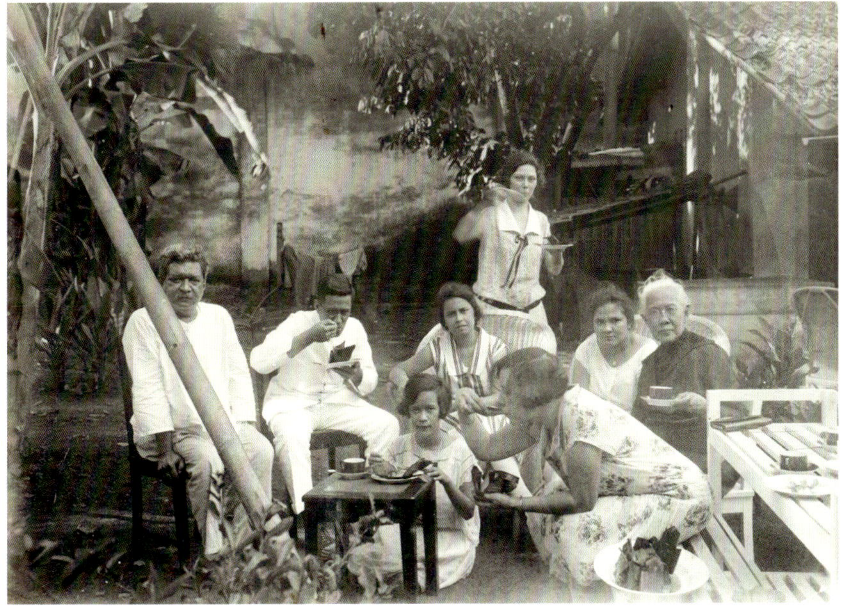

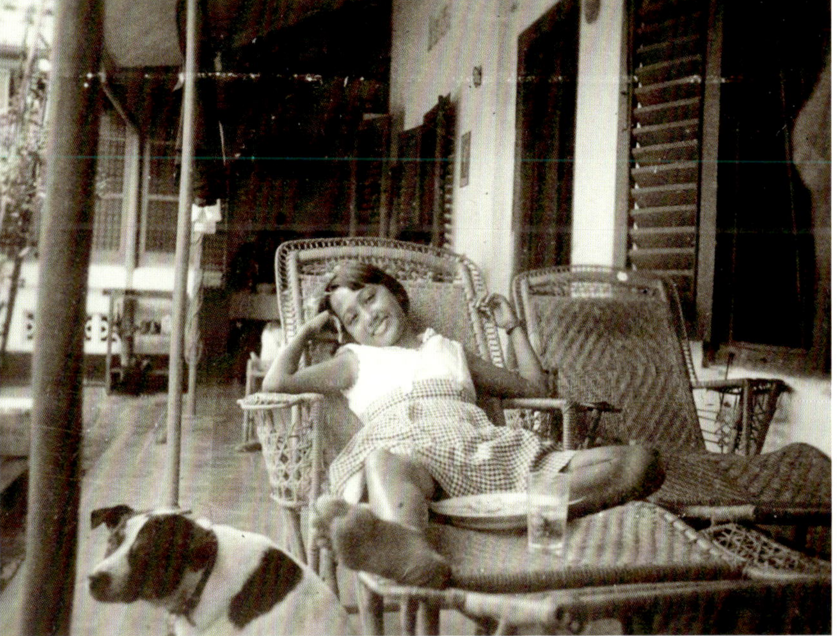

118
Group portrait of Indo-Europeans enjoying tea, Java
Photographer: unknown
silver gelatin developing-out paper
13 x 18 cm
c. 1920
30012875. Gift: Indo Scientific Institute (IWI), 2006

119
Elly Maagdenberg, on a rattan deckchair (*krossie malas*) on the veranda of Haverkamp guesthouse, Batavia
Photographer: Vane
silver gelatin developing-out paper
3 x 4 cm
1932–38
60029006. Provenance: via M.J. Hillerström, 1979

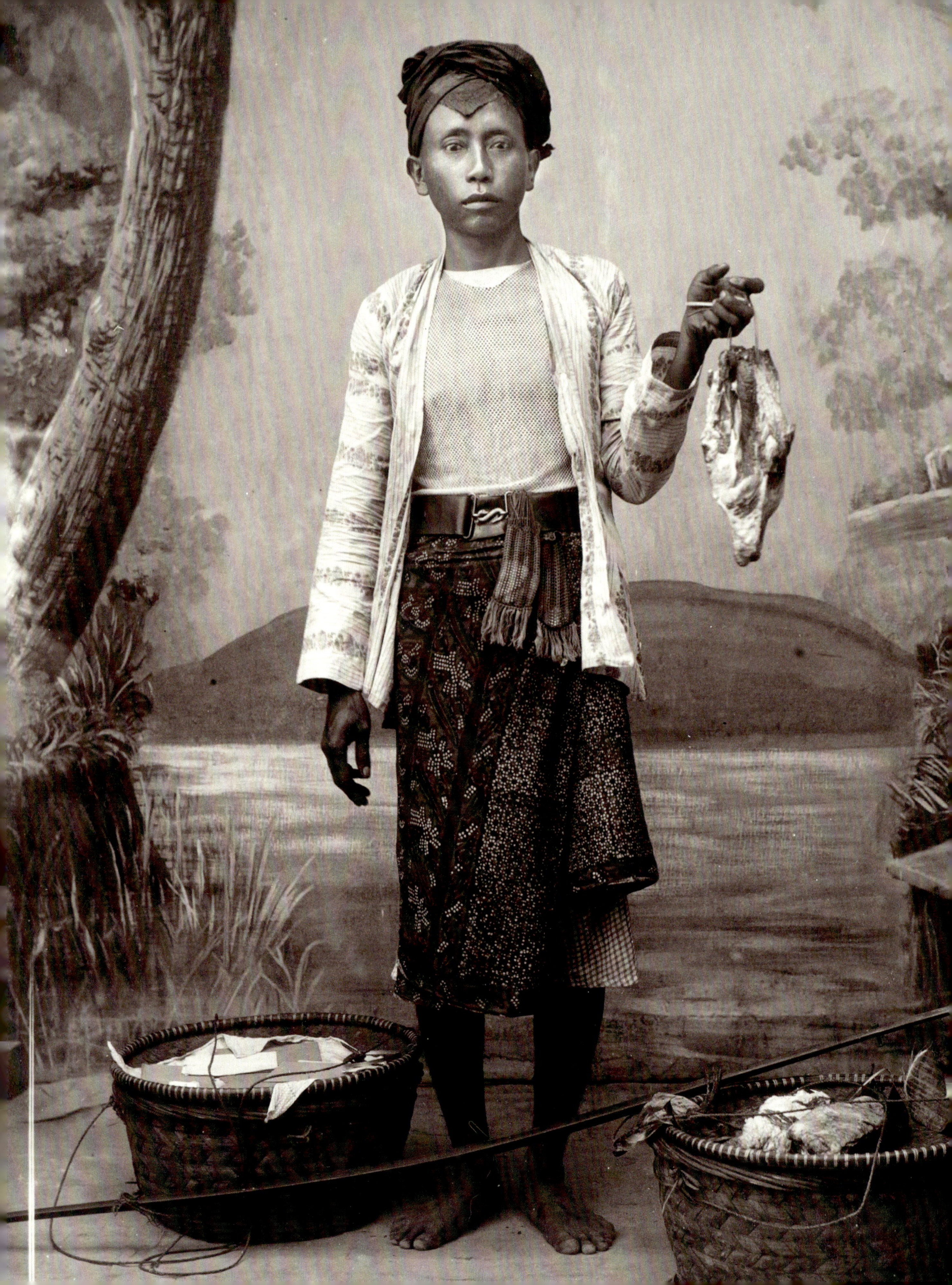

EPILOGUE – SOUVENIRS FROM THE PAST

WIMO AMBALA BAYANG

120
Studio portrait of a meat seller in Batavia
Photographer: unknown
albumen print
24.7 x 17.7 cm
1880–1900
60012415. Gift: P. Altherr via P.W. Osieck (1951). Former collection J. Altherr

My mother just received a digital camera. She carries it in her bag everywhere she goes, and often has her pictures taken against the backgrounds of the places she visits, the food she eats, or simply pictures of herself wearing the clothes she has just bought. One day I asked her why she liked being photographed so much. She answered, 'Photographs are a way for me to exist forever'.

This statement about photography and mortality is similar to Susan Sontag's observation about *memento mori*. In her book *On Photography*, Sontag wrote: 'To take a photograph is to participate in another person's (or thing's) mortality, vulnerability, mutability. Precisely by slicing out this moment and freezing it, all photographs testify to time's relentless melt.'[210] Different from film, photography has a poetic charge, full of nostalgia and sentiment because it is a slice of time, not a flow. Each still photograph is a privileged moment that is transformed into a slim object that can be kept and looked at again and again. Through her own efforts, my mother consciously photographed herself and the objects she found appealing; by taking pictures she remembers and even reminds others that she once existed, and will continue to exist.

My mother's answer also reminds me of George Eastman, the founder of Kodak in 1934, who developed an intriguing marketing concept that was summarised in the slogan: 'Kodak doesn't sell film; it sells memories'.

The notion of 'to exist' in photography is related to how reality is represented. It is also related to how memories of the past are constructed. During its infancy, camera technology was considered as capable of recording reality perfectly, and photographs were therefore often used in science as proof. Over the years, scholars have rigorously critiqued these ideas of photographic objectivity. A photograph constitutes a choreographed visual record: to take pictures is to select what one wants to present in a single frame. When a photographer takes a picture, he or she is not capturing reality, but is constructing it instead.

Presented with a collection of photographs taken in photographic studios in the Netherlands East Indies from 1860 to 1940, I tried to focus on how these photographs have articulated reality and memory. Unlike my mother's photographs, an individual who has been represented through her own pictures, these images are not representations of individuals. Instead, we only see surfaces, facades of human types: an itinerant satay seller wearing a broad woven bamboo hat, surrounded by three customers, each of whom holds a stick of satay; two sarong-wearing bare-chested females, each with a bamboo basket on her head; and two frowning men wearing sarongs, standing beneath broad banana leaves as if protecting themselves from rain. All these scenes were reconstructed in a photographer's studio.

When taking pictures of the locals in a studio, the colonial photographers were trying to focus their attention on the symbols of status while maintaining their distance from the subjects of the photographs. What was interesting for the photographer was not who was being photographed, but what the person was wearing or carrying, or what he or she was doing: these were the things the photographers found unusual. They were collecting cultural artefacts of a colony. Viewed with the perception of a conventional anthropologist, these pictures framed 'Orientals', or in this case Indonesians, as primitive tribes in a distant land who were disconnected from the progress of the age.

Imagining how photographers selected and constructed reality in their studios provides insights into how the West viewed the East at that time. Yet, in my reading of these images, I also see frightened expressions and rigid or awkward gestures. While more research would be required to investigate the relationships between the photographer and the persons who were portrayed, I am inclined to ask whether these subjects were photographed under duress? Were they paid, like photographic models? I suggest that their discomfort might be indirect forms of defence or resistance. The photographers could direct their poses, clothes and backgrounds, but the subject's expressions did not lie. When these photographs were published, was it true that they were cultural artefacts representing clothes and culture? I think that the fear and rigidity of the subjects reflected their perception that colonisation had forced them to become 'the Other' – they were nothing more than mere 'primitive curiosities'. Compare this to the efforts of the offspring of wealthy aristocrats who had access to camera technology, which enabled them to portray themselves more simply in unpretentious poses in extravagant costumes. These pictures were intended to display their pride and dignity. Although the West might see such images and the people they portray as exotic, for me this effort contrasted the image that was constructed by Western photographers. Like my mother, they started portraying themselves in an attempt to 'exist' in their own way.

The studio photographs in the Tropenmuseum collection remind me of a corner near the cashier's compartment in the Mirota Batik souvenir shop at one end of Jalan Malioboro, in Yogyakarta. Mirota Batik sells a wide array of arts and crafts such as sculptures, batik clothing and fabric, key chains, and postcards. One series in the collection intrigues me: the series of 'olden days' pictures that depict the Indonesian archipelago of yore. One of the pictures in the series is of an itinerant locksmith carrying his equipment in two containers hanging from a yoke over his shoulders. The picture was taken in a studio against a background of the tropical rainforest. The style of this photograph is similar to that of some other images in the Tropenmuseum collection, and I think it was part of a group of photographs. What is interesting is why these old photographs were deemed valuable, either aesthetically or as mementoes, and worthy of being made into postcards. Also, I was interested in why they circulated in Indonesia. Considering that the photographs were certainly produced by colonial or Dutch photographers, it means that ultimately, we Indonesians also perceive the 'reality' of our past from a Western perspective. Much like Kassian Céphas, who took his photographs from a Western perspective, we also experience the images like a Dutch visitor to Indonesia. Apparently, the only visual records we have of the nation's past are found in trivial exotic souvenirs. This publishing project by the Tropenmuseum is a highly valuable effort and needs to be seen as a way to contextualise the collection, which is treated with great care and examined with attention to history.

It remains important, however, to not only discover and analyse photographs of Indonesia taken by colonial photographers, but to pay particular attention to photographs made by Indonesians. In this way we can better understand how 'Orientals' perceived their own identity.

The Javanese aristocrat, Raden Ajeng Kartini (Fig. 114), already expressed this sentiment in one of her letters published posthumously in the book titled *Door Duisternis Tot Licht* (*Through the Darkness*

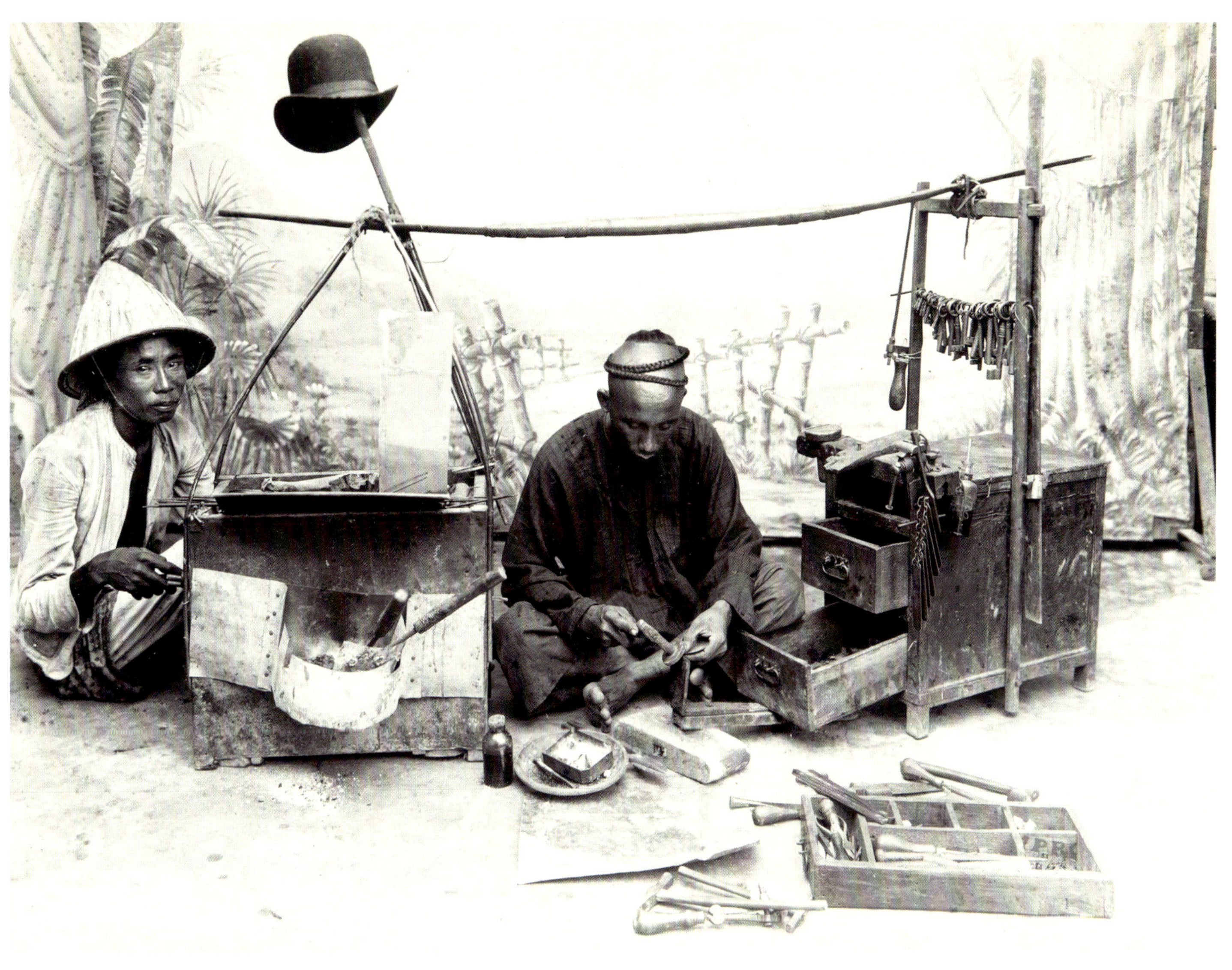

121
Studio portrait of a Chinese locksmith, Java
Photographic Studio: H. Salzwedel
gelatin printing-out paper
21.2 x 28.5 cm
1880–95
60022746. Provenance: H. de Booy

to the Light, 1990): 'I often wish I had photographic equipment and was able to take pictures of our people – in ways that only I could do, not in the ways of the European. There are so many things that I want to convey in words and in pictures so that the European can have the true image of us, the Javanese.'

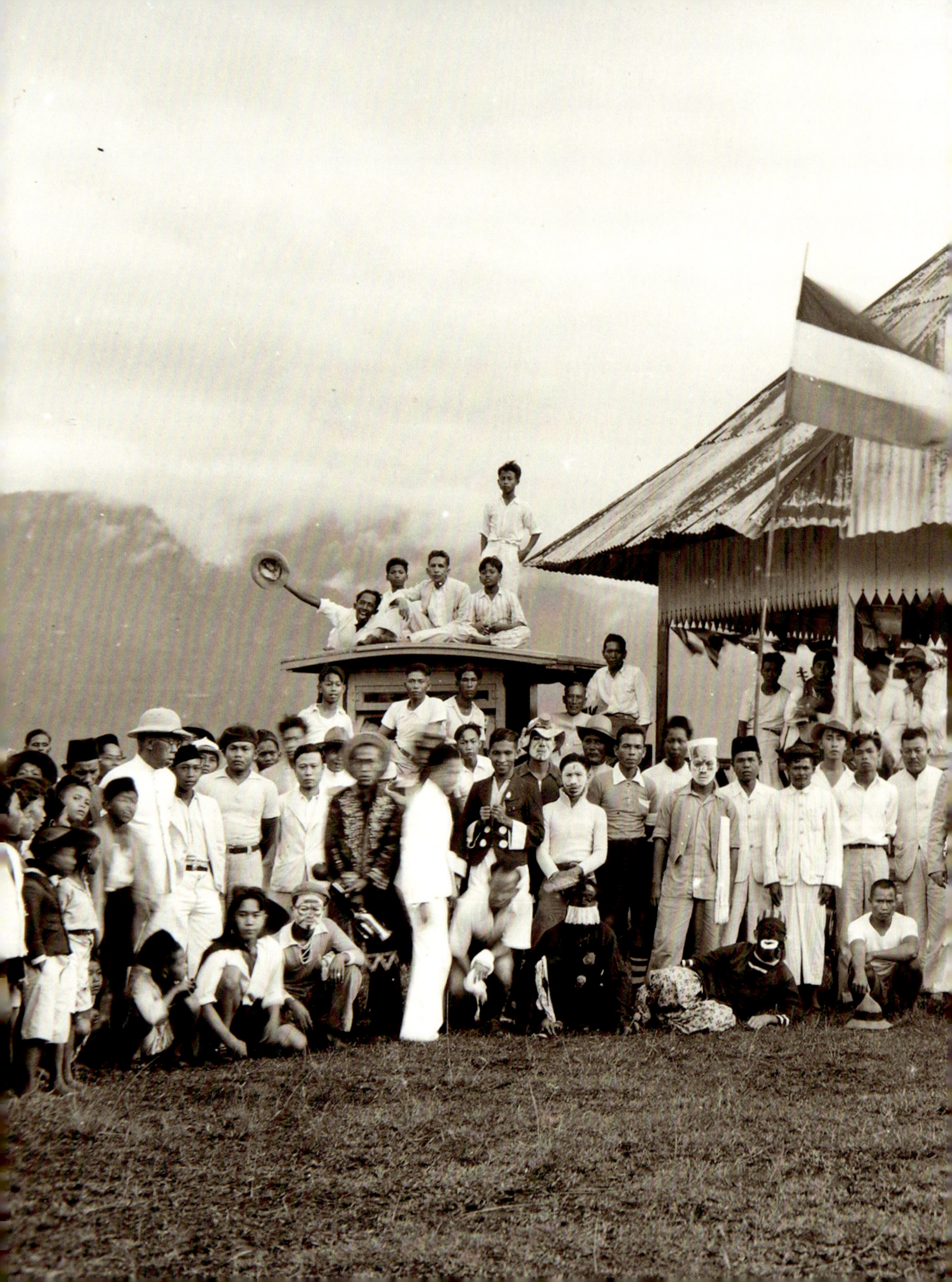

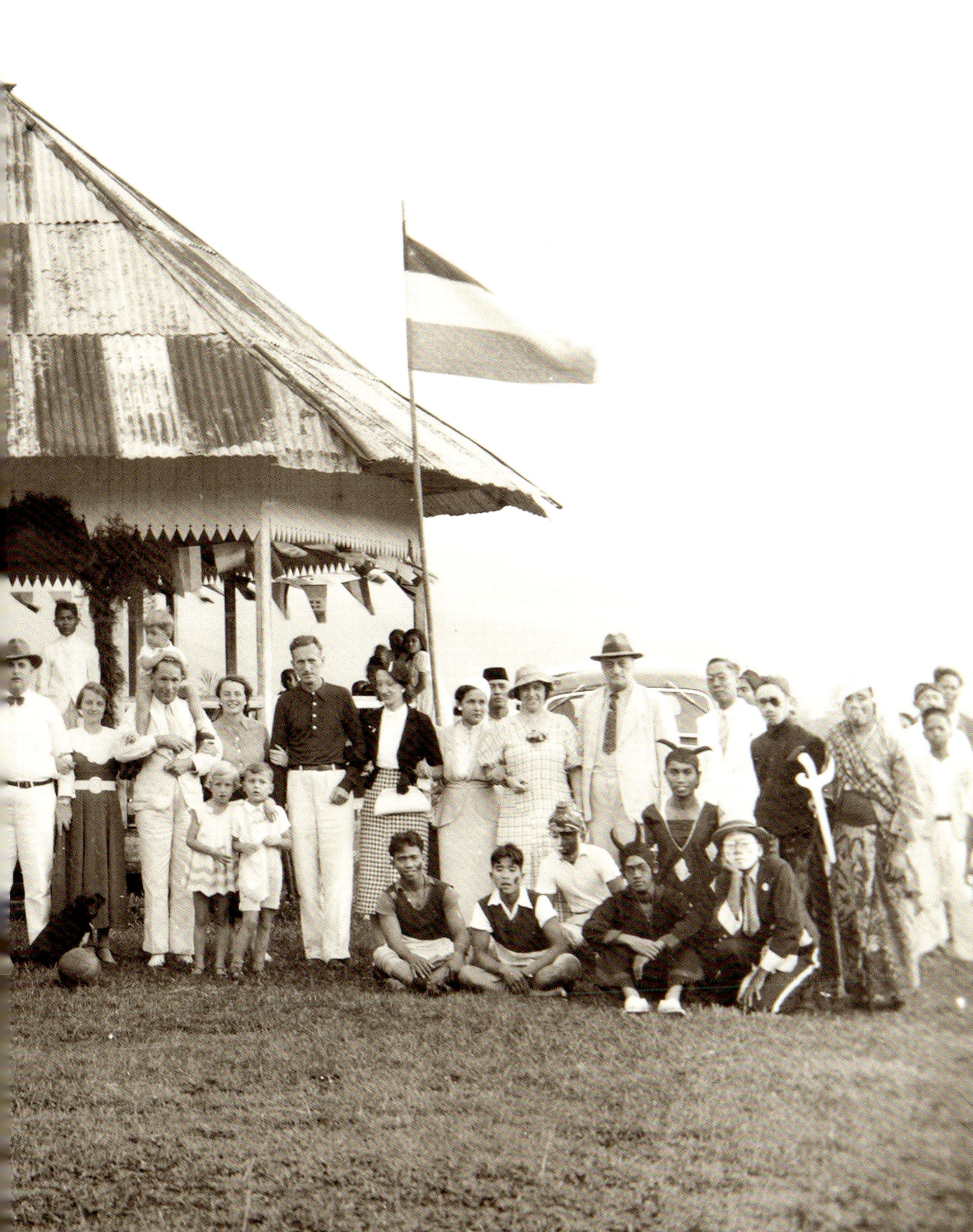

NOTES

< 122
Group portrait in Lebong Donok during a football match played by the Indonesian staff at the Redjang Lebong Mining Company, to mark the departure of the Sanders' family to the Netherlands
Photographer: unknown
silver gelatin developing-out paper
14.8 x 19.6 cm
6 June 1937
60043540. Gift: N.W. van Santen, 1980. Former collection H.J.A. Sanders and W.M. Sanders-Hock

1 According to Wachlin (1994, p. 24), Woodbury & Page presented an identical album (probably this copy, Alb. 1461) to King Willem III in 1877. The accompanying letter, preserved in the Royal Archives (Koninklijk Huisarchief), is dated 19 October 1877. A Woodbury & Page photographer was active in Aceh in 1877. After presenting this gift, the photographic studio requested the designation 'Purveyor to the Royal Household' (Hofleverancier), which was eventually granted. Governor-General J.W. van Lansberge (1830–1905) acted as the mediator and wrote a glowing letter of recommendation. Woodbury & Page started using the Royal coat of arms in their advertising from 1879.

2 This is in contrast to later albums with titles like *Gezigten op Atjeh (Views of Aceh)*; Alb. nos. 0298–0301) in which the military encampments and groups portraits of soldiers are more prevalent.

3 At this time, people thought that the war had truly ended. This photograph is a striking example of this misunderstanding, as was the Aceh monument that represented 'Victory' at the 1883 World Exhibition in Amsterdam. This World Exhibition, the 'International Colonial and Export Exhibition' ran from 1 May until 31 October.

4 Bosma 2003, p. 133. Wealthy planters families were among those who commissioned photographs of their private sphere as well as of their companies from the handful of photographers who were active in the Netherlands East Indies during the 19th century.

5 Bossenbroek 1994, p. 409

6 'Buitengewesten' ('Outer Regions') was the name used for all areas in the Netherlands East Indies beyond Java and Madura

7 Bossenbroek 1994, p. 245

8 A daguerreotype is a polished, silver-coated copper plate that is treated with chemicals to make it sensitive to light. The representation appears directly on the plate. It is a unique original: there is no negative from which multiple prints can be made. It was the first photographic technique to be used on a wide scale.

9 See Groeneveld 1989, pp. 16–17; Theuns-de Boer 2005; and Van den Berg 2005, pp. 227–28.

10 Bosma 2003, p. 226.

11 According to Theuns-de Boer (2005, p. 139), photography was used increasingly to convey Dutch colonial self-awareness during the 19th century. Photography played a greater role than ever before at the 1883 World Exhibition in Amsterdam: the display included more than 1500 photographs from the Netherlands East Indies by, among others, Hendrik Veen, Anthonie Meessen, Woodbury & Page, Daniel Veth, the Topographical Service and Van Kinsbergen. There was a direct link between the medium of photography and actual reality. The Dutch control over the numerous regions of the archipelago was clearly evident and legitimised the Dutch government's desire to profile itself as a successful colonial power. All the Indonesian indigenous peoples and landscapes appeared to have been recorded. The progress of city and harbour developments was documented, the railways symbolised the opening up of Java, and the Borobudur had been restored to its former glory. Even the war in Aceh seemed to be won! The million-and-a-half visitors to the World Exhibition were supposed to leave with the impression that 'The Netherlands was a successful colonial power'.

12 *Idem*, pp. 130–33. Veth published a variant of this photograph in his article: the same photograph as Tropenmuseum inv. no. 60022798.

13 Woodbury & Page also submitted material to several World Exhibitions, including the one held in Amsterdam in 1883.

14 See, for example, the Woodbury & Page catalogue (1879) in Wachlin 1994, pp. 201–9. The Tropenmuseum collection includes photographs showing the aftermath of the tsunami caused by the eruption of Krakatoa in 1883.

15 See Van den Berg 2005, pp. 227–31.

16 Peterson 2009, p. 114

17 *'De Millioenen uit Deli'* was written by Mr. J. van den Brand, a lawyer in Medan. In the Netherlands it provoked uproar in the Lower House ('Tweede Kamer'), resulting in the Public Prosecutor, Mr. J.L.T. Rhemrev, being asked to hold an inquiry; his report was published in 1904.

18 The exact period that the branch operated in Medan is not known. Falconer (1987, p. 33) provides the dates 1885 to 1891, Groeneveld (1989, p. 108) suggests the dates 1888 to 1891 in the running text, but the lists of commercial photographers and professional studios on pp. 179–92 note the dates 1885 to 1895. Boom (2005, p. 254) states that it was the period 1883 to 1895. Bool (2007, p. 309) also maintains that the studio was already present from 1883.

19 For more about this company, see Falconer 1987. The later renowned photographers J.F. Charls and J.C. van Es also worked for G.R. Lambert & Co before they opened a photographic studio together in Java.

20 Nieuwenhuis 1901. On the first page he writes, 'As far as I know, a professional photographer has never before been granted permission to accompany expeditions such as this in Indonesia'.

21 His work appeared in a number of publications by Isaäc Groneman (1832–1912).

22 Albums numbered 0075 to 0079, titled: 'Journey in the Netherlands East Indies 1920–21' ('Indische Reis 1920–21'). The collection also includes two albums relating to Sumatra (alb. nos. 0282 and 0283) that are probably derived from the same or another journey.

23 According to Gonggryp (1934, p. 143) 193,618 Europeans lived on Java and Madura in 1930; the total number of Europeans living in the Netherlands East Indies amounted to 242,372.

24 Indo-Europeans were of mixed European and Indonesian origins. The synonym 'Indo' used to have negative connotations that have now disappeared. It is often used with pride today.

25 *Totok* are 'full-blooded' Europeans. This term could be applied to new arrivals from Europe as well as to 'full-blooded' Europeans who had lived in the Netherlands East Indies for generations. Like the notion 'Indisch', it is used in several different ways.

26 See the lists of commercial photographers and photographic studios in Groeneveld 1989, pp. 179–92.

27 See Karen Strassler's essays and book (2007, 2008 and 2010).

28 This took flight after the publication of the book with the same title, *Daar wèrd wat groots verricht... Nederlandsch-Indië in de XXste eeuw* (Elsevier 1941, edited by Willem Henri van Helsdingen and Hendrik Hoogenberk). The foreword states that this was a response to the pronouncement by Jan Pietersz. Coen, 'Daer can in Indien wat groots verricht worden' ('Something monumental can be achieved in the Indies').

29 See chapter on colonial portrait photography

30 Although the Second World War ended in Indonesia on 15 August 1945 with Japan's surrender, the violence continued: the battle for Indonesia's independence had begun. Soekarno and Hatta announced the Republic of Indonesia on 17 August 1945, but the Netherlands refused to recognise it. Indonesian armed resistance tried to fill the power vacuum left by the Japanese, by force if necessary. This bloody Bersiap period lasted until the spring of 1946. The Indonesian government had barely any control over the armed resistance. Dutch and Indo-European citizens in republican-controlled areas were interned in camps for their own safety, but also to isolate them.

31 Alb. no. 0270, donated by A.P. van Duyn.

32 Tillema 1920–1921, p. 43. The photograph used here (inv. no. 60018615) also appeared in the KPM albums that are discussed on p. 79. Tillema's photograph archive is preserved in the collection of the National Museum of Ethnology in Leiden.

33 Including, among others, the Tropenmuseum (Amsterdam), the National Museum of Ethnology and KITLV (Leiden) and the Wereldmuseum (Rotterdam). The photo collection of the Wereldmuseum has meanwhile been moved to the Museum of Photography (Nederlands Fotomuseum) in Rotterdam.

34 See Bijl 2011.

35 For more about photographs of desolate, scarred landscapes, also see Roosenboom 2009.

36 Bloembergen 2002, pp. 68–69.

37 Roodenburg 2002, p. 40.

38 Adam (1930, p. 140) wrote about the practise of teeth filing: 'With the growing "civilization", this operation will doubtless disappear, together with many other old Batak customs'.

39 There is a copy of the film in the EYE Film Institute Netherlands collection (the former Filmmuseum). One of the first subtitles accurately describes it as a 'documentary cultural film in seven acts' ('een documentair cultuur-filmwerk in zeven acten').

40 There are multiple copies of this photograph album. The Tropenmuseum has three in its collection – one from Queen Wilhelmina (on loan since 1924), Governor-General Fock's copy, and the copy belonging to Resident Dingemans (both were donated). Dingemans was not Resident of Yogyakarta in 1923; he fulfilled this function from 1924 to 1927. We do not know when the album was presented to him.

41 This was accompanied by an exhibition catalogue, see Adam 1919.

42 Nieuwenhuys 1981, 1982 and 1988, and the book that appeared under his pseudonym, E. Breton de Nijs, in 1961.

43 *Tempo doeloe* means 'De vroegere tijd' ('Days gone by') and symbolises a nostalgic look back at the colonial past in the Netherlands East Indies.

44 Among others, also see Boom 2005, and the essay by Pattynama in Legêne and Van Dijk 2011, pp. 160–69.

45 See the forthcoming publication by Daan van Dartel in the framework of PhotoCLEC (Photographs, Colonial Legacy and Museums in Contemporary European Culture), an international research project about colonial photograph collections.

46 The Russian-born, German painter, choreographer, author and photographer Walter Spies (1895–1942) was a great friend of Paul Spies, but not a member of his family.

47 This photograph is no longer preserved in the collection.

48 Journal published by the Dutch Society for the Advancement of Industry (Nederlandsche Maatschappij ter bevordering van Nijverheid), vol. 4, issue VII (part XLVI of the entire series), Haarlem 1883, p. 168.

49 *Ibid.*, vol 4, issue X (part XLIX of the entire series), Haarlem 1886 p. 184.

50 Marie-François-Xavier-Joseph-Jean-Honoré Brau de Saint-Pol Lias (1840–1914) headed the various expeditions. He departed for Malaysia and Sumatra in 1880 with the mining engineer M.J. Errington. He gave a lecture at the 1883 International Colonial and Export Exhibition in Amsterdam in which he used transparencies that documented his experiences in Aceh.

51 P.J. Veth, G.A. Wilken, H.C. Klinken 1883, part I, p. 55.
52 Prints made by the Amsterdam-based photographer P. Oosterhuis
53 A.D. Veen worked as a taxidermist at the Colonial Museum in Haarlem.
54 See *De locomotief: Samarangsch handels- en advertentieblad*, between January 1865 to December 1866.
55 He later became a coffee grower in Menado. Thanks to Steven Wachlin for the information about H. Veen.
56 The series of photographs is numbered 60011604 and 60018024–26. The location is different in image no. 60018024.
57 For J.E. Jasper, see the first volume in this series of books about the Tropenmuseum collections: Legêne and Van Dijk 2011, pp. 123–24.
58 Jasper and Mas Pirngadie 1912, p. 9. The caption translates as 'Tanggerang plaiters'.
59 In the Tropenmuseum collection, inv. no. 4765-111.
60 Bloembergen 2002.
61 Legêne 2010, pp. 118–55. Examples in the Tropenmuseum collection include inv. nos. 4925-1 and 2, 4765-89 and the series 3278-1045*, 5244-1* and 6173-1c-*.
62 Vink 1997.
63 Colonial Museum, bulletin, July 1895.
64 Huub Jans and Hans van den Brink 1980, p. 40.
65 Annual Report of the Colonial Institute Association, Amsterdam, vol. 4, 1914, p. 21.
66 Janneke van Dijk, Jaap de Jonge, Nico de Klerk 2010.
67 Annual Report of the Colonial Institute Association, Amsterdam, vol. 3, 1913, p. 28.
68 Annual Report of the Colonial Institute Association, Amsterdam, vol. 5, 1915, p. 14.
69 *Nieuwe Rotterdamsche Courant*, 3 September 1915; also see Prof Dr J.C. van Eerde, *Gids voor de tentoonstelling betreffende Oud-Javaansch en Hedendaagsch Balisch Hindoeïsme*, Amsterdam: Drukkerij J.H. de Bussy, 1915.
70 See page 8 in the notes from the Board of Directors, KIT 22/11/1915, KIT inv. no. 215.
71 Catalogue to the jubilee exhibition in 1923.
72 According to the descriptions of Hinduism and the work undertaken by the Archaeological Service: '[…] The difficulties that the Archaeological Service has to deal with can be understood from several series of photographs that depict the temples in a state of decay and after restoration. The Archaeological Service has to be thanked for its courtesy in making these pictures available for this exhibition' (from the catalogue to the 1923 jubilee exhibition, p. 37b).
73 Letter from Bley to Mr Mees dated 20 September 1938. Bley advised: 'Als U eens daar komt, vraag dan maar inzage'. ('If you ever visit the Colonial Institute's museum, ask if you can take a look in the albums.')
74 H.F. Wagenaar Reisiger, Demmeni, *Indië in Beeld*, published by the ANWB, the Royal Dutch Touring Club, Haarlem, De Tulp, 1911.
75 H.F. Wagenaar Reisiger in: 'Korte, toelichtende tekst bij het plaatwerk Indië in Beeld uitgegeven door den ANWB', Toeristenbond voor Nederland, Haarlem: N.V. Tulp, 1911.
76 See, for example, inv. nos. 4765-112, 4765-119, 4765-65, and 4765-74 to 76.
77 Annual Report of the Royal Colonial Institute Association, Amsterdam, 1927, pp. 76–77.
78 Annual Report of the Royal Colonial Institute Association, Amsterdam, vol. 32, 1942, p. 12.
79 Annual Report of the Royal Indies Institute Association, Amsterdam, vol. 35, 1945, pp. 11–12.
80 Annual Report of the Royal Tropical Institute, Amsterdam, vol. 40, 1950, p. 11.
81 Annual Report of the Royal Indies Institute Association, Amsterdam, vol. 38, 1948, pp. 16–17.
82 NIWIN, Pelita, Rapwi (Relief and Aid to Prisoners of War in Indonesia), see: *Kortsluiting*, vol. 4, no. 18, 22 September 1978.
83 Annual Report of the Royal Indies Institute Association, Amsterdam, vol. 39, 1949, p. 17.
84 *Moesson*, vol. 23, 1978, no. 5, pp. 4–5.
85 Letter to the 'Indo-European' journal *Moesson*, dated 26 August 1980 from L. Ducelle, received 8 September 1980, and a thank-you note dated 10 September from E.G. Spruyt.
86 The revised edition was published in 1998 under the same title.
87 E.G. Spruyt (1922–2011), Indologist and director of Netherlands East Indies agricultural companies (tea, cinchona, coffee, rubber). He was manager of KIT's historical photograph archive from 1975 to 1987.
88 Funded in the framework of the Indonesian–Dutch Cultural Accord; historical maps and prints were duplicated in addition to the photographs. Besides the KIT, the National Archive, KITLV and the Department of Military History of the Royal Netherlands Army (Sectie Krijgsgeschiedenis van de Koninklijke Landmacht) were also involved. In total 40,000 photographs, 12,000 maps and 1500 prints were documented and added as 35 mm negatives.
89 Steven Vink, Internal memorandum for the Department of Visual Documentation, May 1986.
90 Janneke van Dijk, VIDOC Cijfermatig, internal memorandum, October 1988.
91 Els Barents and Kees Kuil 1984. Forty exhibitions were held in various locations in Amsterdam.
92 The Tropenmuseum was given a unique daguerreotype in 2002 that is dated to between 1852 and 1857 (Sayers collection), see Fig. 109.
93 Among others, the albums numbered 1460, 1472, 1461 and 1467.
94 The commission members were Douglas Newton, emeritus curator The Metropolitan Museum of Art in New York; Philippe Peltier, curator Musée National des Arts Africains et Océaniens in Paris; and Elizabeth Edwards, curator Pitt Rivers Museum, University of Oxford.
95 Elizabeth Edwards, December 1998, *idem* p. 10, Summary.

96 Slides 25,652, photographs 111,360, albums 2983, negatives 54,280, picture postcards 8291, lantern slides 528. The museum works closely with other Dutch ethnographic museums on creating a single online resource of all ethnographic collections in the country. The collections of all the ethnographic museums can be viewed on The Netherlands Ethnographic Collection Foundation (Stichting Volkenkundige Collectie Nederland; SVCN) website (www.svcn.nl). Other collaborations, such as the 'Geheugen van Nederland', also display the museum's collection on the Web, where it is classified by topic. The museum's partnership with Wikimedia facilitated an active collaboration with the Wikipedia community, including providing a context for the material.

97 The museum used funds from the Bankgiro Loterij to purchase these important series of portraits of Moluccans and Indo-Europeans who came to the Netherlands after Indonesia gained independence.

98 Tropenmuseum, 23 September 2011 – 15 January 2012.

99 The term 'Indo' is used to describe Indo-Europeans in the Netherlands East Indies. The IWI was more recently renamed the Indo Scientific Institute for Culture and History.

100 Interview Janneke van Dijk with Cees Taillie, 8 September 2004.

101 De Graaff, Locher-Scholten 2007.

102 Yogyakarta and Surakarta.

103 So-called long-term political agreements in which relationships are arranged in minute detail; a brief declaration included fewer details.

104 From the fifth impression (author's second revised edition) of Multatuli's *Max Havelaar of de koffiveilingen der Nederlandsche Handelmaatschappij*, 1881, p. 59.

105 For more on tiger fights, see Wessing 1992, pp. 287–308.

106 Bossenbroek 1995, p. 823.

107 On this occasion D. Fock was presented with two albums: one about the post office in Medan (alb. no. 0145), and another by Medan city council (alb. no. 0277).

108 'Reis van Z.E. gouverneur generaal Mr. D. Fock naar Sumatra´s Oostkust, 9 tot 21 september 1925'.

109 On this occasion the Sultan of Yogyakarta presented Fock with a number of items, including an album of a special *wayang* performance; Tassilo Adam took the photographs (alb. no. 1470).

110 Gloudemans 1997.

111 Tapes of the interviews conducted in 1976 and 1977 are preserved in the Catholic Documentation Centre (Katholiek Documentatie Centrum) in Nijmegen.

112 In 2006 the anthropologist Marie-Antoinette Thérèse Willemse obtained her doctorate with a biography of the missionary and researcher Jilis Verheijen (1908–97); she previously edited a book of letters by another missionary, Willem van Bekkum (1910–98).

113 A *puputan* is a mass ritual suicide that was preferable to facing the act of surrender, an honourable 'fight to the death', which a ruler and his followers chose in preference to defeat.

114 J. Jongejans 1939.

115 *Nieuws van den dag voor Nederlandsch Indie*, 25 July 1939; and *Het Vaderland*, 24 July 1939.

116 The expedition was under the command of H.J.T. Bijlmer.

117 *Het Vaderland*, 24 July 1939.

118 J. Jongejans 1922.

119 *Idem*, pp. 221–22.

120 Letter from N.F. Jongejans to Van der Pijl, 18 April 2001.

121 Painted in 1938 by Hendrik Paulides; also see inv. nos. 10016339–41.

122 The photograph collection is separated into albums and single photographs. A collection of single photographs that belong together is also treated as an album.

123 Tropenmuseum employees only started photographing on location from the 1970s; see chapter 2.

124 This also includes loose-leaf album photographs that for conservation reasons are stored in archive boxes.

125 See the Annual Reports of the Redjang Lebong Gold Mining Company (Goud-Exploratiemaatschappij 'Redjang-Lebong', Batavia, from 1898: Mijnbouwmaatschappij 'Redjang-Lebong'), 1897–1918 and 1920–38, in the IISG, NEHA archive.

126 The Sanders family also had a film camera. For more on this family's amateur films, now preserved in the EYE Film Institute Netherlands collection, see the essay by Noordegraaf and Pouw 2009.

127 See, for example, inv. no. 60037579, 'Group of decorated workers from the Bandjardawa Sugar Factory', 1926.

128 See, for example, inv. no. 60010422, 'View over the Pasir Banda rubber plantation', c. 1930.

129 Breman 1987.

130 See alb. no. 0264, inv. nos. 60016333 and 60016334.

131 See, for example, *Het Nieuws van den Dag voor Nederlandsch-Indië*, Batavia, 26 May 1920.

132 See *NV. Machinefabriek ´Braat'*, pp. 44–45.

133 *Het Vaderland, Staat en Letterkundig Nieuwsblad*, The Hague, 10 February 1920.

134 Especially the IWI Collection (see p. 58) has several albums that provide impressions of post-war trade and industry.

135 NIMEF was a successor to The First Netherlands-Indies Coffee Roasting House (Eerste Nederlandsch-Indische Koffiebranderij), W.M. Scheuel 1991.

136 Inv. no. 60012131.

137 See inv. no. 60012152, 'Group portrait of the office staff at the NIMEF factory, Bandung', c. 1950.

138 Alexander von Humboldt (1769–1859) was a naturalist and explorer. He conducted research in Central and South America.

139 Franz Wilhelm Junghuhn in Nieuwenhuys 1982; and Nieuwenhuys and Jaquet, 1980.

140 These included: 1. The Department of 's Lands Plantentuin; 2. The Botanical Garden at Buitenzorg; 3. The Herbarium and Museum for Systematic Botany; 4. The Botanical Laboratory; 5. The Zoological Museum; 6. Laboratorium for Marine Research; and 7. The Phytochemical Laboratory.

141 De Bussy also made several films that are now part of the EYE Film Institute Netherlands collection, Amsterdam.
142 David van Duuren 2011, pp. 52–55.
143 www.knag-expedities.nl.
144 'Midden-Sumatra. Reizen en onderzoekingen der Sumatra-expeditie, uitgerust door het Aardrijkskundig Genootschap 1877–1879, beschreven door de leden der expeditie, onder toezicht van prof. P.J. Veth', Part 1, 1882. Album no. 0367 contains 145 photographs documenting the expedition.
145 David van Duuren 2011.
146 David van Duuren, *et al.*, 2007.
147 Preserved in Leiden University's Print Room.
148 Alb. no. 1642
149 Folders 8, 9 and 18.
150 Donated to the Colonial Institute by Van Erp in 1929.
151 N.J. Krom 1933.
152 Including from Rob Nieuwenhuys and Hein Buitenweg.
153 Bosma and Raben, 2003, p. 12.
154 See pag. 24
155 E. Locher-Scholten, 'Mr. P. Brooshooft, een biografische schets in koloniaal-ethisch perspectief', in *Bijdragen tot Taal-, Land- en Volkenkunde*, vol. 132, 1976, no. 2/3, Leiden: KITLV p. 333.
156 The Suez Canal drastically reduced the time it took to travel between Europe and Indonesia, and the Agrarian Act permitted private individuals to hold land in a long lease.
157 E. Breton de Nijs, 1977, p. 9.
158 For details about the prices of ordered photographs, see Norbert van den Berg and Steve Wachlin, 2005, p. 125.
159 Bosma and Raben 2003, p. 12.
160 In the book *Heren van de Thee*, Haasse describes the heat in Batavia, and the loneliness and boredom on the plantations. Additionally, the Tropenmuseum has three post mortem photographs, but considering the high death toll, these seem to be exceptions. Photographing the dead had to happen soon after the event, as the heat necessitated rapid burials.
161 The word 'Asians' here is understood to include Indonesians, Chinese and Arabs.
162 The house now belongs to the Brimob Polri (Korps Brigade Mobil Polisi Republik Indonesia) and is located on the Jl. Prapatan in Jakarta; the museum only has five photographs by Meesen.
163 Her full name was Johanna Adriana Louise Holle-van Motman; see Van den Berg and Wachlin, 2005, p. 238.
164 Haasse 1992, pp. 71, 79 and 80.
165 For example, Van der Hucht, Holle and Kerkhoven; also see Van den Berg and Wachlin.
166 Bosma & Raben 2003, pp. 127, 184 and 211.
167 The word 'servants' is expressly used here; 'employees' implies a different relationship.
168 Haasse 1992, p. 89; and Hein Buitenweg, *Soos en samenleving in tempo doeloe*, The Hague: Servire, 1965, pp. 120–23; for advertisements promoting European products and (canned) food, wines, etc., see Heather Sutherland, *The Making of a Bureaucratic Elite; The Colonial Transformation of the Javanese Priyayi*, Singapore: Heinemann Educational Books (Asia) Ltd. 1980, p. 14.
169 Van den Berg and Wachlin 2005, pp. 149 and 164; the gamelans are now preserved in the Prabu Geusan Ulun Museum, Sumedang also see Henry Spiller 2004, p. 146.
170 The *wedana* (district chief) of Cicuruk, West Java, see Van den Berg and Wachlin 2005, p. 150.
171 See inv. no. 60022734.
172 Bosma and Raben 2003, p. 128.
173 *Ibid.*, pp. 108, 112, 113 and 118.
174 Sutherland 1980, pp. 16, 17 and 20.
175 *Ibid.*, p. 43.
176 For additional biographical details, see KITLV inv. no. 4184, dated 1900.
177 Bosma and Raben 2003, p. 13.
178 Esther Wils, 2005, for a detailed description of how European houses were laid out and decorated.
179 Strongly influenced by the imperial style; see A. Heuken, 2007, p. 250.
180 For European women this was a white blouse with lace.
181 Bosma and Raben 2007, p. 92.
182 For example, inv. nos. 60004386 and 10013642; and Haasse 1992, p. 89.
183 Paintings with romanticised representations of nature or of the local population.
184 For example, inv. nos. 10013678 (VOC) and 60026668 (Javanese).
185 Auctions of household goods were called a *lelang*; see Sutherland 1980, p. 42.
186 When he became the Director of the Navy Institute in 1905, he moved into the official residence on the Ujung Road in Surabaya, a colossal house close to the port. After retiring in 1911 he moved to another house on the same road, and again in 1914 to the Ketabang neighbourhood, in a southerly area of Surabaya. The house on Ujung Road was decorated with a blend of European and Indonesian elements. Several different sets of furniture appear to have been ordered, two in Jugendstil and one in Art Deco style.
187 At least one photograph of his interiors shows that he knew the work of Kurkdjian & Co: inv. no. 60025782
188 Interior of the Van Lonkhuyzen family's home, inv. no. 60017980.
189 Inv. no. 60038304.
190 Possibly because these large decorative objects suited the size of the rooms.
191 Sutherland 1980, pp. 31 and 36.
192 For example, the painting by Antonio D. Gabbiani (1652–1726), 'Portrait of Four Servants of the Medici Court', c. 1684. Jean Gelman Taylor, 'Costume and Gender in Colonial Java', in Henk Schulte Nordholt 1997.
193 Inv. nos. 10026898 and 60026217.
194 Bosma and Raben 2003, p. 71.
195 Peter Mingaars, *et al.*, 2005.
196 Sutherland 1980, pp. 14 and 15; and Bosma and Raben

2007, p. 29.

197 Daniella Stötefalk, 'Stille Invloeden, Een onderzoek naar de invloed van Nederlandse vrouwen op de ontwikkeling van de Indische Kunstnijverheid, 1900–1942', unpublished thesis, Tropenmuseum Reference Library, 2011, p. 16.

198 *Het pauperisme onder de Europeanen in Nederlandsch-Indië*, Batavia: Landsdrukkerij, 1901–1902.

199 The KITLV collection has photographs of the Indo-European Ament family, who lived in Yogyakarta at the end of the 19th century.

200 For the most part, these were photographed by Europeans.

201 See Fig. 107. The celebrated painter Raden Saleh also had his photographic portrait taken in the Netherlands East Indies during the 19th century. During a long stay in Holland, Cornelis Kruseman and others taught Raden Saleh portrait painting. Portraits were an important source of income after he returned to the Netherlands East Indies in 1851. This photographic portrait shows the proud Raden Saleh with his sketchbook, indicating that he was a man of his time.

202 Also see the first chapter and the epilogue.

203 Also see De Jongh 1986, p. 23.

204 Koos van Brakel 2004, p. 129.

205 The little jacket made by Santje Wieseman-Dom (1833–1909) is now preserved in the Tropenmuseum collection (inv. no. 1595-2). Also see Shatanawi 2009, pp. 256–57.

206 Also see Knaap 1999.

207 For the picture postcard, see Haks and Wachlin 2004, p. 194.

208 Besides a few other photographs in the series, the Tropenmuseum also has a painting made after the photograph by H. de Rhijnlander in 1950 (inv. no. 60046593).

209 A. Groeneveld, *et al.*, 1989, p. 55.

210 Sontag 1973, p. 15.

REFERENCES

Adam, Tassilo, *Delische Kunstkring. Tentoonstelling der Bataksche Etnografische Verzameling en der Fotografien van Batakland en Volk van den heer Tassilo Adam*. Medan, Delische Kunstkring, 1919.

Adam, Tassilo, 'Battak Ways and Days', in *Asia. The American Magazine on the Orient* 30, 1930, pp. 118–41.

Ballard, Chris, Steven Vink and Anton Ploeg, *Race to the snow, photography and exploration of Dutch New Guinea,* 1907-1936. Amsterdam, KIT Publishers, 2001.

Barents, Els & Kees Kuil (eds.), *Foto '84 Amsterdam. Eerste internationale fotomanifestatie in Nederland.* Amsterdam, Stichting Amsterdam Foto, 1984.

Barger, M.S. & W.B White, *The Daguerreotype, Nineteenth-Century Technology and Modern Science*. London, Smithonian Institution Press, 1991.Batchen, G., *Each Wild Idea; Writing, Photography, History*. Cambridge, MIT Press, 2002.

Batchen, G. *Burning with Desire: the Conception of Photography.* Cambridge MA, The MIT Press, 1997.

Batchen, G., *Forget Me Not, Photography and Remembrance.* Princeton, Princeton Architectural Press, 2006.

Berg, Norbert van den & Steven Wachlin, *Het album van Mientje. Een fotoalbum uit 1862 in Nederlandsch-Indië.* Bussum, Uitgeverij Thoth, 2005.

Bergen, Leo van, *Van Koloniale geneeskunde tot internationale gezondheidszorg. Een geschiedenis van honderd jaar Nederlandse Vereniging voor Tropische Geneeskunde.* Amsterdam, KIT Publishers, 2007.

Bernard, Ch., 'De heer G.F.J. Bley 70 jaar', in *De thee: korte aanteekeningen van het Algemeen proefstation voor thee,* 1925, p. 98.

Bestuur van de Planters Vereeniging Semarang-Kedoe, Het, 'G.K.F.J. Bley 80 jaar', in *De bergcultures: orgaan van het Algemeen landbouw syndicaat, het Zuid- en West-Sumatra syndicaat, de Centrale vereniging tot beheer van proefstations voor de overjarige culturen in Indonesië en de Algemene vereniging van rubberplanters ter oostkust van Sumatra* 36, 1935, pp. 806–7.

Beumer, Marjolein, *Capturing Museum Knowledge. A Twenty-Year Evolution in Digitally Recording the Tropenmuseum Collection*, Bulletin 386. Amsterdam, KIT Publishers, 2008.

Bijl, Paulus, *Emerging Memory. Photographs of Colonial Atrocity in Dutch Cultural Remembrance.* Utrecht, Utrecht University Press, 2011.

Bloembergen, Marieke, *De koloniale vertoning. Nederland en Indië op de wereldtentoonstellingen (1880–1931).* Amsterdam, Wereldbibliotheek, 2002.

Boer, Dr. M.G. de, *De Koninklijke Paketvaart Maatschappij.* Amsterdam, Bureau Industria, 1924.

Bool, Flip (ed.), *Dutch Eyes. Nieuwe geschiedenis van de fotografie in Nederland.* Zwolle, Uitgeverij Waanders, 2007.

Boom, Mattie, 'Fotografie in de Sumatra-albums van Paul Sandel', in *Bulletin van het Rijksmuseum* 3, 2005, pp. 243–68.

Boom, M. *et al.*, *Stilstaande beelden; ondergang en opkomst van de fotografie.* Amsterdam, Boekmanstichting / Van Gennep, 1996.

Boonstra, J., M. van den Heuvel *et al.*, *In atmosferisch licht, picturalisme in de Nederlandse fotografie 1890–1925.* Zwolle, Uitgeverij Waanders, 2010.

Bosma, Ulbe & Remco Raben. *De oude Indische wereld 1500–1920.* Amsterdam, Uitgeverij Bert Bakker, 2003.

Bossenbroek, Martin, *Holland op zijn Breedst, Indië en Zuid-Afrika in de Nederlandse cultuur omstreeks 1900.* Amsterdam, Uitgeverij Bert Bakker, 1996.

Bossenbroek, Martin *et al.*, *Weerzien met Indië. 10: Koloniaal bestuur tot 1870. 17: Landbouw.* Zwolle, Uitgeverij Waanders, 1994

Bossenbroek, Martin *et al.*, *Weerzien met Indië. 34: Zending en missie.* Zwolle, Uitgeverij Waanders, 1995.

Bossenbroek, Martin *et al.*, *Weerzien met Indië. Het beeld van tempo doeloe.* Zwolle, Uitgeverij Waanders, 1996.

Brakel, J H. van, *Charles Sayers 1901–1943: Pioneer Painter in the Dutch East Indies.* Amsterdam, KIT Publshers, 2004.

Brand, J. van den, *De millioenen uit Deli.* Amsterdam, Höveker & Wormser, 1902.

Breton de Nijs, E. (Rob Nieuwenhuys's pseudonym), *Tempo doeloe. Fotografische documenten uit het oude Indië 1870–1914.* Amsterdam, Querido, 1961.

Breton de Nijs, E., *Batavia, koningin van het oosten,* The Hague, Thomas & Eras Uitgevers, 1977.

Buitenweg, H., *Soos en samenleving in tempo doeloe.* The Hague, Servire, 1965.

Campo, J.N.F.M à., *Koninklijke Paketvaart Maatschappij. Stoomvaart en staatsvorming in de Indonesische archipel 1888–1914.* Hilversum, Verloren, 1992.

Dijk, Jan van, *Handboek herkennen fotografische en fotomechanische procedés. Historische en moderne procedés en digitale afdruktechnieken.* Leiden, Primavera Pers, 2011.

Dijk, Janneke van, Jaap de Jonge & Nico de Klerk, *J.C. Lamster, een vroege filmer in Nederlands-Indië.* Amsterdam, KIT Publishers, 2010.

Drissen, E., *Vastgelegd voor later. Indische foto's (1917–1942) van Thilly Weissenborn. Verzameld door Ernst Drissen.* Amsterdam, Sijthoff, 1983.

Duuren, D.A.P. van, *et al.*, *Physical Anthropology Reconsidered. Human Remains at the Tropenmuseum.* Amsterdam, KIT Publishers, 2007.

Duuren, D.A.P. van, *et al.*, *Oceania at the Tropenmuseum.* Amsterdam, KIT Publishers, 2011.

Edwards, E., *Anthropology and Photography 1860–1920*. New Haven CT, Yale University Press, 1992.
Edwards, E., *Raw Histories: Photographs, Anthropology and Museums*. Oxford, Berg, 2001.
Edwards, E., *Photographs, Objects, Histories: On the Materiality of Images*. London, Routledge, 2004.
Edwards, E. (ed.), *Sensible Objects: Colonialism, Museums and Material Culture*. Oxford, Berg, 2006.
Erp, Th. van & Krom, N.J., *Beschrijving van Barabudur*. The Hague, Nijhoff, 1920–31.
Falconer, John, *A Vision of the Past. A History of Photography in Singapore and Malaya. The Photographs of G.R. Lambert & Co., 1880–1910*. Singapore, Times Editions, 1987.
Gloudemans, Cees, *Dwars door Borneo*. Amsterdam, Atlas, 1997.
Gonggryp, G.F.E., *Geïllustreerde encyclopaedie van Nederlandsch-Indië*. Leiden, NV Leidsche Uitgeversmaatschappij, 1934.
Gouda, F. *et al.*, *Tempo Doeloe: koloniale cultuur in Nederlands Indie*. Groningen, Groniek, 2007.
Gouda, F. & J. Clancy-Smith, *Domesticating the Empire: Race, Gender, and Family Life in French and Dutch Colonialism*. Charlottesville VA, University Press of Virginia, 1998.
Gouda, F., *Dutch Culture Overseas: Colonial Practice in the Netherlands Indies, 1900–1942*. Amsterdam, Amsterdam University Press, 1995.
Graaff, B.G-J. de & E.B. Locher-Scholten, *J.P. Graaf van Limburg Stirum 1873–1948: tegendraads landvoogd en diplomaat*. Zwolle, Uitgeverij Waanders, 2007.
Griffioen, Dirk, *Christelijke zendingen en wereldgodsdiensten*. Boekencentrum BV Zoetermeer, 2007.
Groeneveld, Anneke *et al.*, *Toekang Potret. 100 jaar fotografie in Nederlands-Indië 1839–1939*. Amsterdam, Fragment, 1989.
Groeneveld, Anneke *et al.*, *Beelden van de Oriënt: fotografie en toerisme, 1860–1900*. Amsterdam, Fragment, 1986.
Haasse, H., *Heren van de Thee*. Amsterdam, Querido 1992.
Haks, Leo & Steven Wachlin, *Indonesia. 500 Early Postcards*. Singapore, Archipelago Press, 2004.
Hecht, P., *125 Jaar openbaar kunstbezit met steun van de Vereniging Rembrandt*. Zwolle, Uitgeverij Waanders, 2008.
Heuken, A., *Historical Sites of Jakarta*. Jakarta, Cipta Loka Caraka, 2007.
Hight, E.M. & G.D. Sampson, *Colonialist Photography: Imag(in)ing Race and Place*. London, Routledge, 2002.
Hoedt, Th. G. E., 'G.F.J. Bley', in *De bergcultures: orgaan van het Algemeen landbouw syndicaat, het Zuid- en West-Sumatra syndicaat, de Centrale vereniging tot beheer van proefstations voor de overjarige culturen in Indonesië en de Algemene vereniging van rubberplanters ter oostkust van Sumatra* 38, 1935, pp. 878–79.
Hoedt, Th. G. E., 'Vader Bley bevorderd tot Officier in de Orde van Oranje-Nassau!', in *De bergcultures: orgaan van het Algemeen landbouw syndicaat, het Zuid- en West-Sumatra syndicaat, de Centrale vereniging tot beheer van proefstations voor de overjarige culturen in Indonesië en de Algemene vereniging van rubberplanters ter oostkust van Sumatra* 40, 1935, pp. 956–58.
Jans, H. & Hans van den Brink, *Tropen in Amsterdam. 70 jaar Koninklijk Instituut voor de Tropen*, Amsterdam, Royal Tropical Institute, 1980.
Jasper, J.E. & Mas Pirngadie, *De Inlandsche Kunstnijverheid in Nederlandsch Indië. Deel 1: Het Vlechtwerk*. The Hague, Mouton, 1912.
Jongejans, J., *Uit Dajakland; kijkjes in het leven van den koppensneller en zijn omgeving*. Amsterdam, Meulenhoff, 1922.
Jongejans, J., *Land en volk van Atjeh: vroeger en nu* (with a foreword by H. Colijn), Baarn, Hollandia, 1939.
Jongh, E. de, *Portretten van Echt en Trouw, huwelijk en gezin in de Nederlandse Kunst van de zeventiende eeuw*. Zwolle, Uitgeverij Waanders, 1986.
Jongmans, Rob, 'De missionaris als voer voor antropologen. Reisalbums van Martien Gloudemans', in *Nieuwsbrief Nederlands Fotogenootschap* 56, 2007, pp. 22–23.
Jongmans, Rob, 'Religieus schouwspel op Bali. Fotografen vereeuwigen het leven in een aards paradijs', in *Fotografisch geheugen* 58, 2008, pp. 6–7.
Jongmans, Rob, 'Reis door de Indische archipel met de Paketvaart. Het stoomschip als leidmotief', in *Fotografisch geheugen* 66, 2010, pp. 13–15.
Kielstra, E.B., *Onder de Atjehers, verhaal van een Franschman voor Nederlandsche lezers bewerkt*. Haarlem, Uitgeverij De Erven F. Bohn, 1885.
Knaap, Gerrit, *Cephas, Yogyakarta. Photography in the Service of the Sultan*. Leiden, KITLV Press, 1999.
Knol, Meta *et al.*, *Beyond the Dutch, Indonesië, Nederland en de beeldende kunsten van 1900 tot nu*. Amsterdam, KIT Publishers, 2009.
Koninklijke Paketvaart Maatschappij (Royal Packet Steam Navigation Company), *Guide Through Netherlands India*. Amsterdam, De Bussy, 1911.
Krom, N.J., 'Het Karmawibhangga op Barabudur', in *Mededeelingen der koninklijke academie van wetenschappen, afdeeling letterkunde*, part 79, Amsterdam, 1933.
Legêne, Susan, 'Uitsparing en inkleuring – Batik en koloniale beeldvorming in Nederland', in *Spiegelreflex. Culturele sporen van de koloniale ervaring*. Amsterdam, Uitgeverij Bert Bakker, 2010, pp. 118–55.
Legêne, Susan & Janneke van Dijk, *The Netherlands East Indies at the Tropenmuseum*. Amsterdam, KIT Publishers, 2011.
Locher-Scholten, E., 'Mr. P. Brooshooft, een biografische schets in koloniaal-ethisch perspectief', in *Bijdragen tot Taal-, Land- en Volkenkunde* 132, no. 2/3, Leiden, KITLV Press, 1976.
Maxwell, Anne, *Colonial Photography and Exhibitions: Representations of the 'Native' and the Making of European Identities*. London, Leicester University Press, 1999.
Merrillees, Scott, *Batavia in Nineteenth Century Photographs*. Singapore, Archipelago Press, 2000.
Meyer, A.H., 'Bley en de kapokcultuur', in *De bergcultures: orgaan van het Algemeen landbouw syndicaat, het Zuid- en West-Sumatra syndicaat, de Centrale vereniging tot beheer*

van proefstations voor de overjarige culturen in Indonesië en de Algemene vereniging van rubberplanters ter oostkust van Sumatra 36, 1935, pp. 808–9.

Mingaars, P., *et al.*, *Indisch Lexicon, Indische woorden in de Nederlandse literatuur*. 't Goy-Houten, Hes & de Graaf Publishers BV, 2005.

Multatuli (Eduard Douwes Dekker's pseudonym), *Max Havelaar of de Koffiveilingen der Nederlandsche Handelmaatschappij*. Rotterdam, Elsevier, 1881.

Newton, Gael, *Picture Paradise: Asia-Pacific Photography 1840s–1940s*. Canberra, NGA Publishing, 2008.

Nieuwenhuis, C., *De expeditie naar Samalanga (Januari 1901). Dagverhaal van een fotograaf te velde*. Amsterdam, Van Holkema & Warendorf, 1901.

Nieuwenhuys, Rob & Frits Jaquet, *Java's onuitputtelijke natuur, Reisverhalen, tekeningen en fotografieën van Franz Wilhelm Junghuhn,* Alphen a/d Rijn, Sijthoff, 1980.

Nieuwenhuys, Rob, *Baren en oudgasten. Tempo doeloe – een verzonken wereld. Fotografische documenten uit het oude Indië 1870–1920*. Amsterdam, Querido, 1981.

Nieuwenhuys, Rob, *Komen en blijven. Tempo doeloe – een verzonken wereld. Fotografische documenten uit het oude Indië 1870–1920*. Amsterdam, Querido, 1982.

Nieuwenhuys, Rob. *Met vreemde ogen. Tempo doeloe – een verzonken wereld. Fotografische documenten uit het oude Indië 1870–1920*. Amsterdam, Querido, 1988.

Noordegraaf, Julia J. & Elvira Pouw, 'Extended family films. Home Movies in the State-Sponsored Archive', in *The Moving Image* 9. Minneapolis, University of Minnesota Press, Spring 2009, pp. 83–103.

N.V. Machinefabriek "Braat", Soerabaia 1901–1921. Batavia, Ruygrok, 1921.

Ouwehand, L., *Herinneringen in beeld, fotoalbums uit Nederlands Indie*. Leiden, KITLV Press, 2009.

Pattynama, Pamela, 'Collective memory. The Interactions Between Literature, Museums, Cinema and Photography', in Legêne, Susan & Janneke van Dijk, *The Netherlands East Indies at the Tropenmuseum*. Amsterdam, KIT Publishers, 2011, pp. 160–69.

Het pauperisme onder de Europeanen in Nederlandsch-Indië. Batavia, Landsdrukkerij, 1901–1902.

Peterson, Karin *et al.*, *In het voetspoor van Louis Couperus. Pasoeroeran door de lens van Salzwedel*. Amsterdam, KIT Publishers, 2009.

Pinney, Christopher, *Camera Indica. The Social Life of Indian Photographs*. London, Reaktion Books, 1997.

Pinney, Christopher, *The Coming of Photography in India*. London, The British Library, 2008.

Protschky, S., *Images of the Tropics*. Leiden, KITLV Press, 2011.

Raden Mas Noto Soeroto, *Bij het 100ste geboortejaar van Raden Saleh: Javaansch schilder geb. te Semarang 1814, gest. te Buitenzorg 1880*. Batavia, publisher unknown, 1913.

Reed, Jane Levy (ed.), *Toward Independence. A Century of Indonesia Photographed*. San Franciso, The Friends of Photography, 1991 .

Reijly, J.M., *Care and Identification of 19th-Century Photographic Prints*. USA, Eastman Kodak Company, 1986.

Reis van Z.E. gouverneur generaal Mr. D. Fock naar Sumatra's Oostkust, 9 tot 21 september 1925. Medan, Varenkamp, 1925.

Roodenburg, Linda, *De bril van Anceaux / Anceaux's Glasses. Volkenkundige fotografie vanaf 1860*. Zwolle, Uitgeverij Waanders, 2002.

Roosenboom, Hans, 'Een foto zegt (soms) minder dan duizend woorden. Tempo doeloe: bedrieglijke rust', in *Fotografisch Geheugen* 64, 2009, pp. 28–29.

Schulte Nordholt, H.G.Ch., *Outward Appearances: Dressing State and Society in Indonesia*. Leiden, KITLV Press, 1997.

Schreuel, W.M., *En de Brantas stroomt: de geschiedenis van een koffiebranderij en een blikfabriek: tijdvak 1876–1940, planter 1890–1901, fabrikant 1901–1940*. The Hague, Moesson, 1991.

Shatanawi, Mirjam, *Islam in beeld. Kunst en cultuur van moslims wereldwijd*. Amsterdam, SUN, 2009.

Sontag, Susan, *On Photography*, New York, Farrar, Straus and Giroux, 1973.

Spiller, H., *Gamelan: The Traditional Sounds of Indonesia*. Santa Barbara, ABC-Clio, 2004.

Stötefalk, D., *Stille Invloeden, Een onderzoek naar de invloed van Nederlandse vrouwen op de ontwikkeling van de Indische Kunstnijverheid, 1900–1942*. Unpublished graduate thesis, 2011.

Strassler, Karen, 'Photography's Asian Circuits', in *IIAS Newsletter* 44, Summer 2007. Leiden, pp. 1, 4–5.

Strassler, Karen, 'Cosmopolitan Visions: Ethnic Chinese and the Photographic Imagining of Indonesia in the Late Colonial and Early Postcolonial Periods', in *The Journal of Asian Studies* 67, May 2008, pp. 395–432.

Strassler, Karen, *Refracted Visions. Popular Photography and National Modernity in Java*. Durham and London, Duke University Press, 2010.

Sutherland, H., *Pangreh Pradja: Java's Indigenous Administrative Corps and its Role in the Last Decades of Dutch Colonial Rule*. Ph.D. Dissertation, Yale University, 1973.

Sutherland, H., *The Making of a Bureaucratic Elite; The Colonial Transformation of the Javanese Priyayi*. Singapore, Heinemann Educational Books (Asia) Ltd., 1980.

Theuns-de Boer, Gerda & Saskia Asser, *Isidore van Kinsbergen (1821–1905). Photo Pioneer and Theatre Maker in the Dutch East Indies*. Zaltbommel / Leiden, Uitgeverij Aprilis / KITLV Press, 2005.

Theye, Th.,'Anmerkungen zu Franz Wilhelm Junghuhns Photographien aus Java', in *Forschen, Vermessen, Steiten. Franz Wilhelm Junghuhn (1809–1864)*. Jakarta, Goethe Institute, 2010, pp. 199–235.

Thompson, K.A., *An Eye for the Tropics: Tourism, Photography, and Framing the Caribbean Picturesque*. Durham NC, Duke University Press, 2006.

Tillema, H.F., *"Kromoblanda". Over 't vraagstuk van "het Wonen" in Kromo's groote land,* vol. III. Wassenaar, Uden Masman, 1920–1921.

Vanvugt, Ewald, *Een propagandist van het zuiverste water. H.F. Tillema (1870–1952) en de fotografie van tempo doeloe*. Amsterdam, Uitgeverij Jan Mets, 1993.

Velde, Paul van der, *Een Indische Liefde,* P.J. Veth (1814-1895) en de inburgering van Nederlands-Indië. Amsterdam, Uitgeverij Balans, 2000.

Veth, P.J., 'Schetsen van Java III. De Javaanse Gratiën', in *Eigen Haard*, 1875, pp. 300–2.

Veth, P.J., G.A. Wilken & H.C. Klinken, *Catalogus der afdeeling Nederlandsche Kolonien van de Internationaale koloniale en uitvoerhandel tentoonstelling (1 mei tot ult. october 1883) te Amsterdam.* Leiden, Brill, 1883.

Vickers, Adrian, *Bali: A Paradise Created.* Singapore, Periplus, 1989.

Vink, Steven, *'Fotografie tijdens expedities'.* In: A. Wentholt (red.), *In kaart gebracht met kapmes en kompas, met het Koninklijk Nederlands Aardrijkskundig Genootschap op expeditie tussen 1873 en 1960.* Heerlen/Amsterdam, ABP/KNAG, 2003, Pag. 344 – 349.

Vink, S. *'Cultural properties from the South: projects for conservation of the historical collection of photographs in the Tropical Museum.'* CR: interdisciplinair vakblad voor conservering en restauratie. 2004, Vol. 5, nr. 4, p. 34-41.

Wachlin, Steven, *Woodbury & Page. Photographers Java.* Leiden, KITLV Press, 1994.

Weber- van Bosse, Mevrouw A, *Een jaar aan boord H.M. Siboga.* Leiden, E.J. Brill, 1903 (Herdruk Amsterdam, Uitgeverij Atlas, 2000).

Wessing, Robert, 'A Tiger in the Heart: the Javanese *rampok macan*', in *Bijdragen tot de Taal-, Land- en Volkenkunde* 148, Leiden, KITLV, 1992, pp. 287–308.

Westerkamp, P., *How Smout became Smut; the Making and Use of Mannequins in the Colonial and Post-Colonial Displays in Amsterdam.* Forthcoming, 2012.

Willems, Wim *et al.*, *Uit Indië geboren. Vier eeuwen familiegeschiedenis.* Zwolle, Uitgeverij Waanders, 1997.

Willemsen, Marie-Antoinette Thérèse, *Een missionarisleven in brieven. Willem van Bekkum, Indië 1936–1998.* Zutphen, Walburg Pers, 2005.

Willemsen, Marie-Antoinette Thérèse, *Een pionier op Flores. Jilis Verheijen 1908–1907, missionaris en onderzoeker.* Zutphen, Walburg Pers, 2006.

Wils, E., *Wonen in Indië, House and Home in the Dutch East Indies.* The Hague, Stichting Tong-Tong, 2005.

Zoete, J. de, *et al.*, *In het volle zonlicht, de daguerreotypieën van het Museum Enschedé te Haarlem.* Haarlem, Koninklijke Joh Enschedé / Gottmer Groep, 2009.

Zweers, Louis, *Sumatra. Kolonialen, koelies en krijgers.* Houten, Fibula / Unieboek, 1988.

INDEX

ABOUT THE AUTHORS

Janneke van Dijk (JVD) is a freelance photograph researcher who specialises in colonial visual culture. For many years she was the curator of the photography collection at the Tropenmuseum. In this capacity, she was a member of the exhibition work group 'Netherlands East Indies, a colonial past' (Nederlands-Indië, een koloniaal verleden). She co-authored *Augusta Curiel, fotografe in Suriname 1904–1937* (2007); *J.C. Lamster, een vroege filmer in Nederlands-Indië* (2010); and *The Netherlands East Indies at the Tropenmuseum* (2011), the first in the ten-volume series about the Tropenmuseum collections.

Rob Jongmans (RJ) has worked for EYE (the former Filmmuseum), the Netherlands Architecture Institute (NAi) and the International Institute of Social History (IISG) as a visual collection registrar. He mostly worked with collections of film posters, posters collected by architects, the ReclameArsenaal (Advertising Arsenal) collection, and political cartoons. He joined the Tropenmuseum in 2004 as a collection registrar and researcher, focusing on the museum's photography collection.

Anouk Mansfeld (AM) is an art historian who specialises in historical colonial photography. Her research into the Tropenmuseum collection has resulted in a number of articles and exhibitions, including *Fotografie in India (1860–1890); Julius Muller, Suriname 100 jaar geleden; Familiefoto's uit Nederlands Indië (1880–1942)*; and *Indië in scène – Fotostudio Kurkdjian & Co (1888–1936)*. She is currently developing a policy for contemporary photography collecting for the Tropenmuseum.

Steven Vink (SV) is a historical geographer. He started working on the Tropenmuseum photographic collection in 1981 and was senior researcher of the visual collections. He has published several books and articles about the Tropenmuseum's photographic collections that focus on Suriname, New Guinea and Yemen. One of his areas of focus is expedition photography during the Dutch colonial era.

Pim Westerkamp (PW) has been the Tropenmuseum's curator of the culture and history of Southeast Asia since 2005. Prior to this, he worked for fourteen years as curator for Indonesia at the Nusantara Museum in Delft. He studied cultural anthropology and theatre sciences. His research interests include contemporary material and immaterial heritage, colonial and modern history, the history of collecting and exhibiting in the Tropenmuseum, and ethical issues relating to museums.

Wimo Ambala Bayang was born in Magelang, Central Java. He studied interior design at the Modern School of Design and at the Department of Photography at the Indonesian Art Institute, Yogyakarta. He works with photography and video and was one of the founders of Ruang Mes 56, a Yogyakarta artists' collective. His works offer a unique perspective on culture, which he sees less as a critique than a call for a return to tradition. His 2008 solo exhibition, 'Belanda Sudah Dekat!' ('The Dutch Are Close!'), was part of a residency at Cemeti Art House. His solo exhibition, 'Not So High (Heels)', at D Gallery, Jakarta in 2010 was followed by a more recent exhibition 'You See Half, You Get Half'. Wimo has participated in many residency programmes including Lijiang Studio China (2005); Heden Kunst van Nu, The Hague (2008); and South Project/Monash, Melbourne (2009).

The authors are grateful to the many scholars, both in the Netherlands and abroad, who have explored aspects of the history of photography in the Netherlands East Indies in recent decades. We are especially grateful go to Mattie Boom, Susan Legêne, Liane van der Linden and Pamela Pattynama for their valuable comments on the manuscript.

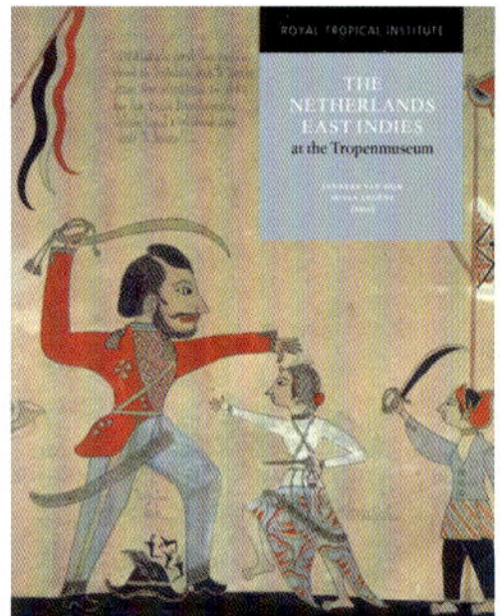

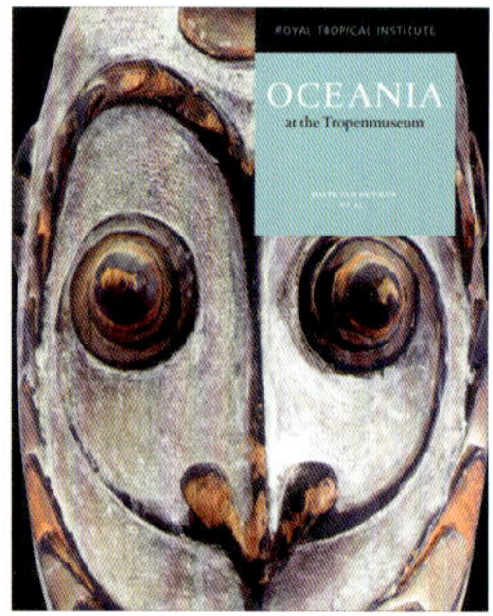

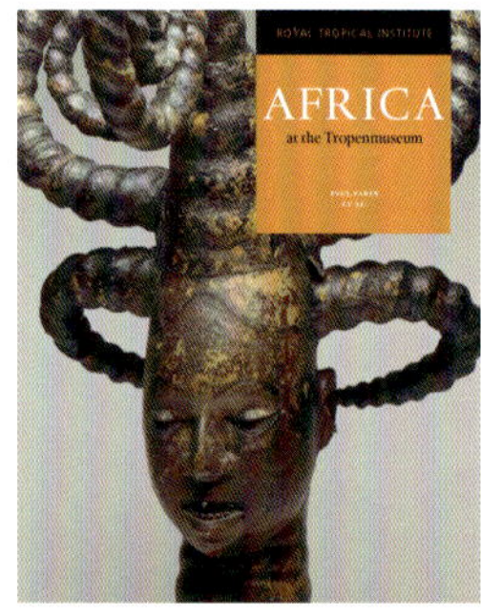

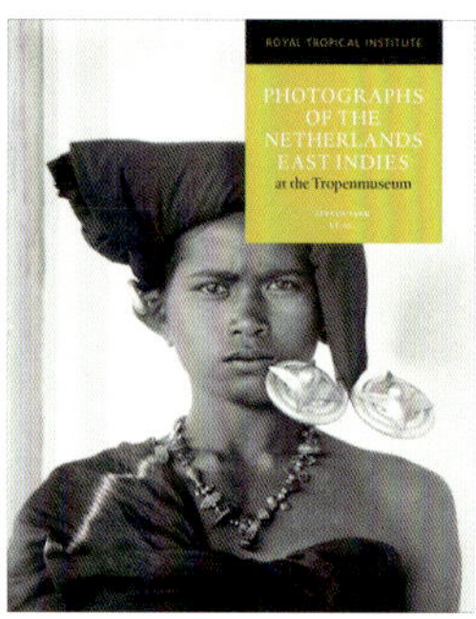

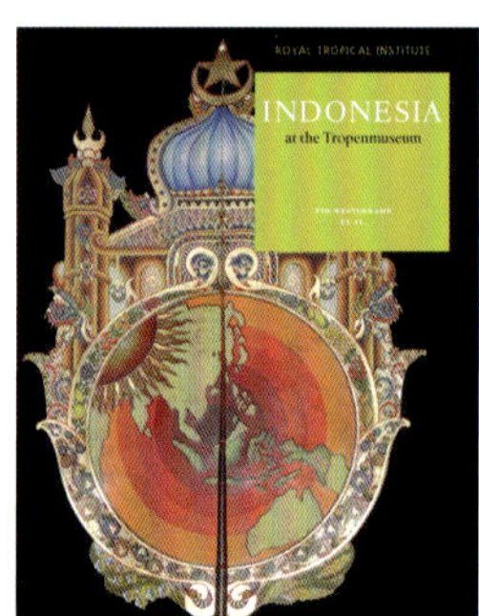

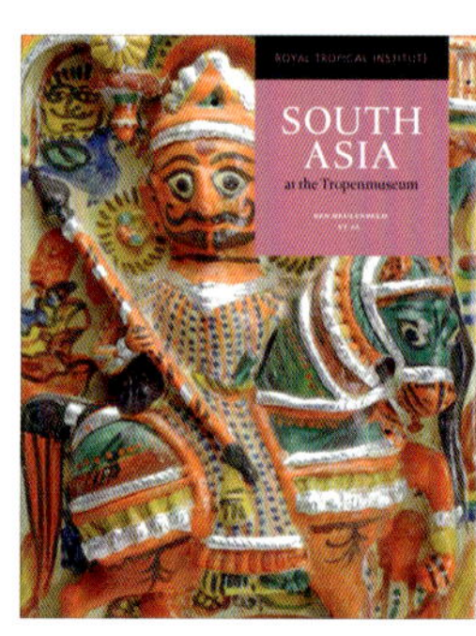

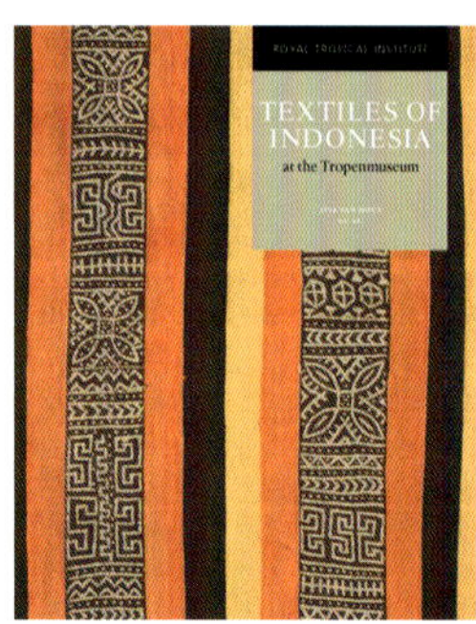

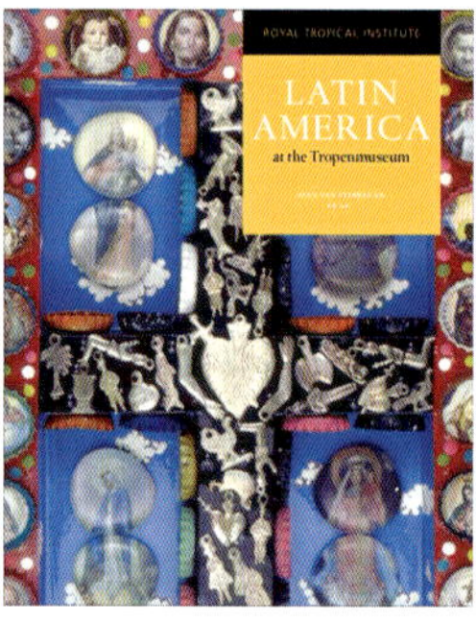

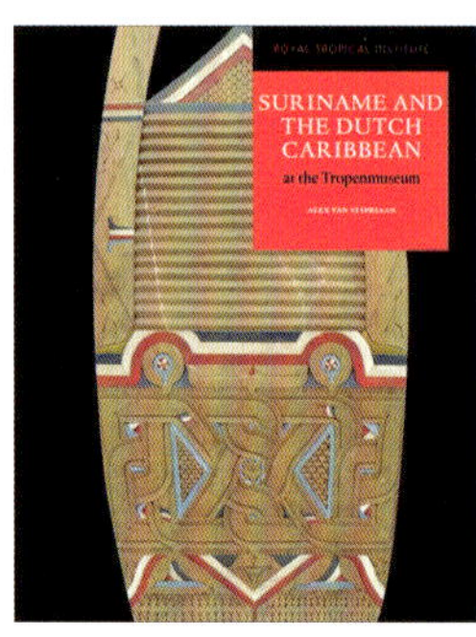

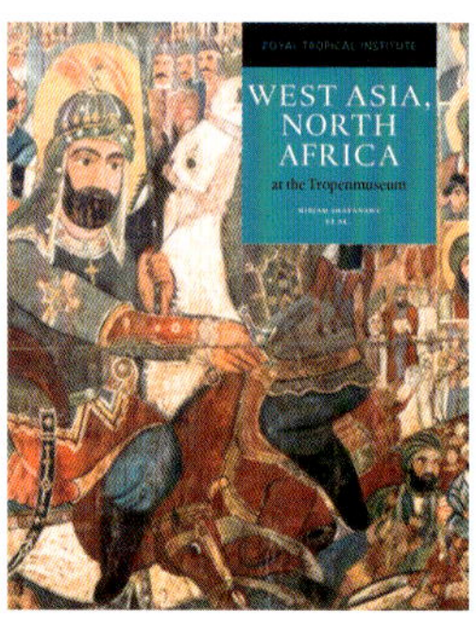

KIT Publishers
Mauritskade 63
P.O. Box 95001
1090 HA Amsterdam
The Netherlands
E-mail: publishers@kit.nl
www.kitpublishers.nl
www.tropenmuseum.nl

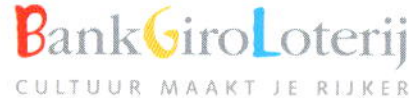

The publisher gratefully acknowledges
the support of the BankGiro Loterij

Editorial board
Koos van Brakel, Daan van Dartel, Paul Faber,
Arlette Kouwenhoven, Wayne Modest, Sonja Wijs

Translation and editing
Mark Poysden, Amsterdam, the Netherlands

Photography
KIT Tropenmuseum / Irene de Groot / Paul Romijn

Design
Studio Berry Slok, Amsterdam, The Netherlands

Production
High Trade BV, Zwolle, The Netherlands

Printed in Slovakia

Cover illustration: *Portrait of a Karo Batak woman*
Photographer: Tassilo Adam (1878–1955)
gelatin glass negative, 9 x 12 cm, 1918, 10005392
Gift: Tassilo Adam via Dr. Hamberisser, 1921

ISBN 978 946022 1934
NUR 640

Photographs of the Netherlands East Indies at the Tropenmuseum is volume four of a ten-volume series of the Royal Tropical Institute, published between 2011-2015.